Attachment, Evolution,
and the Psychology of Religion

ATTACHMENT, EVOLUTION,
and the
PSYCHOLOGY OF RELIGION

Lee A. Kirkpatrick

THE GUILFORD PRESS
New York   London

© 2005 The Guilford Press
A Division of Guilford Publications, Inc.
72 Spring Street, New York, NY 10012
www.guilford.com

Printed in the United States of America

This book is printed on acid-free paper.

Last digit is print number: 9 8 7 6 5 4 3 2

Library of Congress Cataloging-in-Publication Data

Kirkpatrick, Lee A., 1958–
  Attachment, evolution, and the psychology of religion / Lee A. Kirkpatrick.
     p. cm.
  Includes bibliographical references and index.
  ISBN-10 1-59385-088-3   ISBN-13 978-1-59385-088-3
  1. Psychology, Religious.   2. Attachment behavior.   3. Evolutionary
psychology.   I. Title.
  BL53.K56 2005
  200′.1′9—dc22   2004013003

About the Author

Lee A. Kirkpatrick, PhD, is Associate Professor and Director of Graduate Studies in Psychology at the College of William and Mary in Virginia. He has published numerous research articles and book chapters on topics related to adult attachment, the psychology of religion, and evolutionary psychology.

Preface

Between these covers lie, in effect, two different but related books. The first—at least in the sequence I have chosen here—presents an application of attachment theory to the psychology of religion. Since its introduction by John Bowlby, Mary Ainsworth, and others in the 1960s and 1970s, attachment theory has become a dominant force in developmental psychology and other subdisciplines of social, personality, and clinical psychology. I argue that the theory provides a powerful framework for approaching the psychology of religion as well. In the first part of the book I show how a diversity of research findings from the psychology of religion can be organized and interpreted in attachment terms, and review the rapidly growing body of empirical research that has been motivated by, and tests hypotheses derived from, an attachment perspective.

Although attachment theory is, in my opinion, considerably deeper and broader than most other psychological theories of religion, it by no means provides a comprehensive theory thereof. It seems particularly well suited for understanding certain aspects of certain religions, such as beliefs about, and perceived relationships with, the God of most varieties of Christianity, but there is much more to religion than this. The second half of the book thus presents a comprehensive theoretical framework for the psychology of religion, within which attachment plays an important but circumscribed role. Drawing upon the emerging paradigm of evolutionary psychology, my thesis is that religion can be understood not as an instinct or adaptation designed by natural selection by virtue of survival or reproduction benefits, but rather as a collection of by-products of numerous specialized psychological systems that evolved over the course of human history for other (i.e., nonreligious) functions. The attachment system is, in this larger view, just one among many. A host of other social-psychological systems can similarly be applied to the supernatural—systems related, for example, to social exchange (reciprocal altruism), kinship relations, coalition formation and maintenance, intrasexual competition (for status, resources, and mates), and so forth—which give rise to very different kinds of beliefs, expectations, and behavior in relation to God or the gods. For any particular religious phenomenon of interest, I suggest, the theoretical task is one of identifying the underlying mechanism involved and applying what we know about the operation and function of that mechanism.

Of course, I hope that this volume will read not like two distinct books but rather one coherently integrated one. Theoretically, the structural relationship is clear: It is a part-to-whole relation in which attachment represents one component of the larger evolutionary metatheory—one tree within the forest, so to speak. I have chosen here to focus on one tree first, and then to zoom out for a perspective on the forest.

* * *

I am not a big fan of autobiographical book prefaces. Frankly, I am not usually too interested in an author's life history, and I don't expect readers to be especially interested in mine. However, readers might gain a useful perspective on my views by understanding how I came to them, particularly with respect to the way the book is organized and the sequence in which I develop the arguments.

As is probably true for many academics, my intellectual development is largely the tale of a few great books. In my case, the first was Richard Dawkins's *The Selfish Gene*, which I read for a class in college not long after it was first published in 1976. (Thank you, Chuck Shull.) This was my first serious introduction to evolutionary theory, and it blew my mind. The modern theory of evolution by natural selection, as brilliantly explicated by Dawkins, struck me as an immensely elegant theory, beautiful in its simplicity yet astonishingly deep and powerful. As a psychology major, I naturally was intrigued by the book's focus on the evolution of behavior, but my excitement actually had little to do with that. Indeed, I found it difficult, if not impossible, to map the ideas presented by

Dawkins onto anything I was learning in psychology; the concepts, language, and ways of thinking were so different that I could not begin to imagine how they could be integrated meaningfully. I was hooked on evolutionary theory, not so much as a foundation for psychology, but more or less as an intellectual hobby. Over the next decade or so I read numerous other books by Richard Dawkins, Stephen J. Gould, and others. I also discovered and digested some of the early "pop sociobiology" books that made various attempts (unlike Dawkins, for the most part) to apply evolutionary thinking directly to human behavior. I found most of these efforts at human sociobiology somehow unconvincing, though at the time I was unable to put my finger on exactly why. Nevertheless, they provided some intriguing hints that my separate interests in evolutionary theory and psychology might some day come together.

At the University of Denver in the 1980s, attachment theory was in the air. I was exposed to it in several different classes as a graduate student, and everyone seemed to be talking about it in one context or another. My fellow student and dear friend Cindy Hazan, along with our shared adviser Phil Shaver, were busy working on what turned out to be an enormously influential application of attachment theory to romantic love. Attachment theory at this time struck me as plausible and somewhat intriguing, but not significantly more so than any number of other major theories to which I was being exposed in social, personality, cognitive, and developmental psychology. However, this initial assessment was based entirely on secondary sources. I still remember the day that Cindy urged me to read Bowlby's first volume of the *Attachment and Loss* trilogy, emphasizing that I could not properly appreciate the theory otherwise. She was right. (Thank you, Cindy.) I found Bowlby's approach to the problem qualitatively different from, and far more exciting than, anything else I was reading in psychology. He went beyond explaining what the attachment system was and how it worked, to explaining exactly why it was this way and not some other way. In particular, he showed me for the first time how the ideas from evolutionary theory could be applied convincingly to a problem in human psychology, developing hypotheses about how we should expect human psychology to be designed and examining them in light of multiple, diverse sources of data. I came away convinced not only that attachment theory might be true, but that it virtually had to be true, in much the same way as I had felt about the theory of natural selection based on my reading of Dawkins a decade earlier.

Denver also turned out to be the right place for someone interested in the psychology of religion, mainly because of the presence of one of the giants of the field, Bernard Spilka. I was familiar with a fair amount of psychology of religion literature from my master's thesis project at the University of Texas at El Paso, and learned much more about it working with Bernie and Phil Shaver. However, I found it troubling that little of this research literature seemed directly connected to the rest of psychology as I was coming to know it. The topic of religion almost never came up in books or lectures in my graduate course work (as, I recalled, it had not in my undergraduate courses), as if psychologists had no interest in religion. At the same time, researchers in the psychology of religion were only rarely drawing upon theoretical perspectives from the "mainstream" of psychology, as if religion researchers had no interest in psychology. This seemed like an absurd state of affairs to me, and the solution seemed obvious: The psychology of religion needed to import theories from other areas of psychology. Once I discovered Bowlby and attachment theory, choosing a topic for my doctoral dissertation was a no-brainer. "Book One" here (Chapters 1–8) reviews this research program as it has been developed and extended by myself and other researchers over the last 15 years.

After finally settling at the College of William and Mary in the early 1990s, I continued to work on a variety of research problems in both adult attachment and the psychology of religion. I was still enamored of attachment theory, but it was clear that it was useful only for explaining certain domains of human psychology and experience (both within and outside of religion). However, I had yet to come across any other theory in psychology that even began to approach the depth and breadth of Bowlby's ideas. Countless theories offered mainly descriptive accounts of what people do and think, usually within some narrowly circumscribed domain, and some of the particular situational or individual-difference factors thought to underlie them. Unlike Bowlby, though, almost nobody seemed very interested in asking deeper questions about why.

One day a graduate student named Martie Haselton came into my office and excitedly showed me a book she had just come across in the university library, and asked if I had seen it. I had not. It was an edited volume entitled *The Adapted Mind*, and she urged me to drop everything and start reading it—particularly a now classic chapter by John Tooby and Leda Cosmides that articulated in abundant detail everything that was wrong with the social sciences, and offered a new paradigm called "evolu-

tionary psychology" to fix it. (Thank you, Martie.) It took me a very long
time to get through that chapter, not so much because it was quite lengthy
but because I found that I could only read a dozen pages or so at a time without taking a day off to fully consolidate and digest the arguments. When I
finally got to the end, I went back and read it again. It changed my whole
way of thinking about psychology. In particular, it showed me how to approach all areas of psychology in the same way that Bowlby had approached
attachment, and how to think about the place of attachment in the larger
scheme of things. Now, a dozen years later, an evolutionary perspective
pervades my thinking about everything.

* * *

When The Guilford Press first approached me about writing a book
on attachment theory and religion, I was already well on my way down
this evolutionary-psychology path. In particular, I had done a lot of
thinking about how my work on attachment theory and religion fit
within a broad evolutionary framework, and how this perspective provided a powerful, nonarbitrary basis for carving up the psychological
world of religion into functional parts or domains based on the evolutionary logic of adaptive problems and adaptations. Ultimately we agreed
on the two-books-in-one approach.

Now that I've arrived at this more general evolutionary-psychological
model of religion, part of me wants to go back and rewrite the entire thing
in the opposite order. The general evolutionary framework for psychology
would come first, and specific theories about particular domains or aspects
of religion would be laid out subsequently. Attachment, in this scheme,
would be just one of many domain-specific aspects of the story, with no
privileged status above the others. The problem with this perfectly logical
organization is simply that I have much more to say about attachment than
the rest. Some day I hope that book-length treatments will develop more
fully the various other approaches that I outline only briefly in the latter
half of this book. In my more optimistic moments I can almost envision a
multivolume series entitled something like "The Evolutionary Psychology
of Religion," in which one volume is subtitled "Attachment" and others
are subtitled "Coalitional Psychology," "Social Exchange," "Kinship,"
"Intrasexual Competition," and so forth.

Nevertheless, I have decided to stick to an organization for the book
that follows my own intellectual evolution. I begin by describing the application of attachment theory to religion, drawing upon both the psy-

chology of religion literature and my own empirical research on the topic. I then introduce evolutionary psychology as an emerging paradigm for psychology and the social sciences, emphasizing how attachment theory fits squarely within it. Finally, I introduce and briefly review a variety of other psychological mechanisms and systems that I think explain other aspects of religion. The book thus tells a story in an order that to me is autobiographical. To readers uninterested in my autobiography, I hope this organization will still make for a good story, perhaps offering some sense of an unfolding mystery or drama—at least to the extent this is possible given that I have already summarized the plot and given away the ending.

* * *

I am grateful to Brandy Burkett, A. J. Figueredo, Pehr Granqvist, Ray Paloutzian, Phillip R. Shaver, and Linda Zyzniewski for reading and providing extensive comments on earlier drafts of the manuscript. I also owe a special debt of gratitude to the University of Canterbury in New Zealand for a generous Erskine Fellowship that allowed me to spend several months on the other side of the planet, away from most other obligations and distractions, working feverishly on the book. Special thanks also go to my friends Bruce Ellis and Garth Fletcher, for making this possible and being such gracious hosts while I was there, and to the College of William and Mary for making special accommodations to allow me to take that opportunity. Finally, I thank my editor, Jim Nageotte, for somehow always knowing exactly how much support and guidance I needed—never more and never less.

Contents

CHAPTER ONE

Introduction

Religion, broadly defined, might be the most thought- and written-about topic in the history of human civilization. There are vast literatures devoted to religious beliefs, values, and practice—what people ought to believe and how they should live their lives as a consequence. Theologians and spiritual leaders attempt to ascertain the mind of God or the gods. Devotional literatures attempt to lead people to live satisfying and righteous lives. Philosophers debate religion's logic and values, sometimes endorsing them and at other times tearing them down. Scholars in numerous fields document the variety of religious beliefs around the world and across time, in search of the elusive common thread running among them all. Social scientists examine empirical and theoretical relationships between religious beliefs, behaviors, and practices and other dimensions of human experience at psychological and sociological levels of analysis.

Behind all of these diverse perspectives are agendas; everyone has one. Wafting on the breeze blowing across this crowded territory is a symphony of grinding axes. Strategically or inadvertently, writers seek to promote their own preferred version of religion, undermine others, somehow integrate or reconcile seemingly disparate perspectives, or understand religious phenomena scientifically. This is all fine, so long as everyone is clear about what their agendas are and do not mistake one for another.

AN AMBITIOUS AGENDA

I too have an agenda. I believe that our goal should be: to formulate a *scientific, comprehensive, explanatory psychology of religion.*

I have no delusions about fulfilling such an ambitious goal in this book. Indeed, I doubt that anything like it will be achieved in my lifetime, much less within this (or any other single) volume. Nevertheless, I think it is extremely important to articulate, here at the beginning, the larger agenda to which this book is intended to contribute, for two reasons.

First, I want to be entirely clear up front about the matter. There are any number of goals one might have in approaching the study of psychology and religion, and the agenda I have specified is just one among them. As I will discuss shortly, divergent agendas in the psychology of religion are often confused with one another, to the detriment of all concerned. I am not going to offer any kind of defense of this agenda, but rather will assume its value is self-evident. I am not suggesting that other agendas are any less valid or valuable; I merely want to ensure that mine is not confused with others.

Second, I maintain that we must be cognizant of our long-term goal from the beginning in order to effectively develop a strategy for getting there. We do not currently have a "scientific, comprehensive, explanatory psychology of religion"—this much seems beyond debate—but, more important, I believe that the field is not currently on a path that will lead us to one. Instead, the field is meandering aimlessly with no clear direction. For reasons I will explain in this chapter, we must keep our eyes on the prize from the beginning in order to reach it, starting with a clearly identified goal.

Specifically, I contend that in order to eventually achieve a scientific, comprehensive, explanatory psychology of religion, we must begin with an outline—if only a preliminary, general one—of a large-scale framework within which to organize research and theory. That is, we need a rough sketch of what an eventual "big picture" might generally look like so we can work toward it. Had the proverbial blind men known in advance that they were investigating different parts of a large, terrestrial mammal, the subsequent discussion of their observations would have been infinitely more fruitful. The purpose of this book is, first, to provide a preliminary sketch of such a framework, at a level of analysis perhaps roughly equivalent to identifying the subject of investigation as "a large terrestrial mammal," and, second, to describe one part of the animal in some detail. With such a framework in place, we will be in a position to organize our observations according to what we know about large terrestrial mammals, fitting our observations into meaningful categories such as trunks, ears, and legs. In this sense I hope this book will provide an impetus and direction for future research in the field.

In the following pages I explain, term by term, exactly what I mean by a (1) *scientific* (2) *comprehensive* (3) *explanatory* (4) *psychology of* (5) *religion*, as well as describing some of the obstacles that stand in the way of constructing one. In the second half of the chapter I then provide a brief overview of my approach in this book, specifically regarding how it offers a potential solution to these problems.

Scientific

By *scientific*, I refer to an approach that treats religion as a topic of inquiry to be studied using empirical research methods and theories consistent with those both within psychology and within the sciences more generally. Religion, like any other topic studied by social scientists, is taken to refer to a suite of cognitive, emotional, physiological, social, and cultural human phenomena to be described, understood, and explained in terms of empirically testable theories and hypotheses. Irrespective of whether a particular religious expression or belief is thought to be true or false, or whether it is valued personally or socially as desirable or undesirable (more follows on these issues), a scientific approach to religion should ask the same kinds of questions it asks of any other human phenomenon. How can it be described in terms of broader principles? How does it actually happen, that is, what kinds of enabling or disabling factors are involved? Why does it occur, particularly relative to alternative beliefs or expressions that might otherwise occur? What are the commonalities and differences across individuals and groups, and across time within individuals and groups, in terms of processes and cause?

Unfortunately, however, this scientific agenda for the psychology of religion has long been conflated with other agendas with which it fundamentally has little in common, or with which it is strictly at odds. This is perhaps more true in the psychology of religion than in the "psychology of" virtually anything else. The term "psychology of religion" means many things to many people, but only one meaning refers to the kind of psychological science of religion I have in mind. These often-conflicting agendas create deep rifts—some wide open and obvious, others hidden below the surface—within the field. The failure to clearly differentiate these highly disparate agendas has been a major factor throughout the last century in inhibiting progress in the psychology of religion. To do better, we need to be clear from the start whether the goal toward which we are working is scientific or otherwise.

There are many ways to combine the terms "psychology" and "religion" in the same sentence to produce very different meanings. Similarly, the words "children" and "doctor" can be combined in many ways, but the sons and daughters of physicians have for the most part little in common with pediatricians. This fanciful example offers an analogy to one of the deepest rifts in the psychology of religion, characterized by Beit-Hallahmi (1989) as the distinction between "psychology of religion" as a scientific discipline and "religious psychology." The latter serves as an umbrella term for a variety of ways in which personal religious belief is brought into the psychological fold, in the service of advancing the cause of religion in general or some particular religious viewpoint in particular.

Another increasingly popular way of combining "religion" and "psychology" in the same sentence involves the pursuit of some kind of higher-order metatheoretical (metaphysical?) framework for *integrating* psychology and religion. The interdisciplinary journal *Zygon* regularly publishes various attempts to "integrate" science and religion in sundry creative ways. Hood (1994) has argued for "a compromise position to get beyond the rift—neither a psychology of religion nor a religious psychology, but rather psychology *and* religion" (Hood, Spilka, Hunsberer, & Gorsuch, 1996, p. 445). Jones (1994), in a highly visible article in the prestigious *American Psychologist*, presents a proposal "for how religion could participate as an active partner with psychology as a science and as an applied professional discipline" (p. 184). Countless other examples could be cited as well, of course, from fields ranging from theology to philosophy to religious studies.

The blurring of these distinctions is evident in the organizations and publication outlets associated with the "psychology of religion" field. Division 36 of the American Psychological Association, now named Psychology of Religion, was until a few years ago Psychologists Interested in Religious Issues—a title which well represents the diversity of perspectives housed therein.[1] The Religious Research Association and its journal, *Review of Religious Research*, are similarly ambiguous in name. Although these are in part concerned with fostering scientific research about religion as a topic of investigation, they do so within an applied agenda of providing information and resources to assist religious congregations and organizations.

The problem is not that these different agendas exist, of course, but rather that they are so easily and often confused with each other. For example, Beit-Hallahmi (1989) argues that an implicit religious-psychology agenda is responsible for the fact that so much of the empirical psychology of religion is driven by value-laden distinctions between "good religion" and "bad religion," from James's religions of the "sick-souled" versus "healthy-minded" to Allport's "mature" versus "immature," and later "intrinsic" versus "extrinsic," religious orientations. Numerous theories and measures exist for studying "religious development" or "spiritual development" using stage-like models that begin with extrascientific assumptions about what "mature" (read "good") religion should be. In the latest incarnation of this implicit good–bad dichotomy, "religion" is now viewed by many in the bad-guy role opposite the protagonist "spirituality" (Emmons & Paloutzian, 2003; Hill et al., 2000; Pargament, 1997). All of this gets in the way if the goal is to establish a scientific understanding of religious belief and behavior in all its forms.

A truly scientific approach to the psychology of religion should, of course, steer clear of such evaluative assumptions as much as possible. Whether religion is associated with particular forms of mental health, social relations, war or peace, and so forth are *empirical questions* and within the purview of scientific investigation. The questions of which kinds of psychological states or qualities of interpersonal relations are deemed desirable, or whether war is preferred to peace, reflect ethical, moral, and practical matters beyond the scope of science.

Moreover, the idea that religion is broadly "good" or "bad" is absurd on its face: Like virtually any aspect of human experience and behavior, it no doubt is *both* in myriad ways (and *neither* in other respects). It seems patently obvious from thousands of years of human history that religion can be a powerful force in promoting either peace or war, mental health or mental illness, prosocial or antisocial behavior, racism or universalism, happiness or misery. The role of science is to determine which of these is true under what conditions, and why and how it occurs. The question of how this knowledge might be put to use, and toward what ends, is an entirely different question, one I avoid entirely in this book.

Of course, one common basis for assumptions about whether religion is "good" or "bad" is whether one believes it (or some particular belief) to be ontologically true: true belief presumably being "good," of course, and false belief "bad." It is often assumed that the scientific study of religion is inherently grounded in an extrascientific assumption that religious beliefs are false—that a scientific approach to religion must be inherently atheistic. This line of reasoning leads many people who are themselves religious to be (understandably) skeptical of, if not outright opposed to, a truly scientific study of religion. To explain religion is to explain it away, it is assumed. However, it is simply wrong to assume that a scientific understanding of why and how people come to believe in X has any bearing on the question of whether or not X is true. Philosophers have long referred to this misconception—that the truth value of a proposition can be determined by the source (genesis) of that proposition—as the *genetic fallacy*.

This is a big philosophical question about which I offer just a couple of brief comments. First, consider the fact that psychologists study the origins and causes of all sorts of attitudes, beliefs, and knowledge that are assumed to be true; they do not study only false beliefs. Developmental psychologists, for example, study the ways in which children learn everything from language to physics. Understanding the psychological processes and environmental conditions that contribute to a child's learning that $2 + 2 = 4$ surely does not undermine our confidence in the accuracy of the sum. A psychological theory might explain that a person came to hold a particular attitude in part because of, say, exposure to a persuasive communicator with certain characteristics, quite independent of whether that attitude or belief or attitude also happens to be true—or whether there is a "right" or "wrong" answer at all. Likewise, a scientific understanding of how people come to believe they have a personal relationship with a loving God can be construed from an atheistic perspective in terms of the question of why and how false beliefs are constructed and maintained, or just as well from a Christian perspective of the enabling conditions that permit someone to successfully apprehend the true nature of God.

Second, any question about a belief can be easily turned around and asked in its reverse form: The question of why some people believe X is the flip side of the question of why other people do not, and any strong explanation for either must ultimately speak to both. Whichever version you personally believe to be true (i.e., X or not-X), half of the explanation is about what you consider false beliefs and half about what you regard as true beliefs. A researcher studying conversion (to religion) and deconversion or apostasy (from religion) necessarily must see both sides of the coin, whether he or she personally feels the beliefs are better embraced or rejected.

At this point I should probably acknowledge that the idea of an *evolutionary* psychology of religion strikes many people as ironic to the point of amusing. The joke, of course, is that evolutionary theory and religion are perceived as diametric opposites. But this is not at all the case, except perhaps for a tiny fraction of particular beliefs that directly contradict evolutionary theory (e.g., that our planet is only a few thousand years old) held by a tiny fraction of the population. In part the confusion stems from the genetic fallacy, and in part from a failure to acknowledge that there is nothing internally inconsistent about the (widely held) belief that, for example, evolution is one natural process through which God works. The crucial point is that the theoretical perspective I adopt in this book in no way rests on any particular assumptions about the truth or falsity of the religious beliefs I am trying to explain. Indeed, I will make an even more ironic claim in the final chapter: that the evolutionary perspective I have adopted is *especially* well suited to the task of examining religious beliefs scientifically without any presumption about their veridicality.[2]

Comprehensive

By *comprehensive*, I mean two things. First, of course, I mean that I want to understand everything about religion: not just images of God, or religious attributions of causality, or spiritual experiences, or religious development, or prayer—all of it. I am intellectually greedy.

It might seem completely self-evident that a scientific agenda in the psychology of religion, or any other domain of psychology, would seek a comprehensive understanding in this sense. I doubt many researchers explicitly choose to investigate one particular topic and deliberately exclude other related topics. However, this is another place in which I believe we must make the goal explicit so we can keep our eyes on the prize. The problem is that if we focus narrowly on one small piece of the puzzle, we are likely to wind up with a theoretical understanding that is largely specific to that piece. When we move on to a different phenomenon it becomes necessary to start over from scratch, or, perhaps worse, the theory spun in the context of one problem needs to be squeezed, twisted, or otherwise distorted to make it fit another.

This leads to my second meaning regarding the goal of a "comprehensive" psychology of religion: I want to understand it all in terms of a *coherent, integrated* perspective. This is not to say that we should be seeking a single, specific theory that will explain it all; as I discuss later, "religion" is far too complex and multifaceted for that. However, I am not satisfied with a compromise position that simply acknowledges the need for multiple theories and perspectives to understand different aspects of the problem. I do indeed think this is true, but not just any old set of theories and perspectives will do. All of the parts of the explanatory framework must fit together into an organized, singular whole that gives me a sense of true understanding.

One way to say this is that if a new aspect of the phenomenon, for which an explanation was not already extant, were to appear, we would have a clear plan for approaching the problem, conceptually based on a larger framework. Informed from the outset that he was examining part of a "large, terrestrial mammal," one of the proverbial blind men could certainly conduct a thorough and accurate investigation of an elephant's foot. The independent investigations of tusks, trunks, and ears by others could later be discussed and assembled by the group into a comprehensive report. To use a less fanciful example, a paleontologist has a broad framework in mind when she discovers a new, unidentified piece of bone. She brings to bear on the problem an anatomical framework of the ways in which skeleton parts tend to be arranged, and a comparative framework regarding differences between mammalian skeletons and reptilian skeletons. She has a historical framework that, once the bone piece is dated, narrows the search for viable candidates. These background perspectives provide powerful tools for quickly developing an understanding of the particular skeletal part from which the piece comes and the kind of animal to which it belongs. Specifically, the larger frameworks provide a wellspring of hypotheses to be tried out and empirically tested, and simultaneously constrain the hypotheses worth examining.

In a word, what we need for a comprehensive psychology of religion in this sense is what Kuhn (1962) famously referred to as a *paradigm*. In a paradigmatic discipline, researchers have at their disposal a general, big-picture view of the entire puzzle in terms of what it generally contains and the kinds of methodological and theoretical approaches to be applied to it. One of the benefits of such a paradigm is that each new puzzle piece can be viewed as just that, rather than as a new puzzle altogether. It probably goes without saying that the psychology of religion currently lacks such a paradigm, but I want to go ahead and say it and suggest some reasons why this is the case, to provide a context for the solution to be offered in this book.

The first impediment to a comprehensive paradigm for the psychology of religion concerns the organization of contemporary psychology and related disciplines. Simply put, the psychology of religion is organized around a *topic* or phenomenon—religion—but the principal organizational and institutional structure of psychology is not. Psychology departments recognize historical boundaries (for better or worse) between such areas as developmental, social, personality, cognitive, and clinical psychology, which are defined more along lines of theoretical, metatheoretical, and methodological approaches rather than content or topic. Graduate programs, course schedules, and introductory psychology textbooks, as well as many of the most prestigious conferences and journals, are largely divvied up along these lines as well.

This structural disconnect is problematic for several reasons. First, the psychology of religion has no natural home within the larger discipline of psychology: It is a square peg and the holes are all round. An academic psychologist must be a developmental or social or clinical psychologist first, and then approach the topic of religion from within that subdiscipline. It seems as if there are no generalists anymore, which is more or less what one would need to be in order to obtain the bird's eye view required for a truly comprehensive psychology of religion. At a more practical level the problems are legion: What kind of graduate program should an aspiring psychologist of religion attend? Which journals are appropriate for publishing research in the field? Where does psychology of religion fit into the teaching of psychology? An Introductory Psychology text, for example, contains chapters on developmental, social, cognitive, and other subdisciplines within the field. Where would material on religion go?[3]

This structural issue would not pose much of a problem if the various domains of psychology were conceptually well integrated within a clearly defined metatheoretical framework or paradigm to facilitate effective cross-fertilization and truly collaborative work across the subdisciplines of psychology. Students should be forgiven for wondering what, if anything, the various chapters in their Introductory Psychology textbooks have in common with each other. Such texts reflect the reality that contemporary psychology comprises a host of only loosely connected subdisciplines. If psychology itself were paradigmatic, the paradigm could be adapted for the study of religion. An integrated psychology of religion needs to be based on an integrated psychology, and we do not currently have one.

Some of the chasms between subdisciplines and approaches are old and all too familiar. One is the ancient nature–nurture morass (in its various forms, such as genes vs. environment, biology vs. culture, hardwired vs. learned, etc.), which continues to muddle thinking in many subdisciplines and specific research areas. Although most social and personality psychologists would explicitly endorse (or at least give lip service to) an "interactive" model, the fact remains that most researchers tend to look for causes of behavior primarily or exclusively on one side or the other. Even within specific subdisciplines there is frequently a lack of a single unifying, integrative framework. In social psychology, for example, there has long been a strong underlying tension between the social-cognition camp, which appears to have gained precedence in recent years, and other areas dealing with emotion, relationships, and so forth. Given this disconnect between (and within) psychology's subdisciplines at a deep conceptual level, the prospect of bringing together multiple psychological perspectives on a topic as diverse and complex as religion is daunting at best.

This lack of a coherent paradigm in psychology (and the social sciences generally) is problematic in many ways not specific to the psychology of religion. However, these problems are exacerbated in the study of religion by the nature of the topic itself. One would be hard pressed to identify a topic for social-scientific research with greater inherent complexity and breadth than religion. From the standpoint of psychology alone, virtually every subdiscipline has a legitimate claim to the topic: Changes in religious understanding and belief across childhood, and across the lifespan generally, call out for a developmental perspective; the structure and nature of religious beliefs, attributions, and reasoning is the province of cognitive psychology and/or social cognition; the many interpersonal processes involved in religion, including group dynamics, require a social-psychological perspective; the adaptive and maladaptive causes and effects of religious belief, as well as the role of religious belief in therapeutic contexts, is of interest to clinical psychologists. The causes, consequences, and other correlates of individual differences in religiousness, as well as the place of religion in grand questions about human nature and what it means to be human, offer religion a natural home in personality psychology. Like other psychological processes, how religion "works" inside the brain raises fascinating questions for neurology and cognitive neuroscience. But none of these approaches alone could begin to provide a comprehensive theory of the psychology of religion.

Cross-cutting these disciplines are numerous general categories or foci of psychological investigation, all of which represent important aspects of religion. The psychology of religion poses questions about motivation, emotion, cognition, phenomenology, and behavior. It undoubtedly includes both conscious and unconscious processes, and both rational and irrational ones. There are as many questions about religious change (e.g., conversion) as there are about stability across time (e.g., enduring personality characteristics). Any comprehensive theory of religion must be capable of addressing all of these issues.

For all these reasons, the contemporary structure and sociology of psychology is poorly suited for the goal of constructing a comprehensive theory of anything, much less something as complex and multifaceted as religion. We need a paradigm for psychology in general, which we can then apply to religion. In the second half of this book I argue that the needed paradigm is currently just beginning to emerge, and demonstrate how it might be usefully applied to the psychology of religion.

Explanatory

By *explanatory*, I mean that I want to understand the answers to the deep, tough questions about religious phenomena. I want to know *why* religion has throughout history been universal in human societies; *why* on the one hand religious belief takes on such a remarkable diversity of forms, but on the other hand certain common themes seem to emerge consistently; *why*, in many modern societies, people differ quantitatively and qualitatively with respect to religious belief. It is often said that the three principal goals of science are description, prediction, and explanation. I do not want to quit after the first two.

Empirical research in the psychology of religion, however, has long been strong on description but weak on explanation. A disproportionate amount of research has been devoted, for example, to developing questionnaire measures and determining the factor-analytic structure of God images, religious orientations or motives such as Allport's intrinsic–extrinsic framework, or religiousness broadly defined, independent of any theoretical context. Gorsuch (1984) identified this prevailing approach to psychology of religion as its "measurement paradigm." But this is not a paradigm in the Kuhnian sense, because it is utterly devoid of theory. We may know how many factor-analytic dimensions God has (actually, we have many answers to this), but we do not know why or wherefore.

I believe that this state of affairs derives in large part from the structural problem, outlined in the previous section, regarding the organization of the field. The fact that the psychology of religion is defined by its topic of investigation, rather than by a theoretical or metatheoretical approach, encourages researchers to approach it from a "bottom-up," inductive perspective. That is, they begin with the *of religion* part which, for whatever their personal reasons, is what interests them. They then cast about for ideas about how to study it. This is a perfectly reasonable thing to do, but I think it is largely responsible for having bogged the field down theoretically.

If you start with the topic, the first reasonable step to take is to define what it is exactly that you mean. You have to define it before you can study it, right? (Actually, I think not, but we will come to that shortly.) And as we all know, defining "religion" is a black hole: Scholars of all stripes have been trying to nail down exactly what it is that makes religion "religion," as distinct from other human phenomena, with little consensus in sight. Consequently, we have yet to move far beyond this first step.

Closely related to the definition problem is the measurement problem. Once you have defined the phenomenon of interest, you then have to figure out how to measure it. The two problems are closely intertwined, however, because measurement results—in particular, from factor-analytic research—often drive definition. The consequence of this is the current "measurement paradigm," the result of which is that we have lots of religion measures all dressed up with nowhere to go. We have been so tied up with this task that few have actually put these measures to use in the service of asking substantive, theoretical questions.

The solution to this problem, in my opinion, is to import solid explanatory theories from psychology into the psychology of religion—to start with the explanatory framework and then apply it to the topic of interest rather than the other way around. In other words, the field needs to shift its focus away from the ". . . of religion" half of its rubric to the "psychology of . . ." half. A scientific understanding of religion must ultimately be situated within a larger psychology of human beings generally. Questions about, for example, why people are religious, or are religious in certain ways versus others, must be considered in the context of why people do *anything*. To understand religious motivation, we need to begin with a good theory of motivation in general. To understand how people conceptualize personal relationships with deities, we need to begin with a good theory of personal relationships in general. To understand why religion appears (at least to many) as somehow inherent in human nature, we need to begin with a good theory of human nature.

Psychology of . . .

By *psychology of* (religion), I mean to emphasize an approach in which theory and research about human psychology—including all its behavioral, cognitive, and conative dimensions—plays a central role in the attempt to understand religion. A strong scientific psychology of religion must be first a strong scientific *psychology*, within which our approaches to describing and explaining religion are deeply embedded. Indeed, an ideal approach to psychology of religion would begin with a comprehensive, scientific, explanatory psychology, and then apply this psychology to the topic at hand (in this case, religion). This would be "psychology of" in its most extreme form.

I have already noted that such an integrated, paradigmatic psychology does not currently exist, and that because psychology of religion is defined by its topic, it has no natural home within the discipline of psychology. Both of these factors have contributed to the field's "of religion," rather than "psychology of" orientation. In turn, these problems are further exacerbated by the fact that this "of religion" focus is now institutionalized. Perhaps in response to its estrangement from the rest of psychology, the field packed up and left home to create its own professional organizations, meetings, and journals. Within psychology, Division 36 of the American Psychological Association provides a home for the psychology of religion, which meets annually as part of the larger APA convention, at which it organizes its own program of symposia, paper and poster sessions, and plenary addresses. Several specialized journals are devoted to the topic, including the *Journal of Psychology and Theology*, the *Journal of Psychology and Christianity*, and the (relatively newer) *International Journal for the Psychology of Religion*. In addition, psychologists of religion participate in a larger specialized discipline of "the scientific study of religion," including the Society for the Scientific Study of Religion, its cousin the Religious Research Association, and their respective journals (the *Journal for the Scientific Study of Religion* and the *Review of Religious Research*).

Unfortunately, there is no more conceptual integration and paradigmatic agreement under the psychology-of-religion tent than there is within the discipline of psychology generally. The psychology of religion has inherited all of the traditional subdisciplinary distinctions and the deep theoretical rifts therefrom. Most of its practitioners are, back home, developmental or social or clinical psychologists, and they have much more in common with colleagues in those subdisciplines that with psychologists of religion trained in different subdisciplines. In many ways, a blind man studying elephants has much more in common with other blind men than with deaf men studying elephants. Consequently, the psychology of religion has no greater theoretical or conceptual integration than psychology as a whole.[4] It sounds like a wonderful idea to bring together researchers from disparate backgrounds under the same tent, introducing one another to alternative perspectives and celebrating diversity, but it does not solve the fundamental problems necessary to propel the field in the direction my agenda points.

In some ways, the existence of societies and journals dedicated to the psychology of (or scientific study of) religion has created more problems for the field than it has solved. By institutionalizing its estrangement, the psychology-of-religion field has come to provide a context in which research on religion can thrive despite being poorly informed by psychology generally. Major conceptual approaches too often have little in common with the theories of mainstream psychology. Allport's *intrinsic–extrinsic (I-E)* religious orientation framework, which has dominated the psychology of religion for some time, exemplifies this problem. Although originally situated within a broader theory of personality, I-E has taken on a life of its own without any clear theoretical guidance. (There is an enormous body of research in social psychology on the topic of "intrinsic" versus "extrinsic" motivation in general, but the I-E tradition in the psychology of religion is almost completely unrelated to it.) Such work would be extremely difficult to publish in "mainstream" psychology journals because editors and reviewers demand that new ideas be connected closely and explicitly to existing ones. Without such constraints, the research tradition has gradually drifted further and further from the remainder of psychology. Independence has become isolation, and the influx of theoretical ideas to the field from the rest of psychology has slowed to a trickle.

I hasten to add that my reasons for adopting a *psychological* perspective are not because I think psychology, as a discipline, is any better or more important than sociology, anthropology, or political science. Indeed, the framework I adopt in this book very much emphasizes the need for interdisciplinary cooperation to achieve the goal of a comprehensive scientific understanding of religion. We will need to integrate levels of analysis ranging from biology, through individual psychology, to the sociology and anthropology of groups, societies, and cultures; each of these levels of analysis is important. Situated at the nexus, if you will, between biology "below" it and sociology and political science "above it" (in the traditional vertical representation of these levels of analysis), psychology must play a pivotal role—the lynchpin, so to speak—in such an integration. (See Tooby & Cosmides, 1992, for a discussion.)

With respect to the long-term agenda I have laid out, the only solution to this self-perpetuating and destructive cycle is to reinvigorate the scientific study of religion with a fresh batch of theoretical ideas from psychology. The purpose of this book is to provide some direction for doing so.

Religion

Finally, by *religion* I mean. . . . Actually, at this point I am not going to tell you what I mean. This is not because I do not know how to define it (although it is true that I do not), nor because I am hiding some kind of special, unusual definition of religion to spring on you later. I assure you that I generally mean by "religion" pretty much what most people mean by the term, but I refuse to attempt to define it.

I expect most readers will be surprised by this. It is so typical for writers to begin any work related to religion by offering a working definition of religion that we assume it must be a necessary first step. However, I maintain that this is not the case. Indeed, not only is it unnecessary to define religion formally at the start, but it would be (and frequently has been in the past) counterproductive to do so.

I suggested earlier that if you start out conceptualizing the psychology of religion terrain in terms of the "of religion" part, you find yourself obligated to first define exactly what you mean by it. Because the problem of defining religion in a satisfactory manner appears to be intractable, the field has been unable to get out of the starting gate. Where, for example, does "religion" end and "spirituality" begin? Does belief in magic constitute religion? What about astrology? But if we start instead from the other direction, beginning with a theory (and/or metatheory) of psychology first, and then apply it to religious phenomena, the nagging problem of finding a precise definition of "religion" simply goes away.[5] A general psychological theory can be imported into any specific domain and applied to any particular phenomenon of interest, and it does not make a bit of difference whether you call the phenomenon "religion" or not. If you want to explain a highly specific phenomenon, you may be able to accomplish the task by drawing upon one or two specific theories; if you want to explain a broader range of phenomena, you will reach for a broader array of theories and components of the metatheory.

For example, certain specific aspects of (especially Christian) "religion," such as perceptions of having a personal relationship with a parent-like deity, can be well understood as manifestations of an evolved psychological system called the *attachment system*. Other qualitatively different aspects of "religion," such as religion-based morality, sacrifices to gods, and religiously motivated warfare, can be explained in terms of other (i.e., than attachment) psychological systems. Later in the book I try to show how the same psychological theory can be applied as well to topics at the margin of "religion," such as beliefs about parapsychology and other things supernatural, and then to other forms of belief and thought that clearly are not within the purview of what most people would call "religion." In the end I say a few things about how this science of psychology might be turned on science itself.

The point is that if you begin from the "psychology of" direction rather than the "of religion" direction, the definitional boundaries of those topics are irrelevant. But as we all know, there is no such thing as a free lunch. In this case, one problem is traded for another. Although the theory-driven approach circumvents the problem of defining the boundaries of "religion," it creates the problem of defining the boundaries of your *theory*. That is, if you begin by showing that the theory neatly explains a narrow range of observations, and then you broaden your scope and ask about related phenomena, you sooner or later run up against the question of the limits of generalizability of your theory.

So why would you want to make this trade? Judgments about the boundaries of a theory are not inherently easier to make than ones about the boundaries of topical definitions. This is where the importance of a paradigm, or *metatheory*, comes to the fore. If a specific theory represents one functionally distinct component of a coherent metatheory, there is no need to push the generalizability of a theory any further than its clear range of applicability. It is assumed from the outset that different psychological processes, explained by different specific theories, will be required to understand different phenomena. You can then render unto Caesar what is rightfully Caesar's.

Of course, this is not going to be as easy as it sounds: For many if not most phenomena, there will be multiple theories or components of the metatheory that all offer viable alternative solutions to the problem. But, to borrow a phrase from computer programmers, this is a feature, not a bug. It is much better to have too many hypotheses than too few. To the extent that the metatheory provides multiple hypotheses, you have some clear direction as to how to proceed in designing your empirical research, testing these competing hypotheses directly against one another.

A NEW DIRECTION

At least partially because of the kinds of reasons outlined earlier, the psychology-of-religion field has made sadly little progress toward the ambitious, long-term goal of a comprehensive scientific understanding of religion. This is not to say, however, that we have not learned anything, but rather that we have bits and pieces that overlap in some ways and fail to fit together into any kind of meaningful framework. What we *have* learned is this: From the endless debate over the definition of religion, it is clear that the topic of investigation is enormously complex and multifaceted; thus, any comprehensive theory will have to be commensurately multifaceted to accommodate it. From the measurement work in psychology we have learned that beliefs about God, religious motivation, and other psychological aspects of religion are similarly complex and multifaceted, again pointing to the need for a large-scale, all-encompassing framework. Cutting through the countless debates over interpretation, we have learned from anthropology that religion is (in some form or another) universal across human societies, yet also is highly variable in specific form across cultures. Again setting aside the details, we have learned from sociology that religions more often than not involve groups, which compete with one another, splinter, and evolve in various ways over time. A comprehensive approach to religion will have to provide a framework for dealing with these issues as well.

In this book I propose a couple of starting points: first, one particular psychological theory that I believe is useful for understanding a wide range of religious phenomena, and then a larger metatheory within which the theory fits and which provides a paradigm for organizing and integrating psychology in general as well as the psychology of religion in particular. In this section I briefly preview these two starting points and the ways in which they promise to forward the proposed agenda.

Attachment Theory

In the absence of a complete and comprehensive explanatory psychology from which to operate, the next best place to start will be a strong explanatory psychological theory that is sufficiently broad and deep to cover a lot of important ground. *Attachment theory*, as introduced by John Bowlby (1969, 1973, 1980) and since extended by a host of researchers in developmental, social, personality, and clinical psychology, provides a good place to start.

First, attachment theory is a fundamentally *psychological* theory. It was developed initially as a theory of infant social development, particularly focusing on the ways in which experience with caregivers shapes subsequent behavior and social relations; it was in no way developed specifically for the purpose of describing or explaining religion. Applying the theory to religion thus illustrates the process of importing theory from psychology to the study of religion, and offers a theoretical context for understanding religion in terms of the same processes and principles as other domains of motivation, emotion, and behavior. Such a theory has the potential to help reintegrate the psychology of religion with its parent discipline in a way that promises not only to benefit the psychology of religion but to feed back new observations and applications of the theory to psychology more generally.

Second, attachment theory is more *comprehensive* than most alternatives currently extant in the psychology of religion. It is one of few theories whose influence has been felt across many subdisciplines of contemporary psychology: From its initial (and continuing) powerful effect on developmental psychology, attachment theory has fanned out into clinical psychology, social psychology, and personality psychology in various ways, thus providing one path toward a psychology of religion that integrates numerous subdisciplines within psychology. It is not a theory about emotion, behavior, cognition, or physiology; it is a theory about all of these and, most important, about how all of these are integrated in an organized, functional way. The theory includes both normative and individual-difference components, which are needed if we wish to answer both normative questions (Why are people religious?) and individual-difference questions (Why are different people religious in different ways?) about religion.

Third, attachment theory is deeply *explanatory*. It does not merely describe how infants interact with their mothers, or adult romantic partners with one another, but purports to explain *why* humans are built in such a way that they behave this way. It not only provides a descriptive typology for conceptualizing individual differences in people's orientations toward personal relationships and intimacy, it purports to explain *how* these differences come about and *why* the system works in this rather than some other way. This functional, process-oriented approach enables its application to other phenomena such as religion, offering a basis for addressing questions about both the causes of and individual differences in religious belief and behavior.

Fourth, attachment theory is unambiguously a *scientific* theory. It has been supported by countless empirical studies reflecting a multitude of methodologies and populations, meaning not only that we can have considerable confidence in it, but also that it has clearly been demonstrated to be amenable to empirical testing. Perhaps equally important, however, is the fact that its application to religion is not laden by evaluative baggage. In contrast to earlier psychoanalytic formulations that presuppose religion to be inherently infantile, regressive, and mentally unhealthy, attachment theory provides a more value-neutral theoretical basis for understanding many of the same aspects of religious belief in which Freud was interested. Like Freud's theory, attachment theory focuses on human concerns about comfort and protection, and God is psychologically represented as a kind of parent figure. However, from an attachment theory perspective, there is absolutely nothing assumed to be "infantile" or "regressive" about any of this. As Bowlby argued cogently and other researchers have subsequently explored in depth, attachment system processes are designed to operate across the entire lifespan. Attachment theory thus provides a scientific view of how humans are designed with respect to these issues in a way that is inherently neither pro- nor anti-religious.[6]

Finally, there is one additional reason why attachment theory is particularly valuable for the psychology of religion, in the context of my pie-in-the-sky goal of a comprehensive theory. It is that attachment theory fits comfortably within a much larger and broader metatheory that has begun to emerge over the past decade or so, one that has the potential to be the overarching, paradigmatic framework that truly can integrate the many diverse areas and topics across the various subdisciplines of psychology.

Evolutionary Psychology

As broad and deep as attachment theory is, however, it is by no means a "comprehensive" theory of psychology, and thus is an unlikely candidate for a comprehensive theory of religion. I hope to convince you in the coming chapters that it can potentially explain a great deal about religious belief and behavior, but even if we stretch the theory to its limits, it will leave enormous chunks of religion untouched. Once we have exhausted the explanatory power of attachment theory, then what? Where will we go from there?

I propose the emerging paradigmatic framework of *evolutionary psychology* as the solution to this problem. In short, evolutionary psychology refers to an approach to psychological science that begins by acknowledging that the brain—the organ primarily responsible for producing and organizing all thought and behavior—is, like all other organs and physiological systems, the product of eons of evolution by natural selection. As such, it is assumed to have evolved to perform particular functions that reflect solutions to adaptive problems entailing (directly or indirectly) survival and/or reproduction. Much as the remainder of the body is well understood in terms of functional systems—a heart for pumping blood, a liver for detoxifying blood, lungs for exchanging gases with the atmosphere, and so forth—the brain/mind can be understood as a complex aggregation of evolved functional systems or *psychological mechanisms*. The "design" of these systems, then, should reflect the principles of natural selection as they operated on ancestral humans and prehumans, thus providing a wellspring of hypotheses for investigating thought and behavior in functional terms.

Evolutionary psychology, as the moniker suggests, is ultimately a *psychological* approach to understanding human behavior and experience. As noted earlier, it is about brains and minds: how they are organized, what they do, and how and why they do it. Moniker notwithstanding, however, the evolutionary paradigm itself is actually much broader than this: It has the potential not only to organize and integrate the various subdisciplines and diverse issues within psychology, but also to provide a foundation for organizing and integrating the social sciences as a whole. A proper understanding of the specieswide architecture of the human mind—as viewed from a functional perspective focusing on the question of what brains/minds were "designed" to do—is the fulcrum on which this organization pivots. On the one hand, the approach ties psychology to biology and ethology, from which it takes its fundamental theory. On the other hand, this model of the human mind provides a basis upon which other social sciences such as anthropology and sociology can be firmly founded. (See Tooby & Cosmides, 1992, and Wilson, 1998, for discussion.)

Moreover, evolutionary psychology is inherently *explanatory*, as it is organized around questions of *function*. The fundamental premise of the approach is that our species-universal psychological architecture—our "human nature," if you will—evolved to *do something*, namely, to solve the many specific adaptive problems of survival and reproduction faced by our distant ancestors. Evolutionary theory provides a guide for generating and testing hypotheses about what these problems were, and what kinds of solutions natural selection is likely to have produced in response. It is, in general, a (meta)theory about the *functions* of brains/ minds, not only predicting and describing what they do but also explaining why this is the case.

Evolutionary psychology is inherently *scientific* in several important ways. Like any scientific approach, it provides a source of hypotheses to be tested empirically using established social-scientific research methods. Moreover, it provides a perspective from which to approach religion that is not inherently value laden. Indeed, one of the most important insights of an evolutionary approach is the identification of a small number of clear principles by which natural selection distinguishes (reproductively) successful from unsuccessful designs; these criteria reflect nothing more and nothing less than the degree to which the genes producing alternative designs are differentially successful in producing copies of themselves in future generations. There is nothing inherently "good" or "bad" about the products of this process, including modern humans. However, when we judge these products in the context of our own moral, ethical, and practical criteria, we find that some aspects of human nature are more desirable to us than others. The same evolutionary processes that enable parents to love and nurture their children and romantic partners to love one another, for example, have also enabled humans to deceive, cheat, and wage war. Analogously, the aspects of evolved human psychology that enable religion run this entire gamut, giving rise to both its admirable and seamy sides.

For the purposes of my long-term agenda, however, the most important and unique characteristic of evolutionary psychology is its provision of a *comprehensive* and (especially) *integrative* framework for approaching the study of human behavior. The paradigm is not organized around any particular topic, and indeed is potentially applicable to any aspect of psychology one desires to study. Moreover, this framework is inherently interdisciplinary: It draws upon theory and observations from biology, ethology, primatology, anthropology, archaeology, and other sciences, bringing them together into a coherent perspective from which to view human behavior. In contrast to the *multidisciplinary* scientific study of religion, evolutionary psychology is truly *interdisciplinary*. This is the kind of approach we will need to construct a truly comprehensive science of religion.

THE PLAN OF THIS BOOK

My goal in this book is to sketch a "big picture" of what, ultimately, a comprehensive psychology (and to some extent, a social science) of religion might look like, based on evolutionary psychology. I have no hope of painting the entire picture, given our current state of knowledge in the field (and my own limited knowledge in particular). Instead, I provide a general outline of the entire picture, and fill in just one small part of it.

I try to do this in what may seem an unnatural sequence. I paint one corner (attachment theory) of the picture first, drawing in a fair amount of detail and even adding color and texture. Then I turn to the remainder of the canvas and splash across it a few broad, sweeping strokes, to provide a general impression of the outlines of some of the other parts and where they will go.

To be more specific: Attachment theory is introduced in Chapter 2, and Chapters 3 through 6 show how the theory might explain a variety of aspects of religion, particularly Christianity. Chapters 3 and 4 lay out the general theoretical arguments, and Chapters 5 and 6 review and organize the extant data. After briefly introducing evolutionary psychology (and showing where and how attachment theory fits within it) in Chapter 7, I revisit attachment theory in Chapter 8 to discuss some recent theoretical developments that have been motivated directly by an evolutionary perspective, and their implications for the attachment theory of religion.

The remaining chapters then turn from attachment theory in particular to evolutionary psychology more generally. I argue that the attachment system is just one of a large number of evolved behavioral systems that collectively comprise human nature, and that different aspects of religion reflect, to varying degrees, the operation of these various psychological mechanisms. In the second half of the book I introduce a number of other such systems and mechanisms and illustrate some ways in which this evolutionary-psychological perspective can organize our thinking about both the universality and the diversity of religion. This general approach is sketched out in Chapter 9 and contrasted with some alternative approaches.

The next two chapters examine other specific theories within evolutionary psychology, which are each briefly reviewed and accompanied by a variety of examples—drawing heavily upon the work of a handful of recent researchers whose work fits together nicely within this framework—of how the particular theory might be applied to various religious phenomena. Chapter 10 is comparable to the earlier attachment chapters in suggesting theoretical explanations for the specific forms that religious beliefs take; Chapter 11 digs down a bit more deeply to address the question of the very origins of religious belief in our evolved psychology. In Chapter 11 I discuss the application of this same theoretical framework, first, to other kinds of beliefs that are related to, but not typically included under the rubric of, religion, and, second, to science itself in order to demonstrate the generality of the approach.

If we ultimately are to achieve the goal of a truly comprehensive scientific account of religion, this general evolutionary–psychological model must be placed within a still broader framework. The design and organization of human brains/minds provide a crucial psychological foundation for religious belief and behavior, but the myriad ways in which these beliefs and behaviors actually play out and become distributed within and across populations involve a host of other processes that must also be understood. In Chapter 12 I sketch a framework for conceptualizing processes such as individual learning, complex reasoning, social learning, and cultural transmission as manifestations of higher levels of analysis layered on top of an evolutionary-psychological foundation—neither reducible to principles of evolutionary psychology nor alternatives to it.

It might well occur to you that the order of presentation would make more sense the other way around: that is, to start out with the broad, sweeping-outline strokes (evolutionary psychology), and then zero in on one particular area (attachment) to develop in more detail. I confess that in many ways this would indeed be a more sensible organization. But there are advantages to the order I have chosen as well, one of which is that it follows the progression of my own thinking over the last decade in more or less chronological order. By leading you along the same path I have taken myself, I hope it will be easier to show the way because I already know it. Nevertheless, in the final chapter I will provide a retrospective review of the book, this time telling the story in the other direction. You can then decide for yourself which version you prefer.

CHAPTER TWO

Introduction to Attachment Theory

John Bowlby may well have been the first modern evolutionary psychologist. Darwin was, of course, the first to apply the theory of evolution by natural selection to humans, a full century earlier, and the depth and breadth of his contribution is remarkable. However, I bestow the title of first *modern* evolutionary psychologist because Bowlby's conceptualization of the attachment system is a prototypical example of the way evolutionary psychologists today view the organization of behavioral and cognitive systems—a view he developed at least a decade (maybe two, depending on where you start counting) before modern evolutionary psychology arrived on the scene.

Since the publication of Bowlby's seminal 1969 volume, the first in his classic trilogy, attachment theory has steadily developed into one of the most successful theories in psychological science. It changed the face of research on children's personality and social development almost immediately after its appearance, and remains highly influential in this area to the present day. Thirty-five years is a very long time for a theory to remain "in vogue" in modern social science. A bit later, researchers in other areas of psychology began to take notice, and in the last decade or so attachment has developed into a leading approach in (adult) social and personality psychology, having found application to a diversity of topics, including romantic relationships, friendships, coping with stress, loneliness, grief, and miscellaneous other topics.

In order to make the case in subsequent chapters that attachment theory provides a powerful framework for understanding many aspects of religion as well, a review of the theory and some previous empirical research inspired by it is necessary. This is a formidable task, given the truly vast amount of work out there. Bowlby himself wrote four full books, not to mention numerous other articles and chapters, to spell out the theory. The recent *Handbook of Attachment* (Cassidy & Shaver, 1999), an encyclopedic edited volume covering the field in true "handbook" fashion, fills almost 1,000 pages. Moreover, many overviews of the theory and research have been published previously—just summarizing these summaries would require more than a chapter here. My review therefore will necessarily be incomplete and selective, focusing on those aspects of the theory and research most directly relevant to my present task.

BACKDROP

Bowlby was a psychiatrist, trained in the object relations school of psychoanalysis under Melanie Klein. His road to attachment theory began from this clinical focus: He was trying to understand a substantial mass of data demonstrating that children raised in institutional environments with limited contact with caregivers "failed to thrive." For Bowlby, existing psychoanalytic theory was simply not up to the task of explaining the devastating effects of maternal deprivation and separation on these children. His efforts to construct an alternative theoretical perspective that could make sense of these observations led him to something much larger, and ultimately far more influential, than the rather less ambitious goal with which he began.

Later in this chapter I discuss some of the reasons why Bowlby decided to break with his psychoanalytic past, and how his theoretical and methodological approach differs in several crucial ways from that of psychoanalysis. At this juncture I emphasize just one: his observation that much progress had occurred in sciences other than psychology and that psychoanalytic theory needed substantial updating to keep pace with these other developments. The most profound influences came from the then just-emerging field of *ethology*.

Several developments in this new field of ethological theory were of particular importance. First, such research had produced some striking examples of behavioral systems related to parent–offspring relationships in other species that clearly seemed relevant for thinking about human development. Lorenz's (1935) famous work on imprinting in geese suggested the existence of a behavioral system in hatchlings that worked according to a simple rule: Follow around the first large moving object you see. Ordinarily (i.e., in natural environments) this object would be the mother, of course, but Lorenz showed it could just as well be a rather silly-looking ethologist. Moreover, such a system made good evolutionary sense as a means of maintaining proximity between hatchlings and their mothers, thus providing the youngsters with protection when danger appears and maintaining a steady diet of observational learning. An imprinting system would not work in humans or other primates, of course, because infants are not capable of following their mothers around. But primates and their ancestors surely would have faced the same ecological problem of maintaining proximity between infants and their primary caregivers—in some ways more so because of the utter helplessness of the former and their initially complete dependence on the latter.

Another striking set of observations came from the equally famous work of Harlow (1958) with cloth and wire monkeys. In what was to become his most famous research, Harlow separated baby rhesus monkeys from their mothers and raised them in social isolation. He then provided them with two surrogate "mothers": one a vaguely mother-shaped cage of bare wire, equipped with a bottle for nursing; the other a similarly shaped object cloaked in fur and designed to be warm and fuzzy. Harlow found, of course, that the infant monkeys clung to the furry surrogate most of the time—particularly when they were frightened—using the wire surrogate merely to feed themselves. These findings are legendary in psychology, as well they should be. They demonstrated convincingly that, at least in rhesus monkeys, infants' interest in their mothers was not reducible to the need or desire for food or breast; they spontaneously sought physical contact and comfort for, presumably, entirely other reasons.

The second crucial influence of ethology was the radically new conceptualization it offered for the organization of behavior and motivation. Ethologists were beginning to draw upon *control systems theory* as an alternative to the simpler conceptualizations of "instincts" that had gone before. Previous theories of motivation—most notably, Freud's psychic energy model—viewed instinctive motives as generalized drives seeking expression. An instinctive drive for sex, for example, was thought to build up until it found an outlet and released its energy. Using control systems theory, however, ethologists were beginning to think about motivation in terms of behavioral *systems* that are turned on and turned off by particular kinds of stimuli. In the simple case of fixed action patterns, the connection is immediate and direct: The system is organized to activate a particular behavior or suite of behaviors whenever a stimulus appears, as in the classic example of male stickleback fish that attack anything with a large red spot (which, in its natural environment, would invariably be attached to a rival male). In more complex systems, positive and negative feedback loops are postulated for regulating behavior, including *homeostatic* systems. In the classic example of a climate-control system, a thermostat monitors the environment for deviations from a preprogrammed baseline temperature. If the ambient temperature falls below a threshold value, the heating system switches on; once the temperature comes back to criterion the system switches off.

THE ATTACHMENT SYSTEM

Although the story is actually more complex—Bowlby (1969) presented a lengthy and detailed analysis of ethological and psychological data to support his case—the general outline of attachment theory can be essentially reconstituted by combining these three sets of observations.[1] Bowlby postulated the existence of the attachment *system* as an evolved behavioral system in humans and other primates, which was designed by natural selection to maintain proximity between infants and their *attachment figures* (i.e., primary caregivers), with the ultimate purpose of protection of helpless infants from environmental dangers such as predators. That is, the evolutionary function of the system parallels to a large extent the imprinting system in geese. He further argued persuasively that this system is functionally distinct from other behavioral/motivational systems concerned with reproduction and nutrition. Babies do not love their mommies simply for their breasts.

The attachment system Bowlby postulated is, in line with control systems theory, a goal-corrected, or homeostatic, system. Instead of a thermostat monitoring ambient temperature and comparing it to a criterion of desired temperature (i.e., a *set point*), the system instead monitors proximity to the primary caregiver and compares it to a set point representing desired level of proximity. At one end of the continuum is physical contact (i.e., being held, hugged, swaddled); at the other end is out of sight and out of mind. The system constantly asks the question "Is my attachment figure sufficiently close/available?" (Hazan & Shaver, 1994).

The system is more complex than a simple homeostatic system, however, because the set point itself is variable. Other mechanisms are designed to monitor a variety of both external and internal cues and adjust the set point—that is, the degree of proximity to the attachment figure desirable under the current circumstances—accordingly. In particular, a higher level of proximity is desirable if the environment appears dangerous, or if one's current health status makes one especially vulnerable. Bowlby argued, using sound ecological and evolutionary reasoning, that certain families of stimuli were, in ancestral environments, reliably correlated with danger: for example, unfamiliarity, heights, looming objects, and loud and sudden noises; consequently, fear of such stimuli is "hardwired" in the infant. Such stimuli activate both the fear system and the attachment system, with the former motivating efforts to avoid or escape from the stimulus, and the latter motivating efforts to increase proximity to the attachment figure. Second, he pointed out that the system also monitors internal states such as illness, fatigue, and injury; the presence of such conditions, like external danger, calls for greater proximity and enhanced caregiving from the attachment figure.

It is also important to note, particularly for the thesis of this book, that the *set point* of the system tends to change over the course of development as well. Infants and very young children are typically comforted after a scare only by physical contact, but as they grow older they are reassured by the caregiver being close by, or even simply by vocal or visual contact. In adulthood—a topic to which we will turn shortly—a telephone call or even an e-mail might do, at least in times of moderate distress; actual physical comforting may be required to fully deactivate the system in highly stressful circumstances.

If, compared to the current system set point, the attachment figure is regarded as insufficiently proximal and available, a suite of behavioral options is activated. These *attachment behaviors* are designed to bring the attachment figure into closer proximity, as the heating system is designed to restore the warmth of a room. At birth human infants come equipped with one all-purpose attachment behavior—crying—but as they get older other behavioral options begin to appear, which include clinging, reaching with outstretched arms, and (eventually) physical locomotion.

If these efforts are successful and a sufficient level of proximity is restored, the behavioral system is deactivated. If the attachment figure is indeed sufficiently available, however, no further care-seeking action is immediately required. The attachment system is deactivated (though it continues to monitor the situation for change), thus enabling the activation of other behavioral systems which otherwise receive lower priority.

Other Related Systems

The most commonly discussed "other" behavioral system in this context is the *exploration* system. In some ways this is the "flip side" of attachment, to the extent that some researchers (Bretherton, 1985) prefer to think of attachment and exploration as two complementary parts of a larger system. Human (and other primate) youngsters need to spend time exploring their environments, acquiring and practicing new skills and knowledge—and the more, the better. Were this not true, a more efficient protection system (at least from the infant's point of view) would be one in which the child never leaves his or her mother's arm, but this is not what natural selection has fashioned in humans.

Instead, attachment and exploration are linked in a kind of "dynamic equilibrium" (Cassidy, 1999): The exploration system is activated under normal, familiar circumstances, with the child metaphorically or literally keeping one eye on the mother's whereabouts while at play. (Actually, the child is likely to periodically move back closer to the attachment figure at regular intervals to check in and make sure he or she is still attentive and available, a phenomenon labeled *social referencing* by Campos and Stenberg, 1981.) If the attachment figure moves away, or if the child becomes frightened or injured, the attachment system is activated and attachment behaviors appear; the exploration system is simultaneously deactivated. Assuming that attachment behaviors are successful in restoring adequate proximity, the attachment system is then deactivated and exploration can begin anew. It is in this sense that attachment figures offer two relational provisions: a *haven of safety* to which to turn in times of distress or danger, and a *secure base* for exploration at other times. Confidence in the accessibility and reliability of the attachment figure enhances the ability to explore and to do so with confidence.

Most theorists would agree that these provisions are two of the crucial defining characteristics of an attachment relationship—as distinguished from other kinds of interpersonal relationships. For example, Cassidy (1999) notes the existence of another relational behavioral system in childhood, an *affiliative* or *sociable* system regulating relationships with peers. Although both attachments and affiliative peer relations have some things in common—both are bonds with people with whom one desires proximity, for example—each represents a unique kind of relationship with its own distinct functions. From an evolutionary perspective, it seems likely that natural selection has fashioned functionally differentiated, though perhaps in some ways partially overlapping, systems to perform these functions. This idea of functional *domain-specificity* of evolved mechanisms is a hallmark of modern evolutionary psychology, and I make much use of the idea later.

On the other side of the equation, another behavioral system that obviously plays a crucial role in this scenario is a parental *caregiving* figure in the attachment system. The attachment system could not have evolved unless caregivers were already designed to nurture and care for their offspring; it must instead have evolved subsequently as a means of eliciting and regulating the care provided by parents. Like the infant's attachment system, the caregiving system can also be conceptualized as an integrated complex of evolved mechanisms activated by certain cues (e.g., infant attachment behaviors and the infant's own perceptions of danger) and producing organized patterns of behavior (picking up and holding the infant, comforting the infant with "baby talk"). In subsequent chapters we revisit the caregiving system in several contexts, including the issue of how the caregiving and attachment systems may be related across the lifespan.

The Phenomenology of Attachment

Many of these ideas can be expressed in other ways, given a shift in viewpoint. For example, Sroufe and Waters (1977a) suggest that from the phenomenological stance of the child (or other attached person), the barometer in the attachment system is the level of *felt security*. That is, a feeling of "insecurity" is what one experiences when the attachment figure is too far away relative to the proximity desired (as a function, in turn, of perceived danger, own health, and so forth), thus activating the attachment system. In contrast, a reduced level of danger and/or close proximity to the primary caregiver leads one to feel "secure," motivating one to enthusiastically and confidently explore the environment. In Bowlby's (1973) words, "When an individual is confident that an attachment figure will be available to him whenever he desires it, that person will be much less prone to either intense or chronic fear than will an individual who for any reason has no such confidence" (p. 202). The secure base provided by the attachment figure gives rise to a sense of security and confidence with which to approach and master one's environment. In the face of threat, the haven of safety provided by the attachment figure offers solace and comfort.

The dynamics of attachment are experienced to large extent in terms of the major emotions. Many of the most intense emotions, according to Bowlby (1980), are associated with attachment dynamics. In an oft-cited quote, Bowlby (1980) wrote that

> many of the most intense emotions arise during the formation, the maintenance, the disruption and the renewal of attachment relationships. The formation of a bond is described as falling in love, maintaining a bond as loving someone, and losing a partner as grieving over someone. Similarly, threat of loss arouses anxiety and actual loss gives rise to sorrow while each of these situations is likely to around anger. The unchallenged maintenance of a bond is experienced as a source of security and the renewal of a bond as a source of joy. (p. 40)

As with many, if not most, psychological processes or mechanisms, people are not generally privy to the internal dynamics governing attachment in their brains: Our phenomenological experience is not that of a set point being crossed or a behavioral system being activated; instead, we feel the push and pull of emotional states. We simply find ourselves feeling anxious or secure. If it is the former, we take action, such as reestablishing contact with our attachment figure, that we know from experience has the intended effect of making us feel better. We love our mommy and feel sad when she leaves, and we feel devastated if she leaves and is not expected to return.

In general, we feel a strong affectional *bond* with our attachment figures. As noted by Bowlby in the preceding quotation, an attachment relationship is experienced as loving and/or feeling loved. It is important to bear in mind, however, that attachment represents only one of many kinds of psychological bonds. Ainsworth (1985) distinguished "affectional bonds" from role-oriented relationships, emphasizing that an attachment bond is formed with a particular *individual* rather than a class or category of people. Most researchers seem to agree that the defining features of an attachment relationship include the provision of feelings of comfort and security, the role of the attachment figure as both a haven of safety (in the presence of threat) and secure base for exploration (in the absence of threat), and the distress and/or protest occasioned by potential or actual separation from the attachment figure. Weiss (1982), focusing mainly on adults, distinguished six functions provided by qualitatively distinct kinds of bonds or close relationships. Whereas attachment relationships are characterized by the provision of security, other relationships offer such provisions as affiliation or social integration, opportunity for nurturance (caregiving), collaboration and reassurance of worth, a sense of persisting alliance, and obtaining help or guidance.

One other important implication of this conceptualization is that attachment is a property of a *relationship* between two individuals, as experienced from the perspective of one of them (the "attached" person). It is not strictly a property of the individual (e.g., a personality trait), but neither is it a property of the relationship per se. Instead, it is "a bond that one individual has to another individual who is perceived as stronger and wiser" (Cassidy, 1999, p. 12). This idea is particularly important in the context of individual differences, to which we turn in the next section.

Although it is tempting to think of attachment differences in terms of the *strength* of the bond, Cassidy (1999) advises against this. For example, it would certainly be a mistake to equate strength or frequency of attachment behaviors with strength of bond: A behavior such as fearful clinging could result from either secure or insecure attachment, depending on context (see next section). Instead, Cassidy suggests Hinde's (1979) term *penetration*, in reference to the extent to which a relationship with an individual pervades many diverse aspects of the attached person's life. Thus, for example, when parental attachments "fade" in adolescence to be replaced by peer attachments, it is more accurate to think in terms of reduced penetration of the parental bond than to its "weakening."

Individual Differences in Attachment in Childhood

The picture of attachment sketched so far sounds rather idyllic, with mothers (or other primary caregivers) and children living in a harmonious, symbiotic relationship. Children confidently explore their environment, playing and learning, under the watchful eye of the caring parent and feeling secure and loved. When distressed, they reunite with the loving, nurturing caregiver, who can always be counted upon to offer solace and protection. Once the danger has passed, the recharged child heads back out to the world at the end of a secure tether until the next frightening episode.

The real world is not quite so idyllic, of course—at least not for everybody. Infant–mother relationships do not always follow the pattern just described. From the beginning, attachment theorists have been cognizant of this reality. In fact, the best known aspect of attachment theory, particularly to those outside a few areas of specialization in developmental and social psychology, concerns the nature and measurement of *individual differences* in attachment.

Empirical research on attachment was pioneered by Mary Ainsworth and her colleagues, who developed a laboratory procedure known as the *Strange Situation* to assess individual differences in infant–mother attachment (Ainsworth, Blehar, Waters, & Wall, 1978). In this structured-observation methodology, mothers (or fathers, though more often the former) and their infants come to the lab and are put together into a room containing a variety of toys. A standardized series of episodes then unfolds, involving the mother leaving the child alone in the room, and the entrance and exit of a stranger both in the mother's presence and in her absence. The sessions are observed and/or videotaped surreptitiously and evaluated by coders according to an elaborate and detailed scoring system. The primary focus of the observations concerns the child's responses to separation from the mother, reunion with the mother following separation, and interactions with the stranger.

Based on extensive research with this system, Ainsworth and colleagues (Ainsworth, Blehar, Waters, & Wall, 1978) identified three general *patterns* of attachment. In brief, "Type B" (subsequently labeled *secure*) infants are moderately distressed by brief separation from their mothers, but are quickly comforted upon her return. Type A (*avoidant*) infants behave as if they were indifferent to separation and reunion in the Strange Situation: They outwardly appear nonplussed by the mother's exit, and seem to ignore her (while continuing to play) upon her return. (However, physiological measures indicate that despite their behavior, they are no less distressed by these episodes than other children; Sroufe & Waters, 1977b). Type C (*resistant*; often referred to alternatively as *anxious*, *ambivalent*, or *anxious/ambivalent*) infants are in some ways the opposite of the avoidant infants, displaying extreme distress when separated from their mothers and failing to evince confident exploration of the environment in her presence. Upon reunion they are very difficult to calm and alternate between clinging, proximity-promoting behaviors and resistant, angry behaviors. Table 2.1 summarizes the differences among these patterns. In American samples, the relative proportions of infants classified across these categories averages roughly 60% for secure, 25% for avoidant, and 15% for anxious.[2]

TABLE 2.1. Strange Situation Classification Groups

Group	Brief description
Secure (B) (Ainsworth et al., 1978)	Uses mother as secure base for exploration. Separation: Signs of missing parent, especially during the second separation. Reunion: Actively greets parent with smile, vocalization, or gesture. If upset, signals or seeks contact with parent. Once comforted, returns to exploration.
Avoidant (A) (Ainsworth et al., 1978)	Explores readily, little display of affect or secure-base behavior. Separation: Responds minimally, little visible distress when left alone. Reunion: Looks away from, actively avoids parent; often focuses on toys. If picked up, may stiffen, lean away. Seeks distance from parent, often interested instead in toys.
Ambivalent or resistant (C) (Ainsworth et al., 1978)	Visibly distressed upon entering room, often fretful or passive; fails to engage in exploration. Separation: Unsettled, distressed. Reunion: May alternate bids for contact with signs of angry rejection, tantrums; or may appear passive or too upset to signal, make contact. Fails to find comfort in parent.
Disorganized/ disoriented (D) (Main & Solomon, 1990)	Behavior appears to lack observable goal, intention, or explanation-for example, contradictory sequences or simultaneous behavioral displays; incomplete, interrupted movement; stereotypies; freezing/stilling; direct indications of fear/apprehension of parent; confusion, disorientation. Most characteristic is lack of a coherent attachment strategy, despite the fact that the baby may reveal the underlying patterns of organized attachment (A, B, C).

Note. Descriptions in Groups A, B, and C are based on Ainsworth et al. (1978). Descriptions in Group D are based on Main and Solomon (1990). From Solomon and George (1999, p. 291). Copyright 1999 by The Guilford Press. Reprinted by permission.

The origins of these individual differences, according to attachment theory, are found in large part in maternal behavior—that is, the child's experience in relevant situations across the first year or so of life. Unlike Lorenz's goslings, human infants do not bond to their mothers immediately after birth; rather, their attachments develop slowly over the first year to 18 months of life. According to research by Ainsworth and by other researchers (e.g., Ainsworth et al., 1978; see Weinfield, Sroufe, Egeland, & Carlson, 1999, for a recent review), the crucial variable appears to be the degree to which mothers are *reliably sensitive* to the infants' attachment behaviors. Thus, mothers of secure infants are characterized by sensitive and appropriate responding to the infants' signals of distress and attempts to gain and maintain proximity. Mothers of avoidant infants are consistently the opposite, rebuffing their infants' attempts to gain proximity and failing to be psychologically and/or physically available when called upon. Mothers of anxious babies are characterized by insensitivity to the infant's signals, being inconsistently available when proximity is desired and sometimes intrusive at inappropriate times. Their mothers tend to reject the infant's attempts to gain proximity and largely try to avoid physical contact with the infant. Although the empirical relationship between caregiver sensitivity and subsequent attachment security is not always large in individual studies, the relationship has been confirmed in a meta-analysis of 66 studies (De-Wolff & van IJzendoorn, 1997).[3]

From the control theory perspective, one way to think about these individual differences is in terms of the activation of the attachment system. In *anxious* infants, the attachment system can be thought of as being on a "hair trigger": Due to chronic uncertainty about whether the attachment figure will be available when needed, the system is hypervigilant with respect to monitoring the caregiver's whereabouts and thus readily activated by any hint of potential separation. In contrast, the attachment system in *avoidant* infants is activated under only the most extreme conditions. Routine threats of separation or danger fail to engage the behavioral system, even though physiological measures reveal that the infants are in fact experiencing distress (Sroufe & Waters, 1977b), presumably as a consequence of a developmental history in which attempts to gain proximity to and comfort from the caregiver have been repeatedly rebuffed. Bowlby (1969) described a variety of ways the avoidance may be accomplished, including a process of *defensive exclusion* of information, related to various kinds of defense mechanisms in psychoanalytic theory.

Multiple Attachment Figures

I have been speaking so far as if infants and children have only one attachment figure, but Bowlby acknowledged from the beginning that in
many or most cases an individual may have multiple attachment figures.
For children, other attachment figures may include older siblings, other
kin, or regular day care providers. However, he argued that the number of
such figures is relatively few, and importantly, these attachments are not
entirely interchangeable: A *hierarchy* of attachment figures typically
exists, with one special individual (usually, but not necessarily, the
mother) at the top. Bowlby (1969) referred to this principle as *monotropy*.
Empirical evidence shows that most children prefer to turn to their
mothers when distressed, but in her absence will approach other attachment figures as well. Cassidy (1999) suggests several good evolutionary
reasons why the system might be built this way: to establish a relationship with an individual who will take primary responsibility for the
child's care (i.e., to avoid the child "falling between the cracks"); to facilitate rapid decision making about whom to approach in the face of immediate danger; and to identify which caregiver provides the most
sensitive and reliable care and (presumably) is the most invested in the
child's welfare.

Importantly, individual differences in attachment patterns may well
differ across these relationships. Numerous studies have employed the
Strange Situation to classify infants with respect to attachment patterns
to both mothers and fathers separately, with varied results. Fox,
Kimmerly, and Schafer (1991) concluded from a meta-analysis of 11 such
studies that, although many researchers previously had found little or no
correlation between maternal and paternal attachments, there is substantial concordance between an infant's attachment classification to its
mother and to its father. In my own view their data can easily be interpreted either as a half-empty glass or a half-full glass (the kappa coeffi-
cient from only one of their six analyses was above .60, and examination
of the cross-tabulation tables reveals sizeable proportions of off-diagonal
cases). In any case, the less-than-perfect correspondence reinforces the
notion that an attachment is a relationship-specific bond between persons, not a general personality trait—that is, a property of a relationship
rather than of an individual. Most researchers agree, however, that in the
case of multiple attachment figures there is always (or at least typically)
one *primary* attachment figure. If the child were suddenly frightened and

all of his or her attachment figures were lined up in a row, the primary attachment figure is the one to whom the child would run first.

Internal Working Models and the Stability of Attachment Patterns

The theoretical link between maternal behavior and infant patterns of attachment is Bowlby's (1973) notion of *internal working models* (or *mental models*) of attachment (see also Bretherton, 1985; Collins & Read, 1994; Main et al., 1985). Based on repeated experience, infants and children develop a set of expectations and beliefs—a *schema*, in cognitive terms—about the availability and responsiveness of their primary caregivers which guides future behavioral, emotional, and cognitive responses in social interactions. In essence, mental models represent the child's answer to the question: "Can I count on my attachment figure to be available and responsive when needed?" The three possible answers are yes (*secure*), no (*avoidant*), and maybe (*anxious*; Hazan & Shaver, 1994).

Internal working models (IWMs) are also generally invoked to explain the consistency of attachment patterns, as well as other correlates of attachment patterns, across time. Main, Kaplan, and Cassidy (1985) showed that classifications based on the Strange Situation paradigm are fairly stable between 1 and 6 years of age. Other longitudinal studies have shown that various theoretically relevant aspects of personality and social behavior throughout childhood are predictable from infant Strange Situation classification, including such variables as self-reliance, dependency on teachers and other adults, empathy, anger-proneness, aggression, social skills and competence, and psychopathology (see Weinfield et al., 1999, for a review and references). Although IWMs are understood to be malleable (indeed, they are constructed from experience which, of course, may change across time), they are assumed to be relatively stable and resistant to change once established.

Another important aspect of IWMs concerns perceptions and evaluations of the self. Bowlby argued that in early life, IWMs concerning the degree to which caregivers are reliable providers of love, care, and protection are linked inextricably to mental models of the self as worthy of love, care, and protection. As a consequence of cognitive development, along with more varied experience with individuals other than the primary attachment figure, the models of self and others can become decoupled. The conceptual differentiation of self versus others models is a useful theoretical tool in understanding attachment in adulthood (and later, in religion), as will become evident in the next section.

ATTACHMENT IN ADULTHOOD

Bowlby clearly believed that attachment processes were important across the entire lifespan—"from the cradle to the grave," in an oft-quoted phrase. Specifically, he intimated that early attachment experience, and the IWMs of attachment developed early on, were carried forward into adulthood as models of close relationships. Bowlby did not develop these ideas in detail, but subsequent researchers have taken up the idea and run with it in various directions.

Research on adult attachment generally is built upon the premise that IWMs constructed based on early attachment experience provide the cognitive and emotional building blocks from which close relationships later life are constructed (Sroufe & Fleeson, 1986). In light of research noted earlier showing that individual differences in attachment are relatively stable across time, and are predictive of a variety of social and personality variables throughout childhood, it seems reasonable to expect that such influences continue throughout the lifespan. Although IWMs are thought to be malleable and certainly can and do change in response to new experiences and changes in life situation, Bowlby argued that they are conservative and tend to remain stable by default. Such thinking has led to several applications of the theory to adulthood.

Attachment and Adult Romantic Relationships

Perhaps the most direct application of Bowlby's ideas to adulthood is the idea that certain kinds of interpersonal relationships between adults function psychologically, at least in part, as attachments. In one early application of the theory, Weiss (1973) carried the notion of the functional specificity of attachment into the study of loneliness. He distinguished two types of loneliness in adulthood: *emotional isolation*, resulting from the lack of a single deep, intimate attachment, and *social isolation*, resulting from a lack of friendships and acquaintances of other kinds. This idea has received some empirical support from research by Cutrona and Russell (1987). As noted previously, Weiss (1974, 1986) later went on to outline six functionally distinct relational provisions offered by different kinds of adult relationships, one of which was attachment.

However, it was not until the publication of two seminal papers by Cindy Hazan and Phil Shaver in the late 1980s that a sustained research program on the topic emerged—one that has now grown into an enormous literature. In a theoretical chapter, Shaver, Hazan, and Bradshaw (1988) outlined a case for conceptualizing adult romantic love relationships as the "integration of three behavioral systems": *attachment*, *caregiving*, and *sex/reproduction*. In such relationships, they argued, romantic partners serve as attachment figures for one another, turning to each other for comfort and support in times of distress and using each other as a secure base. Shaver et al. reviewed a diverse array of research findings and observations to demonstrate the many similarities and parallels between infant–mother interactions and interactions between adult lovers. For example, prolonged eye contact, cooing or talking "baby talk," and other intimate behaviors are similar to the sorts of behaviors displayed by infants to elicit and maintain contact with an attachment figure.

Individual Differences in Adult Romantic Attachment

Hazan and Shaver (1988) subsequently reasoned that if adult love relationships function in part as attachments, then patterns of individual differences—"attachment styles"—may exist among adults that parallel those documented by Ainsworth et al. (1978) in infants. In two empirical studies, they presented college students and respondents, respectively, to a newspaper survey, with a self-report measure developed to assess such differences. Respondents were simply asked to indicate which of three paragraph-length prototypes, designed to reflect what the authors construed to be the "grown-up" versions of infant attachment patterns, best described them. The three prototypes, which have been widely used in subsequent research (including research on religion to be discussed later), were as follows:

1. *Avoidant*: I am somewhat uncomfortable being close to others; I find it difficult to trust them completely, difficult to allow myself to depend on them. I am nervous whenever anyone gets too close, and often, others want me to be more intimate than I feel comfortable being.

2. *Secure*: I find it relatively easy to get close to others and am comfortable depending on them and having them depend on me. I don't worry about being abandoned or about someone getting too close to me.
3. *Anxious/ambivalent*: I find that others are reluctant to get as close as I would like. I often worry that my partner doesn't really love me or won't want to stay with me. I want to get very close to my partner, and this sometimes scares people away.

These and literally hundreds of studies since have consistently demonstrated that individual differences on this and other related measures correlate consistently with a wide variety of theoretically relevant variables. A review of the findings is impossible here (for a book-length review, see J. Feeney & Noller, 1996). Much of this research has focused on aspects or correlates of IWMs of (adult) attachment—that is, differences among these groups in their perceptions, beliefs, and values concerning close relationships—as well as the nature and quality of individuals' intimate relationships. Table 2.2 summarizes some of the principal themes that have emerged from this research. Other research using longitudinal designs and laboratory experiments has shown that people self-classified as secure have longer-lasting love relationships (Kirkpatrick & Davis, 1994; Kirkpatrick & Hazan, 1994); show different patterns of behavior (Simpson, Rholes, & Nelligan, 1992) and physiological responses (Carpenter & Kirkpatrick, 1996; B. Feeney & Kirkpatrick, 1996) to stressful situations in the laboratory; and exhibit a multitude of other differences consistent with the theory.

As in childhood, IWMs of self and others in adulthood are postulated to mediate the kinds of effects reviewed earlier. Although the level at which such mental models operate is a matter of some debate, it seems likely that people maintain in part both (1) mental models concerning attachment figures in general, and (2) mental models specific to particular relationships. Collins and Read (1994) suggest that such models are hierarchically arranged, with a top level characterized by a highly general model of self and others, a second level comprising models of parent–child relationships versus peer relationships, and so on. The moderate degree of correspondence between maternal and paternal attachment classifications (Fox et al., 1991) provides some support for Collins and Read's (1994) hierarchical framework: That is, there is greater correspondence than would be expected if relationship-specific mental models

TABLE 2.2. Attachment Group Differences in Working Models

Secure	Avoidant	Ambivalent
Memories		
Parents warm and affectionate	Mothers cold and rejecting	Fathers unfair
Attachment-related beliefs, attitudes		
Few self-doubts; high in self-worth	Suspicious of human motives	Others complex and difficult to understand
Generally liked by others	Others not trustworthy or dependable	People have little control over own lives
Others generally well-intentioned and good-hearted	Doubt honesty and integrity of parents and others	
Others generally trustworthy, dependable, and altruistic	Lack confidence in social situations	
Interpersonally oriented	Not interpersonally oriented	
Attachment-related goals and needs		
Desire intimate relationships	Need to maintain distance	Desire extreme intimacy
Seek balance of closeness and autonomy in relationships	Limit intimacy to satisfy needs for autonomy	Seek lower levels of autonomy
	Place greater weight on goals such as achievement	Fear rejection
Plans and strategies		
Acknowledge distress	Manage distress by cutting off anger	Heightened displays of distress and anger
Modulate negative affect in constructive way	Minimize distress-related emotional displays; withhold intimate disclosure	Solicitous and compliant to gain acceptance

Note. From J. A. Feeney (1999, p. 364). Copyright 1999 by The Guilford Press. Reprinted by permission.

were independent, but less than would be expected from a singular, generalized mental model alone. Whether or not various levels of attachment-relevant mental representations are arranged in this precise hierarchical structure, it seems certain that mental models of various levels of generality are interconnected at least to some degree.

Factorial and Dimensional Models

Since the publication of Hazan and Shaver's seminal work, numerous researchers have attempted to improve and expand the measurement of individual differences in romantic attachment. Perhaps the most important theoretical development was introduced by Bartholomew (1990; Bartholomew & Horowitz, 1991), who proposed the existence of a fourth attachment style. Specifically, Bartholomew suggested a distinction between two distinct forms of *avoidance*, reflecting different motivational bases for avoidant behavior in relationships: in short, a *dismissing* avoidant style, reflecting a devaluing of close relationships (i.e., a self-reliant, who-needs-'em attitude), and a *fearful* avoidant style, reflecting an avoidance of intimacy due to fear of being hurt (i.e., an others-can't-be-trusted attitude). Moreover, Bartholomew showed how the resulting four styles can be meaningfully represented in a 2 x 2 framework, as illustrated in Figure 2.1. One dimension—contrasting *secure* and *preoccupied* (i.e. *anxious/ambivalent*) versus the two avoidant (*fearful* and *dismissing*) types—reflects differences in mental models of *others*, whereas the second dimension—contrasting *secure* and *dismissing* versus *preoccupied* and *fearful*—reflects differences in mental models of the *self*. Several self-report measures have been developed by Bartholomew and others to assess the four attachment styles (e.g., via self-classification on prototypes, as per Hazan & Shaver, 1987) and the two dimensions (e.g., via multi-item scales), and Bartholomew has also introduced a structured interview procedure as well.

Other researchers, concerned primarily about the psychometric reliability of the prototype measure, have introduced multi-item scales to assess the Hazan–Shaver attachment styles (e.g., Collins & Read, 1990; Simpson et al., 1992). Much factor-analytic work on these and the Bartholomew scales has converged on the notion that individual differences can be captured well by a two-dimensional model in which one factor generally contrasts *security* versus *avoidance* and the other (more or less orthogonal) factor reflects *anxiety* (versus the lack thereof). This conceptualization overlaps considerably with Bartholomew's 2 × 2 model, with IWMs of *self* largely related to the *anxiety* dimension (i.e., people who doubt their own lovability are more fearful about being rejected) and models of *others* largely related to the *avoidance* dimension (i.e., comfort with and desire to have close, intimate relationships with others). (See Brennan, Clark, & Shaver, 1998, for a complete discussion.) Table 2.3 summarizes some of the empirical correlates of these dimensions.

The Formation and Development of Adult Love Bonds

The vast majority of work on adult romantic attachments has focused on individual differences, particularly correlates of attachment styles as measured in the ways discussed earlier. In some important recent work, Hazan and Zeifman (1999; Zeifman & Hazan, 1997) have revived a normative perspective to reexamine the crucial question of whether adult romantic bonds are, in fact, attachment bonds in the technical sense, and to explore the development of such bonds vis-à-vis the ontogeny of infant attachment bonds. Unlike most of the research reviewed earlier, the

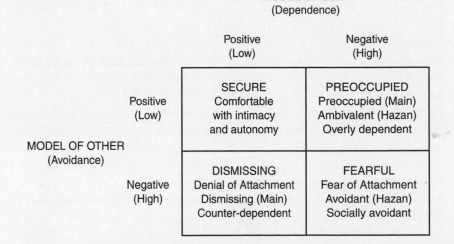

MODEL OF SELF
(Dependence)

	Positive (Low)	Negative (High)
Positive (Low)	SECURE Comfortable with intimacy and autonomy	PREOCCUPIED Preoccupied (Main) Ambivalent (Hazan) Overly dependent
Negative (High)	DISMISSING Denial of Attachment Dismissing (Main) Counter-dependent	FEARFUL Fear of Attachment Avoidant (Hazan) Socially avoidant

MODEL OF OTHER
(Avoidance)

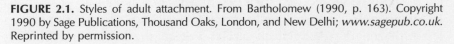

FIGURE 2.1. Styles of adult attachment. From Bartholomew (1990, p. 163). Copyright 1990 by Sage Publications, Thousand Oaks, London, and New Delhi; *www.sagepub.co.uk*. Reprinted by permission.

Hazan–Zeifman model does not assume (though it also does not necessarily reject) continuity of attachment, with respect to either function or patterns of individual differences, from childhood to adulthood.

Zeifman and Hazan (1997; Hazan & Zeifman, 1999) review a wide variety of data to support their claim that the psychology and biology underlying the two kinds of relationships are highly similar for such features as responses to separation and loss; the characteristics desirable in a partner (e.g., kindness, understanding); the process of bond development; the nature of intimate, physical contact and behavior (that is taboo in other relationships); overall effects on psychological and immune functioning; and underlying biochemistry (e.g., the role of oxytocin, phenylethylamine, and endorphins). They further outline a developmental model of adult attachment formation—through stages of *preattachment* (attraction and flirting), *attachment in the making* (falling in love), *clearcut attachment* (loving), and *goal-corrected partnership*. Hazan and Zeifman (1999) report two empirical studies showing that the transfer of attachments from parents to peers follows a progression in which three primary components of attachment—proximity seeking, haven of safety, and secure base—shift one by one rather than simultaneously, and that all three of these components are found together in peer attachments only among adults in committed, pair-bond relationships.

TABLE 2.3. Key Aspects of Relationship Quality Associated with Subjects' Own Attachment Style

Comfort with closeness (cf. secure vs. avoidant attachment)	Anxiety over relationships (cf. ambivalent attachment)
Trust	Lack of trust
Relationship satisfaction (M)	Relationship dissatisfaction (F)
Commitment	Jealousy
Closeness/interdependence	High levels of conflict (F)
Supportiveness	Coercion, domination, and distress in response to dyadic conflict
Self-disclosure, including flexibility and reciprocity of disclosure	Lack of compromise in dyadic problem solving
Involvement and satisfaction in daily interactions with partner (M)	Low involvement and satisfaction in daily interactions with partner (F)

Note. (M) indicates that these associations have been reported primarily for males; (F) indicates that these associations have been reported primarily for females. From J. A. Feeney (1999, p. 368). Copyright 1999 by The Guilford Press. Reprinted by permission.

An Alternative Approach to Adult Attachment

Perhaps attesting to the richness of Bowlby's ideas, a second school of adult attachment research has developed contemporaneously, and almost entirely independently, of this romantic attachment tradition. (Actually, it predates the romantic attachment school by several years.) Based on a very different conceptualization of attachment in adulthood, this line of research has centered on a structured interview technique known as the *Adult Attachment Interview* (AAI; see George & Solomon, 1999, for a historical review and description of the procedure). Although this approach has played little role to date in the research on religion to be discussed in subsequent chapters, I would be remiss by not saying at least a few words about it.

The AAI assesses one's "current state of mind with respect to attachment." The interview includes a variety of questions about one's current feelings and childhood memories of relationships with one's parents. The scoring of the interview, however, has little to do with the actual content of people's responses to these questions, in terms of the positivity or negativity of these memories or thoughts about one's relationships with one's parents. Instead, scoring focuses on such matters as the consistency and coherence of discourse—for example, the degree to which respondents can support generalizations about parents with illustrative concrete examples, and the degree to which they present and organize responses in a "collaborative" manner. Trained coders later classify respondents into three principal categories: *secure/autonomous*, *preoccupied*, or *dismissing*—which roughly parallel the three Ainsworth infant categories and the three Hazan–Shaver romantic attachment categories.

The scoring procedure was initially developed according to a specific criterion: maximizing the statistical prediction of respondents' own infants' classification in the Strange Situation. Much research has since confirmed this criterion validity in independent samples (see Hesse, 1999, for a review), including studies in which AAI measures were obtained prior to the birth of the child (Fonagy, Steele, & Steele, 1991). Other studies have extended these findings to show that parental AAI classification is predictive of various other child characteristics beyond infancy.

The problem, however, is that it is simply not clear exactly what the AAI measures. The interview itself contains no reference to adult romantic relationships, and indeed recent research shows only a very weak positive relationship between classifications on the AAI and the Hazan–Shaver measures (see Crowell, Fraley, & Shaver, 1999, for a review). My own perspective is that, given its focus on predicting one's children's attachment patterns, the AAI more likely captures something about individual differences in the parental *caregiving* system rather than the attachment system per se. Indeed, AAI classification is correlated with observational measures of parental caregiving, which in turn are predictive of infant Strange Situation classification.[4] Or, perhaps more likely, it taps into some kind of combination of the two.

The relevance of this work for understanding the theoretical role of the attachment system in religion is therefore unclear at present. Moreover, because only one empirical study to date (Granqvist, 2002a) has examined the relationship between AAI classification and religion variables, the utility of the AAI as a tool for religion research similarly remains unknown. Theoretically, the general conceptualization of adults' "states of mind" with respect to attachment and the focus on mother–child relationships (in contrast to romantic relationships) suggest that this approach should be highly pertinent to the kinds of applications of attachment theory to religion that will be the subject of the next few chapters. Future research incorporating AAI attachment measures might well contribute to an attachment theory in important and unexpected ways. In light of our limited knowledge at this point, however, I will have little more to say about the AAI tradition of attachment research in the coming chapters.

ATTACHMENT AND EVOLUTIONARY PSYCHOLOGY

Bowlby was a psychoanalyst who attempted to bring an evolutionary and ethological perspective to his discipline. In many ways his own views straddled a fine line between these divergent approaches. His focus, particularly in the first (Bowlby, 1969) volume on attachment, on evolved behavioral systems and ethology was a fine example of modern evolutionary psychology. On the other hand, Bowlby retained (at least in modified form) many analytic concepts from his area of training, particularly with respect to defense mechanisms. My reading of the volumes is that as the next two volumes of his trilogy unfold, the evolutionist in Bowlby gradually waned and the analyst in him gradually reemerged.

The first sustained empirical research to grow out of the theory was Ainsworth et al.'s (1978) empirical research on infant–mother attachment, which was firmly based in the ethological tradition theoretically and behavioral observation methodologically. A crucial turning point occurred with a highly influential paper by Main et al. (1985) subtitled, "A Move to the Level of Representation." In addition to introducing the AAI, this paper developed at length the construct of IWMs in adulthood from an attachment perspective.

If one takes a long historical view of attachment theory as an extension of psychoanalysis, however, this "move to the level of representation" seems akin to Volkswagen announcing that they are about to begin building small cars.[5] Psychoanalysis has, of course, always been about mental representations. Bowlby's ethological perspective, along with Ainsworth's empirical research, had effectively shifted the focus away from this direction; Main et al. were now reintroducing it. The field was about to come full circle. The AAI research tradition has largely turned back toward a more analytic perspective, and has not taken an organized behavioral-systems approach to understanding caregiver behavior, perhaps because "as a reflection of the psychoanalytic roots of attachment theory, and in the absence of a broad biological and developmental view of caregiving, attachment theorists and researchers have emphasized caregiving as the developmental endpoint of early attachment experiences" (George & Solomon, 1999, p. 655). From an evolutionary perspective, discussed in Chapter 8, caregiving must surely be a functionally distinct psychological system with its own crucial inputs, outputs, and rules of operation. George and Solomon (1999) have recently begun to formulate a model of caregiving from a systems perspective, but I feel confident that had researchers not lost sight of Bowlby's ethological perspective, such a model would have been well developed more than a decade ago.

Other scholars have gone even farther in backing away from the evolutionary edifice Bowlby worked so hard to erect. West and Sheldon-Keller (1994), for example, note that psychoanalysts such as Winnicott arrived from other directions at conclusions similar to Bowlby's; they conclude that therefore the evolutionary/ethological underpinnings of Bowlby's approach provide "a firm foundation, but not a necessary one" for attachment theory (p. 169). What these authors seem to miss is the fact that psychoanalysts have produced an immense collection of ideas about what is happening inside people's heads; it should come as no surprise that some of these ideas overlap with some of the ideas within attachment theory. The authors of several chapters in a volume edited by Sperling and Berman (1994) abandon the evolutionary/ethological model entirely and seem determined to tow attachment theory back into traditional psychoanalytic terrain (see Kirkpatrick, 1996). Other scholars have worked toward "integrating" attachment theory and Freudian psychoanalysis in ways that seem to miss the point entirely that attachment theory was intended to update and replace earlier psychoanalytic theory, not merely amend it. For example, Silverman (1991) offers a model that essentially tacks an attachment component onto an otherwise intact Freudian drive model. The evolutionary, systems perspective is exactly what from the beginning has distinguished attachment theory from psychoanalysis, and to lose sight of this perspective is to return to the psychoanalysis that Bowlby rejected: a psychoanalysis unconstrained in its theorizing by ethological observation and evolutionary principles.

In contrast, the romantic attachment perspective of Hazan and Shaver fits more squarely within the evolutionary/ethological perspective. The conceptualization of adult love as the integration of attachment, caregiving, and sex/reproduction systems makes this conceptualization explicit, as does their retention of a model in which the attachment system is activated and deactivated by particular classes of stimuli, and their assumption that individual differences are rooted in actual experience. Hazan and Zeifman's extensions of the model to the development of adult attachment bonds pushes attachment theory further in this direction, drawing heavily upon evolutionary theory and a variety of ethological and physiological observation. As discussed in Chapter 8, other researchers (including myself) have continued on this course, reconceptualizing many aspects of adult attachment and related systems in an explicit evolutionary context that has led to a variety of important new developments in the field.

A crucial reminder of the importance of retaining the evolutionary/ethological perspective is the continuing work on attachment and related processes in other species. Suomi (1999; see also Reite & Boccia, 1994) reviews the extensive literature on attachment and related processes in rhesus monkeys based on both field and experimental laboratory research. The litany of unambiguous parallels with humans is striking, including behavioral patterns of infants reflecting adaptations for eliciting maternal care; individual differences in the organization of infant behavior as a function of quality and quantity of maternal caregiving; responses

to separation from and loss of the attachment figure; interactions between maternal caregiving and heritable variability in temperament; and
cross-generational transmission.

I believe it is imperative that we keep such work firmly in mind
when venturing into the abstract theoretical world of mental representations. If other species possess evolved behavioral systems including attachment that produce patterns of behavior so highly similar to what is
observed in humans, and presumably do so without the kinds of abstract
and complex mental representations of which only humans (again presumably) are capable, it is unparsimonious (not to mention potentially
very misleading) to construct elaborate analytical theories to explain
these processes in humans when other evolutionary/ethological approaches are needed to explain the same behavior in our primate cousins.
As summarized by Suomi (1999),

> One insight that the nonhuman primate data bring to discussions about
> long-term consequences of early experiences is that strong developmen-
> tal continuities can unfold *in the absence of language or complex imagery.* It
> is difficult to argue that rhesus monkeys, for example, possess sufficient
> cognitive capabilities to develop "internal working models" requiring
> considerable self-reflection, given that they are probably not capable of
> "self-awareness" or "self-recognition." (pp. 193–194; emphasis in ori-
> ginal)

Humans are surely capable of constructing, entertaining, and manipulating mental representations far more complex than those of rhesus monkeys (and certainly more so than birds, mice, and other species with attachment-like systems of one form or another). It would be a mistake to
go too far and adopt a we-are-nothing-but-animals view, but we must certainly keep in mind that such complex cognitive processes are constructed partly from, and influenced in many ways by, more primitive
(and more phylogenetically ancient) mechanisms. Consequently, our
theories of mental representations need to be constrained and guided by
an understanding of these evolved systems.

My own view, as will be evident through most of this book, is that
we need to finish what Bowlby started. Bowlby got halfway from psychoanalysis to evolutionary psychology, and it is time to finish the job.
Modern developments in evolutionary theory, as well as their recent applications in the emerging field of evolutionary psychology, provide a

powerful set of theoretical tools that can now be brought to bear on attachment processes and the rest of evolved human nature. As we shall see, most of these important developments were not available to Bowlby; he went about as far as he could given the knowledge available in his time. Armed with these new theoretical tools, however, we are now in a position to go further along the course Bowlby charted.

SUMMARY AND CONCLUSIONS

The sketch I have outlined of attachment theory in this chapter might be called the "traditional" model of attachment—the model within which most attachment researchers continue to operate. Although researchers in recent years have done much interesting work in the way of extending the theory—for example, to adult romantic relationships—it is remarkable that the basic outline of the theory has remained almost entirely intact since Bowlby first formalized it in 1969. If anything, the theory's popularity continues to grow as we begin a new millennium. There are few other psychological theories about which the same could be said.

However, a variety of new theoretical developments have emerged in the last decade, spurred largely by explicit evolutionary perspectives. I defer discussion of these recent ideas until Chapter 8, after I have introduced evolutionary psychology in Chapter 7. As we shall see then, this emerging evolutionary perspective attempts to accomplish something that the theory discussed in this chapter leaves wanting, namely the tying together of attachment, love, caregiving, and mating into a larger, coherent framework.

Because most of this work builds directly upon the literature reviewed in this chapter, extending it rather than directly contradicting it (for the most part), I will continue in the succeeding chapters to spell out my theory of how attachment processes are involved in many aspects of religious belief. Later, after introducing some of the more recent thinking about attachment and individual differences in attachment, as well as about evolutionary psychology more generally, I will return to the topic of religion to see what aspects of the attachment–religion theory require modification in view of these ideas. I hope to be able to show how these new perspectives extend, and shed additional light on, the theory to be developed in the next few chapters.

CHAPTER THREE

God as an
Attachment Figure

If you were thinking about potential applications to religion as you were reading Chapter 2, you probably have already anticipated many of the basic ideas developed in these next few chapters. The principal and most obvious point of departure for my discussion of religion is the observation that the perceived availability and responsiveness of a supernatural attachment figure is a fundamental dynamic underlying Christianity and many other theistic religions. Whether that attachment figure is God, Jesus Christ, the Virgin Mary, or one of various saints, guardian angels, or other supernatural beings, the analogy is striking. The religious person proceeds with faith that God (or another figure) will be available to protect and comfort him or her when danger threatens; at other times, the mere knowledge of God's presence and accessibility allows him or her to approach the problems and difficulties of daily life with confidence.

I am not the first writer to suggest resemblances between attachment and religion. The analogy of the attachment relationship to Christian belief was acknowledged by Reed (1978), who noted that "every form of attachment behavior, and of the behavior of the attachment-figure, identified by Bowlby, has its close counterpart in the images of the relationship between Israel (or the Worshiper) and God which we find in, for example, the psalms" (p. 14). For Reed, alternation between exploration (i.e., using a secure base) and seeking comfort (haven of safety) represents just one component of his larger (mainly sociological) "oscillation theory" of religion. Wenegrat (1990) includes a discussion of attachment in a book on sociobiology and religion that has much in common with the present book (and I will draw liberally from it throughout the following chapters).

At least one modern theologian has also been impressed by the applicability of the attachment model to people's beliefs in God. Kaufman (1981) discussed the tremendous psychological importance of secure attachments and noted that, unfortunately, humans are at best limited and fallible attachment figures. By comparison,

> the idea of God is the idea of an absolutely adequate attachment-figure.
> . . . We need not debate here whether mother-imagery or father-imagery
> would be more to the purpose: the point is that God is thought of as a
> protective and caring parent who is always reliable and always available
> to its children when they are in need. (p. 67)

We will return often to this theme of God as an *ideal* attachment figure in the coming chapters.

RELIGION AS RELATIONSHIP

Before jumping into a discussion of the idea that people perceive themselves to have attachment relationships with God, let us begin with the issue of interpersonal relationships in the context of religion more generally. According to Ferm (1945) the word *religion* derives from the Latin *religare* ("being bound") or *relegere* ("gather together")—a relationship, if you will. Of course, etymology goes only so far, but this is as good a way to start as any.

The centrality of relationship themes in religious life has been noted by numerous scholars. According to Greeley (1981), "just as the story of anyone's life is the story of relationships—so each person's religious story is a story of relationships" (p. 18). Stark (1965) described religious experience as a form of dyadic interaction involving "the divinity and the individual as a pair of actors involved in a social encounter" (p. 99). The object relations school of psychoanalysis has a long history of conceptualizing religious belief and experience in terms of relationships between the self and others. For example, Guntrip (1961, as cited in Beit-Hallahmi, 1992) illustrates the theme in observing that

> religious experience is so very much an expression of human nature as rooted in the primary need for good personal relationships. . . . Religion is *about* the human being's innate need to find good object-relationships in which to live his life. (p. 255)

The relationship conceptualization of religion is not just a theoretical invention by academic scholars; it is clearly understood and articulated by believers themselves. Consider these examples:

- When asked "Which of the following four statements comes closest to your own view of 'faith': a set of beliefs, membership in a church or synagogue, finding meaning in life, or a relationship with God?," 51% of a national Gallup sample chose "a relationship with God," compared to 19%, 4%, and 20% for the other alternatives, respectively (Gallup & Jones, 1989).
- In this same survey, more than half of these respondents rated "growing into a deeper relationship with God" as (at least) "very important" to them, with only 16% saying that this was not at all important (Gallup & Jones, 1989).
- In a study of clergy, the most common response to the question "How does faith help you in daily life?" was "access to a loving God who is willing to help in everyday life" (Hughes, 1989).
- My own research has consistently revealed that two-thirds or more of both newspaper survey respondents and college students respond affirmatively to the question "Do you feel you have a personal relationship with Jesus Christ and/or God?" (e.g., Kirkpatrick & Shaver, 1992).
- In the building in which I work, a poster advertising a meeting of the Inter-Varsity Fellowship on our campus recently announced: "Christianity is not a religion: It is a RELATIONSHIP!" (The sign was hot pink, with capitalization and punctuation as quoted.)

Of course, the "relationship" under consideration in all these cases is people's—Christians', in these examples—perceived relationships with God or Jesus.

The nature of this relationship can vary tremendously from person to person and from culture to culture. Gods may be one or many, benevolent or malevolent, actively involved in human affairs or more distant, partly human or unimaginably abstract. In all of these cases, however, people typically think of these beings in relationship terms.

Relationships come in many flavors, however, of which attachment is only one. Perhaps Bowlby's most crucial insight in many ways was his recognition that attachment represents a functionally distinct behavioral system that operates in particular ways in particular circumstances, and that attachment bonds or relationships differ functionally for other kinds of interpersonal relationships. Thus, the fact that people perceive that they have a relationship with God or Jesus leaves open the question of whether this is an *attachment* relationship. In this chapter I will try to make a convincing case that the answer is yes.

BUT IS IT REALLY AN ATTACHMENT RELATIONSHIP?

Although it is easy to draw analogies between beliefs about God and mental models of attachment figures, I take a stronger position and argue that the resemblances are more than mere analogies: that God "really" is an attachment figure for many believers. There is a philosophical sense in which this is a difficult distinction to make because all theories are analogies at some level of analysis. However, there seems to be a clear difference between suggesting that there are some interesting resemblances between one thing and another, on the one hand, and that one thing actually is a product of the other, fulfilling the same functions according to the same principles. In the former case the resemblances may be interesting, and may lead to some testable hypotheses, but there is not necessarily any reason to think that these hypotheses would in fact pan out. All analogies break down at some point, and there is no way to know where that point is.

In contrast, my proposed extension of the theory to religion is intended to take seriously such constructs as IWMs, the haven of safety and secure base provisions offered by attachment figures, and regulation of felt security. The stronger case that I make, stated more precisely, is this: The attachment system is a "real" system in the brain/mind, instantiated in brain circuitry to organize a variety of more domain-specific modules in a particular way, as designed by natural selection to fulfill the adaptive functions identified by Bowlby. For many people in many religions, I suggest that this attachment system is fundamentally involved in their thinking, beliefs, and reasoning about God and their relationship to God. This strong position suggests that, beyond apparent (and potentially only superficial) similarities, our knowledge of how attachment processes work in other relationships should prove useful in understanding the ways in which people construe God and interact with God.

How does one tell if God "really" functions psychologically as an attachment figure? A good place to start is by identifying the principal criteria for defining an attachment figure—specifically, criteria that distinguish attachments from other functionally distinct kinds of interpersonal relationships—and examine how well beliefs about God meet these criteria. Ainsworth (1985) summarized five defining characteristics that are widely acknowledged to distinguish attachment relationships from other types of close relationships: (1) the attached person seeks proximity to the caregiver, particularly when frightened or alarmed; (2) the caregiver provides care and protection (the haven of safety function) as well as (3) a sense of security (the secure base function); (4) the threat of separation causes anxiety in the attached person; and (5) loss of the attachment figure would cause grief in the attached person. In the remainder of this chapter I test the idea that God (or other religious figures) "really" does function as an attachment figure to many worshipers.

SEEKING AND MAINTAINING PROXIMITY TO GOD

The proximity-seeking criterion is probably in general the least diagnostic of the five criteria, given that virtually all positively valenced relationships involve the desire to be close to the other. We like to spend time with, and keep in touch with, many people who would not be considered attachment figures per se. As much as fans might like to hang out with their favorite movie stars, or teenyboppers with their pop idols, it would be a real stretch to suggest that Helen Hunt or Britney Spears function as attachment figures for these people. Surely parents enjoy (usually) spending time with their children, but the children are not the parents' attachment figures.

Nevertheless, proximity seeking is an important criterion to discuss with respect to God, given the obvious problem that one cannot be physically proximal to God in the same way as to other persons; by definition (usually), God is not present in a physical, corporeal form. For that matter, one might ask whether it makes sense to talk about proximity seeking with respect to God at all, at least in anything more than a vague metaphorical sense. I think it does. In his second volume, Bowlby (1973) moved away from a definition of the set point of the attachment system in terms of physical proximity to a more psychological view: "By presence is meant 'readily accessibility,' by absence 'inaccessibility'" (p. 23). He then added an even more stringent criterion: In order for the attachment figure to provide a sense of security to the child, the attachment figure must also be perceived as *responsive* (Kobak, 1999). Thus, as long as God is perceived by believers to be readily accessible as well as responsive, the attachment model is potentially applicable.

Similarly, recall from Chapter 2 Ainsworth's (1982) observation that both the nature of attachment behaviors and the criteria for what counts as "proximal" change predictably over the course of development. During the first 6 months of life, infants depend heavily on *proximal* behaviors to initiate and maintain contact with their mothers. These behaviors include signaling behaviors such as crying and upraised arms and approach behaviors such as clinging and cuddling. Under normal conditions these proximal behaviors are progressively replaced with more distal behaviors as children mature. Older children can often be comforted or have their sense of security restored via visual or verbal contact, and adolescents and adults can often be satisfied by the mere knowledge that the attachment figure is potentially available if needed (Bretherton, 1987). Soldiers overseas write letters to their sweethearts back home, and both children and adults call their parents on the phone. Today these connections can be maintained electronically via e-mail or "chat" programs over the Internet.

Beyond infancy and early childhood, then, the efficacy of an attachment figure depends not on physical but, rather, psychological proximity. And if such "mere knowledge" of an attachment figure's accessibility and responsiveness can suffice under most circumstances, it seems only a small step to suggest that a noncorporeal deity can function fully as, and offer the psychological provisions of, an attachment figure. There are many ways in which religions facilitate perceptions of God's (or gods') proximity and accessibility.

Proximity in Belief and Myth

Of the several supernatural qualities typically attributed to God or gods, one of the most common is that God is *omnipresent*. Although it may seem, at least to Westerners, that omnipresence is a necessary and essential defining quality of what it means to be God (or a god), in fact this is not as self-evident as it appears. In many religions gods are assumed to be in particular places at particular times; consider, for example, classic Greek and Roman mythology. There is no necessary *logical* reason why a supernatural being could not have other qualities such as omniscience, while still being limited in space and time. Omnipresence is a highly counterintuitive idea that turns out, according to several interesting experiments, to be quite difficult to maintain: Although people can maintain and report this belief in an abstract sense, their actual reasoning on laboratory tasks reflects a strong tendency to drift toward an anthropomorphized image of God as limited in space and time (Barrett & Keil, 1996; more on this research later).

Thus, the question remains as to why the Christian God (and gods of many other religions) is often attributed with omnipresence. I suggest that it makes it possible for all believers to feel that they are in close proximity to God simultaneously. According to most Christian faiths, God (or Jesus) is always by your side, holding your hand and watching over you. Believers are reminded constantly in Scripture, sermons, and religious literature that God is always nearby and available when needed. It would be difficult for people to logically maintain that this is true for all believers simultaneously were God not omnipresent. Note that an alternative is for each person to have his or her own "guardian angel" or similar kind of personal deity, dedicated full-time to one individual without being distracted by other responsibilities.

Another aspect of belief that helps people maintain a sense of proximity to God is that most religious mythologies include stories about deities coming to earth in human or quasi-human form and interacting directly and concretely with real people. The example of Jesus in Christianity provides a clear illustration. Again, it is not self-evident why this should be such a common belief, as it is not in any way logically necessary. Why isn't God widely perceived as merely an abstract entity with no worldly manifestation? I suggest that such stories serve to inject concreteness into an otherwise abstract concept, rendering much more "real" the idea of being—literally, concretely, physically—close to God.

Facilitating Psychological Proximity

Despite our remarkable abilities for abstract representation and imagination, attachment to a purely abstract being poses a formidable challenge. Thus, although God is typically thought to be omnipresent, virtually all religions provide tangible places such as churches and shrines where worshipers can go to be "nearer to" God. It is of course true that houses of worship serve other functions as well, such as bringing people together for sermons, group activities and interaction, and so forth. Yet the role of the church as a place one can go to be close to God should not be underestimated. People often visit churches spontaneously at times other than formal services, especially when troubled, to speak with and feel the presence of the deity. Theoretically one could do this anywhere, so why else is the church a preferred location for this purpose?

There are many other ways to maintain a sense of psychological, if not perceived physical, proximity to God as well. Each religious tradition has it own set of images, icons, and other physical representations that serve as concrete reminders of God's presence. Catholics wear crucifixes on necklaces; Christians of all stripes hang paintings of Jesus or other religious imagery in their homes. In some religions, believers construct elaborate shrines to deities in their homes. Even a well-placed Bible can provide a regular cue to bring God's image into consciousness. Religions have forever been the source and motivation for the construction of elaborate cathedrals that (among other things) provide constant reminders of God's presence to passersby, as well as an enormous diversity of idols, icons, graven images, painting and sculpture, and other forms of art. Each of these objects can be seen to serve the function (as well perhaps as other functions) of making God psychologically salient and available in concrete ways.

Prayer

The activity of prayer presents a particularly illustrative example of proximity seeking in relation to God. Reed (1978) was clearly struck by this point when he observed that

> crying and calling [by an infant] find a close parallel in supplicatory prayer. The prominent place of prayer in most religions is perhaps the most striking point of contact with Bowlby's observations. (p. 15)

In his classic study of prayer, Protestant historian Friedrich Heiler (1932) emphasized the theme that prayer is a direct manifestation of the perception of having a relationship with an immediate, personal God. According to Heiler, prayer is in its essence a "living communion of man with God, bringing man into direct touch with God and into a personal relation with Him" (p. 362). When a devout person prays, Heiler observed, he "believes that he speaks with a God, immediately present and personal" (p. 356).

Researchers have classified a variety of forms of prayer, which vary in function and circumstance. In their comprehensive textbook on the psychology of religion, Hood et al. (1996) review several such varieties, two of which seem clearly related to proximity maintenance: *contemplative* prayer, which they describe as "an attempt to relate deeply to one's God," and *meditational* prayer, reflecting "concern with one's relationship to God" (p. 394 ff.).

Other attachment behaviors seem to display intriguing analogues in religion as well. Going to a church or other place of worship to feel closer to God, as discussed earlier, can be thought of as an approach behavior. Upraising of the arms in worship, a common behavior in many Pentecostal and other Christian worship services, has always struck me as looking remarkably like an infant waiting to be picked up by its mother.

A particularly interesting example that may have origins in the attachment system is *glossolalia*, or "speaking in tongues." Oates (1967) observed that, at least to an outside observer, glossolalia sounds very much like infant babbling or a "childlike form of language." The parallel to infant attachment behavior is particularly striking when glossolalia is combined, as is often the case, with head back and arms raised to the sky. In his extensive study of glossolalia, Kildahl (1972) quoted one of his respondents' descriptions of a glossolalic experience as "I felt like a child who could only say 'Goo'" (p. 64).

I hasten to add that although this discussion of attachment behaviors, in Freudian terms, makes them sound like a form of "infantile regression," this is not at all my intended meaning—just as it is not the intended meaning of Shaver et al. (1988) in noting similar parallels between adult love relationships and infant-like attachment behaviors such as cooing, talking "baby-talk," and cuddling. Instead, I merely intend to suggest that behavioral systems designed to operate in infancy or childhood, but which tend to dissipate in priority and importance during subsequent development, may be activated later in life under certain circumstances. There is no suggestion that people displaying such behaviors are "regressing" in any more generalized sense, and there is no intended evaluative component as implied (at least to my ear) by terms such as "regression." (I hope I do not sound as if I doth protest too much here, but it seems important to make this explicit, given the possibility of readers reading between the lines something that is not there.)

GOD AS A HAVEN OF SAFETY

As discussed in Chapter 2, Bowlby (1969) identified three classes of stimuli hypothesized to activate the attachment system: (1) frightening or alarming environmental events, that is, stimuli that evoke fear and distress; (2) illness, injury, or fatigue; and (3) separation or threat of separation from attachment figures. If God functions psychologically as an attachment figure, then we should find that people turn to God, and evince attachment-like behaviors toward God, under these conditions. Moreover, the experience of God as a haven of safety in these circumstances should give rise to the same kinds of feelings of comfort and security provided by secure human attachments.

In fact, considerable research suggests that these are indeed the very conditions under which people, at least in Western Christian traditions, are most likely to seek God's support and comfort. In their textbook treatment of the topic, Hood et al. (1996) conclude that people are most likely to "turn to their gods in times of trouble and crisis," and list three general classes of potential triggers: "illness, disability, and other negative life events that cause both mental and physical distress; the anticipated or actual death of friends and relatives; and dealing with an adverse life situation" (pp. 386–387)—in short, the same list provided by Bowlby. Each of these is discussed in more detail.

Crisis and Distress

The idea that religion is associated with psychological distress and crisis has, of course, a very long history (see, e.g., Hood et al., 1996, for a review). Many contemporary writers have continued to focus on the particularly important role taken on by religion at such times (e.g., Argyle & Beit-Hallahmi, 1975; Pargament & Hahn, 1986). It is not only scientists who see this pattern: Believers often freely recognize it themselves. For example, when Ross (1950) queried over 1,700 religious youth about why they prayed, the two reasons most frequently cited were "God listens to and answers your prayers" and "It helps you in time of stress and crisis."

There appear to be at least two important limitations on the nature of this stress–religion link, however: Not all kinds of distress lead to changes in all aspects of religion. First, based on their review of the literature, Argyle and BeitHallahmi (1975) emphasized that people specifically turn to *prayer*, rather than the church, in stressful circumstances. This is a crucial insight from an attachment perspective because it suggests that it is the relationship with God per se, and not some other aspect of religiousness—such as church membership, group processes, or cognitive meaning structures—to which people are turning under these circumstances. As discussed earlier, prayer is a specific example of attachment behavior toward God.

Another religious attachment behavior that appears to follow the same pattern is glossolalia. Kildahl (1972) concluded from his study that "more than 85 percent of tongue-speakers had experienced a clearly defined anxiety crisis preceding their speaking in tongues" (p. 57). Typically, he noted, this crisis involved feelings of "worthlessness and powerlessness." Moreover, Kildahl reported that the glossolalic experience invariably resulted in increased feelings of confidence and security, which he attributed to worshipers' perception that they had proof that they were loved and protected by God.

The second important constraint on the stress–religion link is that religion is more likely to be invoked in *unusually* stressful times than in response to more mundane stressors. Pargament (1997) reviews several studies demonstrating that, for example, people are more likely to pray over catastrophes and health crises than such minor stressors such as job-related concerns (Lindenthal, Myers, Pepper, & Stern, 1970), and fisherman engage in more religious-like rituals before long trips to sea than shorter ones (Poggie, Pollnac, & Gersuny, 1976). One of the clear differences between attachment in childhood and in adulthood is that the attachment system is activated far less readily in adulthood than in childhood (Weiss, 1982). Adults do not run to attachment figures every time they stub a toe or are startled by a car backfire, as do young children. The fact that people primarily turn to God only when *severely* distressed is thus consistent with an attachment interpretation.

The haven of safety provision offered by God is captured neatly by the adage that there are no atheists in foxholes. It is difficult to imagine a situation more deserving of the term "unusually stressful times" than finding oneself on a battlefield. Allport (1950) conducted interviews with a large number of World War II combat veterans about the role of their religious beliefs while on the battlefield, and came away with the conclusion that "the individual in distress craves affection and security. Sometimes a human bond will suffice, more often it will not" (p. 57). (Had attachment theory been available at the time, I suspect that Allport might have written the present book 40 years ago.) Indeed, a number of empirical studies point to the role of prayer and God as providing a haven of safety in times of fear and distress. The no-atheists-in-foxholes maxim was literally supported by Stouffer et al. (1949), who showed that soldiers in battle do in fact pray frequently and feel that such prayer is beneficial. In a study of religious attributions, Pargament and Hahn (1986) concluded that "subjects appeared to turn to God more as a source of support during stress than as a moral guide or as an antidote to an unjust world" (p. 204).

Perhaps the most widely cited effect of stress and crisis in the psychology of religion concerns its role in sudden and dramatic religion conversions. As this is a sizeable and very important topic in its own right, I will treat it separately and at length in Chapter 6.

Illness and Injury

Numerous studies have examined prayer and religious change in the context of health-related problems. Several studies show prayer to be an especially common coping method for dealing with serious physical illnesses of various types (Duke, 1977; Gibbs & Achterberg-Lawlis, 1978; O'Brien, 1982). Again, prayer seems to be reserved mainly for dealing with the most life-threatening situations and health symptoms (Bearon & Koening, 1990), rather than minor complaints.

Moreover, prayer appears to be effective in helping people cope psychologically with serious illness. In an indepth study of patients suffering from renal failure and facing the prospect of longterm hemodialysis, O'Brien (1982) demonstrated that religious faith was an important variable in predicting successful coping and in combating feelings of alienation. Excerpts from interviews with these patients suggested that God was seen by many as providing comfort, nurturance, and a source of personal strength for getting through this difficult time. For example, one patient who had recently suffered several cardiac arrests was quoted as saying "Each time I knew everything would be all right because I asked God to carry me through—I know that He's got His arms around me" (p. 76). Other studies have similarly shown religion to be particularly helpful to people in coping with chronic illness (Mattlin, Wethington, & Kessler, 1990). In particular, a belief that God is in control is related to several positive psychological effects among cancer patients (Jenkins & Pargament, 1988). Such effects seem to be particularly valuable to the elderly (see Hood et al., 1996, pp. 390–391), perhaps because older people are more likely to have lost their primary (human) attachment figures.

Death and Grieving

Since loss of an attachment figure is an event particularly likely to activate attachment behavior, the attachment model would predict that religious behavior and belief should increase during periods of bereavement. Loveland (1968) showed that bereaved persons feel more religious and engage in more prayer than they did prior to the death, yet the specific *content* of their basic beliefs does not appear to be affected. Loveland, along with Parkes (1972) and Haun (1977), also showed that religious belief and commitment correlated positively with adjustment and coping to loss of a spouse.

There are at least three distinct but correlated factors related to attachment operating in religious responses to bereavement. First, as noted by Bowlby, the loss of a loved one per se is one kind of event that activates the attachment system. Second, such losses (particularly in adulthood) are typically accompanied by a host of other stressors as one struggles to make the transition to a life without the lost person. Loss of a spouse, for example, means there is a funeral to arrange and other bills to pay (and possibly financial strain as a result), and one must learn to take on any number of tasks that the spouse previously performed. Thus a second path to attachment-system activation is set in motion as well. Third, the loss of a principal attachment figure, such as a parent or a spouse, may activate a search for a *substitute* or *surrogate* caregiver, or at least increased reliance on a previously secondary figure. In such circumstances one may turn to God or Jesus for this reason. I will return to a more general discussion of substitute attachment figures, and the conditions under which God may serve as one, in Chapter 6.

From an attachment perspective, the reason death of an attachment figure is so traumatic is because it means a permanent separation from the caregiver. Similarly, it has been suggested that fear of death—that is, one's *own* death—is related to separation anxiety. Wenegrat (1990) concludes that several published studies of children

> are indeed remarkable for the attachment concerns they uncover beneath the child's idea of death. When questioned, children often equate death with vanishing, becoming lost, or being trapped or kidnapped. These fears, which are of losing valued contact and protection, take the same form as other childhood separation fears described by attachment theorists. (p. 41)

Wenegrat further notes that adult defenses against death anxiety also point to attachment dynamics. Yalom (1980) described two patterns of such defenses, one of which involves dependence on an "ultimate rescuer."[1]

The role of religion in coping with bereavement is probably one of the principal factors underlying the widely observed finding that religiousness tends to increase as people reach their later years. One inescapable consequence of getting older is that loved ones pass away. In line with my suggestion, this means that one experiences both an increased frequency in bereavement episodes, and simultaneously the loss of attachment figures. God or Jesus may become particularly valuable as an alternative attachment figure during this stage of life for a combination of these two reasons.

GOD AS A SECURE BASE

In their zeal to examine the ways in which people turn to God in times of stress and danger—the haven of safety function, in attachment terms—researchers have unfortunately paid far less attention to the psychological importance of God in people's lives under ordinary conditions. From an attachment theory perspective, however, the secure-base function of attachment is every bit as important as the haven of safety function, as it facilitates confident exploration of the environment and provides a source of courage and efficacy in going about one's daily affairs. According to Bowlby (1973) and others, the availability of a secure base is the antidote to fear and anxiety: "When an individual is confident that an attachment figure will be available to him whenever he desires it, that person will be much less prone to either intense or chronic fear than will an individual who for any reason has no such confidence" (p. 202).

Evidence comes from many sources for the idea that religious beliefs, and a personal attachment relationship to God (or Jesus, etc.) in particular, offer this provision. In this section I make more liberal use of quotations than I typically do, in order to illustrate the uncanny resemblance to Bowlby's (1969, 1973) own descriptions of the secure base and its psychological effects that are seen in religion (and because of the paucity of pertinent empirical research just noted).

Phenomenology

It would be easy to assemble a lengthy book containing nothing but illustrative quotes from believers emphasizing the imagery of God or Jesus being by one's side, holding one's hand, standing over one, and so forth. For present purposes I present just a few. One of Poloma and Gallup's (1991) survey respondents, for example, described a moment in which she strongly felt the presence of God as feeling "all warm—like God had wrapped me up in a blanket and was holding me close to him" (p. 50). Pargament (1997) quotes a woman describing advice given to her by a friend:

> "That when Jesus said, I will never leave you or forsake you, he meant it. That once you take this step, once you step over this line and ask me to come in, then I'm always there with you. . . . And boy, that hit me right between the eyes. I felt like that was written for me. And when she told me that, I just thought, my God, he's been there with me this whole time. He never left. From the moment I asked him into my life, in 1972, Jesus has been standing right by me." (p. 169)

Casual inspection of any inspirational literature similarly reveals a pervasive secure-base theme, according to which one's relationship with God or Jesus provides one with strength, self-assurance, and a sense of peace to tackle the problems and challenges of everyday life. For example, Billy Graham's (1984) *Peace with God* "points the way, the *only* way, to authentic personal peace in a world of crisis," according to its preface (p. 10).

Secure-base themes are in clear evidence throughout much of Christian Scripture, particularly in the Psalms (Wenegrat, 1990). Perhaps best known is the 23rd Psalm: "Yea, though I walk through the valley of the shadow of death, I will fear no evil: for thou art with me; thy rod and thy staff, they comfort me." Countless other examples from the Psalms could be cited, in which God is described or addressed as "a shield for me" (3:3), "my rock, and my fortress," (18:2), and "the strength of my life" (27:1). Similarly, Young (1926) showed that 33% of 2,922 Protestant hymns classified involve the theme of "infantile return" to a powerful and loving protector who shields humankind from all harm.

Other scholars have picked up on the same themes. William James (1902) observed that "the sense of Presence of a higher and friendly Power seems to be the fundamental feature in the spiritual life," adding that "in the Christian consciousness this sense of the enveloping friendliness becomes most personal and definite" (pp. 274–275). He illustrated the point with this quotation from Voysey (1882; cited in James, 1902):

> It is the myriads of trustful souls, that this sense of God's unfailing presence with them in their going out and in their coming in, and by night and day, is a source of absolute repose and confident calmness. It drives away all fear of what may befall them. That nearness of God is a constant security against terror and anxiety. (p. 275)

Other psychologists of religion have similarly remarked on the function of faith in providing a generalized sense of emotional security. For example:

> The emotional quality of faith is indicated in a basic confidence and security that gives one assurance. In this sense faith is the opposite of fear, anxiety, and uncertainty. Without emotional security there is no relaxation, but tension, distress, and instability. Assurance is the firm emotional undertone that enables one to have steady nerves and calm poise in the face of danger or confusion. (Johnson, 1945, p. 191)

Although I am focusing mainly on Christianity in the present chapter, it is important to note that the idea of God or gods as providing a secure base is by no means limited to this religious tradition. In his study of the Nuer people of the southern Egyptian Sudan, Evans-Pritchard (1956) offers the following:

> The believer, who has communicated with his god, is not merely a man who sees new truths of which the unbeliever is ignorant; he is a man who

is *stronger*. He feels within him more force, either to endure the trials of existence, or to conquer them. It is as though he were raised above the miseries of the world, because he is raised above his condition as a mere man; he believes that he is saved from evil, under whatever form he may conceive this evil. (p. 61)

Whereas prayer was discussed earlier in terms of God's role as a haven of safety and comfort—that is, in times of danger and/or distress—at other times prayer is more consonant with God's provision of a secure base. Recall from Chapter 2 the phenomenon of *social referencing* (Campos & Stenberg, 1981), in which young children exploring their environment check back with their mothers visually, verbally, and/or physically from time to time to reassure themselves that she is still available and attentive. Some forms of prayer, such as those discussed earlier in this chapter, might similarly be construed as "God referencing" that provides reassurance that God remains an available and responsive secure base.

Psychological Outcomes

To the extent that God functions psychologically as an attachment figure and provides a secure base for believers, belief in God should confer certain psychological benefits—that is, it should function as "an antidote to fear and anxiety." A variety of empirical studies suggest that this may be the case. In Western, predominantly Christian samples, measures of religious commitment (including intrinsic religious orientation) have been shown to correlate positively with a sense of internal locus of control (Kahoe, 1974; Strickland & Shaffer, 1971), a sense of personal competence and control (Ventis, 1995), an active, flexible approach to problem solving (Pargament, Steele, & Tyler, 1979), and a sense of optimism and hope with respect to both the long-term and short-term future (Myers, 1992). At the same time, religiousness has been shown to correlate *inversely* with trait anxiety (Baker & Gorsuch, 1982; Entner, 1977; McClain, 1978) and fear of death (Kahoe & Dunn, 1975).

More important, however, is the fact that this is not merely a case of religion measures correlating equally strongly with all kinds of measures of mental health or other psychological outcomes—findings which might be explained, for example, in terms of self-report response biases such as social desirability or general negative affectivity. Although the research literature on religion and mental health is replete with conflicting and ambiguous results (Bergin, 1983), a dimension of religiousness focusing specifically on a secure attachment to God appears to be strongly associated with positive mental health outcomes. In a large national survey, Poloma and Gallup (1991) found that *prayer*, and particularly the "experience of God during prayer," were more strongly correlated than other religion variables with their measures of well-being. Pollner (1989) analyzed data from the General Social Survey to assess the role of divine and human relationships on well-being and life satisfaction. His measure of "divine relationships," designed to "tap the psychological proximity of a divine other and the frequency and depth of interaction with that other" (p. 95), proved to be the strongest among several predictors of well-being in multiple regression analyses. Similar results were found even when background variables and church attendance were statistically controlled. Galanter (1989) reported the two best predictors of emotional well-being among Unification Church members to be the survey items "My religious beliefs give me comfort" and "I feel a close connection to God."

In an empirical study of newspaper survey respondents designed explicitly from an attachment perspective, Kirkpatrick and Shaver (1992) found very few significant correlations between a diverse collection of religion variables and measures of life satisfaction, loneliness and depression, and physical symptoms, with one important exception: An item designed to assess individual differences in the security of respondents' attachments to God was strongly associated with the mental and physical health variables. Specifically, respondents reporting an *avoidant* attachment relationship with God (i.e., God is perceived as impersonal, distant, and "doesn't care about me") scored significantly lower on a variety of measures of well-being—including loneliness, depression, psychosomatic symptoms, and life satisfaction—than respondents reporting *secure* (God is perceived as warm, responsive, caring) or *anxious* (God is perceived as sometimes warm and responsive, sometimes not) attachments to God. These results closely paralleled results for a similar variable measuring individual differences in security of attachment in human love relationships.

More recently, Rowatt and Kirkpatrick (2002) constructed a two-dimensional scale for measuring individual differences in attachment to God by breaking down each of the three Kirkpatrick–Shaver prototypes into multiple questionnaire items. Factor analysis confirmed the presence of two factors corresponding to those typically found among adult-attachment items (e.g., Brennan et al., 1998): an *avoidance* (vs. security) dimension and an *anxiety* dimension. In a sample of 374 college students, the anxious attachment-to-God scale was significantly correlated with well-established measures of *neuroticism, negative affect,* and (inversely) *positive affect.* More important, these relationships were then reexamined in multiple regression analyses in which a variety of other measures were statistically controlled, including social desirability, intrinsic religiousness, doctrinal orthodoxy, and loving images of God. Even with these variables partialed out, anxious attachment to God remained a significant predictor of the well-being measures. This suggests that the correlations cannot be explained by individual differences in socially desirable responding, nor by other dimensions of religiosity correlated with attachment to God. As in the Kirkpatrick–Shaver study, attachment to God per se appears to predict (at least certain aspects of) psychological well-being in ways that other dimensions of religiosity do not.

Based on a comprehensive review of extant empirical research on religion and mental health, Batson and Ventis (1982; see also Ventis, 1995) found intrinsic religious orientation (i.e., genuine religious commitment) to be positively correlated with two conceptualizations of mental health, *freedom from worry and guilt* and *personal competence and control,* but *not* to several other aspects of mental health. In addition, mental health conceptualized in terms of "freedom from worry and guilt" was positively associated with religious involvement only in studies of elderly populations. This latter finding may reflect the fact, as suggested in the previous section, that elderly people are less likely to have living parents and spouses available to provide a secure base.

In sum, it seems clear that beliefs about a personal God who watches over one functions psychologically as a secure base, just as do human attachments. It is easy to see why: An attachment figure who is simultaneously omnipresent, omniscient, and omnipotent would provide the most secure of secure bases. As the theological Kaufman (1981) noted, God is an "absolutely adequate attachment-figure."

RESPONSES TO SEPARATION AND LOSS

I noted in a previous section that religious belief and prayer increase in response to bereavement, which was interpreted in terms of the haven of safety function of religious attachment. However, the fourth and fifth defining criteria given by Ainsworth (1985) concern responses to separation from, or loss of, the attachment figure per se: The threat of separation causes anxiety in the attached person, and loss of the attachment figure causes grief. If God functions psychologically as an attachment figure, then separation from or loss of God should engender these same kinds of responses.

Determining whether God meets these criteria is a difficult matter, because one does not become separated from, or lose a relationship with, God in the same ways that people typically lose human relationship partners. God does not die, sail off to fight wars, move away, or file for divorce. Indeed, this is a primary reason why God is "an "absolutely adequate attachment-figure" in the first place.

On the other hand, beliefs about what happens after death reflect issues of potential separation from God. The potential for true separation from God is usually seen by believers to come only in the hereafter, at which time one spends eternity either with God or separated from God. In most Christian churches, separation from God is the very essence of hell.

The most common way of "losing" God is simply ceasing to believe in the existence of God (or at least of a particular image of God). However, because this scenario generally involves the believer separating him- or herself from God rather than the other way around, it is not clear whether grief per se would be the expected emotional reaction. On the other hand, the situation is in many ways analogous to divorce or the dissolution of other close interpersonal relationships (Wright, 1987). According to Wright, defectors from cults commonly experience psychological symptoms, including "separation anxiety," similar to those associated with marital separation and divorce.

There are, however, situations in which people feel as if they have indeed been abandoned by God, and the consequences are invariably traumatic, particularly if this is perceived to occur at time that God is most needed. Brenner (1980; cited in Pargament, 1997) quotes a concentration camp survivor who lost his religious faith, and much more:

> "I used to have a very personal intimate relationship with God. I thought everything I did and every move I made God knew and was right there. . . . He'd be there just above me, watching and admonishing and saying 'tut-tut-tut' about those inner thoughts I might have. . . . Then the Nazis came, and where did He go? God was no longer near me. Disappeared. And I am no longer the person I was." (p. 134)

Mahedy (1986; cited in Pargament, 1997), a Vietnam chaplain, discusses at length the difficulties faced by combat soldiers trying to square their beliefs about God in the face of the atrocities of war. On the one hand, they were always told that God was "on their side," but the killing and devastation led many to conclude that God was in fact no longer there. Once they came to this conclusion, their deconversions were emotionally charged and angry. As summarized by Mahedy,

> the veterans' rejection of God is active, passionate, almost physical, and rooted in the best of reasons. They have been betrayed. On some level they had believed that God had promised something and then didn't or couldn't deliver. (p. 106)

One of the principal observations that led Bowlby (1969) to attachment theory was that children separated from their mothers consistently displayed a predictable set of responses, beginning with angry protest and subsequently moving through stages of despair and detachment. Loss of faith in God, then, might be expected to follow these same stages. The cases discussed by Brenner and Mahedy (both in Pargament, 1997) seem to point in this direction, but further research is clearly needed to examine explicitly the similarities and differences between religious deconversion and separation processes as described by attachment theory.

SUMMARY AND CONCLUSIONS

Bowlby's choice of the term "attachment" was in many ways unfortunate, because the word carries such a broad meaning in colloquial usage. We speak of feeling "attached to" almost anything of personal value to us, from a stamp collection to a favorite pen to an old car. But these cannot be attachments in Bowlby's sense, because they are not personal relationships. Moreover, we might loosely describe ourselves or others as "attached to" persons whom we have never met and never expect to meet, but whom we admire or otherwise value for other reasons. I do not know how many times I have been asked whether "Deadheads"—fans of (the American improvisational rock band) the Grateful Dead, who are legendary for traveling long distances from concert to concert—are "attached" to Jerry Garcia or the band as a whole. (The answer is no.)

Bowlby was quite clear, as discussed in Chapter 2, that "attachment" is not synonymous with "close relationship"; rather, attachments are a special category of relationships or psychological bond, identifiable by several criteria that distinguish them from other kinds of relationships, as discussed in this chapter. Your stamp collection may be of enormous personal importance to you, but I doubt that you perceive it as "someone" with whom you have a personal relationship. You might "seek proximity" to it, in the sense that you like to keep it handy, but I doubt that it really provides you psychologically with a secure base and a haven of safety. Although you would be upset if you lost it, it surely would be considered pathological if your response were the kind of true grief one feels in response to the loss of a parent or spouse.

In contrast, I have tried to demonstrate in this chapter that many people do indeed perceive themselves as having a personal relationship with God, and that beliefs about God and about this relationship meet all of the defining criteria laid out by Ainsworth (1985). I am suggesting that attachment is not merely a metaphor for people's perceived relationships with God, but "really" is an attachment relationship in every important sense. Attachments differ from other kinds of relationships not by strength, but by function, and I have tried to show here that relationships with God function in the same manner as relationships with parents during childhood.

There is another way to think about the question of what distinguishes "true" attachments from other kinds of relationships. As we saw in Chapter 2, Bowlby's theoretical account of *why* and *how* attachment relationships work as they do is that they reflect the operation of a functionally organized, evolved behavioral system, one designed by natural selection with the function of solving particular adaptive problems related to protection and survival. We might turn the usual way of thinking around and say that an attachment relationship is one in which the *attachment system*, with all its various cognitive, affective, and behavior-regulation components, is importantly involved in guiding one's thoughts, feelings, and behaviors in that relationship.

This conceptualization of the problem is useful in two ways. First, it means that if perceived relationships with God are "really" attachments in this sense, then we should see other evidence of the operation of the attachment system in religion as well. In the next chapter I examine some other manifestations of attachment processes in religion, focusing particularly on the emotion of love, and in Chapters 5 and 6 I review research in which hypotheses derived from this conceptualization have been tested empirically.

Second, this way of thinking serves as a reminder that the attachment system is only one of numerous evolved systems for regulating cognition, emotion, and behavior in functionally distinct classes of relationships. We have already seen how the attachment system has been distinguished from other cognitive–emotional–behavioral systems underlying other kinds of relationships, such as caregiving and reproduction. Beginning in Chapter 10, we look at these and numerous other systems and examine some of the ways in which they, side by side with the attachment system, influence religious belief and behavior.

CHAPTER FOUR

More on Religion as an Attachment Process

Some Extensions and Limitations

In Chapter 3 I examined images of and beliefs about God, and tried to show that God does indeed meet the criteria for an attachment figure. In this chapter I extend the argument by examining other aspects of religious belief that appear to fit the model as well, as would be expected if such relationships are in fact constructed and shaped by the operation of the attachment system. I then turn to the question of how far the model might—or might not—be extended to other aspects of religious belief and behavior beyond the haven of safety and secure-base functions of perceived relationships with a personal God.

RELIGION AND LOVE

To the extent that the attachment system is operative in certain aspects of religious belief, the emotional as well as the cognitive machinery of attachment should be in evidence as well. In particular, if a person is attached to a deity or other religious figure, the person should feel *love* toward, and the sense of *being loved by*, that figure, just as children love and feel loved by their parents and adults in romantic relationships love each other.

The emotion of love is, of course, central to Christianity. Bumper stickers proudly proclaim "I [picture of a heart] Jesus" or, conversely, that "Jesus loves me," or more broadly, "God is love." We are encouraged by Christian teachings to love not only our neighbors, but our enemies. Most important, of course, we are to love God and/or Jesus, and to experience and feel their love for us. This may also be why religious experience is so often described as ineffable, and why religious emotion—like romantic love—is so widely expressed in song and other art forms. The experience of being in love is an extraordinarily powerful emotional state that words are woefully inadequate to describe, as any poet will quickly attest. Thouless (1923) reflected on the "tendency of religious emotion to express itself in the language of human love," particularly among the mystics (p. 132). Song, dance, and other nonverbal expressions have proven for centuries to be infinitely better suited than prose for the communication of such emotional states.

In particular, numerous scholars including William James (1902), have likened the process of religious *conversion* to that of falling in love. In the words of Pratt (1920),

> the convert feels the presence of a new friend who loves him and to whom he is endlessly grateful and whom he is coming to love passionately. In many cases getting converted means falling in love with Jesus. (p. 160)

Although a quest for answers to existential questions and other philosophical matters undoubtedly play an important role in many people's religious development (e.g., Batson, Shoenrade, & Ventis 1993), they do not appear to be the stuff of sudden and dramatic religious conversions. Ullman (1989) came to this conclusion, much to her own surprise, on the basis of an in-depth study of 40 religious converts (a study to which we will return repeatedly over the next few chapters):

> What I initially considered primarily a change of ideology turned out to be more akin to a falling in love. . . . Conversion pivots around a sudden attachment, an infatuation with a real or imagined figure which occurs on a background of great emotional turmoil. The typical convert was transformed not by a religion, but by a person. The discovery of a new

truth was indistinguishable from a discovery of a new relationship, which relieved, temporarily, the upheaval of the previous life. This intense and omnipresent attachment discovered in the religious experience promised the convert everlasting guidance and love, for the object of the convert's infatuation was perceived as infallible. (p. xvi)

Given that Ullman began her investigation with a decidedly cognitive theoretical bias, this is a particularly ringing endorsement of the centrality of love—in the context of a perceived relationship with a deity—in the process of religious conversion.

WHAT KIND OF LOVE?: ROMANTIC ATTACHMENT VERSUS ATTACHMENT TO GOD

Although drawing parallels between romantic love and various aspects of religion is useful in pointing toward the kinds of psychological theories (such as attachment theory) that might be useful in understanding religion, it can also lead to serious confusion. For example, the many apparent resemblances between romantic love and religious conversion, in conjunction with the well-established finding that the most common age for sudden religious conversion is during adolescence, has led some previous scholars to postulate that religious beliefs are linked to puberty or sexual instincts (Coe, 1916; Thouless, 1923). As Greeley (1990) observes, however, "The usual reaction . . . to a comparison of human love with divine love is to insist that it is utterly different from sexual attraction ('not at all physical,' my students tell me)" (p. 249). Of course, the love one feels for, and from, God is quite different from that experienced in adult romantic relationships, and it is important to understand why.

Psychologically, I suggest, a worshiper's love for God is more akin to a child's love for her mother or father than to an adult's love for a romantic partner or spouse. God's love for oneself, conversely, is perceived in terms analogous to a mother's love for her child rather than a spouse's love. Writing specifically about Roman Catholicism, Greeley (1990) reached a similar conclusion: "The Mary Myth's powerful appeal is to be found . . . in the marvelous possibility that God loves us the way a mother loves her baby" (p. 252). Or, as one of his interviewees put it, "If you've ever held in your arms a child you have just given life to and been filled with love for that wondrous little being, you know that's how God feels about us" (Greeley, 1990, p. 252).

From an attachment theory perspective, the matter can be understood by considering some crucial differences between romantic and infant–mother relationships identified by Weiss (1982) and acknowledged by Shaver et al. (1988; Hazan & Shaver, 1987) and other adult-attachment researchers. First, adult relationships are typically with *peers*, who are not necessarily perceived as consistently stronger and wiser. In order to serve as attachment figures to one another, adult romantic partners must also serve as *caregivers* to one another, alternating between roles as dictated by individual needs and circumstances. This is in clear contrast to infant–mother relationships in which, except for some unusual (and generally pathological) examples of role reversals, the infant is the one who is "attached" and the mother (or other attachment figure) is the caregiver. According to Weiss (1986), with the change in attachment figure from parent to peer, "there has taken place a change in the character of the object from the awesomely powerful, usually protective, parent of childhood to a peer whose frailties, once the relationship has passed its initial idealizations, are apt to be well recognized" (p. 102). Skolnick (1985) criticized Bowlby's emphasis on representing the attachment figure as the "stronger and wiser Other" (a phrase commonly used by Bowlby), primarily because this conceptualization of the attachment figure seems inapplicable in many romantic relationships. The asymmetry of the worshiper–God relationship more closely resembles the infant–mother relationship in this regard, in that the roles of caregiver and carereceiver are nearly always clearly defined and invariant across time. Unlike romantic love partners or other peers, however, God retains the character of the "awesomely powerful, usually protective" attachment figure of childhood. In a word, God is the quintessential "stronger and wiser Other."

Second, adult romantic attachments, unlike infant–mother relationships, typically involve a partner with whom a *sexual* relationship exists. This complication is, of course, typically absent from people's perceived relationships with God or other religious figures. There are fascinating exceptions to this, such as certain forms of mysticism (Moller, 1965) and various sects or cults in which a charismatic leader (who may serve as an attachment figure) also engages in sexual activity with cult members. (I revisit this important latter example in a different context, in a subsequent chapter.) But in most religious traditions, relationships with God,

Jesus, or other supernatural figures do not include an explicitly sexual component. The exceptions may provide interesting insights concerning the larger question of how attachment and sex are linked in adulthood (cf. Shaver et al., 1988).

Another way to think about these differences is to recall Hazan and Shaver's (1987; also Shaver, Hazan, & Bradshaw, 1988) model of romantic love as representing the confluence of three distinct behavioral systems, of which attachment is only one. Attachment in adult romantic relationships is confounded with two other (functionally distinct) behavioral systems: caregiving and sex/reproduction. The infant's relationship to its caregiver, in contrast, is purely an attachment relationship, unconfounded by these other systems. Likewise, the caregiver's relationship to the infant is guided purely by the caregiving system, unconfounded by attachment and sex/reproduction systems. With these distinctions in mind, perceived relationships with God are particularly interesting from an attachment theory perspective because they can be seen to represent a "pure" form of attachment, as in infants' attachments to their primary caregivers.

To return to the question of love, then, the love felt by a worshiper toward God more closely resembles a child's love for a caregiver than an adult's love toward a romantic partner because, stripped of its sexual and caregiving components, love of God reflects a relatively pure manifestation of the attachment system. It is "attachment-love," if you will. Conversely, the love felt by a worshiper *from* God resembles the love a parent feels for his or her child; it is "caregiver-love," unconfounded by attachment or sexuality. Both of these differ from "mating-love," as reflected in lust and sexual attraction and as managed by the sex/reproduction. (I return to the nature of love in relationship to attachment, caregiving, and mating in Chapter 8 from a somewhat different perspective that I hope will clarify the meaning of the informal terms introduced above in quotation marks.)

For the sake of completeness, I should mention the third important difference between infant–mother and romantic attachments identified by Weiss (1982) and others: The attachment system is not as readily activated in adulthood as in childhood. Infants have few behavioral options for dealing with illness, distress, or danger, so restoring proximity to the attachment figure is the only solution available for all of these problems. With maturity, however, comes self-reliance, and we become more capable of dealing with problems in various other ways. Typically, then, only situations of extreme distress or danger fully activate the attachment system in adults. However, as I discuss in some detail in Chapter 6, many such situations are also ones in which (human) romantic partners are not adequately or uniquely suited to solving the problem, and it is in these situations in particular that people are most likely to turn to God.

GOD AS A PARENTAL FIGURE

Apart from the question of love per se, the general idea of God as a parent-like figure has a long history in the psychology of religion. Freud (1927/1961) is of course the most (in)famous example, arguing that God was an exalted, protective father figure. Drawing such parallels is not only an academic exercise: Gods are often described by believers themselves in explicit parental terms, such as "God, the Father."

Motivated primarily by a Freudian framework, researchers have long debated whether images of God are essentially "masculine" and "paternal" or "feminine" and "maternal" (e.g., Godin & Hallez, 1965; Nelsen, Cheek, & Au, 1985; Nelson, 1971; Nelson & Jones, 1957; Strunk, 1959; Vergote & Tamayo, 1981)—that is, whether God more resembles, or functions psychologically as, a "mother figure" or a "father figure." The results of several early studies suggested that, contrary to Freud's "exalted father" notion, God images are perceived as more closely related to maternal than paternal images (Godin & Hallez, 1965; Nelson, 1971; Strunk, 1959) or, alternatively, to one's images of the preferred parent (Nelson & Jones, 1957). Both findings are more consistent with an attachment process than with a strict Freudian interpretation: If the preferred parent represents the primary attachment figure, which seems a plausible assumption, it is the image of this parent that God should most resemble. Moreover, since the primary attachment figure is more likely to be the mother than the father in Western culture (Lamb, 1978), it would follow that the God image would on average resemble the mother more closely than the father.[1]

Wenegrat (1990) has observed that the deities of the oldest known religions were largely maternal figures and that modern Protestantism is unusual in its lack of significant female deities. Freud himself puzzled over this fact, confessing that "I am at a loss to indicate the place of the great maternal deities who perhaps everywhere preceded the paternal deities" (quoted in Argyle & Beit-Hallahmi, 1975, p. 187). The question of whether maternal deities actually did precede paternal deities in the ancient history of religion remains a matter of considerable debate, but there is no doubt that over the course of human history gods have by no means been restricted to male figures.

The most sensible conclusion from this and other research seems to be that images of God combine elements of both stereotypically maternal and stereotypically paternal qualities (Vergote & Tamayo, 1981). Indeed, a theoretically ideal attachment figure would involve a kind of hybrid image, combining the "stereotypically feminine" qualities of being loving and nurturing and the "stereotypically masculine" qualities of being strong and protective. Such an individual would function ideally as a secure base and haven of safety, irrespective of gender. The masculinity–femininity question in regard to God is a red herring.

Of course, it still remains to be explained why the principal or only god in many major religions, including Christianity, tends to be viewed as a male rather than a female figure. I suspect this is because although God is perceived, at least by some people in some religions, in attachment terms, God plays other psychological roles for people as well. God is an exalted attachment figure, but also many other things, and it may well be from some of these other dimensions or roles that the perceived maleness of God images derives. For example, I argue in Chapter 10 that God is perceived by people in many religions as a kind of "big chief" or coalitional leader, a role historically (or, perhaps prehistorically) occupied by men.

INDIVIDUAL DIFFERENCES IN IMAGES OF GOD

Another way in which beliefs about God appear to parallel those about parents is with respect to patterns of individual differences. To the extent that God functions psychologically as an attachment figure, we might expect the structure of *individual differences* in God images to resemble that of parental images. Indeed, much factor-analytic research on God images confirms this expectation.

God as a Benevolent Caregiver

In virtually every factor-analytic study published, irrespective of the particular kinds of items used, the first (and largest) factor to emerge invariably reflects the idea of God as loving, caring, and benevolent. Gorsuch

(1968) performed a hierarchical factor analysis of 100 God-image variables and found two second-order factors, one of which was labeled *Benevolent Deity*. Items loading positively on this factor included "comforting," "loving," and "protective"; items loading negatively included "distant," "impersonal," and "inaccessible." Two of the first-order factors contributing to this higher-order factor were *Kindliness* (e.g., "loving," "comforting,") and the inverse of *Deisticness* (e.g., not "distant," not "impersonal," and not "inaccessible"). Spilka, Armatas, and Nussbaum (1964) found a large general factor in a similar analysis that included the items "comforting," "supporting," "protective," "strong," and "helpful." Using a very different set of descriptors, Tamayo and Desjardins (1976) found a first factor that accounted for 81% of the variance in ratings of God. This factor, which they labeled *Availability*, included items such as "who gives comfort," "a warmhearted refuge," "always ready with open arms," "who will take loving care of me," and "who is always waiting for me." Benson and Spilka (1973) factored 13 adjective pairs and found a first factor, which they labeled simply *Loving God*, to contain such items as "loving," "caring," and "forgiving." It would be difficult to write a list of characteristics that better described an ideal attachment figure.

Evidence for a strong God-attachment dimension has not been confined to studies focusing exclusively on individual differences in God images. Broen (1957) factor-analyzed responses to 133 statements about a wide array of religious attitudes and beliefs, and found a large first factor labeled by two independent judges as *Nearness to God*. According to Broen (1957), "Persons with high loadings on this factor would tend to feel that God was very real and constantly near and accessible. These persons feel they commune with God—'walk and talk' with Him" (p. 177)—in a manner characteristic of a secure attachment relationship.

In a rather different vein, Benson and Williams (1982) used cluster analysis to examine the God images of a random sample of members of the U.S. Congress. Two of the three clusters interpreted by the authors, *attentive-parent* God and *companion* God, are described in terms strongly reminiscent of the secure base and haven of safety functions of the secure attachment relationship.

God as Controlling and Demanding

In addition, many factor-analytic studies point to a second major factor, more or less independent of the first, reflecting a very different set of characteristics. On the Benson–Spilka (1973) measure of God images, the *Controlling God* subscale contains such items as "controlling," "demanding," "wrathful," and "punishing"—an "Old Testament God," in contrast to the nurturing "New Testament God" of the first factor, if you will.

The fact that these two dimensions tend to be more or less orthogonal serves as a reminder that perceptions of God as a nurturant caregiver and as a punitive, frightening being are not necessarily opposites, nor mutually exclusive. In some cases, the latter may actually serve to reinforce the former. Bowlby (1969) noted that lambs and puppies develop and maintain attachments despite receipt of unpredictable punishments from their caregivers and, moreover, that attachment behaviors actually *increase* as a result of such treatment. Similarly, human infants are attached to parents who mistreat them (Egeland & Sroufe, 1981). The basis for this seemingly paradoxical behavior is that the punishments, like other sources of fear and distress, activate the attachment system and hence the seeking of proximity to the primary attachment figure. The same individual is, in a sense, both the source of the problem and the solution.

Belief in a god that rains fire and brimstone upon the world, but who also serves as an attachment figure, may function in a similar manner. In fact, this may explain why beliefs about vindictive, frightening gods have persisted throughout the history of humankind despite the negative emotions they elicit. It may also help to explain why conservative Christian churches, which generally give greater attention to this aspect of God, are growing, while mainline and liberal denominations continue on a downward spiral (Kelley, 1972; Stark & Glock, 1968).

These two dimensions—*loving God* versus *controlling God*, as labeled by Benson and Spilka (1973)—appear to map neatly onto the two primary dimensions of *parenting* that have been widely studied in the developmental psychology literature. Baumrind (1971), who first identified them as separate dimensions, referred to them as *warmth* and *control*, respectively. Subsequent researchers have introduced other names for essentially the same two constructs: Maccoby and Martin (1983) refer to them as *responsiveness* and *demandingness*, whereas Parker, Tupling, and Brown (1979) refer to them as *care* and *overprotection*. Thus, it appears that the two principal factors underlying individual differences in images of God closely parallel the primary dimensions of individual differences in parenting styles—just as would be expected if thinking about God is guided by the psychological mechanisms designed to process information about parental caregiving.[2]

These two dimensions are not the only ones to emerge from factor analyses of God images: In some cases additional factors are extracted as well (e.g., Gorsuch, 1968). Many of these, I suspect, have little to do with attachment, but, rather, other psychological processes that are discussed in subsequent chapters. For example, the degree to which God is perceived to be *just* and *fair* may reflect thinking about equity in the context of *social exchange* rather than attachment per se. As Chapter 10 demonstrates, there is good reason to believe that another evolved system of psychological mechanisms in humans, independent of the attachment system, is "designed" (i.e., by natural selection) specifically for reasoning about social exchange and to detect "cheating" in such relationships. Although such positive notions as justice and fairness might seem at least loosely compatible with the idea of secure attachment, it would be rather a stretch to maintain that the importance of this dimension in people's thinking about God derives from attachment processes—a theme to which I turn in the next section.

At the same time, it should be noted that the "controlling" or "wrathful" factor may reflect other processes in addition to attachment. Measures of God images analyzed in these studies tend to be personality-like, asking about the degree to which God is perceived as one way or another *in general*. I doubt that many people believe that God is angry and wrathful all the time, however, any more than they think other people are. If we were to ask under what *conditions* God becomes angry, we may find that other psychological processes are implicated. To continue with the previous example, it is widely believed that God (like people) becomes enraged when others violate implicit or explicit "social contracts" with him, failing to fulfill promises or otherwise meet agreed-upon obligations. The belief that God thinks in this way may well have more to do with psychological mechanisms designed for reasoning about social exchange and cheater-detection rather than attachment.

Children's Beliefs about God

Heller (1986) observed a number of "personality themes" in children's images of God that seem to illustrate attachment phenomena (although he did not interpret them in attachment terms). His *God, the Therapist* image refers to "an all-nurturant, loving figure" which closely resembles a secure attachment figure. Two alternative God images described by Heller appear to parallel the two insecure patterns of attachment: The *Inconsistent God* seems to correspond to anxious/ambivalent attachment, and *God, the Distant Thing in the Sky* parallels avoidant attachment. Heller also noted several themes that appeared to him to transcend common familial and cultural influences, including *intimacy* (feelings of closeness to God) and *omnipresence* (God is "always there"). While Heller seemed to find some of these themes enigmatic, there is nothing mysterious about them from an attachment perspective.

Unfortunately, research by Heller and others has not typically examined correlates of these individual differences—for example, in terms of their empirical relations with attachment experience in the home. In the next chapter we turn to the question of how such individual differences in religious belief are related to attachment.

BEYOND GOD: EXTENSIONS AND LIMITATIONS

Up to now I have focused on the most obvious applications of attachment theory to religion. The parallels have been, I trust, fairly transparent: Many people believe that they have a personal relationship with a God who looks after them, protects them from harm, and thereby provides them with a source of strength and courage. To the extent that a relationship with God is explicitly conceived in terms similar to children's relationships with parents, the extension of attachment theory to this domain seems natural and reasonable.

The next question, of course, is how useful the theory might be in explaining aspects of religion other than the straightforward connections developed here so far. When I have presented these ideas at conferences and other fora over the years, I have regularly been asked this question in two general forms. The first concerns the degree to which attachment theory can address other aspects of Christianity (and similar religions) beyond traditional images of and perceived relationships with God. The second concerns the degree to which these ideas have any applicability outside Christianity, particularly with respect to Eastern religions such as Hinduism and Buddhism. For that matter, we might as well ask about the myriad other aspects and manifestations of religious belief seen throughout history and around the world, from "primitive" beliefs in animistic spirits and ancestor worship to the social and cultural processes observed in modern religious institutions. In general, how far can attachment theory be extended? How much of religion can it explain?

Before attempting to answer these questions, this is a good place to pause to consider the issue of generalizability. As foreshadowed back in Chapter 1, I intend to place fairly strict limits on how far attachment theory is pushed. The term "religion" covers an exceedingly vast and complex landscape and, as I argued earlier, no single psychological process or mechanism should be expected to explain it all. I do indeed believe that attachment theory is relevant to understanding a variety of aspects of religion other than those discussed so far. At some point, however, the general problem of determining the boundaries of generalization must inevitably be confronted. Let me first explain the strategy by which I intend to approach the problem generally, and then illustrate this with some examples of potential extensions—and also potential overextensions—of the theory.

To Generalize, or Not to Generalize?

Questions about generalizability are faced (or simply ignored) by authors of virtually every theory in psychology. Psychological theories are typically constructed to explain a fairly narrow range of observations, such as the results of experiments conducted on university college students using a particular set of procedures and measures. In the end, the question invariably arises as to how "generalizable" the phenomenon is. In Research Methods textbooks, this is typically referred to as the *external validity* of the finding. Would it be replicated in other kinds of populations? Using other kinds of manipulations and measures? And so on.

These questions arise regularly within the psychology of religion as well. Constructs, measures, and theories concerning religious motivation or orientation, religious or spiritual maturity, cognitive processes (e.g., attribution), and so on are constructed to explain a certain range of observations, and then the question invariably arises as to whether the questionnaire would be applicable to other religions, whether people in other cultures make the same sorts of attributions, and so forth. At least in part, this way of thinking is a direct consequence of the general "bottom-up" approach that characterizes so much research in the psychology of religion (and many other areas of psychology). As I discussed in Chapter 1, working from this direction leads researchers to begin with description and measurement, and subsequently construct (induce) hypotheses and theories based upon their observations. This path leads eventually to the question of how far the idea or measure generalizes beyond its original context.

At this juncture, the researcher is faced with a conundrum: to generalize, or not to generalize? One option is to regard discretion as the better part of valor, and restrain oneself from attempting to extend the theory to anything beyond its most direct and obvious applications. This seems to be the road less traveled, perhaps because confessing that one's theory has limited generalizability seems like an admission of defeat: If your theory can only explain X and Y, and you need to import other theories to account for the rest of the alphabet, the theory is regarded as narrowly circumscribed and of only limited interest—mainly to the (usually) small circle of researchers who happen to be particularly interested in X and Y. The perceived value of a theory is predicated largely on the amount of terrain it can gobble up. Thus when colleagues ask me whether attachment theory can explain the psychological dynamics of Buddhism or Hinduism, the implication has usually seemed to me to be that the theory is of limited value if the answer is no. However, I think this reasoning is flawed, for reasons I explain shortly.

The road more traveled—at least within the social sciences—is instead to see how far the theory can be pushed, to test the limits of its generalizability. If it applies initially to A and B, see if it can explain C, D, and E. To the extent that empirical tests are successful, the theory's perceived explanatory power grows as it is applied more and more widely.

This is a perfectly logical manner in which to proceed, but eventually it is bound to run into trouble. Sooner or later, the now-expanding theory will brush up against the border of an adjacent theory that is also out there on the same mission, trying to explain as much as *it* can, and before long their territories will overlap. Now there are two or more theories claiming to explain the same phenomenon, often in incommensurate ways—or at least ways that are not easily distinguished or reconciled.

In some cases the outcome can be fairly readily decided by a clever researcher, who is able to figure out the "crucial experiment" that decides convincingly which theory lays claim to which adjacent areas. But such crucial experiments are not easy to come by, and more often than not the two theories continue to coexist in the field for long periods of time. The problem here is not simply that there are multiple explanations for a particular observation. Indeed, in many cases they might all be true, either simultaneously (because the phenomenon is in fact multiply determined) or alternatively, depending on moderating factors as yet undiscovered.

The problem is that the field becomes a patchwork of overlapping theories that have very little to do with one another, and that do not fit together in any kind of coherent way. The puzzle picture, if one backs away to admire it, is a mess. Some form of higher-level organization is needed to impose structure that would make the larger picture interpretable and provide a clearly defined context for each piece.

For example, Pargament's (1997) theory of the psychology of religion and coping and Galanter's (1978, 1989) theory of the "relief effect" experienced through affiliation with charismatic groups such as religious cults both overlap in many ways with the attachment approach presented here. All three have much to do with the ways in which people draw upon religious beliefs to deal with adversity; all focus largely on interpersonal relationships; all deal largely in the currency of emotions such as fear and anxiety; and so on. They all aspire to explain many of the same religious phenomena. At the same time, however, each theory addresses some issues and topics more directly than others. Pargament focuses more than I have so far on personal relationships between fellow worshipers, for instance, and Galanter more on groups and group membership than individual relationships. In contemplating the generalizability of attachment theory, I am faced with the question of whether to leave interworshiper relations to Pargament's theory and group relations to Galanter's, or whether to try to show how all of these can be subsumed under attachment theory, or something else.

How to decide? As I argued in Chapter 1 and develop through the latter half of the book, my answer will involve a third approach. I believe we need to take a step back and survey the terrain from the perspective of a broad metatheoretical framework—I am suggesting one based on evolutionary psychology—which can be used as a nonarbitrary basis for carving up the religion landscape in an orderly manner. Unlike the current theoretical landscape, however, the pieces will fit together in a logically coherent way. Attachment dynamics will explain some of this terrain, but other psychological processes and mechanisms will explain others. I have chosen the particular examples discussed here because they will be useful, later in this chapter, for illustrating just how I propose to go about this.

The Problem with Parsimony

Another reason why researchers seek to maximize generalizability involves the desire for parsimony—loosely, the ability to explain the "mostest" with the "leastest." Social (and other) scientists have long been enamored of parsimony as an important criterion in evaluating theories, and to some extent for good reason: A theory that itself is no less complex than the phenomenon under investigation is of little value. From this standpoint, a theory that is widely generalizable, and can thereby explain a vast amount of terrain, is preferable because presumably fewer additional theories will be needed to explain what is left over. We would like to explain all of religion, for example, in terms of a few broad, highly generalizable principles or theories.

The problem here is that the ultimate goal is for our theories to be *right*, not just simple. We want our theoretical understanding to reflect accurately what is really happening out there in the world. (I understand that there are many philosophical complications here surrounding issues like "accuracy" and "really happening," but bear with me. I do not think they are crucial for the particular point I wish to make.) Reducing the natural world to four fundamental elements, such as fire, earth, air, and water, is tantalizingly simple, but that theory has long been abandoned in favor of a catalog of over 100 distinct elements. The goals of accuracy and simplicity are compatible only so long as the phenomenon under investigation is itself assumed to be, at a fundamental level, simple. Religion, however, is not simple. I suspect that the periodic table for the psychology of religion will ultimately contain perhaps 100 elements as well, and certainly cannot be meaningfully reduced to just one. Any theory that is pushed too far is bound to be trying to explain too much.

Moreover, true parsimony is not so much a function of the number of elements in a theory, but rather their arrangement or organizational structure. In the former sense, the earth–air–fire–water framework seems simpler than one comprising more than 100 different varieties of atoms, but this apparent simplicity is misleading. The beauty of the modern theory is the way in which those 100 or more elements are understood to be neatly arranged, based on a few clearly defined functional principles, in the periodic table. There are many, many distinct parts, but they fit together in a precise, orderly way. It is this organizational structure that is "parsimonious" and that powers the application of the framework to understanding the physical and chemical laws by which elements are combined into molecules and so on.

Let me abuse this metaphor a bit longer to return to the main point. A comprehensive psychology of religion will need to contain many functionally distinct elements, whose organization and interrelations can be understood in terms of an evolutionary metatheory akin to the periodic table. Attachment theory is about just one or two of these elements, albeit important ones—akin, say, to carbon or oxygen. This renders it limited in applicability, but indispensable. Attempting to extend its generality beyond the particular elements to which it applies would be analogous to applying the principles of organic chemistry to non-carbon-based molecules. To do so would not be parsimonious, just wrong.

In summary, I believe that attachment theory can explain more about religion than Christian images of God, as I discuss later and in the next several chapters. At the same time, however, its explanatory range will be fairly limited, but not because it is a weak or only marginally relevant theory. Instead, I approach the problem from the perspective of a larger framework in which attachment theory is just one of many parts, and consequently should be *expected* to explain only a limited range of observations. Other theories within the larger framework, discussed in later chapters, explain other sets of observations that reflect other, functionally distinct processes. In the end, this approach has the potential to lead toward the kind of coherent "big picture" sought in my agenda, in which the various pieces fit together rather than creating an overlapping, multilayered mess.

OTHER FORMS OF ATTACHMENT (OR NOT) IN RELIGION

With these general points in mind, let us return to the question of whether attachment theory is applicable to other kinds of relationships, and other kinds of religion, beyond the kind of perceived relationship with a Christian God discussed in the first part of this chapter. As should be clear from the preceding comments, a conservative approach is indicated. Any potential application should be approached in a manner similar to that modeled in Chapter 3, in which I examined beliefs about a Christian God in terms of the defining criteria of an attachment figure. In addition, we need to ask whether it is better explained by an alternative process from the larger framework (the "periodic table"). That is, with a metatheoretical framework in place, we can hold the puzzle piece in our hand and scan the table for the place it fits most neatly, rather than first trying to force it into one spot and then giving up only after being convinced it will not go there. I have not yet laid out the details of the framework I am proposing, but I have alluded to some examples previously and do so in the next section to illustrate what I have in mind.

Relationships with Other Supernatural Beings

Throughout the text so far I have regularly referred to "God," or sometimes "God (or Jesus)," but there is no reason to think that God is the only potential attachment figure in the supernatural world. In many Christian traditions, it is Jesus with whom one maintains an active day-to-day relationship, while God remains a more distant background figure. Furthermore, it seems at least plausible that the operation of attachment system dynamics and internal working models underlie beliefs and inferences about other deities both within and outside of Christianity.

Wenegrat (1990) suggests that due to its lack of significant female deities, modern Protestantism "provides a particularly poor vehicle for attachment concerns" (p. 143). In contrast, he notes that Catholicism provides division of psychological labor, in which a desexualized Virgin Mary adopts "maternal" characteristics (and attachment functions) while God assumes other "paternal" functions. I think Wenegrat may have been misled here by the red herring of the paternal–maternal or masculine–feminine distinction, and consequently overlooks the degree to which Jesus serves as an attachment figure in Protestant beliefs. However, his point is well made that a kind of division of psychological labor is common in polytheistic religions, with some gods perceived as attachment figures and others in terms of other psychological functions and dynamics.

Wenegrat's observation about Mary in Catholicism is an interesting one that finds theoretical and empirical support in the work of Andrew Greeley. Although he never cites attachment theory, Greeley's understanding of this process is clearly consonant with the attachment perspective. In *The Mary Myth*, for example, he writes that

> mothering is part of any intimate human relationship in the sense that we expect those who love us to be at least on occasion passionately tender toward us, to assume the responsibility of "taking care" of us. In marriage, then, a spouse does indeed mother the other. . . . (1977, p. 108)

In Greeley's view, the image of Mary as fulfilling this role is a crucial, defining aspect of Catholicism; it is an image of great power with deep psychological and biological roots. "The Mary Myth's powerful appeal is to be found . . . in the marvelous possibility that God loves us the way a mother loves her baby" (Greeley, 1990, p. 252). Drawing heavily on Greeley's work, Donahue (1995) concludes that the power of this Mary image constitutes an important reason why modern Catholics remain Catholic, (often) despite doctrinal dissension.

Beyond Christianity, it seems reasonable to suppose that beliefs about gods in any theistic religion are *potentially* understandable in terms of attachment dynamics. Insofar as one perceives oneself to have a relationship with a god or gods, particularly one that provides a secure base and/or a haven of safety, the attachment model may prove useful in understanding religious belief and experience. In monotheistic religions in particular, there is the potential for God (by whatever name he or she is identified) to serve as an attachment figure. In Islam, for example, to put faith in God is to entrust in and submit to God. The root of the Arabic word for faith (*amn*) means "to be secure, trust, and entrust," and those who have faith experience security from God (Woodberry, 1992). Although the God of Islam may differ in important ways from the God of Christianity or of Judaism, similar psychological processes rooted in attachment dynamics may well be involved.

In polytheistic belief systems, such as the ancient folks religions of Asia and Africa, gods and spirits play any number of different roles. Although one of these roles might be as an attachment figure, in most of these cases I suspect people's perceived relationships with deities are *not* attachment relationships. For example, one such mechanism to which I have alluded already is that of perceived relationships with gods predicated on principles of *social exchange* rather than attachment. The typical pattern in polytheistic systems is for gods to be specialized, in the sense that different gods are seen to be responsible for different kinds of effects in the world: the weather, the bounty of the harvest, success or luck in the hunt or on the battlefield; disease and good health; and so forth. To the extent that these effects are important to the human condition, people enter into implicit or explicit social contracts with these deities to influence their behavior, with different gods presumed to expect or demand different kinds of sacrifices or investments. In most cases, then, supernatural beings are seen to offer a particular provision or set of provisions in exchange for a particular obligation—the sine qua non of social exchange. On the other hand, attachment dynamics may well be involved in some of these perceived relationships, as in the example from Nuer religion cited earlier.

Relationships with Religious Leaders

Another possible application of attachment theory in the domain of religion is the role of clergy and other religious leaders. Can relationships with religious leaders be meaningfully conceptualized as attachments in Bowlby's sense?

It certainly seems reasonable to suggest that pastors, rabbis, priests, ministers, and other clergy can function as attachment figures. Indeed, such relationships would hardly necessitate any theoretical explanation unique to religion, beyond what is already known about attachments in general. Human religious leaders are typically perceived as wise, knowledgeable, and strong, and people turn to these persons for comfort, help, and advice in difficult times. The same could be said in regard to cult leaders and other such figures outside mainstream churches. Whether these leaders also function as a secure base in the true manner of an attachment figure is a more difficult question, but it surely seems possible. There is nothing necessarily unique about *religious* leaders in this regard: As Bowlby and many others have argued, virtually anyone perceived as a stronger, wiser other can potentially serve as an attachment figure.

It is important to keep in mind here, however, the distinction made by Ainsworth (1985) and others that an attachment is a bond in relation to a particular *person*, not a *role*. A child's babysitter or school teacher serves in the role of primary caregiver for periods of time, but this does not establish these relationships as attachments. In most cases, the relationship is temporary and the child retains the attachment(s) to the parent(s) despite the separation. Likewise, a minister, rabbi, or priest should not be assumed to be an attachment figure strictly on the basis of their role as an "official" stronger, wiser Other. As in the case of a child's teacher or other regular caregiver, the role-defined relationship could well facilitate the development of a true attachment bond, but does not constitute or indicate one in itself.

If priests and rabbis at the congregational level can serve as attachment figures, then what about megaleaders of vast religious empires? Wenegrat (1990) suggests that

> religious leaders can also be attachment figures, particularly if their belief system promotes this role. Charismatic religious leaders such as Maharaj Ji, the Reverend Moon, and Bagwhan Shree Rajneesh un-

doubtedly serve this function for many of their followers. Gurus of every faith may become attachment figures to their close devotees. (pp. 34–35)

Along the same lines, we might ask the same question of closer-to-home figures such as the Pope, Billy Graham, or Pat Robertson.

Wenegrat's (1990) use of the word "undoubtedly" might be a bit strong. Recall that to function as an attachment figure, someone must be perceived as *accessible* and *responsive*. You must feel confident that he or she will be available when needed. I wonder to what degree Unification Church members really feel that way about Reverend Moon, whom they probably could not contact personally if their lives depended upon it. Does just knowing that Reverend Moon is out there really give one a personal sense of comfort and confidence, and is he the person to whom one would turn in times of distress? Are these things true for Catholics with respect to the Pope? It might be possible, but I am skeptical.

Notice that this discussion points to some interesting differences between God and human attachment figures. As discussed in Chapter 3, God typically is perceived as *always* available and accessible, despite the fact that one cannot gain physical proximity with God in quite the same way as with another person. For example, God is typically perceived to be omnipresent. Reverend Moon, on the other hand, is not generally perceived by his followers to have the special supernatural characteristics that enable God to be accessible despite not being physically present in a literal sense. They know he is a human being—albeit a very special one, with other special qualities—to whom, unlike God, one could in principle gain physical proximity. But the reality is that this is very unlikely to be possible in practice.

Finally, it is important to keep in mind that just because something or someone provides a source of security and comfort, it is not necessarily an attachment figure. Adults have many more behavioral and psychological options available for protecting themselves and making themselves feel secure than relying on attachment figures. One's spouse may provide a sense of security when sleeping at home at night, but for some people having a gun under the pillow has a similar effect. We would not want to assume that such a person has an attachment relationship with a revolver, or that the gun serves as an attachment figure. In the present context, the point is that thinking about the Pope might indeed have the effect of enhancing a person's sense of felt security, but perhaps for reasons other than attachment processes. For example, thinking about the Pope may have the effect of re-minding one of the large, powerful coalition that he symbolizes and to which one belongs. *Coalitional psychology*, which is functionally distinct from attachment processes, will be discussed in some detail in a subsequent chapter.

Relationships with Fellow Worshipers and Other Peers

If human religious leaders, such as priests and pastors, can serve as attach-ment figures, what about fellow worshipers? Pargament (1997) and oth-ers have written extensively on the mutually supportive relationships—"horizontal" support—that often develop within religious congregations and other groups. Are these attachments too?

Like the question of clergy as attachment figures, this question is be-ginning to pull us away from the topic of the psychology of religion per se. Although there may be some elements of religious congregations that make them particularly effective at facilitating mutually supportive rela-tionships, the question could be asked equally about peer relationships in the context of any kind of group. Are friendships or other mutually sup-portive adult relationships properly construed as attachments? The gen-eral issues are the same as for other topics discussed earlier. First, one must ask whether the relationship fully meets the defining criteria of an attachment relationship, which may or may not be the case. Second, one must consider what alternative systems other than attachment might be involved, instead or additionally. Chapter 10 examines two other evolu-tionary theories that speak directly to the issue of peer relationships and the ways in which they, rather than attachment, may instead underlie the mutual helping and support found frequently among congregation members.

Relationships with Groups

Can a person be attached, in a strict Bowlbian sense, to a *group*? The idea seems enticing, particularly with respect to cults and other smaller reli-gious units such as local congregations. For example, can Galanter's (1989) "relief effect" be interpreted in terms of attachment processes?

Perhaps I should not have used the term "Bowlbian" in the preced-ing paragraph, as if Bowlby's opinion were the final arbiter, because in this case I think Bowlby was mistaken. Long before the publication of his

Attachment trilogy, he wrote that "probably in all normal people [attachment] continues in one form or another throughout life and, although in many ways transformed, underlies many of our attachments to country, sovereign, or church" (Bowlby, 1956, p. 588).

To my mind, the idea of attachments to groups per se seems too far a stretch of the concept. Earlier I noted that "relationships" with valued stamp collections and rock bands should not be considered attachments, in part because they typically do not meet all of the defining criteria for distinguishing attachment from other kinds of relationships (e.g., providing a secure base, eliciting grief upon loss), and in part because they do not constitute *interpersonal relationships* in the first place. Similarly, relationships defined by roles rather than personal bonds, as noted in the preceding section, are not attachments per se. These same issues apply to the question of attachment to groups. Perhaps most important, I think groups are about something other than attachment—that is, involve psychological systems or mechanisms other than the attachment system—as I discuss in more detail in Chapter 10.

To return to the topic of distant religious leaders, such as the Pope in Catholicism or Reverend Moon in the Unification Church, I suspect that the feeling people may have of an "attachment" to such figures might have more to do with group processes than attachment. That is, such individuals represent powerful *symbols* of the *groups* with which they are associated, and may thereby be effective in activating some of the emotions and schemata associated with the group. Some people have very strong feelings about national symbols such as the American flag, but presumably these feelings are really not directed at the flag itself but rather what it represents. Likewise, feelings about the Pope may reflect more one's identification with Catholicism, for example, than an attachment to the Pope per se. And this group identification, I believe, involves a fundamentally different set of evolved psychological mechanisms from the attachment system.

Nontheistic Religions

A natural question to pose for an attachment account of religious beliefs concerns the applicability of the model to nontheistic belief systems, particularly the noteworthy (and widespread) Eastern religious traditions. How could a godless religion involve attachment processes, given that I have argued that perceptions of a personal relationship are required for a psychological bond to be regarded properly as an attachment?

Indeed, I suspect that a belief system in which there are no personalized gods is unlikely to provide much fertile ground for attachment theory. On the other hand, it is important to realize that many Eastern religions are considerably less devoid of attachment figure-like gods than is commonly thought. This is especially the case with respect to the beliefs of ordinary people which, as in Christianity, often bears little resemblance to those of studious theologians pondering the mysteries of the universe in monasteries and seminaries.

First, the major Eastern religions each are divided into multiple variants, many of which are not at all "godless." Hinduism, for example, presents adherents with three alternative roads to enlightenment. Two of these fit the Westerner's common conceptions of Eastern religion: the path of duty (*karma marga*) is largely ritual-based, and the path of wisdom (*jnana marga*) is largely philosophical and metaphysical. However, according to Hiebert (1992), an estimated 90% of Hindus follow the third path, the path of devotion (*bhakti marga*). This path "offers immediate, unconditional salvation to those who throw themselves on the mercy of God," where God refers to the god of one's caste and/or a personal god chosen by the individual (Hiebert 1992, p. 11). Moreover, Hiebert (1992) observes that

> conversion in the path of *bhakti* is similar to that in Christianity. A person must choose a god or goddess and surrender totally to this deity. The god then saves all those who call on him or her. (p. 11)

Although Westerners typically think of Hinduism more as a nontheistic, metaphysical philosophy than a personal religion in the Western sense, Hiebert's analysis suggests that the vast majority of Hindus may in fact be experiencing a personal relationship with God in very much the same way as their Christian counterparts.

Several of Hiebert's (1992) observations on Buddhism point in a similar direction. For example, Hiebert contrasts the two major traditions of Buddhism by noting that

> for the masses caught in the struggles of life, [Theravada] Buddhism was too austere. . . . They were used to worshiping the many gods of India. Consequently, when sculptors began to carve images of the Buddha, the common people took to worshiping these images. . . . By the third century A.D. the idea of Buddha as the Suffering Savior emerged. It is

> Mahayana that won the Chinese with their belief in spirits and gods, and, through them, the Koreans and Japanese. (p. 17)

Again, it is the metaphysical Theravada tradition (along with Zen) that most of us (Westerners) readily associate with Buddhism, but it is the theistic Mahayana tradition that touched the hearts and minds of everyday people.

A second way in which religion in the East often proves more theistic than is commonly assumed is that traditional folk religions, populated by all manner of gods, spirits, and powers, often continue to exist alongside, or have been blended together with, later imports such as Buddhism. Writing about the spread of Buddhism in China, for example, Smart (1976) notes that

> another factor in the spread of Buddhism in China is a general one which helps to explain its spread elsewhere. Buddhism may be agnostic about the existence of a supreme Creator . . . but it has never felt it necessary to deny popular religion. The gods, spirits, and demons that people the world of the ordinary folk in the lands to which Buddhism has come, including India, are not rejected. . . . Buddhism has tamed, rather than eradicated, such popular religion. Thus in China, Buddhism felt no motive to protest against the cult of ancestors or to wipe out the cults of popular deities.

Of course, there are countless doctrinal and philosophical differences between most Western and Eastern religions, but there may be a surprising amount of similarity when they are parsed in the right way. For example, the idea of a personal god to whom one submits and in whom one places one's faith—in return for salvation and a sense of security— seems practically irresistible to human beings around the globe. To the extent that religious beliefs include such a component, attachment dynamics may lie behind and shape the religious experiences of these individuals. Although empirical research to support these conjectures is sorely needed, it seems reasonable to maintain that attachment may be far more universally applicable to the understanding of religious belief and experience than one might initially suspect. (On the other hand, the widespread idea of gods with whom one expects to receive something *in return* for behaving in certain ways suggests the involvement of a differ-

ent psychological system related to social exchange and reciprocal altruism, as discussed in Chapter 10.)

In sum, we need to be cautious about labeling phenomena as attachment processes. People ask me frequently, for example, what I think
about the concept of "detachment" in Buddhist philosophy. Does it mean
something like insecure (or specifically *avoidant*) attachment? Does it
mean that Buddhists who attempt to attain "detachment" probably grew
up with insecure childhood attachments? I frankly doubt that there is
any meaningful relationship between "detachment" in this sense and attachment processes at all. The only reason it would even occur to anybody, I think, is by virtue of superficial similarities in the words. In Buddhism, one strives to distance oneself from "attachments" (in the loose
sense) to things such as material objects and ambitions. But one's desire
for such things does not constitute attachment in Bowlby's sense of the
word.

SUMMARY AND CONCLUSIONS

In the previous chapter I examined some traditional Christian beliefs
about and images of God, concluding that many people perceive themselves to have a genuine attachment relationship to God. In the first half
of this chapter I extended the argument by reviewing some additional resemblances between perceived relationships with God and attachment
processes, including the role of the emotion of love and other parallels
with parental relationships. In the second half, I explored the question of
how generalizable the attachment model might be in religion, beyond
these images and perceived relationships with a Christian God. I argued
that the question of generalizability takes a rather different form in the
context of a larger metatheory than in the context of the more common
"bottom-up" approach to the problem, because from the beginning the
goal is not simply to extend the model as far as it will go in the interest of
explaining as much as possible with a particular theory. Attachment theory is expected to explain only one part of religion in the first place;
other theories within the metatheoretical framework will be brought to
bear on other matters. It may well be the case that, for example, attachment processes are widely implicated in the religious beliefs and experience within Western Christianity, but much less so in Zen Buddhism.
This in no way implies a weakness on the part of the theory, so long as

other theories compatible with attachment theory—that is, with which attachment theory fits neatly as part of a large, coherent "big picture"—can be brought to bear on these other phenomena.

Consequently, as I have noted occasionally throughout this chapter, in order to seriously consider the question of whether a particular deity functions psychologically as an attachment figure, one needs to know what the alternatives are. In Chapters 10 and 11 I discuss a variety of evolved psychological mechanisms/systems other than the attachment system, and argue that thinking about different deities (or the same deities to different people) may involve any number of such systems. As powerful a theory as attachment is, there is more to life than attachment. Attachment is about a particular kind of relationship with a particular function. From the standpoint of modern evolutionary psychology, there are many, many such systems, each of which can be conceptualized in terms similar to the attachment system. Evolutionary psychologists have identified and researched many, many other evolved psychological mechanisms, each with its own adaptive function and unique design, as we will see in subsequent chapters.

Before doing so, it is time to take a look at some empirical data supporting the arguments developed so far.

CHAPTER FIVE

Individual Differences in Attachment and Religion

The Correspondence Hypothesis

In the previous chapters I have argued that many aspects of religious belief, particularly within Christianity, reflect the operation of attachment processes. To this point I have focused on the normative aspects of attachment theory and religion, for example, by showing that God, as typically conceived in Christianity, displays all of the defining characteristics of an attachment figure. The issue of individual differences was introduced only with respect to normative patterns (e.g., factorial structure) of individual differences in religiousness, particularly with respect to images of God.

In this chapter and the next, the focus switches to two sets of hypotheses about individual differences in attachment and religion. The basic premise is that if the attachment system, including its functional dynamics and internal working models (IWMs), underlies thought and behavior in the context of both human interpersonal relationships and religious beliefs, then individual differences in the workings of the system should be evident within both domains. That is, individual differences in religious belief and experience should be empirically related in one or more ways to individual differences in relationships with parents, adult romantic partners, or other human attachment figures.

In this chapter I review the evidence suggesting a direct relationship between IWMs of human attachments, on the one hand, and beliefs about God and perceptions of relationships with God on the other. These data eventually will lead us to consider the role of socialization and cultural transmission of religious beliefs, which I discuss in the final section of the chapter. In the next chapter I introduce a second, and quite different, way in which individual differences in human attachment and religion may be related.

MENTAL MODELS AND THE CORRESPONDENCE HYPOTHESIS

If God functions psychologically as an attachment figure, in the same manner as children's caregivers and adult romantic partners, then these observations lead to a straightforward set of predictions that I have referred to as the *correspondence hypothesis* (Kirkpatrick, 1992; Kirkpatrick & Shaver, 1990): Individual differences in attachment styles should parallel, in important respects, individual differences in beliefs about God and related aspects of religious belief. For example, people characterized by a secure attachment style would be expected to view God, like their human relationship partners, as an available and responsive attachment figure who loves and cares for them, whereas avoidant persons should be more likely to see God as remote and inaccessible, or cold and rejecting, or simply nonexistent.

One form that such correspondence should take is between IWMs of human attachment figures and beliefs about God at any given point in time. This hypothesis derives from two lines of reasoning. First, if IWMs of attachment figures are arranged at a given point in time in a hierarchical manner, as proposed by Collins and Read (1994), then a set of generalized models of attachment figures as trustworthy, caring, and so forth at a superordinate level should influence more relationship-specific models at the next lower level. As a consequence, IWMs of all attachment figures at a given point in time, including God, should be interrelated to a moderate degree. This model is illustrated in Figure 5.1. Although certain aspects of the IWMs of a given attachment figure are unique to that particular relationship, the superordinate levels of the IWMs provide a basis for correspondence across these models. It would be unusual (though not impossible) for someone to view one attachment figure as highly available and reliable, but another as completely untrustworthy and rejecting. Instead, IWMs are *in part* more global, reflecting beliefs about close-relationship partners and attachment figures as generally loving, available, and reliable, or as generally untrustworthy and inaccessible.

In addition, such correspondence should be observed in adulthood for a second reason. If perceptions of God and of one's relationship with God are constructed from the building blocks of one's own experiences in close relationships (Wenegrat, 1990)—just as adult love relationships are thought to be shaped by early childhood experience with attachment relationships (Sroufe & Fleeson, 1986)—then IWMs of romantic partners and of God in adults should be intercorrelated by virtue of common cause in prior experience, particularly attachment relationships with caregivers in childhood. This model is illustrated in Figure 5.2. Presumably, this common cause is the source of the superordinate IWMs of attachment figures, per the Collins–Read hierarchy, in adulthood.

Moreover, given these assumptions about the origins of God-beliefs in early attachment experience, a second form of correspondence that would be predicted is between individual differences in childhood attachment and subsequent religiosity in adults. That is, correspondence between human attachments and beliefs about God should be observed *longitudinally*, from childhood to adulthood, as well as cross-sectionally in adulthood. In this chapter I review evidence for both of these propositions.

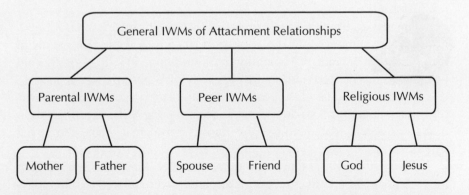

FIGURE 5.1. Hierarchical model of attachment internal working models (IWMs). Adapted from Collins and Read (1994). Copyright 1994 by Jessica Kingsley Publishers. Adapted by permission.

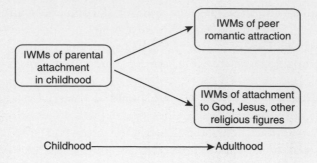

FIGURE 5.2. Continuity of attachment internal working models (IWMs) across time.

Correspondence in Childhood and Adolescence

The development of religious beliefs across childhood has been the subject of considerable research in the psychology of religion. Unfortunately (for our purposes), however, surprisingly little of this research has focused on individual differences in religious beliefs. Instead, researchers have tended to focus on the development across time of children's understandings of religious concepts and of their religious identities as a function of changes in cognitive development, especially from a Piagetian perspective (e.g., Elkind, 1971; Harms, 1944). In those studies in which individual differences in children's belief have been studied, these differences generally have not been correlated with other variables, such as parental relationships.

The few studies that have examined such relationships in childhood, however, are supportive of the correspondence hypothesis. In a study of fifth- and ninth-grade schoolchildren, Tamminen (1991) showed that perceived closeness to and companionship with parents was related to the concept of God as close, real, caring, and forgiving. In addition, the religiously committed students, particularly among girls, described their homes as safer, more caring, and more stimulating than did other students.

Dickie et al. (1997) found in a study of 4- to 11-year-old children that individual differences in perceptions of parents were related to differences in images of God. Different patterns were observed with respect to mothers and fathers and to the dimensions of God images. For example, perceptions of fathers as nurturant were related to the degree to which God was perceived as nurturing, whereas perceptions of mothers as powerful were related to images of God as powerful.

In the first study of this topic motivated explicitly by attachment theory, Jubis (1991) examined the relationship between images of parents and images of God in a sample of 74 fourth graders at a Catholic school. A God-image factor labeled *considerate attentiveness* (e.g., "listens to me"; "pays a lot of attention to me") was correlated positively and significantly with several attachment-related dimensions of maternal images, including *supportive reassurance, affectionate support,* and *tolerant helpfulness.* Moreover, these results remained after a measure of social desirability was statistically controlled—an important observation, demonstrating that the correlations cannot be explained merely as a by-product of variability in children's general willingness to admit to negative, socially undesirable perceptions of their parents or of God. In addition, children's self-reported prayer when "feeling scared, worried, lonely, or sad" and "when really bad things happen to you (like an accident)" were inversely correlated with a measure (derived from a life-events checklist) concerning losses of and separations from attachment figures. That is, children whose parental attachments had been disrupted by losses and/or separations (e.g., divorce, death) were less likely than other children to turn to God as an attachment figure under these kinds of circumstances.

Several other studies have examined the relationship between images of God and perceptions of parents in teenagers. Spilka, Addison, and Rosensohn (1975) found in a sample of 16-year-old Catholic high school students that perceptions of parents as loving and nurturing were correlated with images of God as loving, comforting, and nurturing. Similarly, Potvin (1977) showed in a large, national probability sample of adolescents ages 13–18 that perceived parental affection and parental control were related significantly to loving and punishing God images, respectively. In a study of 14- to 16-year-old working-class Polish boys, Krol (1982; as summarized by Hyde, 1990) found that individual differences in images of God were closely related to images of real fathers, with sons of "bad," alcoholic fathers reporting more negative God images than those with "good" fathers.

Correspondence in Adulthood

Several studies have now been conducted to examine the relationship between adult attachment styles and individual differences in religious belief. In the first of these (Kirkpatrick & Shaver, 1992), over 200 adults responded to a newspaper survey and a follow-up mail survey containing a variety of religion measures and the Hazan–Shaver (1987) measure for classifying subjects into adult attachment styles. With respect to images of God, the strongest differences were observed between the *secure* and *avoidant* adult-attachment groups: People who classified themselves as se-cure were significantly more likely than those classified as avoidant to view God as more loving, less controlling, and less distant/inaccessible. Avoidant persons were significantly less religiously committed than se-cure persons, and were more likely to classify themselves as agnostic than the other groups. Anxious subjects generally fell in between the secure and avoidant groups; however, they were the most likely to say they had had at least one glossolalia experience in their lives (a finding to which I return in the next chapter).

These results were later replicated in two unpublished studies I con-ducted at the University of South Carolina. In another newspaper survey sample of over 400 adults, participants classifying themselves as secure on the Hazan–Shaver measure displayed the highest level of religious com-mitment, and were the most likely to identify themselves as *evangelical* Christians—a Christian orientation that places particular emphasis on one's relationships with God and Jesus. Avoidant respondents, on the other hand, were again the most likely to identify themselves as either atheistic or agnostic. In a second sample of Christian college students, participants classifying themselves as avoidant on the Hazan–Shaver measure scored significantly higher than the other groups on distant God images, and were by far the *least* likely to say that they had a personal relationship with God or Jesus.

Strahan (1991) has also replicated some of these findings among stu-dents at a church-affiliated college in Australia. In one study, avoidant respondents (again on the Hazan–Shaver measure) scored significantly lower than the other groups on the single-item measure, "I know for sure that God cares for me." The avoidant group also scored lowest on intrin-sic religiousness (i.e., genuine religious commitment), although in this sample this result was significant only among male students.

Correspondence Across Cultures

Another source of data that supports the correspondence hypothesis comes from cross-cultural analysis of ethnographies. In two such published studies, Rohner (1975) and Lambert, Triandis, and Wolf (1959) coded numerous cultures with respect to the culturally dominant parenting style, as measured on an *accepting–rejecting* dimension, and the society's beliefs about the supernatural, coded as mainly *benevolent* versus *malevolent*. Both groups of researchers found a strong positive correlation across cultures between these variables: Cultures in which "accepting" (loving, nurturing) parenting styles are predominant tend to embrace benevolent deities, whereas cultures characterized by "rejecting" parenting styles tend to believe in deities that are primarily malevolent toward man. In addition, Rohner (1975) reported a variety of other correlations between various typical patterns of behavior and personality across cultures and the predominant parenting style. For example, in societies characterized by "rejecting" parenting styles, adults and children tend to be less emotionally responsive, emotionally stable, and able to become involved in affectionate relationships, and to show more aggressive and hostile behavior.

Of course, the nature of the causal relationship among these variables represents a complex chicken-and-egg question: Does childhood attachment experience influence the development of religious beliefs, or do religious beliefs influence child-rearing practices? There also are difficulties involved in extrapolating from crosscultural findings to individual differences within cultures. Nevertheless, at least one leading attachment researcher (Bretherton, 1985) has concluded that Rohner's general conclusions should be taken seriously as evidence that parental caregiving influences religious thinking, noting that "I am particularly impressed with the fact that [these religious] correlates of acceptance or rejection among societies read uncannily like the sequalae of secure and insecure attachment reported by Sroufe (1983) for a sample of preschoolers in Minnesota" (p. 26).

It is worth noting here that this interpretation broaches an important general issue concerning the interpretation of cross-cultural variation. Notice that I have used evidence concerning cross-cultural *differences* in religious belief here to argue for cross-cultural *universality* in their underlying psychology. The apparent irony here derives from an outdated notion of "instincts," or evolved psychology in terms of simple stereotyped behavior patterns. The attachment system, in contrast, is far more complex than this, constituting an assemblage of *conditional* rules for responding to different kinds of experience with different kinds of thoughts, emotions, and behaviors. To the extent that people in different cultures experience the same "inputs," they would be expected to generate similar "outputs"; conversely, different inputs lead to different outputs. Thus, a species-universal, psychological attachment system can lead to cross-cultural similarity *or* variability in religious belief, depending on the similarity versus variability of attachment experiences that are normative across those cultures. I return to a more general discussion of this issue, and these particular empirical findings, later in this chapter.

Internal Working Models of Self and Others

Chapter 2 introduced an alternative model of individual differences in adult attachment that was proposed by Bartholomew (1990). She formulated a fourth adult attachment style—distinguishing between *fearful* avoidance and *dismissing* avoidance as two distinct styles—and showed how the four styles could be conceptualized in terms of a 2 x 2 matrix. In this dimensional conceptualization, the secure and preoccupied (anxious) groups share positive IWMs of *others*, in contrast to the negative IWMs of others characterizing the two avoidant groups. The second dimension, contrasting *secure* and *dismissing* versus *preoccupied* and *fearful*, reflects positive versus negative IWMs of the *self*. This 2 x 2 framework, with the four cells labeled according to their corresponding prototypes, was illustrated in Chapter 2 (Figure 2.1, p. 44). This framework provides a useful tool for investigating attachment–religion relationships in a more refined way.

Recall that according to Bowlby (1969), IWMs of self and others tend to be mutually complementary early in life; children who perceive their attachment figures as loving and caring tend to see themselves as worthy of love and care. Several studies in the psychology of religion literature demonstrate a similarly complementary relationship between measures of self-esteem and individual differences in images of God: People who view God as loving and beneficent tend to have higher self-esteem and more positive selfconcepts than those who do not (Benson & Spilka, 1973; Buri & Mueller, 193; Flakoll, 1974; Jolley, 1983; Spilka et al., 1975). From an attachment perspective, these findings reflect a correspondence between IWMs of self and IWMs of God as an attachment figure.

In a more extensive study, Kirkpatrick (1998b) examined the relationship between individual differences in religious belief and adult attachment styles as measured using Bartholomew's four-paragraph prototype measure; as on the Hazan–Shaver measure, participants were asked to choose which of four orientations toward romantic relationships best described them. Participants were more than 1,300 undergraduate students enrolled in Introductory Psychology courses over a 2-year period.

In the cross-sectional analysis of these data (longitudinal results are presented in the next chapter), positive mental models of *both* self and others predicted, independently and additively, higher scores on an aggregate religiousness measure. The finding for self models is consistent with the self-esteem studies just noted. The finding for others models is consistent with the idea that IWMs of multiple attachment figures are interrelated; people who view (human) close-relationship partners as trustworthy, reliable, and so forth are more likely to be religious than those who do not. In terms of attachment "styles," the sum of these two independent effects implies that the secure group (positive IWM of both self and others) was the most religious, the fearful group (negative IWM of both self and others) least religious, and the preoccupied and dismissing groups intermediate with respect to overall religiosity.

When the religiousness variable was disaggregated, however, the individual religion measures displayed different patterns of relationships with the two respective IWM dimensions. Models of *self* were most strongly related to images of God: As in the research described earlier, positive self models were related to perceptions of God as more loving and as less distant. In contrast, positive models of *others* were most strongly associated with belief in a personal (vs. impersonal or nonexistent) God, and belief in having a personal relationship with God (as well as Distant, but not Loving, God images).

These findings are summarized in Figure 5.3, in the upper half of each cell of the table. Within each cell, I have listed the variables for which significant main effects of self and others were found, using plus and minus signs to indicate direction of effects. (Also note that I have used the word "close" to represent "not distant" for ease of interpretation; for example, "God close +" is used to indicate a group that scored low on the Distant God scale.)

Ordinarily I would be hesitant to draw too strong a conclusion from such a subtly different pattern of results. However, it turns out that when the correspondence between the Bartholomew styles and the Hazan–Shaver styles is considered, these results replicate the previously discussed findings reported by Kirkpatrick and Shaver (1992) in remarkable detail. These earlier findings are noted in the lower part of each cell of

	Positive IWM of self	Negative IWM of self
Positive IWM of others	SECURE (Secure)	PREOCCUPIED (Anxious/ Ambivalent)
Self effect:	God loving + God close +	God loving − God close −
Others effect:	Personal God + Relationship with God + God close +	Personal God + Relationship with God + God close +
Kirkpatrick & Shaver (1992):	God loving: high Relationship with God: high God close: high	God loving: low Relationship with God: high God close: intermediate
Negative IWM of others	DISMISSING (N/A)	FEARFUL (Avoidant)
Self effect:	God loving + God close +	God loving − God close −
Others effect:	Personal God − Relationship with God − God close −	Personal God − Relationship with God − God close −
Kirkpatrick & Shaver (1992):	[n/a] [n/a] [n/a]	God loving: low Relationship with God: low God close: low

FIGURE 5.3. Individual differences in religion as a function of adult attachment styles. IWM, internal working model.

Figure 5.3 for comparison. First, recall that God images were the variables on which Kirkpatrick and Shaver found secure respondents to differ from both anxious and avoidant adults on the Hazan–Shaver measure. According to Bartholomew (1990), the "avoidant" style corresponds most closely to her *fearful*-avoidant style. (Bartholomew's dismissing-avoidant style is the one "missing" from the Hazan–Shaver framework). Thus, both insecure styles on the Hazan–Shaver measure differ from the secure style with respect to their *self* models. The finding that secures outscored both insecure groups on God images (Kirkpatrick & Shaver, 1992) thus maps precisely onto the finding that IWMs of self are related to God images (Kirkpatrick, 1998b). The patterns of means for other variables in Kirkpatrick and Shaver (1992) can similarly be mapped onto those of Kirkpatrick (1998b), as shown in Figure 5.3, suggesting that it is specifically a positive mental model of *others* that relates most strongly to perceptions of having a personal relationship with God.

This differentiated pattern of findings suggests that IWMs of self and others may operate separately in shaping people's religious beliefs. Beliefs about what God is like—that is, whether God is viewed as loving and caring or as controlling and wrathful—appear to correlate with mental models of the self. In a word, people who view themselves as loveable and worthy of being cared for are those most likely to see God as the kind of being who loves and cares for people. However, the belief that God has these characteristics is distinct from the question of whether one has—or could possibly have—a personal relationship with him (or her). It is IWMs of *others* that predict the answer to this question: Only those who see attachment figures as trustworthy, available, and accessible see God as available and accessible in a close personal relationship. To have a secure personal relationship with God, both elements are necessary. In Chapter 6 we examine how these separate models of self and others are differentially predictive of religious change across time.

Continuity from Childhood to Adulthood

According to the theory and research reviewed in Chapter 2, individual differences in attachment patterns arise early in life in response to variability in the quality and predictability of parental caregiving. These individual differences remain relatively stable across time as a consequence of IWMs of self and others that are constructed based upon early experience. Secure children develop a set of beliefs and expectations about attachment figures as reliable, available, and responsive; avoidant children develop IWMs of attachment figures as cold, rejecting, and unavailable; and anxious children develop mixed IWMs of attachment figures as unpredictably available at some times but unreliable at others. According to Bowlby and other theorists such as Sroufe and Fleeson (1986), these mental models are carried over into subsequent relationships.

Consequently, a second version of the correspondence hypothesis follows from attachment theory: Adult religious belief—particularly about God and one's perceived relationship to God—should be related to *previous* attachment experience in childhood. To state it more precisely, individual differences in childhood attachment experience should give rise to individual differences in religious belief later in life. This line of reasoning follows the conceptual model discussed earlier in this chapter and illustrated in Figure 5.3.

Previous research on persons at opposite ends of the religiosity spectrum are consistent with this hypothesis. In a classic study, Vetter and Green (1932) surveyed 350 members of the American Association for the Advancement of Atheism to examine causes and reasons for anti-religious attitudes. Members of this organization were disproportionately likely to describe having lost a parent during childhood, and/or to have poor relations with one or both parents. Other studies by Bruder (1947) and Caplovitz and Sherrow (1977) found similar results with respect to apostasy, or loss of religious faith, in adulthood. These findings are consistent with the cross-sectional results from Kirkpatrick and Shaver (1992), in which the avoidant attachment style of romantic attachment was associated with atheism and agnosticism. At the other end of the spectrum, several studies suggest that female seminarians, sisters, and nuns are characterized by unusually secure attachments to their mothers compared to laypersons, and see their mothers as particularly interested, supportive, and helpful (Potvin, 1985; Potvin & Suziedelis, 1969; Vergote & Tamayo, 1981).

In the first study designed explicitly to examine this hypothesis from an attachment perspective, Kirkpatrick and Shaver (1990) simulated a longitudinal study by asking their newspaper-survey respondents to describe their relationships with their parents retrospectively. Three paragraph-length prototypes, one each for secure, avoidant, and anxious childhood attachment "styles," were employed to reflect the respective patterns of parent–child relationships described in the developmental attachment literature. As with the Hazan–Shaver adult attachment measures, participants chose the paragraph that best described their childhood relationships with their mothers and fathers, respectively. A variety of measures of adult religious commitment and belief were included as well.

The results suggested a more complex pattern than was expected from the straightforward correspondence hypothesis. With one very important exception—discussed at length in the next chapter—no significant differences were found on the adult religion variables as a direct function of childhood attachment patterns. Instead, significant statistical *interactions* were observed for most of the religion variables between maternal attachment and mothers' (perceived) religiousness, as summa-rized in Figure 5.4. Specifically, correspondence was observed only when mothers were reported to have been relatively *religious* during the respondent's childhood. In these cases, participants reporting secure maternal attachments, compared to those reporting insecure maternal attachments, tended also to report higher levels of religious commit-ment and church attendance. In addition, those with secure maternal attachments were more likely to endorse a conceptualization of God as a *personal* being, in contrast to pantheistic or deistic alternatives, and were more likely to report that they felt they currently had a *personal relationship* with God or Jesus. On the other hand, these patterns tended to be reversed for participants reporting that their mothers had been relatively nonreligious—a finding to which we return in the next chapter.

With respect to the correspondence hypothesis, the glass can be seen as half empty or half full, depending on whether one focuses on the re-sults for children of religious mothers (which support the hypothesis) or of nonreligious mothers (which contradict the hypothesis). In favor of the "half-full" interpretation, however, it is important to note that at least in samples such as this one, "religious" mothers are much more com-mon than nonreligious ones—at least in the contemporary United States—simply as a function of base rates for religiosity. The vast major-ity of Americans report believing in God and identifying themselves as at least nominally religious (Gallup & Jones, 1989). In some sense, then, the correspondence pattern—secure attachment coupled with high reli-giosity—is probably the statistically predominant one. Cases in which *in-secure* parental attachment is coupled with high adult religiosity, though statistically less common, are particularly interesting and theoretically important, and are discussed at length in the next chapter.

	Religious parents	Nonreligious parents
Secure attachment to parents	*More religious*	*Less religious*
Insecure attachment to parents	*Less religious*	*More religious*

FIGURE 5.4. Adult religiousness as a function of parental religiosity x childhood attach-ment security. Based on results from Kirkpatrick and Shaver (1990).

I was frankly skeptical about the reliability of these interaction findings (as well as the exception to this pattern, discussed in Chapter 6) until Granqvist (1998) replicated them with remarkable precision. In a diverse sample of over 200 students from a Swedish university, Granqvist found significant parental attachment x parental religiousness interactions in the prediction of perceived relationship with God, overall level of religiousness, and amount of positive religious change during adolescence. As in Kirkpatrick and Shaver (1990), results for children of religious parents were consistent with the correspondence hypotheses for these variables, whereas children of relatively nonreligious parents showed the opposite pattern. In contrast to Kirkpatrick and Shaver (1990), however, Granqvist found similar results for both maternal and paternal attachment; indeed, many of these results (as well as others discussed later) appeared somewhat stronger with respect to fathers than mothers.

The Socialized-Correspondence Hypothesis

In my interpretation of the attachment x parental religiousness interaction, I assumed that parental religion moderated the effect of attachment. That is, I suggested that childhood attachment patterns influence adult religiosity, but that this is true only for those with relatively religious mothers. However, the statistical fact of interaction does not require this interpretation. An interaction simply implies that the effect of one variable differs depending on the level of another variable, and cannot alone provide a basis for determining which variable moderates the effect of which.

Indeed, Granqvist (1998; Granqvist & Hagekull, 1999) later introduced an alternative explanation for these data by, in effect, turning my interpretation on its head. According to Granqvist, it may instead be individual differences in attachment that moderate the effects of parental religion. Secure attachment, he suggests, facilitates the *socialization* of children to parental religion, whereas insecure attachment does not. Thus, those with secure childhood attachments become religious if their parents were religious, but not if they were not; those with insecure childhood attachments follow the opposite pattern. Granqvist referred to this process as *socialized correspondence*, where "correspondence" now refers to the parallel between one's religious beliefs and one's parents' beliefs, rather than, as in my interpretation, between one's religious beliefs and security of one's own attachment style (or prior attachment experience).

This interpretation fits nicely with a wide variety of other observations in both attachment theory and the psychology of religion. Kagan (1984), for example, argued that "the major consequence of an attachment is to make the child receptive to the adoption of parental standards" (p. 63), and several attachment theorists have also pointed to the crucial role of attachment figures in the teaching and socialization of their children (e.g., Matas, Arend, & Sroufe, 1978). Minsky (1985) similarly suggested that a principal role of attachment is to establish a context for learning and modeling values and goals. It has long been known that the single best predictor of a person's religiousness is the religiousness of his or her parents (see Argyle & Beit-Hallahmi, 1975, for a review), and much research confirms that children are likely to agree with their parents on religious issues if they come from a stable home in which parents fight infrequently, tend to agree with each other on other important issues, and have parent–child relationships characterized by good communication and sincerity (see Hood et al., 1996, for a review).

Granqvist and Hagekull (1999) provided some additional empirical support for their interpretation as well, by developing two new measures designed specifically for the purpose. One of these new scales, the *Socialization-Based Religiosity Scale* (SBRS), was designed to reflect the degree to which respondents have adopted their parents' religious beliefs and standards. For example, items include "My religious beliefs correspond to my father's religious beliefs," "My mother and I do not at all share the same values regarding religious issues," and "I will probably speak/I speak to my children about religious issues in a similar way as my mother did to me during my childhood." In a sample of Swedish college students, Granqvist and Hagekull found strong support for their hypothesis: Security of childhood attachment was positively related, and avoidance and ambivalence inversely related, to scores on the SBRS scale. Moreover, religious changes described retrospectively by secure participants were characterized by early rather than late, and gradual rather than sudden, onset, as well as with "themes of correspondence" reflecting adoption of significant others' beliefs. The general picture painted here is one of secure children growing into the religious beliefs of their parents in a gradual, conventional manner—perhaps the most common pathway to adult religiousness in most contexts.

Granqvist (2002b) has recently extended these findings in a younger sample of Swedish adolescents ages 14–19, in which he measured attachments to parents as well as to peers. Security (vs. insecurity, as a bipolar dimension) of attachment to both mother and father was correlated positively with SBRS scores. SBRS scores were also related to lower levels of anxious attachment to peers, though unrelated to avoidant peer attachment.

The Two-Level Correspondence Hypothesis

Granqvist's socialized-correspondence hypothesis offers a valuable new perspective on our understanding of the relationship between childhood attachment experience and adult religiousness. It accounts for many of the same findings as my original correspondence hypothesis, as well as additional findings that the original correspondence hypothesis cannot easily explain—in particular, the moderating effects of parental religiousness on the relationship between childhood attachment and adult religiousness. (A complete account of this entire pattern of results requires some additional crucial pieces that are discussed in the next chapter.) Research findings with the SBRS provide additional evidence for the importance of this perspective.

On the other hand, as noted by Granqvist (2002b), the socialized-correspondence hypothesis alone cannot easily account for certain other findings, such as the cross-sectional relationships between attachment security and images of God (as loving, controlling, etc.) reviewed earlier in this chapter. Granqvist (2002b; Granqvist & Hagekull, 2001) has therefore concluded that both versions of the correpondence hypothesis are required to account for all the data. In his proposed *two-level correspondence hypothesis*, "the first level denotes a primary mechanism of social learning of parental standards in the context of a secure relationship and the second level a secondary effect reflecting mental models correspondence between self/other and God" (Granqvist, 2002b, p. 267).

This is certainly a reasonable compromise, and I agree completely that neither perspective can fully account for the data without the other. However, there are some deeper issues involved that deserve additional discussion. First, it is important to acknowledge that despite the convenience of tying the two ideas together under the shared "correspondence" rubric, they address two fundamentally different sets of issues. My original idea of IWM correspondence concerns what happens inside people's heads, and why different people find different kinds of religious ideas more or less plausible or appealing. Socialization, in contrast, focuses on the external source(s) from which such ideas are adopted, particularly the degree to which they come from parents. As such, the two perspectives reflect different *levels of analysis* in trying to understand people's religiousness and individual differences therein. (In this sense the "two-level" part of Granqvist's rubric is fitting, though he does not say it this way.)

Second, because they refer to fundamentally different levels of analysis, the hypotheses are not really competing alternatives to one another. As such, the suggestion that one is "primary" and the other "secondary" is potentially misleading. Chapter 12 examines levels of analysis, and the place of socialization (vis-à-vis the psychology of evolved mechanisms such as the attachment system) in the context of a larger framework, but for now the point is that there are far more reasons to retain both hypotheses other than the fact that both are needed to account for the data.

Finally, there are some potentially serious problems with the idea of "socialization" as an explanatory mechanism that require further examination. Perhaps the oldest and most widely acknowledged fact about the development of people's religious beliefs—as well, for that matter, as much of the rest of their knowledge, attitudes, and values—is that they are transmitted from parent to child via "socialization," and from person to person more generally through "cultural transmission." These assumptions seem so obvious, and are so firmly entrenched in the social sciences, that they are typically taken for granted. In the remainder of this chapter we will take a closer look at this idea.

"SOCIALIZATION" AS AN ALTERNATIVE HYPOTHESIS

Before addressing the specific limitations of socialization as a hypothesis for explaining religion, it is worth noting how serious the issue is for any psychological theory of religion. Mountains of data demonstrate that "socialization" (and/or "cultural transmission") explains the lion's share of the variance in religious beliefs. The best empirical predictor of anyone's beliefs, at least within a multicultural society such as the contemporary United States, is that of their parents (see Hood et al., 1996, for a review). This would be even more true if we took as our population all of humanity, such that cross-cultural variation contributed to the overall variability (i.e., given that worldwide, for example, most Muslim children had Muslim parents, most Taoist children had Taoist parents, and so forth). Therefore, it might be argued from a purely empirical perspective that socialization and cultural transmission should be our default explanations for observed variation in religious beliefs, the baseline against which any other hypothesis should be judged. The crucial test of any other hypothesis would concern the degree to which it can predict additional variance in religious belief, above and beyond what one would predict based on socialization.

From this perspective, the contribution of attachment theory would be limited to explaining any exceptions to the socialization rule—in this case, why unsatisfactory parental relationships lead to failures of socialization. The same line of reasoning could be equally applied to any other psychological theory of religion as well, thereby reducing the entire field to the study of unusual exceptions. This would be a very tough row to hoe, because it is a simple fact that statistically predicting rare events is nearly impossible: If the base rate of a phenomenon is very low (or very high, depending on which way you flip it), there is not much variance available to explain. A theory that simplistically predicts the norm in all cases will be right in the vast majority of cases. This problem is especially well known by researchers in certain areas of psychology, who are interested in predicting statistically rare (but extremely important) behaviors such as suicide.

Consequently, if we are willing to accept socialization as a satisfactory explanation for religious variability, psychologists of religion have very little to do. It is doubtful that we will find any psychological theory that predicts statistical variability better than socialization, so why bother? The reason, I believe, is that socialization (or cultural transmission) is not, *in itself*, a satisfactory explanation for anything. It is a useful construct only in the context of a larger, multi-tiered model of human psychology and behavior.

The Inadequacy of "Socialization" as Explanation

Although at some level the notion of "socialization" (and cultural transmission) is a perfectly reasonable description of a very common process, it is nevertheless a wholly inadequate explanation, and a far more problematic concept than is typically acknowledged by social scientists.

Perhaps the most obvious problem with "socialization" as a theory is the annoying matter of infinite regress. If children get their beliefs from their parents, where did their parents get them? Presumably from their parents, who got them from *their* parents, and so on. This will not work, unless we want to postulate that each bit of cultural information can be traced to some great-great-great- . . . -great grandmother who thought it up. Alternatively, we can try to explain it sideways and point to "culture" as the source of people's (including parents') beliefs. The idea is pretty much the same: The beliefs just move laterally between people rather than vertically through time. But we wind up with the same problem: Where did "culture" get them? For some specific ideas we can identify an original source—a person (or persons) who actually did generate the beliefs and promulgate them, such as a scientist credited with a research finding or theory—and from there they propagate through the population via cultural transmission. Some specific religious beliefs might operate this way, but for the most part religious ideas such as the core beliefs of Christianity have simply been around for too long in too many places to imagine a singular source. In short, a simplistic socialization or cultural-transmission "explanation" cannot be adequate if it leaves unanswered the crucial question of where the transmitted beliefs came from in the first place.

The second problem is that the socialization "rule" is, as a matter of fact, probably false at least as of often as it is true. There are an awful lot of "exceptions" other than the poor parental relationship one addressed here so far. For instance, Sulloway (1996) has amassed an enormous amount of evidence to show that there is generally greater variability in attitudes and values *within* families than between them. Drawing upon standard psychological data as well as historical and biographical data, he shows that first-born children are far more likely to be conventional and conservative in their attitudes and beliefs—supporters of the status quo. Later-borns, in contrast, are "born to rebel" (to quote Sulloway's title): They tend to be the (sometimes radical) opponents of the status quo. An ironic example (in the context of the present book) is Sulloway's empirical demonstration, based on historical and biographical data, that after the publication of Darwin's (radical) theory of evolution by natural selection, opponents of this radical theory were disproportionally likely to be first-borns and supporters (including Darwin himself), later-borns. From these findings it appears that socialization is "effective" for first-borns but not for later-borns; I do not think we would want to argue that this is attributable entirely to quality of parental relations or attachment styles. In any event, given that later-borns are probably a statistical majority in most populations, we would not want to argue that as a group they represent an exception to a general rule.

The point is that, in general, children do not simply soak up parental beliefs and values like a sponge and incorporate them automatically and faithfully. They are much more selective than this, as anyone who has ever tried to get a 4-year-old to eat broccoli, or has complained about the music her kids are listening to, can attest. From an evolutionary perspective, it would not be adaptive for children to be designed in this way. As discussed in subsequent chapters, Trivers's (1974) theory of *parent–offspring conflict* makes clear that parents' and children's interests are not identical, given that they share on average only half of their genes. Thus, what is in a parent's interest for his or her children to do and believe is not necessarily in the child's best interests. Thus, even in the most harmonious family settings, children adopt some parental beliefs, values, and attitudes, but not others. The interesting and important questions are all about the whys and wherefores.

The same general problem can be seen at the cultural level. It is true that fads in fashion, music, and other cultural inventions have a way of spreading rapidly though a population (or subpopulation, such as adolescents) in a manner that clearly implicates "cultural transmission." But in focusing on this obvious fact it is easy to overlook the degree to which this simultaneously is *not* happening. While a majority may quickly adopt the hottest new look or sound, others are rejecting it, ignoring it, or creating their own new variant. And for most such things, everybody loses interest before too long anyway and the whole thing is relegated to scrap heap. Where did it go? In short, some ideas have more staying power than others, and again the interesting and important question is why.

Third, a great deal of what appears to be "socialization" probably is not. The fact that people often behave in ways that mirror information present in culture (or specifically in one's parents) does not necessarily imply that the person learned the behavior or that the exemplar was the cause of the behavior. If children observe their parents, or actors on television, doing X, and then subsequently begin doing X themselves, does that mean they learned X via socialization or cultural transmission? Tooby and Cosmides (1997) offer a hilarious analogy to illustrate the error in this reasoning:

To see this, just think about how easy it would be to argue that girls learn to have breasts. Consider the peer pressure during adolescence for having breasts! the examples on TV of glamorous models!—the whole culture reinforces the idea that women should have breasts, therefore . . . adolescent girls learn to grow breasts. (p. 16)

In the case of breasts, of course, we know that the cause of "resemblances" between people (women, in this case) is not social learning, but rather that all women share the same biological design, which reliably develops under normal circumstances according to a species-universal recipe coded in the human genome. Something very similar can happen with ideas as well.

I have more to say about socialization, in the context of social learning and belief transmission, in Chapter 12. I have no doubt that socialization does occur, and that people do acquire religious ideas in large part via social learning from other people. For present purposes, the essential point is merely that such processes do not constitute an *alternative* explanation for the acquisition of religious beliefs, but rather represent a level of analysis layered on top of, and operating simultaneously and in concert with, psychological and emotional processes such as attachment.

The Epidemiology of Beliefs

The traditional view of cultural transmission and socialization is one of a relatively passive copying process, by which ideas are directly transmitted from one person to the next. Boyer (1994b) takes anthropologists to task for promulgating such a simplistic view, and much of his book is directed toward scholars in this field in an attempt to convince them otherwise. However, psychologists are just as prone to conceptualize cultural transmission in this way. In focusing on the individual as our primary level of analysis, we tend to begin with the assumption that ideas and beliefs are simply "out there" to be sucked up via socialization and acculturation; they are a given to be included as a kind of background variable or constant in our own research.

As Sperber (1994b) has argued at length, however, the transmission of an idea from one person to another is not at all like copying a document from one computer file to another, and the influence of culture on individuals is not at all like downloading the file from hard drive to floppy disk. Instead, individual psychology is involved at every step along the way. Which ideas are attended to is a function of perceptual processes; which ones are retained is a function of memory storage and retrieval processes; which ones are passed along is a function of a variety of motives, communication skills, and so forth. Sperber likens the study of cultural transmission to *epidemiology*: Studying the distribution and spread of ideas is akin to studying the distribution and spread of diseases. Just as the transmission of disease cannot be understood without reference to medicine—one needs to know how particular diseases are contracted, what their symptoms are, and so forth—the transmission of ideas cannot be understood without reference to the psychology that underlies them.

Boyer (1994b) makes many of these same arguments and emphasizes another shortcoming of a simplistic, psychology-free model of cultural transmission: Religious beliefs are vastly *underdetermined* by information provided by culture. The information provided explicitly by culture or parents concerning most topics, including religious ones, is only partial; the receiver must interpret this information and draw a great many inferences to complete the picture. Thus, religious (and other) representations and inferences are strongly constrained by basic knowledge structures in the brain/mind. In Boyer's (1994b) words, "People's inferences go beyond what is given by the cultural input, and they do so in a way that is directed by prior cognitive structures" (p. 92). We impose implicit schemata that are not part of the explicit, culture-given story, and these schemata are such pervasive, fundamental aspects of our psychology that they sometimes seem almost too obvious to discuss. It is rather like asking a fish about water.

This same process applies not only to belief *acquisition*, as in the preceding example, but also to the *transmission* of beliefs from one individual to another. Our shared psychology not only makes it somewhat likely that both person A and person B will independently hit upon similar ideas when faced with similar stimuli under similar circumstances; it also makes it likely that if person B does not hit upon the idea spontaneously herself, he or she will find it understandable and plausible when person A suggests it. In both cases, it is a shared cognitive architecture that makes the process possible.

Boyer (1994b) exemplifies the idea in a discussion of the beliefs about ghosts held by the Fang people of Cameroon:

> People can take singular episodes and ritual statements as the basis for hypotheses about ghosts in general, first of all because they understand

ghost behavior in *psychological* terms. . . . For instance, it is necessary to assume that the ghosts have psychological mechanisms such that they can perceive what people do, form some beliefs on the basis of those perceptions, and store those beliefs in memory. It is also assumed, for instance, that the ghosts have mental capacities such that, if they find a certain state of affairs E to be desirable, and know that another state of affairs, C, is necessary to achieve E, then they will desire to achieve C. For instance, the ghosts are described as *wishing* that certain rituals were performed . . . as *knowing* that people, if afflicted with misfortune, will eventually oblige . . . to *decide*, in consequence, that some illness should be "sent" to the living. . . . (p. 98)

Boyer goes on to point out that it may seem totally obvious or self-evident that, in this example, the ghost would desire to achieve C, but that is precisely the point:

These principles are not given in the utterances and other types of explicit information on the ghosts. They are not "implicitly" transmitted either, in the sense that they could be readily deduced from that explicit information. On the contrary, it is because they are assumed to be valid in the first place that further inferences about the ghosts' behavior can be drawn at all. (p. 99)

In particular, Boyer goes on to suggest that those aspects of religious belief that are explicitly taught by the culture are generally those that are *counterintuitive*; the task is then left to individuals to fill in the gaps in intuitive ways. For example, the idea that a ghost is invisible, or that dead ancestors continue to "live" in some intangible form, may be taught explicitly. Once these beings are identified as "people-like," however, a host of inferential machinery can whir into action to fill in myriad gaps in an image of what these beings are like and what they want.

Although Boyer is focusing in this case on a particular set of species-universal psychological mechanisms known in modern jargon as "folk psychology" or "theory of mind" (about which I have much more to say in Chapter 11), IWMs of attachment may play a similar role in guiding people's perceptions of and inferences about God. For example, a child might be taught explicitly that God is an invisible being who is like a parent to everyone. Even if taught nothing more, the child would easily make a number of spontaneous inferences, such as that God loves people and would intervene on their behalf if something terrible happened. More concretely, the child might infer that God is "up," that you can talk to God and ask for help, that certain behaviors such as upraised arms might get God's attention, and so forth. In effect, all people have attachment schemata, or scripts (i.e., IWMs), that provide the basis for many kinds of inferences about God, once the idea is accepted that God is parent-like. All of these features fit together in a way that makes the entire concept plausible and intuitive, thereby facilitating the transmission of such ideas from one person to the next (as from parents to children) because receivers need only a few key bits of information from which to reconstruct the missing pieces in their own heads.

Individual Differences Revisited

With these ideas in mind, let us return to the topic of individual differences. Early childhood experience with caregivers provides crucial inputs into a system that then produces different outputs, including IWMs of attachment that are subsequently applied to other circumstances, such as other close relationships. Thus, when people bring their attachment machinery to bear on the problem of interacting with a friend, an adult relationship partner, or God, they bring with it their personal history of attachment experience and the resulting IWMs constructed from this experience. When a person with an avoidant attachment style applies his or her attachment machinery to ideas about God, the system is likely to output the idea that this God is distant, inaccessible, and uncaring. A secure person, in contrast, is more likely to infer that God is reliably sensitive and nurturing. Same system, different output.

The same idea can be applied to cross-cultural variability as well, as with the data discussed earlier in this chapter. The observation that a particular set of beliefs or practices is shared by some cultures but very different in others is typically attributed to cultural transmission, which seems to account neatly for the pattern of cross-cultural variability observed. However, the same pattern can also be arrived at by an alternative process related to the Boyer (1994a, 1994b) and Sperber (1996) models described earlier. The same idea or practice might be generated and adopted independently in different places by virtue of the fact that people are bringing the same psychological machinery to bear on a similar problem faced in those places (but perhaps not faced in others). Tooby and Cosmides (1992) introduce the term *evoked culture*—in contrast to the traditional concept of *transmitted culture*—for this process. To borrow an analogy from Williams (1966), we might observe that most people in culture A have calluses on their feet, whereas in Culture B most people have calluses on their fingertips. Hidden beneath the salient cross-cultural diversity is the same underlying physiological callus-producing mechanism, but in one culture most people walk around barefoot and in the other people wear shoes and play guitars. Again, same system, different data.

Earlier in this chapter I discussed studies by Rohner (1975) and Lambert et al. (1959) that showed between-culture variability in normative parenting strategies to be predictive of cultural differences in normative images of God. The reason for interpreting this as evidence for an attachment model of God-belief acquisition is now (I hope) clear. Cross-cultural variability in parenting styles represents a stable ecological difference confronted by the attachment systems of children raised in those cultures, like repeated friction on the soles of the feet versus on the fingertips. One kind of parenting, by virtue of the (universal) design of the attachment system, reliably produces behavioral patterns and IWMs of one variety, which lead (I have been arguing) to certain ways of thinking about God and the perception of some kinds of God-beliefs as plausible and believable and others as implausible and unbelievable; another kind of parenting reliably produces a different pattern. Which kind of belief about God has the most staying power in a given culture depends largely on whatever particular attachment schemata are prevalent or normative in that culture, which in turn depends on the kinds of early attachment experience people typically experience in those cultures.

SUMMARY AND CONCLUSIONS

To the extent that religion really does involve the activation and operation of the attachment system, individual differences in attachment experience should be related to individual differences in religious belief. This chapter provides a review of evidence from numerous studies, some explicitly motivated by an attachment theory perspective and others not, consistent with this expectation. In particular, beliefs about what God or gods are like, and one's ability to have a personal relationship with God, appear to be consistent with one's experience in human relationships with attachment figures. The theoretical mechanism postulated to enable these relations is that of IWMs of attachment.

It turns out that many of the data supportive of this model are equally consistent with an apparently simpler socialization model. However, socialization (or cultural transmission) alone, while in some cases an accurate *description* of the process by which many beliefs are spread, is wholly inadequate as an *explanatory* theory. To say that children acquire their beliefs from their parents (or "culture") is akin to observing that people acquire illnesses from other people. In many cases it is simply not true and, in any case, it is a woefully incomplete explanation of the processes by which people get sick. We need to understand why the psychology of the individuals involved permits specific kinds of beliefs to be attended to, remembered, and interpreted in certain ways that make transmission from person to person possible, just as we need an understanding of immune systems and other elements of medicine and biology to fully understand the transmission of disease. In the end, both levels of the two-level correspondence hypothesis are necessary (Granqvist, 2002b), because each tells a very different part of the larger story.

This view of the "epidemiology of culture" and of "evoked culture" begins to place the theory of attachment and religion into a broader context. In this view, I suggest, the cognitive-emotional machinery of the attachment system provides a kind of deep structure or universal grammar for thinking about gods and other deities. Once a few details are provided from an external source or invented spontaneously, such as the idea that God is like a parent in the sky, this cognitive machinery is employed readily for manipulating these ideas and drawing further inferences from them. Because the attachment system is species-universal, the influence of this same deep structure is evident in the beliefs about gods in many cultures. This is why the God-as-parent idea and other related attachment themes are so widely distributed, and why (unlike hemlines) they have such staying power: Attachment thinking is universal. At the same time, however, the parameters of the attachment system are set differently in different people by virtue of experience, giving rise to individual differences in some of the details of religious belief.

At several points in this chapter I have explicitly put off discussion of some key research findings that are not consistent with either my (working models) or Granqvist's (socialized) correspondence models. There must be more to the story than I have told so far, and it is time now to tell the second part of the story.

CHAPTER SIX

God as a Substitute Attachment Figure

The Compensation Hypothesis

In contrast to the correspondence model presented in the preceding chapter, a more dynamic view of the attachment process leads to a quite different hypothesis, which also seems to be supported by a considerable body of research. This hypothesis emerges from a consideration of the conditions under which the attachment system is activated and the role of attachment in the maintenance of felt security. According to the theory, as discussed in Chapter 2, the attachment system is activated when felt security falls below some criterion level, as when the individual is alarmed or perceives that the attachment figure is not sufficiently available and responsive. Attachment behaviors are then initiated in an attempt to restore proximity to the attachment figure.

From this perspective, the importance of God as an attachment figure might be greatest among those people, in those situations, in which human attachments are perceived to be *unavailable* or *inadequate*. That is, in direct contrast to the correspondence hypothesis, the *lack* of adequate human attachments might be expected to motivate or enable belief in a God who is, in important ways, *unlike* one's human attachment figures. In previous work (Kirkpatrick, 1992; Kirkpatrick & Shaver, 1990) I have referred to this as the *compensation hypothesis*.

To the extent that the correspondence and compensation hypotheses lead to contradictory predictions, of course, they cannot both be true—at least within the same people under the same conditions. Moreover, it may seem troubling that the same theory can lead to such mutually exclusive predictions simultaneously, which would seem to suggest that the theory is unfalsifiable because it would be supported by any set of empirical results (Granqvist & Hagekull, 1999). On the other hand, it is entirely possible that the two hypotheses are both correct, but for different people and/or under different sets of circumstances. Our task is then not one of deciding between them, but rather of identifying which process is responsible when, or for whom.

The point of departure for the compensation hypothesis is the general observation by attachment researchers (e.g., Ainsworth, 1985) that children who fail to establish secure attachments to parents are likely to seek "surrogates" or substitute attachment figures, including teachers, older siblings, other relatives, or, in general, any stronger, wiser other who reliably proves to be accessible and responsive to attachment needs. Although Ainsworth (1985) did not include God in her list of potential surrogates, it seems reasonable to assume that God could potentially fill this role for at least certain people in certain kinds of situations. In this chapter I review research concerning who those "certain people" and those "certain situations" might be.

INDIVIDUAL DIFFERENCES AND RELIGIOUS CONVERSION

In light of Ainsworth's (1985) observation about surrogate attachment figures in childhood, the first place to look for evidence of a compensation effect is to examine the relationship between people's childhood attachment experience and the religious beliefs they subsequently develop. The compensation hypothesis would predict that people with *insecure* childhood attachments might be those most likely to turn to a relationship with God later, to provide the kind of haven of safety and secure base that were not perceived to be available in their childhood attachment relationships with parents or other (human) caregivers.

Childhood Attachment and Adult Religiosity

In Chapter 5 I discussed some of the empirical findings by Kirkpatrick and Shaver (1990) and Granqvist (1998) regarding the relationship between (retrospective reports of) childhood attachments to parents and adult religious belief and experience. In both studies, significant *interactions* were found between maternal religiousness and attachment to mothers (in the Granqvist study, likewise for fathers as well) for several religion measures. People reporting secure attachments with parents were more likely to report religious beliefs in adulthood consistent with those of their parents; that is, they were religious if their parents were religious. Thus, consistent with both aspects of the two-level correspondence hypothesis, one subpopulation of religious adults comes from a history of secure attachment to religious parents, who adopt from parents their beliefs in God as a secure attachment figure.

In contrast, these interactions suggest that a second subpopulation of religious adults grew up with relatively *insecure* attachments to parents. The pattern is clearly inconsistent with either version of the correspondence hypothesis, because the adult beliefs are contrary to both the beliefs of the parents (thus contradicting the socialized-correspondence hypothesis) and to childhood attachment experience (thus contradicting the mental models hypothesis). Instead, the adult religiousness of this one subgroup appears to follow the pattern predicted by the compensation hypothesis. In light of the base rates for both attachment (secure more common than insecure) and parental religiosity (high more common than low), this would be expected to be a relatively small subpopulation, at least in contemporary United States samples. However, as we shall see, it is perhaps the most interesting group.

Sudden Religious Conversion

In reviewing the results of these studies in Chapter 5, I noted that there was one important exception to the interaction pattern, the discussion of which I put off until now. One measure of religion was predicted statistically *not* by an interaction of parental religiousness x parental attachment, but directly by individual differences in attachment (in statistical terms, a *main effect* for attachment). This was a measure of whether one had ever experienced, during adolescence or adulthood, a *sudden religious conversion*. Specifically, participants reporting *insecure* parental attachments had by far the highest conversion rates. In the Kirkpatrick and Shaver (1990) study, 44% of participants classifying their childhood relationship with their mother as *avoidant* reporting having had such an experience, as compared to only 8% and 9% for the secure and anxious groups, respectively.

In one of the unpublished South Carolina studies noted earlier, I attempted to replicate these results in another college-student sample. Retrospective parental attachment classification again predicted sudden religious conversions, but this time it was attachment to *fathers* that emerged as the significant predictor: Of those classifying their paternal attachments as avoidant, 30% reported sudden religious conversions later in life, versus only 5–6% in the other paternal attachment groups. Again, no sign of a parental religion x attachment interaction was evident.

Two studies conducted in Sweden have converged on highly similar results. Granqvist (1998) found that respondents reporting insecure maternal attachment (an aggregate of avoidant and anxious styles, due to sample-size restrictions) were more likely to report an "adult major change" in religiosity (16.3%) than respondents reporting secure maternal attachments (6.5%). In a different sample, employing a different analytic strategy, Granqvist and Hagekull (1999) found evidence of similar patterns with respect to both maternal and paternal childhood attachment. Participants reported childhood attachments (retrospectively) on continuous scales measuring security, avoidance, and ambivalence, and were classified with respect to religious change since childhood as either *sudden convert, other religious change*, or *no change*. Sudden converts scored significantly lower than each of the other groups on *security* of childhood attachment, and significantly higher than each of the other groups on *ambivalence*. They also scored significantly higher than the no-change group, though not significantly higher than the other-change group, with respect to *avoidance*. All of these patterns held for both paternal and maternal attachment measures.

We (Granqvist & Kirkpatrick, in press) have since collected together the data from all of these studies, plus additional unpublished data collected by Granqvist and colleagues, into a meta-analysis of results for predicting sudden religious conversion from childhood attachment. Across all studies (total $N = 1,465$), the rate of sudden religious conversions was significantly higher among those reporting *insecure* (aggregated avoidant and anxious categories) attachments to mothers (9.3%) as compared to secure ones (5.7%). When the data were analyzed differently, sudden converts scored significantly lower than nonconverts on a continuous measure of maternal attachment security. Similarly, those reporting insecure attachments to fathers were significantly more likely to have experienced a sudden conversion (8.5%) than those reporting secure ones (4.8%), and sudden converts scored significantly lower than nonconverts on paternal attachment security. No significant effects were observed for sex or the interaction of attachment x sex: Men and women showed similar patterns of results.

These results are all consistent with previous research on religious converts that has examined (retrospective reports of) childhood relationships with parents. In one widely cited study, Deutsch (1975) interviewed 14 members of a Hindu-inspired cult and found that most reported a history of troubled parental relationships. In the more extensive study by Ullman (1982, 1989) of converts and a matched control group, discussed at some length in Chapter 3, nearly 80% of converts reported serious difficulties in their childhood relations with their fathers, in contrast to only 23% of controls. As summarized by Ullman (1989), the fathers of converts tended to be "absent, passive to the point of psychological unavailability, or actively rejecting." Parallel results were obtained for relationships with mothers, with 53% of converts but only 7% of controls reporting difficulties in maternal relationships. Significant differences in the same direction were also found with respect to measures of having had an "unhappy childhood" and an "unhappy adolescence," as well as the number of specific traumatic events experienced during childhood.

Other Evidence for the Compensation Hypothesis

The fact that sudden religious conversions are statistically related to reports of insecure rather than secure childhood attachments provides only circumstantial evidence for the compensation hypothesis. Fortunately, Granqvist and colleagues have offered several additional lines of evidence to support the idea that these statistical patterns are rooted in emotional compensation processes.

In the previous chapter I reviewed findings from Granqvist and Hagekull (1999) according to which (retrospective reports of) security in childhood attachment—with respect to both mothers and fathers—was correlated strongly and positively with their new measure, the *Socialization-Based* Religiosity Scale (the SBRS). Granqvist and Hagekull (1999) also introduced a second new religiosity scale, an *Emotion-Based Religiosity Scale*

(EBRS) designed specifically to tap attachment-related motives underlying religious belief, including such defining features as haven of safety and secure base functions as well as responses to separation. For example, sample items include "I would experience grief if I knew that I could never get in touch with God again," "I turn to God when I am in pain," and "When I feel lost I find support in my religious faith." In contrast to the results for the SBRS, the EBRS correlated positively with *insecurity* of parental attachment relationships during childhood. Data from this and six other studies relating the EBRS to sudden conversions were subjected to meta-analysis by Granqvist and Kirkpatrick (in press). Across seven studies including more than 800 participants, sudden converts scored significantly and substantially higher on the EBRS than did nonconverts. The reverse was true for the SBRS. In sum, secure childhood attachments to parents is related to socialization-based religiosity, consistent with a correspondence model, whereas insecure attachment is related to emotion-based religiosity, consistent with the compensation model.

Granqvist and colleagues have also presented other evidence examining differences in the *nature* of religious change in relation to childhood attachment variables. In the Granqvist and Hagekull (1999) study discussed earlier, religious change described (retrospectively) by adults with secure childhood attachments tended to be characterized by *early onset, gradualness* rather than suddenness, and "themes of correspondence" reflecting the adoption of beliefs from significant others. In contrast, changes in religiousness by participants with insecure childhood attachments tended to follow the opposite pattern, characterized by *later* rather than earlier onset, *sudden* rather than gradual onset, and "themes of compensation" reflecting emotional turmoil. In the longitudinal study by Granqvist (2002b) of Swedish adolescents, a subsample of participants was identified as having increased substantially in their religiousness over a 15-month intersurvey interval. Within this group, the reported degree of "suddenness" and "intenseness" of that religious change was very strongly correlated ($r = .58$) with reported insecurity of attachment to mother as measured at Time 1. These findings are consistent with the idea, presented in a previous chapter, that the experience of "finding God" may have much in common psychologically with falling in love, which also is experienced frequently as sudden, intense, and dramatic.

Another set of findings casts a particularly interesting light on the compensation hypothesis. In the only other study (of which I am aware) that has shown a compensatory relationship between adult religiosity and self-reports of childhood attachment, Granqvist and Hagekull (2001) examined "New Age" beliefs concerning topics such as astrology, the occult, parapsychology, and UFOs in Sweden, within both a diverse sample of adolescents and a carefully targeted sample of adults likely to be interested in such topics, drawn from alternative book stores, vegetarian cafes, and the like. Within both samples, belief in New Age phenomena was inversely correlated with self-reported attachment security to both parent, and positively correlated with avoidance and anxiousness. Analyzed differently, the two samples differed significantly with respect to mean levels of attachment security, with the presumed New Agers reporting lower levels of security in childhood attachments to parents than the general adolescent sample. Moreover, New Age orientation was correlated positively with the EBRS and negatively with the SBRS within the adolescent sample, providing further evidence for the compensation interpretation.

Although these findings are consistent with the compensation hypothesis, the *nature* of New Age beliefs may seem to be at odds with it. The compensation hypothesis is based on the idea that attachment dynamics lead to religious beliefs for those with insecure attachment histories precisely because those beliefs—in particular, the Christian beliefs that characterize the vast majority of research participants so far—offer the possibility of establishing a secure attachment relationship with God (or Jesus, Mary, etc.). New Age beliefs, in contrast, lack such an attachment component, raising the question as to why and how such beliefs could "compensate" for childhood attachment experience.

One possible answer involves combining the compensation hypothesis with crucial elements of the mental models correspondence hypothesis. From this latter perspective, New Age beliefs might represent precisely the *kind* of belief system to which people with insecure attachment histories would be expected to attracted: that is, one that does not require belief in a loving, caring God that violates their existing mental models of attachment figures. As we saw in the previous chapter, people reporting avoidant adult-attachment relationships tend disproportionately to describe themselves as atheists or agnostics, consistent with the notion that people lacking a secure mental model of attachment relationships would be unlikely to (contemporaneously) hold such a model of God or other deities. As an alternative to unbelief, New Age beliefs represent a manifestation of supernatural thinking that does not require such a mental model. Compensation processes may determine who "finds religion" and who does not, but correspondence processes may be crucial for determining the precise nature and content of that found religion. We will return to this idea, in relation to other research findings, later in this chapter.

A Two-Process Model of Religious Change

The picture that appears to be emerging from the preceding results, in combination with (and in contrast to) the results presented in the previous chapter, is that there are at least two different processes involved in the relationship between childhood attachment and adult religion. There appear to be at least two different pathways (Granqvist, 1998) from childhood attachment experience to adult religiosity, one characterized by correspondence processes and one by compensation processes.

The first process describes what in most populations (at least in the United States) is the most common pattern: In the context of loving, supportive families, children tend to adopt religious beliefs (e.g., images of God as loving and nurturing) that correspond both to the beliefs of their parents and to their own mental models of attachment relationships. This process begins relatively early in life and unfolds gradually over time. According to the two-level correspondence hypothesis, socialization of children to parents' religious views is facilitated both by the presence of a secure attachment relationship and the consistency of the God beliefs with the child's extant IWMs of attachment relationships.

The path to adult religiousness for people with insecure attachment histories, however, appears to be more dramatic. Consistent with the correspondence model, most such persons—specifically, those with highly religious parents (again, statistically more common than irreligious parents in the United States)—are *not* religious as adults; they are the apostates described by Bruder (1947) and Vetter and Green (1932), or the militant atheists described by Caplovitz and Sherrow (1977). However, some insecure persons do eventually "find religion," and those who do arrive there via a very different path—one characterized by one or more sudden and dramatic, emotionally charged experiences later in life, involving the discovery of God, Jesus, or some other religious figure as a substitute attachment figure.

It is easy to see why, from the compensation model perspective, the conversion experiences of these persons would be so emotionally powerful. People with insecure childhood attachments (those most likely to have these experiences) grow up with negative IWMs of attachment relationships, viewing intimacy, closeness, and love as things to be avoided and attachment figures as untrustworthy and unreliable. Indeed, this is what leads most such individuals away from religion or the idea of God as a secure attachment figure in the first place. Among the few who instead experience a subsequent religious conversion, however, something dramatic appears to happen that causes this entire set of conceptualizations to turn around. Converts suddenly come to see God or Jesus as quite the opposite of all this—as someone who loves them, cares about them, faithfully watches over them, and will be there for them when they need support, comfort, and assistance—in direct contradiction to a lifetime's worth of personal experience with attachment figures to the contrary. For someone who has always had confidence in the reliability and loving nature of attachment figures, the idea that God or Jesus is like this fits neatly with existing schemata (i.e., per the correspondence hypothesis). But for someone with an insecure history, this idea must be emotionally very powerful. Perhaps this also explains why such experiences are commonly described as "ineffable": People with long-standing negative IWMs of attachment really do not have the words or concepts at their disposal to describe what is for them an entirely novel experience. It must indeed be, as suggested by many observers cited earlier, similar in many ways to falling in love for the first time. (In Chapter 8 I return to this comparison again and suggest that in many ways it might be true in a quite literal sense.)

Of course, this phenomenon begs the crucial question of what makes such sudden, dramatic change possible. If insecure attachment histories result in IWMs of attachment figures inconsistent with the idea of a loving, nurturing God, how do some individuals with insecure histories come to suddenly adopt beliefs about a loving God? One crucial factor may be that in Christianity, as well as many other monotheistic religions, it is believed that *God's love is unconditional*. One need not be "worthy" of love, or worry that God will reject or abandon one because of one's shortcomings. God loves everybody. This makes God a particularly attractive attachment figure vis-à-vis potential or current romantic partners. Attachment to God is not inherently accompanied by the same emotional risks as attachments to fallible and judgmental people. Although in many variations of Christianity and other religions, God's love is not seen as *entirely* "unconditional"—for example, one might be expected to perform certain rituals or engage in "good works" to earn God's love and forgiveness—such belief systems invariably also provide clear prescriptions for how to accomplish this. Even if God's love is not entirely without conditions, they are clearly defined and achievable. In either case, then, one can be assured of God's love without fear of abandonment or rejection. In addition to this unique feature of God, there are at least two other sets of reasons that help to explain how people with insecure IWMs come to "find God." First, research on adult attachment has led to important refinements in the conceptualization and measurement of IWMs that make it possible to make finer discriminations among types of insecurity, some of which enable religious transformations and others which do not. We will examine this idea in detail in the section on *Individual Differences in Adult Attachment*.

Second, such transformations do not occur in a social vacuum, but generally in response to particular kinds of situational variables that are sufficiently powerful to activate attachment systems that otherwise are relatively quiescent (discussed later in the section *Contextual Factors in Religious Change*).

This two-process model maps neatly onto some much older distinctions and constructs in the psychology of religion. According to Granqvist (1998, in press), we in many ways seem to have rediscovered William James's (1902) 100-year-old distinction between "once-born" versus "twice-born" religionists—also known as conversions of the "healthy-minded" versus the "sick-souled," whose religiosity originates "from within" versus "from without," respectively. It also addresses the long-acknowledged distinction between *gradual* and *sudden* religious conversions, which have always appeared to follow quite different patterns with different correlates—one of which is the powerful emotionality surrounding the latter (see Hood et al., 1996). Two distinct lines of research on conversion in the literature—the "classic paradigm" in (primarily) the psychology of religion and the "contemporary paradigm" in (primarily) the sociology of religion—appear to have grown up around these two very different types of conversion, and the two-pathway model emerging from the attachment theory appears promising for resolving this ongoing debate and integrating the two separate literatures into an integrative framework (see Granqvist, in press, for a complete discussion).

Deconversion and the Instability of Religious Belief

The findings reviewed in the preceding section provide evidence of several kinds to suggest that adult religiosity, particularly in the form of sudden religious conversions, is associated with insecure childhood attachment, in support of the compensation hypothesis. However, the situation is clearly more complex that this because, as discussed earlier, numerous studies suggest that problematic childhood relationships with parents are also associated with adult atheism, as well as increased likelihood of *deconversion* or *apostasy* from religion (Bruder, 1947; Caplovitz & Sherrow, 1977; Vetter & Green, 1932). Although this earlier research was not guided by attachment theory and hence did not measure parent–child relationships explicitly in attachment terms, Granqvist (2002b) has since shown insecurity of attachment to mothers to be positively correlated with (retrospective measures of) both increased religious change and decreased religious change.

Although these results may seem mutually contradictory, they need not be. Instead, the appropriate conclusion appears to be that insecure attachment history is predictive of increased *variability* or *instability* of adult religiosity. Thus, when queried at any particular point in time, some such individuals have recently abandoned a set of beliefs whereas others have recently acquired new beliefs. If the same individuals were surveyed a year later, the previous survey's new convert might well now be a recent apostate.

This line of thinking suggests an alternative interpretation for the finding of Granqvist and Hagekull (2001) concerning the relationship between New Age belief and childhood insecure attachment. In contrast to more traditional religious affiliations, involvement in New Age "religions" tends to be relatively unstable (Barker, 1989). That is, people are more likely to dabble in such beliefs for a brief period before moving on to something else, as if trying them on to see if they fit. Such beliefs might well not be the ultimate destination for people with insecure attachment histories, but instead only one of many dead ends likely explored, but eventually rejected, by individuals searching for something more emotionally satisfying. An intriguing question for future research would be to determine how many of these New Age believers eventually become converts to more attachment-based religious forms.

Another related possibility is that the variability or instability of religious beliefs in this population is not a reflection of mere fickleness, but a function of situational factors. That is, perhaps people with insecure attachment histories are more responsive or reactive than those with secure histories to certain kinds of events or environments, some of which lead to increases in religiosity or conversion and others to decreases. We will return to this important idea later in this chapter.

Of course, the question still remains as to why New Age beliefs would be appealing to anyone in the first place. How would one explain, from the perspective of attachment theory, the existence and popularity of supernatural beliefs that do not include anything remotely resembling a surrogate attachment figure or any clear source of secure base or haven of safety? The likely answer is that attachment theory may well *not* be particularly useful in understanding the specific content of such beliefs, and to try to do so might well result in stretching attachment theory beyond its proper limits (as discussed in Chapter 4). Such beliefs instead probably involve a variety of psychological systems other than the attachment system, as discussed in subsequent chapters.

Individual Differences in Adult Attachment

So far, however, we have identified in childhood attachment insecurity only a relatively *distal* factor that seems to predispose some individuals more than others to have such experiences. From an attachment perspective, it is clear why this kind of attachment history might lead people to activate a search for a substitute or surrogate attachment figure in place of the poor-quality family relationships actually experienced. Exactly how this happens, and the situational factors that might facilitate it, still need to be addressed. In the remainder of this chapter I examine these issues, turning first to individual differences in adulthood and then to the precipitating factors associated with religious change in adulthood.

As discussed in Chapter 2, Bowlby maintained that the attachment system is presumed to be designed to operate in adulthood as well as in childhood. During adolescence (ordinarily), attachments to parents are gradually relinquished and new attachment bonds are formed with peers. In the Hazan–Zeifman theory, the system is designed by natural selection to play a crucial role in the formation and maintenance of pair-bonds in the context of mating relationships. In this sense, then, finding a "substitute" attachment figure to replace one's parents is entirely normative; virtually everyone does so eventually. Our questions about the factors underlying sudden religious conversions in adulthood can therefore be reframed in the context of adult attachment relationships: Why do some people turn specifically to God, either instead of or in addition to romantic partners, as an attachment figure in adulthood?

One way to approach this question is to continue our focus on individual differences. Individual differences in childhood attachment represent a distal predictor of adult conversion, but individual differences in *adult* attachment may well mediate these effects proximally. Specifically, if the attachment system is designed such that attachments are typically transferred from parents to romantic partners, then individual differences in romantic attachment styles are an appropriate place to look.

Recall from Chapter 2 that individual differences in romantic attachment styles have been shown to correlate with a wide variety of variables in the context of adult relationships. In terms of the original Hazan–Shaver (1987) tripartite classification, *secure* adults are happy and comfortable in long-term, committed romantic relationships, and tend to have more satisfying and longer-lasting romantic relationships than others. *Anxious* adults fear that their partners do not love them and/ or will abandon them, desire more closeness than partners are usually willing to provide, and tend to be clingy in their attempts to keep the partner in close proximity. *Avoidant* adults are uncomfortable with, and thus steer clear of, intimacy and closeness, and are less likely to fall in (or even believe in) love. In Chapter 5 we saw the results of several studies showing that, on average, people's contemporaneous religious beliefs seem to mirror these orientations toward romantic relationships in many ways.

Framed in attachment terms, the individual-difference question about conversion in adulthood is the following: Which of these attachment styles is/are associated with a greater likelihood of someone turning to God (or Jesus, etc.) as a substitute attachment figure in addition to, or in lieu of, his or her romantic partners? From a compensation hypothesis perspective, the clear predictions would seem to be as follows. People who are *securely* attached to romantic partners, who have successfully made the transition from parental to peer attachment and are now enjoying satisfying mutual attachment relationships, should have no particular motivation to go off in search of an alternative. People who are *avoidantly* attached are unlikely to be in satisfying romantic relationships, but this is because they prefer it that way: They are not currently seeking an attachment relationship at all. (A hypothesis as to why this might be the case is discussed in Chapter 8.)

Instead, it is the *anxious* (also called *preoccupied*) group that seems to best fit the bill. These persons find their romantic attachments to be insufficiently intimate. They describe relationship partners as failing to meet their needs for closeness and intimacy, and are likely to say that their strong desire for closeness may sometimes drive partners or potential partners away (Hazan & Shaver, 1987). Especially among women, the close interpersonal relationships of anxious adults tend to be characterized by emotional highs and lows, jealousy, conflict, and dissatisfaction (see Shaver & Hazan, 1993, for a review). Moreover, anxious adults are more likely than others to say they fall in love easily and frequently, and to experience "lovesickness," "limerence," and related states (Hazan & Shaver, 1987; Shaver & Hazan, 1988). From an attachment perspective, this constellation of interpersonal characteristics seems to describe the kind of person one would expect to be most likely to turn to God to meet attachment needs.

The psychology of religion literature contains more than a few hints that this may be the case. For example, numerous studies cited by Wenegrat (1990, p. 31) have linked religiousness to "dependent" personality traits and anxiousness to obtain external approval, and Wenegrat describes several case studies suggesting this connection. Simmonds (1977) studied members of a fundamentalist sect and interpreted the various kinds of problems experienced by these members prior to their conversions as reflecting "dependency problems." We have to be very careful with the concept of "dependency," however: Ainsworth (1969) and Maccoby and Masters (1970) review at length the many important differences between attachment theory and earlier "dependency theories" that differ from attachment theory in many crucial ways. Nevertheless, it is not inaccurate to describe anxious/preoccupied adults as more "dependent" than people of other attachment styles in the specific sense of desiring high levels of intimacy and closeness, behaving in "clingy" ways, and obsessing over the fear that their partners do not love them and may abandon them.

The literature on *glossolalia*—another kind of powerful emotional religious experience—also seems to suggest links to something like the anxious or preoccupied adult attachment style. Vivier (1960, cited in Richardson, 1973) found that glossolalics came disproportionately from "disturbed" homes, were more "anxious," had more initial problems in their marriages, and have a "tendency to cling to objects in the environment for emotional support" (p. 382). Wood (1965) suggested that glossolalics "have an uncommon degree of uncertainty concerning interpersonal relationships" and "a strong drive to feel close fellowship with others but they are uncertain that these interpersonal involvements will be satisfactory" (pp. 92–96). Despite many efforts to demonstrate links between glossolalia and psychopathology, very little such evidence has been found (Hine 1969; Richardson, 1973). For example, Plog (1965) found no differences between glossolalics and controls on any dimension of the California Psychological Inventory—except one concerning problems in interpersonal relationships. Consistent with this, recall from Chapter 5 that Kirkpatrick and Shaver (1992) found anxious adults to report a higher incidence of glossolalic experiences than either avoidant or secure adults.

I have conducted two longitudinal studies of adults to examine individual differences in adult attachment styles as a predictor of subsequent religious change. In the first study (Kirkpatrick, 1997), I contacted as many respondents as I could find from a newspaper-survey study that had been conducted 4 years earlier.[1] The response rate was remarkably high (over 80%) among those who presumably received the questionnaire in the mail (that is, not counting the ones returned by the postal service as undeliverable). This follow-up questionnaire was ultimately completed by 146 adult women (data from men were not analyzed due to small sample size). Analysis focused on the prediction of responses to several questions on the follow-up questionnaire concerning religious changes that had occurred over the intersurvey interval, as a function of adult attachment styles as measured 4 years prior.

The results provided considerable evidence for the compensation hypothesis in adulthood. Both *avoidant* (38%) and *anxious* (36%) women were significantly more likely than *secure* women (19%) to report having "found a new relationship with God" during the intersurvey interval. However, it was only the *anxious* group that differed from the others in reporting having "had a religious experience or religious conversion" during that period (25%, versus 7% of avoidant and 9% of secure women). Other findings following this latter pattern, but failing to reach statistical significance, were found for questions about having been "born again" and having "spoken in tongues" (glossolalia). As expected, no significant differences were found on two other questions that were included for comparison purposes, concerning whether respondents had changed churches or denominations during the intersurvey interval. Interestingly, the anxious group was also most likely to report having "lost faith in God" during the previous 4 years. I suspect that the reason for this is that although anxious adults may be the most likely to turn to God as a surrogate attachment figure, they are also most likely to discover later that their relationship with God is not adequate to meet their attachment needs either.

In a second study (Kirkpatrick, 1998b), I switched from studying a small sample over a long time period to a larger sample over a briefer interval. Nearly 300 undergraduates completed measures of attachment and religion at the beginning of a fall semester and then at the beginning of the subsequent semester 5 months later. In this study I employed a measure of Bartholomew's four-category adult attachment measure in lieu of the Hazan–Shaver (1987) three-category measure, permitting the data to be analyzed as a 2 (positive vs. negative IWMs of self) x 2 (positive vs. negative IWMs of others) analysis of variance, predicting religious change over time from these attachment dimensions as measured at Time 1.

In the previous chapter I discussed cross-sectional findings from the Time 1 data. Recall that in those analyses, concurrent religiosity was in general positively related to positivity of both models of self and models of others, consistent with other cross-sectional findings on attachment and religion discussed previously. More specifically, models of self were related to beliefs about what God is *like* (e.g., people who saw themselves as loveable were more likely to have loving God images), whereas models of others were related to perceptions of God as someone with whom one could, or currently does, have a personal relationship. Both findings were attributed to the correspondence of IWMs between the religious and interpersonal domains.

The longitudinal findings were more complex and fascinating, suggesting support for *both* correspondence and compensation processes. For an aggregate religion variable as well as the Loving God scale, significant main effects of both self model and others model were found. Specifically, increases from Time 1 to Time 2 on these variables were associated with *positive* IWMs of others at Time 1, but with *negative* models of self at Time 1. Translated into group terms, this combination of negative self model and positive others model represents Bartholomew's *preoccupied* attachment style, which corresponds to Hazan and Shaver's *anxious* category. Thus, these findings replicate nicely the finding from Kirkpatrick (1997), described earlier, that anxious women were more likely than avoidant or secure women to report, 4 years later, that they had experienced a sudden conversion or other religious experience during the intersurvey interval. The results are summarized in Figure 6.1, with the 1998 results in the upper half of each cell of the table and the corre-

	Positive IWM of self	Negative IWM of self
Positive IWM of others	SECURE (Secure)	PREOCCUPIED (Anxious/ Ambivalent)
Self effect:	Relationship with God – God loving – Aggregate religiosity –	Relationship with God + God loving + Aggregate religiosity +
Others effect:	God loving + God close +	God loving + God close +
Kirkpatrick (1997)	Found new relationship with God: low Religious experience/ conversion: low	Found new relationship with God: high Religious experience/conversion: high
Negative IWM of others	DISMISSING (N/A)	FEARFUL (Avoidant)
Self effect:	Relationship with God – God loving – Aggregate religiosity –	Relationship with God + God loving + Aggregate religiosity +
Others effect:	God loving – God close –	God loving – God close –
Kirkpatrick (1997)	[n/a] [n/a]	Found new relationship with God: high Religious experience/conversion: low

FIGURE 6.1. Individual differences in religious change across time as a function of adult attachment styles. Based on Kirkpatrick (1998).

sponding 1997 results below these. (As in Figure 5.3, the word "close" is substituted for "not distant" for ease of interpretation.)

Analyses of separate religion measures again produced some differentiated patterns. Change in belief that one has a *personal relationship with God* was related significantly only to models of *self*. Specifically, people with *negative* self models at Time 1 showed greater positive change on this variable across time. Again translating back to group labels, the self-model dimension contrasts the secure and dismissing-avoidant categories with preoccupied (anxious) and fearful (avoidant) categories. If we assume, along with Bartholomew (1990), that Hazan and Shaver's "avoidant" category reflects fearful rather than dismissing avoidance, this result replicates exactly the finding from Kirkpatrick (1997) in which both anxious and avoidant women were more likely than secure women to "find a new relationship with God" over the subsequent 4-year period. Both of these insecure groups share negative models of self, in contrast to the positive self models of secure participants.

In addition, change on the Distant God scale was predicted significantly by a main effect of models of others, but not models of self. People with positive models of others at Time 1 (i.e. secure and anxious/preoccupied attachment styles) came to see God as less distant (described as "close" in Figure 6.1) over time, relative to persons of the two avoidant types.

To summarize, adults who are insecure with respect to romantic attachments—both anxious/preoccupied and (fearful) avoidant persons—appear to be more likely to turn to God as a potential surrogate attachment figure over time. However, it is mainly the *anxious* or *preoccupied* group that is likely also to report a sudden religious conversion or other religious experience. This is a subtle pattern, but the fact that it appears in both longitudinal studies warrants some degree of confidence.

How might this pattern of findings be interpreted? The former finding, which contrasts the two groups with positive models of *self* versus the two groups with negative self models, suggests that the likelihood of people turning to God as a surrogate attachment figure is related to the degree to which they *see themselves as unworthy of love and care* from romantic partners. Such individuals consequently either find themselves feeling afraid of being abandoned by their romantic partners (anxious or preoccupied), or maintain distance from close relationships entirely to avoid such dangers (fearful avoidant). Negative IWMs of self may, in effect, provide the *motivation* to turn to God as an attachment figure. However, the second finding, in which only the anxious/preoccupied group evinces a greater likelihood of having a religious experience or conversion, suggests that in order for this to really "work," one also needs to have *positive IWMs of others*. That is, one must believe that attachment figures are indeed loving, trustworthy, and reliable. For someone with negative IWMs of others, "finding God" may prove a disappointing experience: The God one has "found" turns out to be, consistent with one's IWMs of attachment figures in general, a distant, inaccessible God that effectively provides neither a secure base nor a haven of safety. Indeed, recall the finding of Kirkpatrick (1998b; see Figure 6.1) that people with negative IWMs of others came to see God as more distant across time. If one already possesses IWMs of attachment figures as reliable and accessible, however, these can be transferred to one's newly found relationship with God. Thus one can establish not only an attachment relationship with God, but specifically a *secure* attachment relationship. With fears of abandonment out of the way, the person is able to experience the kind of secure attachment with God that was never possible with human attachment figures. This proves to be a powerful emotional experience, a "religious experience" or conversion.

Unfortunately, what we do not know is the relationship between these self-classifications of romantic attachment styles in adulthood and classifications of childhood attachments to parents earlier in life. Even in fairly large samples, the base rates for childhood avoidance, adult anxiousness, and religious conversion are all sufficiently low to preclude reliable statistical analysis of their three-way interconnections. The crucial question, of course, is whether we have discovered a full path from childhood avoidance to adult anxiousness to conversion, that is, whether adult attachment style mediates the link from childhood attachment to sudden conversion and religious experience.

In any case, we at best have only again identified some individual-difference factors that predispose some people to be more likely to have religious experiences than others. Clearly all individuals falling into the "predisposed" category do not have such experiences, situational factors must be involved as well. In the next section I examine some of these from an attachment theory perspective.

CONTEXTUAL FACTORS IN RELIGIOUS CHANGE

The first half of this chapter focused on individual differences in attachment as predictors of religious change, particularly with respect to sudden religious conversion. The data reviewed here provide an answer to the question of *who* is most likely to have this experience: people with a history of insecure attachments to one or both parents in childhood, and people with a *preoccupied* or *anxious* attachment style in adulthood.

Even among these groups who display the strongest predisposition toward sudden conversion, however, not everyone has this experience—indeed, not even a statistical majority. Moreover, recall that people reporting insecure attachments in childhood are more likely than others to deconvert from religion as well as convert to religion. Clearly, other factors are involved that *interact* with individual differences to produce these variable outcomes. In this section, then, I apply the attachment perspective to the question of *when*, or under what circumstances, people are likely to turn to God as a surrogate or substitute attachment figure.

In Chapter 3 I reviewed literature showing that people turn to God under precisely the kinds of circumstances thought to activate the attachment system: in times of severe distress, sickness and fatigue, and separation from or loss of primary attachment figures. According to attachment theory, these are the times at which the set goal of the attachment system is adjusted and desire for proximity to an attachment figure, as a haven of safety, is heightened. However, we must also explain why people sometimes turn specifically to God, rather than human relationship partners, under these circumstances.

In their early study of childhood attachment and religion, Kirkpatrick and Shaver (1990) asked participants who had reported religious conversions to describe any significant life events preceding their conversions. An informal content analysis of these responses revealed a disproportionate frequency of reports of attachment-related crises, such as serious problems in a marital relationship, divorce or separation, or death of a loved one. Using a more rigorous coding methodology, Granqvist (1998) found the most common "themes of compensation" among people reporting a major religious change to include "bereavement or death of significant other" and "relationship problems or divorce." Although these studies point in the right direction, there are many well-known methodological problems in retrospective studies of converts who, for example, may have a tendency to exaggerate differences between their pre- and postconversion selves. Fortunately, better data are now available.

Separation and Loss

Perhaps the most emotionally devastating experiences in people's lives involve separation from and loss of attachment figures. Indeed, Bowlby devoted the last two books of his three-volume series on attachment to these topics, titling them *Separation* (1973) and *Loss* (1980), respectively. According to attachment theory, separation activates the attachment system in an effort to reestablish contact with the attachment figure;

such efforts also characterize the early stages of response to permanent loss. When a primary attachment figure, such as parent or relationship partner, is lost through death, or when other circumstances result in an extended period of separation from the attachment figure, God may be perceived as a particularly attractive and valuable surrogate attachment figure.

Bereavement

Chapter 3 examines several reasons why the death of an attachment figure is particularly likely to lead to the search for a surrogate attachment figure, and reviews literature showing that bereavement is indeed associated empirically with increases in religious faith. More recently, Brown, Nesse, House, and Utz (in press) studied a large number of widows from a representative sample of older adults in the Detroit area, as well as a statistically matched control sample, in a 4-year, multiwave longitudinal study. Importantly, pre-loss measures of religiosity and other variables were available for many of participants, permitting prospective study of religious changes in response to loss. The researchers also included measures of attachment security, permitting the examination of individual differences as well.

Several key findings emerged from this study. First, as expected, both church attendance and self-reported importance of religion increased from baseline to Wave 1 (6 months after loss) significantly more among widows than among matched controls. Second, these changes were temporary: Religious importance returned to baseline levels at Wave 2 (24 months) and church attendance at Wave 3 (48 months). Third, these increases in religiosity evidently were effective in helping widows deal with their grief. Among those widows who did show an increase in religiosity at Wave 1, grief scores were lower at this and all subsequent waves than among widows who did not show such an increase in religiosity. This effect was highly specific, however: It was observed only on the measure of grief per se, and not on measures of anxiety, depression, or general well-being. Moreover, when a parallel analysis was run in which church attendance was used in place of religious importance—that is, differentiating widows whose church attendance increased in response to loss versus those whose did not—these effects were not observed. It is unfortunate that the researchers had not included any religion measures related more directly to beliefs about God and people's perceived relationships with

God, as I suspect that such data would reveal this to be the crucial factor underlying the other results. That is, turning to God as a surrogate attachment figure alleviated the grief associated with the loss (though not necessarily other subsequent or correlated emotional effects).

Brown et al. (in press) also presented some individual-difference results that are intriguing from an attachment perspective. Contrary to expectations based on the studies reviewed previously, widows classified as high in attachment insecurity did not display a significantly greater increase in religiosity in response to loss than those classified as low in insecurity. However, the authors note that, consistent with the compensation hypothesis, insecurity was correlated with religiosity at baseline. This suggests at least two possible interpretations for the null finding regarding religious increase in secure versus insecure widows. First, the pre-existing difference in religiosity between groups raises the potential for methodological artifacts: For example, the baseline religiosity of insecure women may already have been sufficiently high to cause a ceiling effect. A second, theoretically more interesting possibility is that compensation effects have already occurred in this population prior to the study. Because the sample was selected to contain only "older adults"—specifically, households were selected in which the husband was at least 65 years of age—it is likely that many respondents had already experienced significant losses of family members and friends prior to the loss of spouse examined in the study. The higher levels of religiousness among the insecure women at baseline may be the result of earlier increases in religiosity in response to previous losses—increases that did not occur in secure women. (Although these two explanations are quite different, they are not mutually exclusive.)

Relationship Dissolution

Death is, of course, not the only way in which we lose attachment figures. Another common kind of attachment loss is the dissolution of close relationships, particularly breakups of romantic relationships and divorce. As noted earlier, such events are commonly mentioned by religious converts as having been experienced not long before their conversions. However, good data on this topic have been lacking until quite recently.

Data from Granqvist and Hagekull (2000) illustrate the role of a relationship with God vis-à-vis changes in the status of adult romantic attachments. In a sample of Swedish college students, individuals currently involved in long-term, committed love relationships scored significantly lower than "singles" on measures of religious activity, belief in God (i.e., less likely to be atheists), perceptions of having a personal relationship with God, religious change, and emotion-based religiosity (e.g., the EBRS). Although these data do not speak directly to the issue of sudden conversions, the findings, in particular for emotion-based religiosity, suggest, as discussed earlier, "emotional compensation" processes similar to those of sudden conversions. Importantly, this effect for lovers versus singles was statistically independent of the effects of individual differences in attachment styles. It surely is not a coincidence that cult recruiters are trained to target loners in airports and bus depots, presumably because such individuals are known to be most likely to be open to the recruiter's message.

More recently, Granqvist and Hagekull (2003) have examined the role of relationship status more thoroughly in a longitudinal design. Starting with a precollege sample of 196 Swedish adolescents, they identified 15 months later a subsample of 22 individuals who experienced a separation or breakup of a previous committed romantic relationship ("new singles"), and 28 individuals who formed a new romantic relationship over the intersurvey interval ("new lovers"). The effect of change in relationship status on religiosity was striking, but only when individual differences in attachment styles at Time 1 were also taken into account. Among the "new singles," Time 1 romantic avoidance (vs. security) was strongly, positively correlated with Time 2 measures of emotion-based religiosity, relationship with God, and an aggregated religiosity measure. Among the "new lovers," the opposite was observed: Romantic avoidance, and to a lesser extent romantic anxiety, were inversely correlated with the religion measures. That is, insecure persons became more religious in response to breakups and separation, but became less religious when they entered new romantic relationships. Similar results for insecure versus secure persons were found on some religion measures when the romantic attachment measures were replaced with measures of security/insecurity of attachment history with mother and with father, with the trend again showing insecurity to be associated with religious increases among "new singles" and decreases among "new lovers." (In all analyses, gender and Time 1 religiosity were statistically controlled.)

These results are consistent with studies described earlier (Kirkpatrick, 1997, 1998b) in support of the compensation hypothesis, in which attachment insecurity was predictive of positive religious change across time. However, the Granqvist-Hagekull results demonstrate that individual differences in attachment styles are most likely to be observed in particular contexts relevant to the attachment system, much as differences in attachment patterns among young children are most evident in responses to separation from the attachment figure (as in Ainsworth's Strange Situation paradigm). The conclusion seems clearly to be that religious change, and particularly conversion, is explained by neither individual differences nor situational factors alone, but rather by their interaction.

Unavailability of Attachment Figures

Another reason why people might turn to God rather than a human attachment figure is that in some circumstances their primary human attachment figures are, for one reason or another, simply not available. The battlefield, as noted earlier, is one place where this typically is true. The fact that there are no atheists in foxholes results partly from the extraordinary level of stress and fear in such situations, combined with the inadequacy of human attachment figures to function as a true haven of safety, but this effect is no doubt exacerbated by separation from one's primary attachment figures back home. In an amusing twist on the cliché, Allport (1950) quoted a battle veteran as reporting that "there were atheists in foxholes, but most of them were in love" (p. 56). Perhaps the psychological availability of memories of loved ones, bolstered perhaps by a tattered photograph in the pocket, is sufficient for some individuals to maintain psychological proximity transcending geographical distance. (I wonder if these soldiers were more likely to have secure attachment histories.)

Another unusual but illustrative example is provided by the autobiographies of lesbian nuns, as recorded by Curb and Manahan (1985). Nearly all of these writers emphasized that strict rules were in effect prohibiting the development of "particular friendships" within the convent, and measures were often taken to separate pairs of individuals who appeared to be developing close relationships. In addition, of course, contact with loved ones outside the convent was also limited. I strongly suspect that the rationale behind such prohibitions is that by reducing or eliminating attachment relationships with other people, the formation and maintenance of attachments to God or Jesus are facilitated.

On the other hand, these autobiographies suggest a second lesson as well: Despite these prohibitions, many individuals secretly developed and maintained lesbian relationships within the convent. This is not to imply, of course, that most or even many nuns are lesbians, but merely to illustrate that the need for human, interpersonal attachments is extremely difficult to suppress. In attempting to explain why religious conversions occur, we need to keep in mind that, in fact, they most often do *not* occur; most people do not have these experiences. One reason for this, illustrated in Hazan and Zeifman's (1999) theory of attachment-bond development in humans, is that intimate physical contact may play an important role in facilitating the development of romantic attachments (for reasons discussed in Chapter 8). Although I argued in Chapter 4 that people are able to develop attachments to God despite God's noncorporeal nature, at some point this may indeed become a limiting factor in the perceived adequacy of such bonds. Perhaps Allport's (1950) observation, quoted earlier, should be turned around: "Sometimes a bond with God will suffice, other times it will not" (p. 57).

Adolescence: Transition between Attachment Figures

One of the most extensively documented facts in the conversion literature is that *adolescence* is the most common period of life for religious conversion. Early researchers such as Hall (1904), James (1902), and Starbuck (1899) were even inclined to refer to religious conversion as "an adolescent phenomenon." Johnson (1959) reviewed five major studies and found, in an enormous total sample, that the average age of conversion was 15.2 years; and other researchers have produced similar estimates (Gillespie, 1991; Roberts, 1965). It is well known, too, that cult recruiters make teenagers and young adults primary targets for their proselytizing and recruitment activities. Presumably these recruiters are well-versed in the demographic profiles characterizing potential converts.

Because adolescence is such a dramatic and unusual developmental period, it is not surprising that a wide range of explanations have been advanced for the prevalence of conversion at this time, including postulated links to puberty and sexual instincts (Coe, 1916; Thouless, 1923); the need for meaning, purpose, and sense of identity (Starbuck, 1899); and self-realization (Coe, 1916). The hypothesis that adolescent conversion is related to "sexual instincts" makes the common mistake, noted previously, of confusing the attachment system with other, distinct evolved systems related to mating and reproduction.

Attachment theory offers a different perspective on this issue. Adolescence represents a period of major *transition* between primary attachment figures—a time during which attachments to parents begin to wane (not in terms of strength, necessarily, but rather in terms of "penetration") and attachments to *peers* begin to develop. Perhaps if the adolescent is exposed to religious ideas at the "right" time as this process is unfolding—for example, when the search first begins for alternative attachment figures—the primary attachment may be transferred to God rather than to a peer. Weiss (1986) also notes that at this time "there has taken place a change in the character of the object from the awesomely powerful, usually protective, parent of childhood to a peer whose frailties, once the relationship has passed its initial idealizations, are apt to be well recognized" (p. 102). It is easy to see how God—an "ideal" attachment figure—might therefore be seen by some as a more attractive substitute for the once-ideal parents.

The process by which attachments are transferred from parents to peers during adolescence has been discussed by Hazan and Zeifman (1999), according to whom the attachment functions of proximity seeking, haven of safety, and secure base are transferred one by one, in a stepwise manner, rather than all at once. While the adolescent is betwixt and between, he or she is likely to be vulnerable to a variety of psychological stresses. According to Weiss (1982), relinquishing the parents as attachment figures has a number of important implications for the adolescent, including vulnerability to loneliness, and for Weiss, loneliness "indicates the absence from one's internal world of an attachment figure" (p. 178). At such a time, many adolescents may turn to God (or perhaps a charismatic religious leader) as a substitute attachment figure. Some interesting avenues for future research would be to determine (1) whether religious conversions follow the same pattern as the transfer of attachments from parents to peers, and (2) the ways in which adolescent conversions correspond to the formation of peer attachments—for example, whether these tend to co-occur, or instead whether one tends to preclude the other.

On the other hand, we again must keep in mind that conversion is the exception, not the norm. Indeed, the research literature has shown not only that adolescence is associated with increased likelihood of religious conversion, but that it is also associated with increased likelihood of *deconversion* or apostasy, that is, the decline of religiosity among those raised in religious homes (Roof & Hadaway, 1979; Roof & McKinney,

1987). An interesting hypothesis worth examining is whether such deconversions coincide in time (or follow shortly after) the successful transfer of attachment bonds from parents to a peer. That is, for adolescents who "find God" during the transitional period in which they are relinquishing parents as attachment figures but have not yet replaced them with peer attachments, the development of a satisfying romantic relationship may result in turning back away from a God who is, in effect, no longer needed.

Perceived Inadequacy of Attachment Figures

The psychology of religion literature has long identified one of the predominant precipitating factors in sudden religious conversions as the experience of highly stressful events or circumstances or, alternatively, the experience of emotional distress and turmoil. Early studies and reviews generally agreed that sudden conversions are often preceded by a period of general distress, depression, and anxiety (Clark, 1929; Starbuck, 1899). According to Strickland (1924), the subsequent crisis or turning point itself "provides a relief of the nerve tensions and consequent release from fear, anxiety, grief, or other emotional states" (p. 119). In Strickland's analysis, this turning point involves the surrendering of oneself to God, and the placing of one's problems into God's hands.

More recent research has continued to replicate these early findings. Galanter (1979) showed, in a study of members of the Unification Church, that most converts reported that they had been experiencing severe emotional distress at the time of conversion into the church (and displayed a substantial reduction in emotional and neurotic distress after joining). In a subsequent study utilizing a prospective design—thus, importantly, circumventing some of the methodological problems of retrospective reports—Galanter (1980) studied potential converts to the Unification Church. Those that followed through on the decision to convert had reported a higher level of personal distress 1 month prior to their decision, as compared to those who chose not to convert (as well as an additional, nonconvert control group). Studies by Ullman (1982, 1989) and by Kox, Meeus, and Hart (1991), both showed large differences between converts and matched control groups with respect to the report of distress and serious personal problems during the years prior to their conversions.

Unfortunately, most of this research has treated stress and distress as an undifferentiated, global category of events or circumstances. As reviewed in the preceding sections, many of the most stressful or distress-producing events that people experience in life involve various kinds of disruptions of and threats to attachment bonds, and the evidence suggests that these particular kinds of stressors are related to religious conversion and change. Once these particular kinds of events and distress, related to the unavailability, inadequacy, or loss of attachment figures, are taken into account, it is not clear to what extent other kinds of stressors—for example, work-related or financial problems—are responsible for initiating religious change. More research is clearly needed to differentiate the kinds of stressful events associated with religious change.

Based upon his review of the relevant literature, Pargament (1997) concluded that people rarely turn to God in response to mundane, day-to-day stressors, but only or primarily in times of *severe* crisis or distress. From an attachment perspective, there is a good reason why the severity of the crisis or distress is important. The reason that people turn to attachment figures during times of stress and crisis is, presumably, that the attachment figure is or might be able to provide support, comfort, or protection from the threatening event. Certainly this is true in infancy and childhood, when parents are clearly much better equipped to deal with environmental dangers than their children. The issue is more complex in adulthood, however, given that adult relationship partners are in fact not necessarily better equipped to deal with adult-sized crises. In some situations, then, turning to God may be precipitated by the perception that these attachments are *inadequate*, for one reason or another. As an "ideal" attachment figure, God may be preferable to human attachment figures in circumstances in which relatively weak, fallible humans are simply not up to the task at hand.

Those situations in which human attachment figures are inadequate are, in fact, most likely to be the ones that are *severely* stressful or distressing. For example, consider again the case of soldiers on the battlefield. One reason why God may become a substitute attachment figure here is that soldiers' human attachment figures are simply not there. However, even if they were, they are not likely to be very helpful: No spouse or parent would be capable of providing real protection when the bullets start flying. Only a powerful deity could genuinely protect one from harm under such circumstances.

Apart from the nature of the stressor itself, another crucial factor influencing the adequacy of a human attachment figure is his or her behavior. Both parents and romantic partners vary considerably in the degree to which they provide sensitive and reliable caregiving when it is requested or needed; indeed, such differences in childhood are presumed to underlie the development of individual differences early in life. Variability in caregiving by romantic partners has been studied by Simpson, et al., (1992). They invited romantic pairs to the laboratory and created a stressful situation for the female partners (by telling them that the experiment involved something that many people find moderately stressful, but without telling them what). They then left the women with their romantic partners together in a waiting room to await their (unknown) fate, and surreptitiously videotaped the partners' interactions. Among other results, the researchers found that the men's caregiving varied as a function of their (adult) attachment styles: Secure men offered more support as their partner's anxiety increased, whereas avoidant men offered *less* support as their partner's anxiety increased—independent of the level of active support seeking displayed by his nervous partner. It is when "the chips are down" that attachment figures are most needed, and it seems to be exactly at these times that avoidant partners (at least male partners) are most likely to fail. Thus, some romantic partners display severe inadequacies in terms of their ability or willingness to provide a haven of safety in times of distress. This leads to the prediction—another suggestion for future research—that individual differences in the likelihood of utilizing God as an attachment figure should be related to the attachment and/or caregiving styles of people's romantic *partners*.

A complication in this analysis is the fact that differences between romantic partners are probably also correlated with individual differences in one's own attachment style. That is, some people are more likely than others to choose inadequate (in this particular sense) attachment figures as partners in the first place. For example, some research suggests a tendency for avoidant adults to pair with anxious partners (Kirkpatrick & Davis, 1994). This is particularly interesting in the present context, because we have already seen that individuals classified as *anxious* (or *preoccupied*) are the most likely to turn to God as an attachment figure. Earlier I discussed several reasons for this, related to characteristics of anxious persons. The research reviewed here suggests that the effects of being anxious may be exacerbated further by the (correlated) increased likelihood of having an avoidant partner who is inadequate as a haven of safety. If there is a recipe for attachment to God in adulthood, it might be the combination of an anxious/preoccupied attachment style and an avoidant romantic partner.

One might ask in this context why insecurely attached adults do not simply abandon these "inadequate" human partners for more adequate ones, rather than turning to God. This question highlights some of the important differences between perceived relationships with God and relationships with people. The course of an interpersonal relationship is influenced by the behavior of one's partner as well as one's own behavior; the partner's behavior, in turn, is influenced in part by one's own behavior. An anxious person can easily drive away a human relationship partner with excessive dependency and demands for closeness (which, in turn, confirms the anxious person's mental model of others as being insufficiently close and responsive); an avoidant person can drive a partner away by failing to meet the partner's desire for intimacy and closeness. A person desiring greater intimacy from a spouse or lover can easily be frustrated by an intimacy-avoiding partner; a person wishing to maintain emotional distance can feel smothered by a clingy, dependent partner.

These interactive processes often lead to a kind of self-fulfilling prophecy in which a person elicits the kind of behavior from the partner that confirms the mental models one brought into the relationship. (See Caspi and Bem, 1990, for an interesting theoretical discussion of ways in which person–environment interactions contribute to the stability of individual differences.) Moreover, this kind of process may be largely responsible for the fact that attachment styles tend to remain stable across time (Kirkpatrick & Hazan, 1994). It is difficult for insecure individuals to break out of such cycles, in large part because potential opportunities for a secure relationship are easily undermined by one's own self-defeating behavior.

Unlike human attachment partners, however, perceived relationships with God are presumably not influenced directly by God's "actual" behavior, nor, for that matter, is God's behavior influenced by that of the worshiper. A perceived relationship with God characterized by the desired level of intimacy can be maintained over time without being undermined by either "partner's" behavior. An individual might well be able to invent or reinvent his or her perceived relationship with God in secure terms without inadvertently undermining the process through previously established, counterproductive patterns of behavior.

Cultural Factors

A final topic worth mentioning in this context concerns the many cultural factors that influence the nature and shape of attachment relationships in a given place and historical period. Although the influence of such factors presumably is largely mediated by more proximal processes such as those discussed in the preceding pages, they deserve at least brief mention in their own right. In particular, consideration of such factors may be useful in understanding changes in the forms religion takes across cultures, and across time within a given culture.

For example, Caudill (1958) suggests that one consequence of the massive cultural changes that have occurred in human history, in the transition to modern environments from small, kinship-based groups, is that individuals have reduced access to cultural supports for coping with bereavement. In preindustrial societies, grieving over the death of a loved one would be shared with a wide circle of family and friends who would all be in close proximity, and available to one another as a source of support, comfort, and assistance. In contrast, various features of modern societies, such as the geographic dispersal among family members and many competing tasks and stressors, places greater strain on the individual to cope with these events. Similarly, Loveland (1968) suggests that modern society does not provide adequate mechanisms for coping with bereavement. An interesting hypothesis deriving from this observation is that people in the modern United States are more likely to experience sudden religious conversions in response to bereavement than people in most other times and places.

Similarly, many aspects of modern society create enormous strains on the process of developing and maintaining attachment bonds. Living in the midst of millions of strangers in a modern city creates feelings of alienation and loneliness; high divorce rates lead to large numbers of people without primary attachments, at least temporarily; geographic dispersal of kin and friends leaves people alone and unconnected. To the extent that these factors influence the processes of formation, maintenance, and dissolution of attachment bonds, the theory presented here predicts that they should also in turn influence the nature and distribution of religious beliefs. For example, these sorts of factors may be largely responsible for the fact that religion persists with such tenacity, despite many intellectual forces to the contrary, in the modern United States, and why in particular it is charismatic and evangelical churches that continue to grow today, while mainstream denominations decline (e.g., Kelley, 1972).

SUMMARY AND CONCLUSIONS

Since I first proposed the correspondence and compensation hypotheses (Kirkpatrick, 1992; Kirkpatrick & Shaver, 1990), many of my colleagues have suggested that the theory must be inherently flawed if it makes two mutually contradictory sets of predictions. Technically, the problem appears to be one of *falsifiability*, an important characteristic of a strong scientific theory: The theory is "supported" if attachment security, for example, is related either positively or inversely to images of God as an attachment figure. This is a perfectly reasonable criticism, but my own sense has always been that the kind of theory that does this is potentially a rich, heuristically valuable one—particularly for the psychology of religion, which as I argued in Chapter 1 suffers from a paucity of such theory.

Of course, it was never possible for both hypotheses to be true at the same time for the same people, but they both follow so naturally from attachment theory that it would have been foolish to take sides early on for the sake of consistency. In the long run, I think the value of both has been established; indeed, they both seem to be true, but for different people at different times. The emerging synthesis includes two distinct processes by which attachment dynamics and IWMs influence religious belief.

The most common pattern statistically is that of correspondence. Concurrent IWMs of God and human attachment figures tend to be consistent with one another, and adult religious belief tends to correspond to attachment experience in childhood. People with secure childhoods tend to adopt the religious beliefs of their parents, which themselves reflect the security of parents' attachment; the transmission of beliefs about a nurturing, loving God from parent to child parallels the process of the intergenerational transmission of attachment patterns. This process explains the strong predictive relationship between people's religious beliefs and those of their parents, as documented in countless studies. As I argued in Chapter 5, IWMs of attachment are crucial in facilitating this process. The process tends to be slow and gradual.

On the other hand, some individuals with insecure attachment histories display the opposite pattern, finding in God the kind of attachment relationship that has been missing from their interpersonal relationships. When this occurs, "falling in love" with God tends to occur rapidly and dramatically, leading at least sometimes to a sudden religious conversion. In this chapter I have provided evidence for this process, as well as describing some of the situational factors that may play an important role in determining whether or not it will occur. Such "compensation" processes have long been of great interest to psychologists of religion, and illustrate dramatically the role of attachment dynamics in religious development.

We are not quite finished with attachment theory. Over the last decade there have been a number of new theoretical developments that warrant attention before we leave the topic. Because these new perspectives have been motivated and shaped directly by evolutionary biology and evolutionary psychology, it will be useful to introduce evolutionary psychology before proceeding to the new directions in attachment theory that it has spurred. I do this in the next chapter, and then return to attachment theory for one more look in Chapter 8.

CHAPTER SEVEN

Attachment in Context
Introduction to Evolutionary Psychology

Throughout my presentation of attachment theory in Chapter 2, I made a point of emphasizing its evolutionary and ethological origins and argued that it was crucial for attachment researchers to keep this perspective clearly in mind. However, you might well have noticed that since then, evolutionary theory has played very little role, at least explicitly, in my application of the theory to religion. In the preceding four chapters I have proceeded as most attachment researchers have done over the last few decades: The evolutionary basis of the theory provides us with a sense of confidence in the basic tenets of the theory—the idea of attachment as a control system, the secure-base haven of safety functions of attachment figures, the patterns of individual differences that emerge from differential experience, and so on—but evolutionary reasoning has otherwise played little direct role in applications and empirical testing of hypotheses derived from the theory. The theory has in effect taken on a life of its own.

This approach has gotten us a long way so far, but I now shift to a more explicit evolutionary focus for several reasons. First, although it is true that the basic outline of Bowlby's theory has held up remarkably well over time, he did not get everything quite right. Bowlby sought to update psychoanalytic theory in view of many scientific developments, particularly the emergence of ethology and control systems theory, that had occurred in the years since Freud. Likewise, many important theoretical developments in evolutionary biology have occurred since Bowlby's first volume in 1969, and his theory similarly needs to be reexamined and updated accordingly. Recent evolutionary perspectives on attachment will not undermine any of the specific ideas in the preceding chapters about attachment and religion, but Chapter 8 examines some ways in which these newer views suggest some intriguing new directions in which an attachment theory of religion might be extended.

A second reason for shifting our focus to evolutionary psychology is to place the attachment theory of religion into a larger context. As noted previously, attachment theory cannot possibly explain everything about religious belief and behavior, nor should it be expected to do so. Where, then, shall we look for explanations of other aspects of religion that do not fall under the purview of attachment theory? How might we conceptually carve up the vast and variegated topic of "religion" into separate parts to be explained in terms of different theories? And how can we do so in a manner that will lead to a theoretically coherent and integrated view of the psychology of religion, rather than a cobbled-together, incoherent hodgepodge of unrelated ideas? I argue that evolutionary psychology offers the kind of broad metatheoretical framework required for this task, within which attachment theory represents only one important component.

As a first step toward these goals, this chapter provides a brief overview of contemporary evolutionary psychology, with particular emphasis on how attachment theory both illustrates it and fits squarely within it. This review is necessarily brief and incomplete, so I will cover only as much as is needed to develop the rest of my argument about religion in the remainder of the book. For a more complete overview, see especially Buss (1995, 2004), Pinker (1997), and Tooby and Cosmides (1992); for a more concise and easily accessible overview, see Tooby and Cosmides (1997).

EVOLUTIONARY PSYCHOLOGY AS A PARADIGM OR METATHEORY

Evolutionary psychology in its modern form is not a theory per se, but rather a metatheoretical perspective or framework. In all important respects it can be regarded as a scientific *paradigm* in the Kuhnian (1962) sense: It provides a body of background assumptions shared by all researchers in the field, defines the kinds of questions to be asked and the sorts of empirical research methods most appropriate for answering them. In this sense evolutionary psychology is comparable to, say, behaviorism, or to the cognitive revolution that displaced it. It crosscuts the traditional subdisciplinary boundaries of psychology—social, personality, developmental, and so on—and in fact aspires to connect the disciplines of psychology with its neighboring disciplines such as anthropology and biology. It is the kind of overarching, metatheoretical framework that, as I argued in Chapter 1, is lacking but sorely needed to organize research and theory in psychology generally and in the psychology of religion in particular.

Evolutionary psychology can be described as a general approach to psychology that takes seriously the notion that human brains are evolved organs that were "designed" by natural selection, and acknowledges that this fact matters greatly for understanding how the mind works and how behavior is generated. In most areas of social science, including the psychology of religion, this fundamental assumption is widely rejected in lieu of a "Standard Social Science Model" (SSSM; Tooby & Cosmides, 1992) that assumes (1) a tabula rasa view of human nature according to which we are all mainly products of "learning," "socialization," and so forth, and (2) a brain/mind that operates according to a small number of domain-general, content-independent rules/processes of reasoning and inference (e.g., logic). Few psychologists would deny that humans are the product of eons of evolution by natural selection, and few would hesitate to attribute the design of our physical bodies—arms and legs, eyes, internal organs, and so on—to natural selection. However, the prevailing assumption seems to be that somewhere there is an invisible line between psychology and physiology that the effects of natural selection do not cross. Once we evolved big brains and became highly intelligent, and subsequently developed "culture," the mind was reconstructed according to a new set of principles of learning and acculturation. Our big brains are giant, all-purpose information-processing devices that can be used for whatever purposes we choose, and are shaped and molded by our experience and environment. Our evolutionary history no longer matters for understanding how we think and behave.

The incorrectness of this view was apparent to Bowlby, who understood that our species' evolutionary history was highly relevant to understanding the design of the attachment system. He recognized that the attachment system is a species wide adaptation that develops reliably in all human infants as surely as do physical traits such as eyes and hearts, that our close primate cousins share this adaptation (as a consequence of a shared distant ancestor), and that it evolved to perform a specific function (to maintain proximity between infants and caregivers) to solve a particular adaptive problem (protection of helpless, defenseless infants). The system is there because ancestral environments were dangerous; were they not, we would not be so designed. Our evolutionary history really does matter for understanding this aspect of our species' psychological makeup. Evolutionary psychologists merely assert that this is true for other features of human psychology, of which attachment is just one among numerous examples.

ADAPTATION AND NATURAL SELECTION

Protection against predators (including, often, conspecifics, or members of the same species) is an example of an *adaptive problem* faced by most living organisms. Different species face widely different threats and problems. Plants get eaten by herbivores, some microorganisms get eaten by other microorganisms, little fish get eaten by big fish, and so forth. Each of these prey species has evolved different sorts of defenses, both physical and behavioral, in response to these threats. Plants secrete toxins or grow thorns; little fish hide in reeds or swim in visually bewildering schools; turtles grow a hard protective shell. Goslings are protected from environmental threats by their mothers, and have evolved an imprinting system that works to keep them close to their protectors. Humans have evolved the more complex attachment system toward more or less the same end.

But this is the tip of the proverbial iceberg. Although popular depictions of natural selection, such as television documentaries, tend to focus largely on predator–prey interactions as examples of Tennyson's "nature red in tooth and claw," protection against predators is only one of an enormous number of adaptive problems faced by organisms. Other survival problems include identifying, locating, and acquiring food of a particular type; processing the food to free usable energy and eliminating waste products; choosing environments in which to spend one's time according to other needs; thermoregulation; and so forth.

Moreover, survival of individual organisms is only part of the evolutionary game, and in some ways a rather insignificant part. Surviving does not count for anything in natural selection unless one successfully reproduces; reproduction is really the name of the game. In sexually reproducing species such as our own, reproduction poses a vast array of adaptive problems quite independent of survival. In sexually reproducing species, one needs to identify potential mates (same species, opposite sex, reproductively viable), locate and/or attract one or more of them (which may entail competition with rivals that may take any number of different forms), exchange genetic material with them, and in many species defend mates against potential interlopers and/or discourage them from wandering off or defecting to rivals. Each species has evolved biological structures designed to solve the particular versions of these problems posed by its ancestors: penises, vaginas, and other aspects of reproductive biology; particular patterns of coloration that identify species or sex membership (and possibly health or other aspects of quality of individuals within these categories); and so forth.

But even reproduction does not count in the evolution game unless sufficient numbers of one's offspring survive and go on to reproduce successfully: Your offspring, and then their offspring, are (usually) the primary vehicle by which your genes make it into future generations. In some species the solution to this problem involves producing enormous numbers of offspring (e.g., insects and fish that lay hundreds or thousands of eggs at a time); other species produce fewer offspring but invest heavily in their welfare.

Finally, as worked out by Hamilton (1964) in an enormously influential paper, ensuring the survival and reproduction of your offspring is just a special case of a broader rule: Another ticket to immortality for the genes in an individual is any relative of the individual who, by virtue of genetic relatedness, is statistically likely (to varying degrees, depending on relationship) to carry the same versions of genes. Your siblings are in some ways your competitors, but in other ways provide alternative vehicles for your genes in the same way that your offspring do. This fact thus introduces a whole new set of adaptive problems concerning the welfare of close kin vis-à-vis nonkin.

In short, species face an enormous number of adaptive problems specific to their environmental niche, which involve not only survival but also mating, reproduction, parenting, and kinship. Protection and care of immature offspring is only one of these, and is no more important in the scheme of things than any of the others.

Adaptations

In thinking about *adaptations*—evolved solutions to adaptive problems— the first thing that comes to most people's minds are visually salient physical traits. Giraffes have long necks, butterflies have specialized nectar-sucking mouthparts, and tigers have sharp teeth—all solutions to the adaptive problem of acquiring appropriate foods. In the preceding discussion I reinforced this view by deliberately referring only to physical traits as examples. Within human bodies, organs such as hearts and lungs are adaptations designed to solve the particular problems of transporting oxygen and other substances to cells around the body. Livers are designed to detoxify blood, bones to provide support and strength, and so on.

Hardware is useless, however, without software to operate it. There is no point in having nectar-sucking mouthparts if you do not have the motivation to suck or cannot locate or identify flowers containing nectar. Consequently, each species must also be characterized by its own distinct suite of *behavioral adaptations* in addition to other physical traits. Long necks are of no use to giraffes unless they use them by stretching to reach leaves high in trees that other browsing land mammals cannot reach; sharp teeth are of no use to tigers unless they capture meaty prey and apply their fangs in the appropriate way to make the kill. Penises and vaginas are of no use unless you know what to do with them, and choose wisely with respect to the kinds of partners with whom you share them. (The problem of choosing mates itself involves an enormous number of specific adaptive problems, some of which differ between the sexes. More on that later.) Human (and most mammal) parents invest in their offspring in many ways, including protecting them, feeding them, and helping them along in various other ways later on. Each species has its own "nature" with respect to its characteristic patterns of behavior, designed over eons of natural selection in a manner that proved effective in solving the adaptive problems faced by that species' distant ancestors.

All of this should be strongly reminiscent of some of the distinctions discussed in Chapter 2 between attachment, on the one hand, and other systems or relationship types on the other. Learning about one's environment involves a different set of adaptive problems, and thus a different set of behavioral adaptations (recall the "exploration system" from Chapter 2), than do protection and attachment. The observation that a child's relationship with its mother is a qualitatively and functionally different kind of relationship from his or her relationship with peers led Cassidy (1999) to emphasize that a "sociability system" is distinct from the attachment system. In adulthood, mating relationships involve problems of sex and reproduction, as well as mutual assistance and caregiving, such that adult romantic love involves the confluence of at least three distinct behavioral systems (Hazan & Shaver, 1987; Shaver et al., 1988).

"Selfish Genes" and Inclusive Fitness

Although Darwin did a remarkable job in laying out the theory of natural selection in 1859, it was another 100 years before the process was understood correctly. In the wake of Hamilton's (1964) theory of *inclusive fitness* and *kin selection* (more about which later), Williams (1966) crystallized the notion of adaptation and clarified precisely how natural selection works. (See Dawkins, 1976/1989, for an entertaining and brilliant popular exposition of this "selfish gene" view.) Natural selection does not operate in terms of what is "good for the species"; in fact, it does not even operate in terms of what is good for individuals. Individual survival, as I noted briefly earlier, is itself adaptive only to the extent that living longer translates into more offspring, and offspring of offspring, and so on. Genes are "replicators" that build "survival machines" (Dawkins's terms)—both hardware (physical structures) and software (behavioral programs or psychological mechanisms)—some of which are more successful than others in surviving and reproducing. Genes that build survival machines that are better at getting themselves (the genes) replicated than other survival machines are the genes that wind up disproportionately represented in future generations. In many important ways, a chicken really is just an egg's way of making another egg.

This way of understanding natural selection, in terms of the differential success of alternative genetic recipes (replicators) rather than in terms of the survival of individuals (vehicles), has numerous crucial implications for understanding adaptations and their functions. Strictly speaking, a feature is *adaptive* only in the sense that it leads to a relative advantage in the proliferation of genes that specify its construction: that is, to its own *reproductive success* or *inclusive fitness*. Many species would benefit, for example, if all individuals selflessly cooperated with one another at every turn, sacrificing themselves whenever this would benefit the group as a whole. However, such altruism is not found in nature, for the simple reason that a mutant genetic program that instilled a selfish "cheating strategy" in some individuals—enjoying the benefits of others' sacrifices without incurring the costs—would be wildly successful in a population of self-sacrificers. The organisms built by this alternative program would out-survive and out-reproduce the others, and the "selfish" genes would soon displace the altruistic ones in subsequent generations.

Moreover, an adaptation need not necessarily be "good for" the individuals that have it, with respect to their health, happiness, or any other criterion. If you are not convinced, ask yourself this question: In what way is raising children "good for" parents? Wouldn't most parents be happier and healthier if they decided to forgo the terrible twos and all the other nuisances of child rearing, and just focus on having fun? Why do parents the world over invest so much of their time and energy in offspring, when these resources could instead be used in many other ways for their own individual benefit?

Even this situation is far more complex than it may appear. Parents in our and many other species do invest heavily in offspring—but not always. As shown by Trivers (1972) in his theory of *parental investment*, resources funneled toward any particular offspring are resources no longer available for investment in other extant or future offspring. In no species, including humans, are parents designed to invest *indiscriminately* in offspring at their own expense. Consequently, infants are faced with the adaptive problems of obtaining adequate investment from parents, and of dealing with variable levels of parental investment that might be faced. Considerations such as these have led evolutionary psychologists to some new perspectives on the nature and operation of the attachment system—perspectives that were not available to Bowlby when he was developing attachment theory in the 1960s and 1970s—that I discuss in Chapter 8.

DOMAIN-SPECIFICITY AND THE MENTAL-ORGANS MODEL

Unlike physical traits, behaviors per se cannot be naturally selected or evolve; only biological structures can. The structures that organize (most) behavior are found in the brain, and consist of arrangements of neural circuitry, a host of neurotransmitters and their receptors, and so forth. From the perspective of modern evolutionary psychology, the biological details are not the central focus; instead, the heart of the approach is an information-processing perspective, according to which the brain/mind, like the remainder of the human body, consists of a collection of adaptations designed to solve recurrent adaptive problems faced by our distant ancestors. These *psychological mechanisms* are both highly numerous and *domain-specific*, reflecting the diversity and specificity of problems to be solved, such as those mentioned in the preceding section. The general notion that cognition is organized in a highly modular and domain-specific manner has been converged upon from a variety of directions (e.g., research in neuroscience, cognitive development, etc.) independently of an evolutionary perspective. The contribution of evolutionary psychology is to provide a powerful heuristic for predicting, and basis for understanding the function of, the specific assortment of mechanisms that characterize our species' evolved psychology (Cosmides & Tooby, 1994).

Psychological mechanisms are conceptualized as information-processing devices designed to attend to certain features of the environment, process this information according to certain rules, and generate behavioral, cognitive, and emotional output. Thus the attachment system in infancy is designed to respond to internal cues of hunger or pain, and external cues of potential danger, by producing behavioral output of certain kinds (i.e., attachment behaviors). To choose a different example, a *sexual jealousy* mechanism is designed to attend to environmental cues indicative of potential or actual infidelity by one's mate; when activated, it initiates a suite of emotional and behavioral responses designed to punish the transgressors and preclude future occurrences (Daly, Wilson, & Weghorst, 1982; Symons, 1979). The adaptive problem solved for males concerns the genetic costs of investing resources in offspring carrying a competitor's genes; for females, the principal danger is diversion of resources from self and (especially) offspring to a competitor. Thus jealousy is an example of a sex-differentiated mechanism resulting from the sexes having faced somewhat different adaptive problems in ancestral environments (Buss, Larsen, Westen, & Semmelroth, 1992; Daly et al., 1982). In domains in which the sexes faced identical adaptive problems, they are expected to share similar evolved architectures.

Thus, one crucial aspect of the evolutionary-psychological paradigm is the rejection of a view of the brain/mind as a general, all-purpose information-processing device. Natural selection has designed human brain/minds, as well as those of other species, as a collection of mechanisms designed specifically to solve specific adaptive problems. There is no such thing as a general problem-solving mechanism because there is no such thing as a general problem, just as there is no such thing as a single kitchen tool that serves as a general, all-purpose food-processing device (Symons, 1992). A mechanism designed to guide food preferences cannot be the same as one designed to guide mate preferences, or we would wind up with some very strange diets and relationships. "Human nature" is the complete package of species-typical psychological mechanisms we have inherited from our ancestors, and that differs in some ways (but is similar in others) to "dog nature," "ant nature," and so on.

This distinction between *psychological mechanisms*, which are species-universal (and presumably have been so since the late Pleistocene), and *observed behavior*, which is highly variable across individuals and groups, is central to the evolutionary-psychology model (Cosmides & Tooby, 1987). Attachment researchers have long recognized the importance of the distinction between an attachment system, on the one hand, and attachment behaviors on the other. Sroufe and Waters (1977a) emphasized the distinction in arguing that attachment should be viewed as an "organizational construct," and noted several important implications of doing so. For example, they noted that one would not necessarily expect measures of attachment behaviors to be intercorrelated because, given their functional organization, specific behaviors may be substitutable, such that the successful use of one particular attachment behavior might preclude the use of others. This makes the attachment conceptualization different from that of most personality traits, in which specific measures would be expected to correlate highly with one another (as measured, for example, by alpha coefficients). Although Sroufe and Waters's perspective on this issue was not explicitly evolutionary, it fits nicely with the evolutionary-psychological view of evolved psychological mechanisms as a crucial level of analysis between behavior and biology.

NATURE "VERSUS" NURTURE

This view of human nature represents, in my opinion, the first coherent framework for thinking about the biggest and most annoying problem in the history of psychology: the age-old nature–nurture debate. Psychologists today agree that this is a false dichotomy, and that behavior is a product of both. Yet there remains much confusion about exactly what it means to say "both."

One meaning concerns the problem of explaining *variability* in a trait or other characteristic. Using particular kinds of data (e.g., twins reared apart vs. together) and statistical techniques, geneticists can compute the *heritability* of a trait in terms of the proportion of variance explained respectively by genetic versus environmental variability (the latter typically further subdivided into shared and nonshared components). In this way of thinking, a trait can be described as being X% genetic and 100 − X% environmental, and in this sense the trait is a product of "both."

But variance partitioning addresses only one kind of nature–nurture question. This question, concerning the variability of a trait, falls in the domain of *behavior genetics*, which should not be confused with evolutionary psychology. Behavior genetics is focused mainly on the question of why people are *different* from one another, and approaches the question as just described. Evolutionary psychology, in contrast, focuses mainly on the opposite question of what makes all people *the same*. The goal of evolutionary psychology is the identification of the universals of human psychology. This is not to say that either approach is better than the other; they are inherently complementary. At present, however, the relationship between the fields is tenuous and somewhat strained.[1]

Interestingly, and perhaps ironically given many people's misconceptions of the field, evolutionary psychology typically turns to *environmental* factors rather than genetic ones to explain variability in behavior. Williams (1966) and Buss (1995) offer as an analogy the evolved mechanism in human skin that produces calluses. All humans have this mechanism, just as they have two legs and a heart, yet there are enormous individual differences both within and across cultures in the presence and location of calluses on bodies. Some variability in callus production may be genetic: no doubt there is some minor quantitative variability in skin sensitivity from person to person, just as some people have longer legs than others. But the lion's share of variance in calluses is produced by environmental effects: People who work with their hands get calluses on their hands; guitarists get them on their fingers; those who walk barefoot get them on their feet. Most psychological mechanisms are thought to work in an analogous way: Everyone has the same system, but the system is designed to produce different outputs contingent on different inputs. Bowlby's conceptualization of the attachment and exploration systems exemplifies this model clearly, with certain classes of environmental cues hypothesized to activate attachment behavior and other classes to deactivate it and activate exploratory behavior.

The other kind of nature–nurture question concerns how to explain not the variability in something, but rather to explain the something itself. This is the part of the question where evolutionary psychology offers a unique and powerful perspective on what it means for human behavior to be caused by "both" nature and nurture. Ask yourself, are calluses produced by "nature" or by "nurture"? On one hand, they are clearly produced by a genetically constructed biological organ (nature). One could have this mechanism in one's skin and go an entire lifetime without ever having a callus, however, so it cannot be only "nature." On the other hand, calluses are clearly produced by the environmental cause of repeated friction on the skin. But it cannot be just "nurture," because friction generally does not generally cause surfaces to build up or get tougher but rather wears them down. The question of whether calluses are produced by "nature" or by "nurture" is meaningless; in a very real sense the answer is 100% both. Neither alone produces anything.

Evolutionary psychologists argue that *all* behavior must be construed as the product of both nature and nurture in this way. As summarized by Tooby and Cosmides (1990), "Evolution acts *through* genes, but it acts on the *relationship* between the genes and the environment. The 'environment' is as much a part of the process of evolutionary inheritance as are the 'genes,' and equally as 'biological' and evolved" (p. 20). It really could not be any other way. Evolutionary psychology is not just another swing to the latter side of the nature–nurture pendulum; it is an inherently interactionist model. Attachment behavior, as well as parental caregiving behavior, sexual behavior, and other domains of behavior, is caused by the interaction of particular classes of environmental stimuli and experience with evolved psychological mechanisms designed to be sensitive to these particular classes of stimuli, and to generate responses that were, on average in ancestral environments, more adaptive than alternatives. Likewise, attachment behavior is the product of environmental stimuli interacting with an evolved attachment system that is designed to attend to certain classes of stimuli and respond to them differentially.

Moreover, evolutionary psychologists by no means ignore the important roles of individual learning, developmental processes, or cultural influences. However, they maintain that simple appeals to "learning" and "culture" are not in themselves explanations of anything; one needs to explain why certain things are learned and others are not, and why culture takes the forms that it does in the first place. That is, both learning and culture are themselves things to be explained. In both cases, understanding our evolved psychological architecture is essential to understanding such processes. For example, it is well known that taste aversions can be learned extremely quickly (often in one trial) when a particular food is paired with certain kinds of experience (nausea, vomiting) but not others (electric shock)—suggesting that an innate mechanism is "prepared" to rapidly construct some kinds of learned connections more than others. Children learn language (and invent it when it is absent) far more readily than could possibly be explained by simple associationist or operant processes (Chomsky, 1957; Pinker, 1994), suggesting the existence of some kind of innate brain/mind structures designed specifically for this purpose. Note that these are the very kinds of research findings that led to the demise of behaviorism which, like the SSSM, sought to explain everything in terms of a few general principles of learning and without regard to the evolved psychology of the organisms being studied.

Attachment theory again provides a nice example: Both the normative model of how the attachment functions generally, and the complementary model of how individual differences emerge, depend strongly on the particular experiences and learning of the infant and child across development. Attachment is partly about the maturation of an evolved brain/mind system, but also about the experience of the child in interaction with a primary caregiver (who may be more or less reliable) and with an environment (which may be more or less anxiety provoking). I discuss some other models of interaction between environments and the attachment system in a subsequent chapter.

STONE AGE MINDS IN MODERN ENVIRONMENTS

I suggested earlier in this chapter that the term *adaptive* is easily misunderstood to be equivalent to *functional* or *useful* in other ways, such as producing happiness or avoiding pain. From an evolutionary perspective, such effects are irrelevant unless they translate into reproductive advantage. Another way to misunderstand the term is to confuse what appears to be "adaptive" (in any sense, including the strict inclusive-fitness sense) in modern environments with what was adaptive in ancestral environments (the *environment of evolutionary adaptedness*, or EEA).[2] Particularly in the human world, things have changed considerably over the last, say, million years or so. In fact, most of that change has occurred in the last 10,000 years or so, since the emergence of agriculture.

Evolution is a slow process, particularly in long-lived organisms (such as human beings) in which generations are measured in scores rather than in years, months, or hours. Ten thousand years is simply not enough time for very much significant specieswide evolutionary change to have occurred in the human gene pool. Consequently, we look like, and more importantly think like, our distant ancestors. It is generally accepted that our evolved psychology has remained virtually unchanged since the late Pleistocene of about 100,000 years ago, when our ancestors lived semi-nomadic lifestyles as hunters and gatherers in small, mainly kin-based groups. Natural selection thus created a psychological design that "worked" for these ancestors under those conditions. In some ways, these old-fashioned brains are virtually obsolete in the new circumstances we have created for ourselves.

A popular and useful analogy for illustrating this issue is that of our evolved taste preferences. Humans love sweets and fats. For Steven Pinker (1997), cheesecake is the perfect food. The reason we crave cheesecake, according to Pinker, is because foods loaded with nutritionally important sugars (ripe fruits) and fats (large game animals) were rare and difficult to come by in the distant past; when you found them, it paid to be motivated to fill up on them. Today, however, with a McDonald's on every corner, these previously adaptive preferences have become a terrible problem for many people in terms of their health, fitness, and appearance. What worked then does not necessarily work now. It is easy to think of other, more "psychological" examples as well. For example, we have inherited a psychology that is well designed for dealing effectively with social relations in groups of perhaps a few dozen people. What happens when such brains are turned loose in midtown Manhattan? What happens to our self-esteem, for example, when we are subjected to thousands of images a day of beautiful, successful people on television and via other media? (See Wright, 1994, for an interesting discussion of this latter point.)

To my mind, this notion is perhaps the single most important contribution that evolutionary psychology will have to make over the long haul. By separating the adaptive value (in a strictly inclusive-fitness sense) of psychological mechanisms in ancestral environments from their apparent utility or functionality by other criteria in modern environments, we open the door to understanding patterns of behavior that seem maladaptive, senseless, or just plain puzzling. The implications for clinical psychology and psychiatry, and specifically the diagnosis and treatment of a wide variety of psychological problems, are potentially enormous (Glantz & Pearce, 1989; Nesse & Williams, 1994).

In fact, the historical development (and thus existence) of attachment theory itself is largely the result of an important example of this issue. The impetus for the development of the theory (and the discarding of existing psychoanalytic and social learning theories) came from Bowlby's early work on the traumatic psychological effects of maternal deprivation on infants and children, particularly in hospitals and other institutions in which children were housed in large numbers with little regard for any kind of regular or sustained contact with primary caregivers. Such institutions are, of course, a modern invention; no child 100,000 years ago grew up in a box with dozens of other parentless children, receiving only basic sustenance from adults. Infants do not come equipped with psychological mechanisms designed to deal with such an artificial environment, and the consequences are disastrous.

Incidentally, another important point to make about this example is that attachment theory (and its evolutionary approach) not only was useful in identifying the nature of the problem, it also led directly to a solution. A widespread misunderstanding (and fear) of evolutionary psychology is based on the misconception that if something is "in our genes," it is therefore immutable—and nobody wants to think that. If it is not immediately obvious to you that this is false, consider the fact that nearsightedness is usually due to genetic causes but is readily and completely fixed by prescription glasses or laser surgery. Recall that, despite the assumption that the designs of psychological mechanisms are "in the genes," evolutionary psychologists largely ascribe *variability* in the output of these mechanisms (e.g., behavior) to environmental factors. Bowlby's work provides a nice example of how an evolutionary theoretical understanding of attachment processes led quickly to practical advice about how infants should and should not be reared.

INDIVIDUAL DIFFERENCES
IN EVOLUTIONARY CONTEXT

If evolutionary psychology posits a universal human psychology, how can it be that stable individual differences are observed within and across populations with respect to almost anything that can be measured? This is a particularly important topic in the present context, given the important role of individual differences in attachment theory and research. Moreover, a number of evolutionary theorists have offered some new perspectives on individual differences in attachment, both in childhood and adulthood, in recent years, which I introduce in the next section. Before doing so, however, I review a few general ways in which stable individual differences can be understood from an evolutionary perspective, drawing heavily on the taxonomy outlined by Buss and Greiling (1999).

Stable Environmental Differences

I have referred several times to the notion that behavioral variability is largely explained by evolutionary psychologists in terms of variability in environments. You get calluses if you experience repeated friction, but not if you do not experience it. My emphasis so far has been on short-term or immediate responses to environmental change, as when the attachment system is activated by the mother moving away or a frightening event. However, the same effect can occur over the long term as well, such that stable environmental differences will lead to stable individual differences. For construction workers and guitarists, calluses become more or less fixed so long as their bearers continue working or playing. Notice that this explanation works for cross-cultural differences, too: Few 21st-century Americans have calluses on the soles of their feet, but people in tribal cultures living in tropical environments generally do.

Such differences in "enduring environmental evocation" (as Buss & Greiling, 1999, put it) undoubtedly account for part of the variance in attachment styles in both children and adults. People living in unstable, unpredictable, or otherwise stressful environments are likely to have their attachment systems more or less chronically activated, resulting in more clingy behavior toward the mother/partner or a search for alternative attachment figures (such as God). People living in stable, benign environments can go long stretches without access to an attachment figure, save perhaps for the occasional phone call; such a person might appear to be "dismissing"of attachment under these circumstances. Although attachment theorists might object that this is not really what is meant by attachment styles, which are generally conceptualized as a property of a person (or of the person in relation to a particular other), people who are "anxious" for environmental reasons and those who are anxious for "dispositional" reasons might well be indistinguishable in terms of overt behavior and emotions. In any event, the point is that stable individual differences in behavior can be generated in this way from a species-typical attachment system faced with stable environmental differences.

Another way in which individual differences in attachment might be explained in terms of enduring situational evocation involves the assumption that there is something about the modern environments in which some individuals (presumably those identified as "insecure") live that is importantly different from the ancestral environments in which the system evolved, causing the system to malfunction. As noted earlier, functionally important mismatches between ancestral and modern conditions are one source of various forms of pathology; if a mismatch is experienced by only some members of the population, it becomes a matter of individual differences. We return to the question of whether secure attachment is "normative," and whether insecure attachment is "maladaptive," in Chapter 8.

Direct Genetic Effects

A second common source of individual differences is, of course, genetic variability. Much heritable variation in traits is random "noise" from a strict evolutionary perspective, with no direct fitness consequences. Natural selection tends to reduce variability in the gene pool by eliminating the less adaptive variants (see Tooby & Cosmides, 1990, for a technical discussion), so that the heritable variability that remains is that which does not much matter with respect to natural selection. For example, the genetic variability in the height to which people grow is largely of this sort: Natural selection has winnowed the range of human stature to one within which there is (or was, in ancestral environments) little adaptive advantage overall to being taller or shorter. If being taller were generally more adaptive for humans, we would no doubt have evolved as a species to be taller than we are. This is not to say that heritable differences in height are of no consequence in individual lives: There are any number of ways in which one's height influences daily life. A very tall person will never ride in the Kentucky derby, and few short people make it to the National Basketball Association.

Few if any psychologists maintain that there are distinct genes (technically, *alleles*) that code for secure, anxious, and/or avoidant attachment, and I am not inclined to argue for them here. However, genetic differences can also express themselves in less direct ways. It is extremely doubtful that we have genes that code directly for basketball-playing ability, yet genetically based individual differences in height correlate strongly (I assume) with such ability. Kagan's (1984) suggestion that heritable differences in infant temperament may largely account for individual differences in Strange Situation behavior falls in this category. It is easy to imagine how a shy temperament, for example, could cause an infant to be easily frightened in novel circumstances and hence display attachment behaviors at a higher frequency than others, independent of parental caregiving quality. Parents may be unable to respond to infant demands for attention that are so frequent, resulting in the kind of "inconsistent" responding associated with the anxious (ambivalent, resistant) attachment style and causing the infant to become even more anxious and fearful. Thus, heritable individual differences can influence the expression of evolved behavior programs in many ways, apart from coding directly for such differences. A genetic explanation for individual differences need not be incompatible with a theory about a species-universal psychological system.

Frequency-Dependent Adaptive Strategies

To this point I have discussed psychological (and physiological) mechanisms as if each is designed to execute a singular strategy. (Here, as elsewhere in this discussion, the word "strategy" is by no means intended to imply that conscious awareness or rational decision making need be involved.) Such strategies are adaptive to the extent that environments, and thus the adaptive problems they pose, are stable across time. However, if environments are more variable such that different strategies are adaptive in different circumstances, evolution can fashion alternative *facultative* strategies, with different members of a species (or the same individual at different times) exhibiting alternative variants.

The evolved design of such alternative strategies can take a variety of forms. In the simplest case, alternative genes (alleles) coding for different traits or strategies can both continue to exist in the gene pool, typically in a particular mathematical ratio that has proved to be *evolutionarily stable*. Specifically, this occurs when a ratio is reached that reflects the relative probabilities of success in inclusive-fitness terms. Imagine a "safe" strategy that is almost always successful to a small degree, and a "risky" strategy that rarely succeeds but, when it does, succeeds wildly. Genes for these respective strategies can become distributed in the population in such a way that the majority of individuals inherit the "safe" genes, but a small proportion inherit the "risky" version—the precise numbers determined by the empirical success rates produced by the two strategies. Such adaptations are referred to as *frequency-dependent*. Perhaps the most familiar example is biological sex, which in most species (including humans, of course) is distributed 50–50. Although being male and being female represent two qualitatively different "strategies" for mating and reproduction across the lifespan, on average there is no (or was not in ancestral environments) probabilistic fitness advantage to being one versus the other.

Mealey (1995) has argued that one form of criminality, which she calls *primary sociopathy*, may be heritable (in very small proportion) in humans as a function of frequency-dependent selection. Theoretically, the argument is that a population dominated by strategies for cooperation and fair reciprocity provides an adaptive niche for a cheater strategy that takes advantage of the do-gooders. Cheating is not a particularly adaptive strategy in a population full of cheaters, but if it occurs only in small proportion it can be wildly successful (again, strictly from a natural selection point of view). I do not believe anyone has proposed that heritable differences in attachment patterns, if there are any, exist as a result of frequency-dependent selection. However, this discussion is relevant with respect to an important topic related to attachment, as follows.

Early Environmental Calibration

In many cases, which of two (or more) facultative strategies is most adaptive varies depending on context. If ancestral environments varied considerably, and if certain aspects of those environments presented observable, reliable cues as to which "kind" of environment one was currently in (and thus which of the strategies was the better bet), then natural selection can favor the evolution of facultative strategies that are "selected" by individuals based on life experience. That is, one strategy or developmental path is switched on if the organism perceives one kind of cue, but an alternative life course is set in motion by perception of the alternative cue. If this seems implausible to you, consider the facts that certain species of fish actually change their biological sex depending on environmental cues indicating it is adaptive to do so (Charnov, 1982), and many species of insects (such as ants and bees) develop into distinct castes depending on the quantity or quality of maternal provisioning

(Gross, 1996). Simply activating one behavioral program rather than another seems a trivial matter compared to these engineering feats. In Mealey's (1995) model, *secondary psychopathy* results from a process like this one, in which an alternative "cheater" strategy is activated by the perception of certain environmental cues early in life.

An Example of Facultative Strategies: Human Mating

There is a clear consensus among evolutionary psychologists that the human mating repertoire comprises a variety of alternative strategies. Cross-culturally, there is evidence among humans of long-term monogamy, polygamy (*polygyny*, multiple wives, and *polyandry*, multiple husbands, with the former being widespread and the latter extremely rare), serial monogamy, and promiscuous short-term mating strategies. Additional evidence that humans are multiple strategists comes from diverse sources, from cross-species comparisons of sexual dimorphism in body size and male testis size (which suggest a history of multiple mating by both males and females) to the existence of psychological mechanisms, such as sexual jealousy, that suggest an evolutionary history in which infidelity was something that needed to be guarded against. (See Buss & Greiling, 1999, for a summary of numerous additional arguments.) It is surely not a coincidence that nearly all of these strategies are observed among our closest relatives. For example, the harem systems of gorillas are polygynous; chimpanzees and bonobos are promiscuous; and gibbons are monogamous.

In general terms, the reason for this variability in mating strategies is that there are many distinct advantages and disadvantages to each with respect to inclusive-fitness benefits, and which strategy is most adaptive depends on how the balance sheet works out in a particular environment. Many of the benefits and costs differ for men and women: For example, a benefit of short-term mating for men is that the number of offspring that can potentially be produced by a single man in a lifetime is virtually unlimited, whereas women are limited by the lengthy periods of gestation and lactation they must invest in each. (For a thorough review of the costs and benefits, outlined separately for males and females, see Buss & Schmitt, 1993.) Not only are these costs and benefits numerous on each side of the ledger, but the situation is complicated further by the fact that members of each sex are not free to pursue their preferred strategy; they are constrained by the availability and preferences of potential partners.

Further discussion of human mating strategies would take us too far astray here, although we revisit the idea subsequently in other contexts. For our present discussion, the crucial point is that adaptations need not take a single form across the members of a species, or even within the same individual across time. Multiple variants of a physical trait or behavioral system can exist within the same population, with individuals "choosing" from the menu of options based on genetic individual differences, environmental cues, or a combination of the two. This general point—as well as the specific example of mating strategies—is central to some of the recent developments in attachment theory research, which in turn have some interesting implications for our theory of religion.

ARE EVOLUTIONARY EXPLANATIONS UNFALSIFIABLE?

At the risk of appearing too apologetic, I think it is important to address a common criticism of evolutionary psychology. Many opponents of this paradigm seem to believe there is nothing more to evolutionary psychology than "Just-So" stories (in reference to the famous Rudyard Kipling children's book) that are unscientific because they are empirically untestable. We cannot go back in time and observe the evolution of an attachment mechanism in human ancestors, for example, so adding an evolutionary veneer to the attachment story is just window-dressing that can be neither confirmed nor disconfirmed empirically. If this is the case, then indeed this entire book is a waste of your time and mine.

I have stolen the title of this section from an excellent article by Ketelaar and Ellis (2000), which I recommend (along with the published commentaries and reply by the authors) to readers interested in this question (see also Buss, 1995). Here I briefly summarize one of the principal arguments in a simple way, and leave the technical philosophical debate (e.g., regarding Popperian versus Lakatosian philosophies of science) to Ketelaar and Ellis.

In short, the idea is that within an evolutionary metatheory or paradigm, more specific theories, subtheories, and hypotheses are hierarchically arranged, and it is only at one level in which empirical testing occurs. This hierarchy, as described by Buss (1995), is reproduced in Figure 7.1. At the core of evolutionary psychology (top of diagram) is a group of

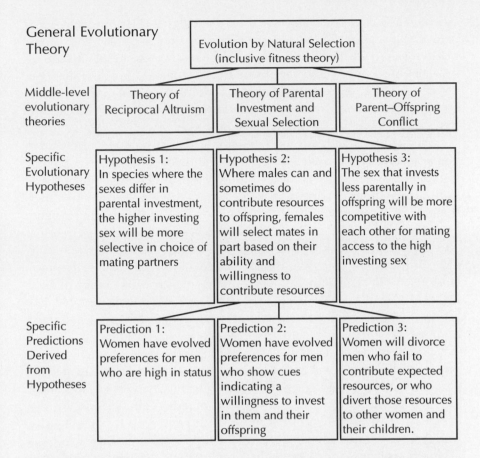

General Evolutionary
Theory

Evolution by Natural Selection
(inclusive fitness theory)

Middle-level
evolutionary
theories

Theory of
Reciprocal Altruism

Theory of Parental
Investment and
Sexual Selection

Theory of
Parent–Offspring
Conflict

Specific
Evolutionary
Hypotheses

Hypothesis 1:
In species where the
sexes differ in
parental investment,
the higher investing
sex will be more
selective in choice of
mating partners

Hypothesis 2:
Where males can and
sometimes do
contribute resources
to offspring, females
will select mates in
part based on their
ability and
willingness to
contribute resources

Hypothesis 3:
The sex that invests
less parentally in
offspring will be more
competitive with
each other for mating
access to the high
investing sex

Specific
Predictions
Derived
from
Hypotheses

Prediction 1:
Women have evolved
preferences for men
who are high in status

Prediction 2:
Women have evolved
preferences for men
who show cues
indicating a
willingness to invest
in them and their
offspring

Prediction 3:
Women will divorce
men who fail to
contribute expected
resources, or who
divert those resources
to other women and
their children.

FIGURE 7.1. A hierarchy of levels of analysis in evolutionary psychology. From Buss (1995). Copyright 1995 by Lawrence Erlbaum Associates, Inc. Reprinted by permission.

basic assumptions that derive from modern evolutionary biology, particularly the theory of *inclusive fitness* as proposed by Hamilton (1964) and subsequently explicated by Williams (1966), Dawkins (1976/1989), and others. This metatheoretical, or "hard-core," level is assumed to be true for all evolutionary-psychological theorizing, and is no longer directly tested (at least by psychologists). This core in turn gives rise to a number of "middle-level" theories which are either formally deduced from, or at least inspired and strongly informed by, the core evolutionary theory at the higher level. Buss (1995) notes three of the most influential middle-level theories in his theory, and I have more to say about each of these in subsequent chapters. In many cases these middle-level theories may compete as explanations for a given phenomenon. These middle-level theories in turn provide the foundation for developing more specific hypotheses about the kinds of observations that ought to hold true if the theory is correct. Finally, empirically testable predictions about expected observations are derived from these hypotheses. A few specific examples are provided in the figure as illustrations.

Empirical research can only be conducted to test the lowest-level predictions; everything else is based on the theory above. If the prediction fails to hold, the hypothesis from which it is derived must be questioned, and either discarded or (more likely) revised. The middle-level theories (such as attachment) are insulated by this level of hypothesis, but if these hypotheses consistently break down, one would have to begin questioning, for example, attachment theory as a whole. The scientific value of the entire enterprise hinges on the progress of the research program as a whole, and does not rise or fall on any particular empirical finding. So yes, evolutionary-psychological theory is empirically testable, but not as a whole. What are testable are the specific hypotheses derived from it.

As a second answer, I would like to suggest a more intuitive way of saying much the same thing: Evolutionary-psychological theories are empirically testable in very much the same way other theories in psychology are. It is true that we cannot go back in time and directly observe the evolution of the attachment system through prehistory, but it is equally true that we cannot directly observe the *hypothetical constructs* of which all psychological theories are built. Psychologists routinely test theories about postulated mechanisms, traits, and other unobservable entities hypothesized to reside in people's heads (at least since radical behaviorism was rejected). The logic of evolutionary-psychology research is no different from any other in the main: You start with a theory, derive hypotheses and ultimately testable predictions, and then collect data to see whether the predictions pan out. Of course, confirming an evolutionary-psychological prediction in this way does not prove the evolutionary hypothesis—or theory, or metatheory—to be true; there are always alternative hypotheses (from both within and outside evolutionary theory) that must be ruled out. But this is true for all theories, whatever their origin. The only real difference between evolutionary-psychological theories and others is that the former derive from a larger hierarchical metatheory.

Third, it is important to note that empirical testing, like theorizing, in evolutionary psychology is inherently multidisciplinary. Many predictions derived from evolutionary psychological hypotheses (and middle-level theories, etc.) can be tested using techniques familiar to research psychologists, from self-report inventories to laboratory experiments. However, the range of sources of data relevant for testing evolutionary theories is much broader than is typical of psychology (or of any specific discipline, for that matter). Evolutionary psychologists draw upon data from evolutionary biology, ethology, anthropology and its various subdisciplines, archeology, paleontology, and other related fields, in addition to the various subdisciplines of psychology. So "empirically testable" need not necessarily mean designing laboratory experiments—though of course this also is true of many psychological research areas in which experimentation plays a more limited role, as in the psychology of religion.

In the end, most of us would agree that the crucial question is whether a particular theory (or metatheory) is useful in generating hypotheses that can be subjected to empirical testing. The previous chapters have illustrated how attachment theory provided a useful theoretical framework for guiding empirical research on religion, and in subsequent chapters I show that the same is true with respect to the application of several other evolutionary-psychological theories to religion as well.

SOME ILLUSTRATIVE EXAMPLES: POLITICS, MUSIC, AND SPORTS

The "Standard Social Science Model" depicted by Tooby and Cosmides (1992) was intended to reflect the general paradigmatic framework predominant across most if not all of the social sciences today. The psychology of religion is no exception. For example, in their excellent encyclopedic textbook on psychology of religion, Hood et al. (1996) begin their second chapter with a subsection title posing the question "Is religion in our genes?," to which their reply is:

> Although the "theory of instincts" that was so popular in the 20th century subsequently lost favor, especially in light of the growing dominance of behaviorism in North American psychology, the idea of a "religious instinct" did not go away. Many behavioral scientists would be

skeptical of this notion, just as they would be suspicious of a claim that we humans are "naturally" inclined to like (or dislike) heavy metal music, or that we have a genetic destiny to be political or to be sports fans. Rather, social scientists would, on the basis of much evidence, point out that our love (or hate) of heavy metal music, and our inclinations toward politics and sports, come more from our socialization experience than from the DNA we have inherited from our parents. (p. 44)

This quotation summarizes fairly well, I believe, the way many psychologists—including most psychologists of religion—would approach religion and many related topics. It therefore provides a convenient example for illustrating some of the general issues discussed in this chapter, as well as many common misconceptions about evolutionary psychology, to begin to set the stage for the evolutionary psychology of religion I propose in this book.

So, how would an evolutionary psychologist respond to these comments? First, an evolutionary psychologist would surely agree that humans do not have genes "for" heavy metal music or politics or sports fandom. Restated, more precisely, human evolved psychology does not contain psychological mechanisms designed by natural selection specifically to produce the behavior of attending AC/DC concerts, or running for Congress, or watching basketball on TV. The same is true with respect to religion, as I argue in Chapter 9. But this does not at all mean that an understanding of the evolved psychological architecture is irrelevant. Recall Pinker's (1997) cheesecake metaphor: No one would argue that our genes code for mechanisms specialized for eating or baking cheesecake, yet an evolutionary perspective is indispensable for understanding its popularity.

At the same time, one is confronted with some interesting observations that require explanation: Why are music, sports, and politics, at least if broadly defined, observable in all known human cultures? Heavy-metal music is not universal, of course, but music in some form *is* universal. So too are competitive games (and the observation of them by others), as well as the struggle for power and dominance within and between social groups. The particular details vary across time and across cultures, but something about "human nature" evidently causes these phenomena to appear in one form or another in all societies. An evolutionary perspective provides a framework for understanding the cross-cultural universality lying beneath the superficial variability.

For example, "political" suggests such general themes as individuals striving for status, dominance, and power (i.e., negotiating status and dominance hierarchies); the construction and maintenance of coalitions and alliances; and the negotiation of conflictual relations between individuals and groups. The exact form taken by these processes varies widely across cultures and even individuals, but they are evident in some form in all cultures. Indeed, similar themes are clearly evident in chimpanzee societies: A book by one of the world's foremost experts on chimpanzee behavior is titled *Chimpanzee Politics* for this reason (de Waal, 1982). There is a very real sense in which politics *are* in the DNA we have inherited from our parents, and an evolutionary perspective is required to understand why and how.

Two other points are raised by the question about heavy-metal music. First, note that the issue raised in the quoted passage is not about universality but rather *individual differences*: Why do some people love it and others hate it? As discussed earlier in this chapter, this question presents a fundamentally different kind of problem than questions about the universality of the psychological mechanisms that give rise to them. It is of course unlikely that people have specific genes "for" liking (or hating) heavy metal music but, as with individual differences in attachment, there are many ways in which an evolutionary perspective provides an organizing framework for understanding individual differences.

Second, heavy-metal music (as well as sports) illustrates a complex modern phenomenon for which an evolutionary explanation is likely to involve *multiple* mechanisms corresponding to qualitatively different aspects of the phenomenon. For example, there is a strong *coalitional* component to most fads: Fans of heavy-metal music (and other popular movements) often dress a certain way, advertise their favorite bands on teeshirts and bumper stickers, and organize social networks around the music and the performers. The musicians themselves, along with other members of their inner circle, often parlay their high status into money and the sexual interest of "groupies"; there is a strong component of *status-striving* and *mating competition* involved. The actual enjoying-the-music part is only one part of the phenomenon, and perhaps a relatively unimportant one with respect to understanding many aspects of the heavy-metal world. My evolutionary-psychological theory of religion will have much in common with this example.

Finally, a proper understanding of these various phenomena in terms of the psychological mechanisms underlying them has considerable promise for developing more detailed hypotheses about what to expect in these behavioral domains. Psychological mechanisms involved in political behavior—for example, those related to status competition, reciprocal altruism, and coalitional psychology—represent sets of inferential rules that individuals use in thinking about and producing such behavior. If we understand the rules by which these mechanisms operate, we will be in a better position to predict such behavior.

In short, behaviors and inclinations that seem clearly to be "socialized" or "learned" at one level of analysis can be seen as founded on an evolved psychological architecture that enables and shapes these phenomena. Evolutionary psychology offers the theoretical framework for addressing these questions, with the potential for constructing a fully integrated model of nature (evolved psychological architecture) and nurture (specific details acquired via instruction, individual learning, and socialization). For these reasons, I believe it has the potential to be a powerful organizing framework for the psychology of religion, as I hope the coming chapters demonstrate.

SUMMARY AND CONCLUSIONS

I began Chapter 2 with the claim that Bowlby was perhaps the first truly modern evolutionary psychologist, and we are now in a position to examine that claim in a bit more detail. Drawing upon ethology and control systems theory, Bowlby conceptualized the attachment system as a functionally organized suite of evolved psychological mechanisms, designed by natural selection as a solution to a recurrent adaptive problem. To reiterate, here are some of the major tenets of attachment theory recast in more explicitly evolutionary-psychological terminology:

1. The attachment system evolved via natural selection for the ultimate adaptive function of providing protection to helpless infants, by way of maintaining proximity between infants and their caregivers.
2. Humans share the basic design of this system with other species, particularly our closest primate relatives. Other species have solved related adaptive problems in different ways, as in the imprinting system in goslings.

3. The attachment system is a domain-specific system that is designed to operate in the context of only certain kinds of relationships; other social relationships, such as those defined by roles, involve other functionally distinct evolved systems.

4. The attachment system operates as an information-processing system that attends to highly specific input from the external environment (e.g., caregiver's whereabouts, cues to danger) and internal environment (e.g., current health status, fear system, memories of previous attachment-relevant experience); processes this input according to a specific set of rules, and produces behavioral or psychological output (e.g., attachment behaviors, or activation of the exploration system) accordingly.

So where does attachment theory fit in the evolutionary-psychological scheme of things? Referring to the hierarchical outline of theories provided by Buss (1995), as reproduced in Figure 7.1, Simpson (1999) places attachment theory within the set of middle-level theories in the second level of the diagram—alongside the theories of reciprocal altruism, parental investment, and parent–offspring conflict. I am not inclined to argue with him. This makes somewhat more concrete my suggestion that attachment theory fits squarely within evolutionary psychology.

In the remainder of this book, I propose to adopt the evolutionary-psychological metatheory described in this chapter as a general conceptual framework for organizing the psychology of religion. The attachment system, which can now be seen as just one of many systems that make up our evolved psychological architecture, is just one of many such systems that shapes and guides religious thought and behavior. To understand the many aspects of religion that are not addressed by attachment theory, we will look to other evolved psychological systems with different adaptive functions. But first, let us take one more look at attachment theory from the perspective of contemporary evolutionary psychology, and examine the implications of this view for the theory of attachment and religion.

CHAPTER EIGHT

Attachment Theory in Modern Evolutionary Perspective

Bowlby's conceptualization of attachment as a control system, his account of its evolutionary origins, his use of cross-species comparative data, and many other aspects of his thinking look as if the theory were constructed by an evolutionary psychologist several decades later. I hope my review of contemporary evolutionary psychology in the preceding chapter has made clear the grounds for this claim.

One of Bowlby's goals in developing attachment theory, as noted in Chapter 1, was to modernize then-current theory—in particular, psychoanalytic theory—in light of scientific developments in related fields such as ethology. Given that he developed attachment theory well before the publication of several important developments in evolutionary biology, it should come as no surprise that attachment theory itself now requires some rethinking. In an excellent chapter that I recommend highly, Simpson (1999) has reviewed a variety of issues that, in light of these theoretical advances, were poorly understood by Bowlby. Application of these newer ideas has led to a variety of modifications and extensions of attachment theory over the last decade. In this chapter I review some of these, and then examine implications of these revised views for the theory of attachment and religion presented in the first half of this book.

CHILDHOOD ATTACHMENT IN MODERN EVOLUTIONARY PERSPECTIVE

Despite three decades of research, Bowlby's basic outline of the operation and function of the attachment system in infancy remains almost entirely intact. The principal patterns of individual differences documented in infants and young children, and the patterns of parental caregiving thought to be partly responsible for them, remain essentially unchanged. However, evolutionary theory has led some researchers to reconceptualize the *nature* of these individual differences to some extent, with respect to the questions of exactly *why* and *how* the evolved design of the attachment system produces them. This reconceptualization does not fundamentally change my theory of attachment and religion in any way, but is important to understand it before moving on to other developments, discussed subsequently, that do lead to some new potential applications of attachment theory to religion.

Parental Caregiving and Parent–Offspring Conflict

Attachment tends to bring to mind idyllic images of infants nursing contentedly, mother and infant gazing lovingly into one another's eyes, and of mothers rushing to their infants' side in response to calls of distress. To many if not most attachment theorists, including Bowlby, this is the way the attachment and maternal caregiving systems were designed to operate. From this widely held perspective, secure attachment represents the *normative* operation of the attachment system, with caregivers reliably responding to infant attachment behaviors, effectively regulating their infants' levels of felt anxiety, and providing the functions of a haven of safety and a secure base. Insecure patterns of attachment, in this view, represent something gone awry: unfortunate imperfections or even pathologies.

Unfortunately, a modern evolutionary view throws a wet blanket over this happy portrait, in two major ways. First, as summarized concisely by Chisolm (1996), "It is increasingly appreciated that the EEA [environment of evolutionary adaptedness] was neither as uniform nor as benign as Bowlby seems to have imagined" (p. 14). At least as much as is true today, parents in ancestral environments would have faced many different (and variable) challenges to successful child rearing, including "unpredictable food supplies, vagaries of climate and weather, diseases, parasites, predators, and, perhaps most important, other conspecifics such as one's parents" (Buss & Greiling, 1999, p. 219). If you consider how difficult parenting is in modern industrialized societies today—aided by such "luxuries" as internal plumbing, central heating, grocery stores, the absence of lions and hyenas, and the availability (in a pinch) of government assistance—it defies the imagination that it could have been any easier 100,000 years ago on the savannah. Despite their best efforts, ancestral parents no doubt struggled to provide for their children in the way they might have desired; many surely did not succeed.

Perhaps more important, however, a modern evolutionary perspective casts serious doubt on the assumption that even given the ability to provide quality caregiving, ancestral parents would have been uniformly *motivated* or willing to do so. It is easy to fall into the trap of thinking about mother–infant bonds as a perfect symbiosis in which the interests of mother and infant are isomorphic, and to therefore assume that mothers have evolved to be single-minded baby-producing/child care machines (Hrdy, 1999). Even (or particularly) from an evolutionary perspective, isn't it obvious that a parent's first priority should be his or her offspring—the primary vehicle for inclusive fitness? What else could possibly be more important?

Subsequent to the publication of Bowlby's early work, Trivers (1974) provided a rather sobering answer to these questions in his theory of parent–offspring conflict—one of the other middle-level evolutionary theories illustrated in Figure 7.1. In fact, there are potentially many things more important to a parent, from an inclusive-fitness perspective, than investing heavily in a given infant. The simple biological fact is that offspring and parents do not have identical interests, because they do not have identical genes. On average, offspring carry only half of a given parent's genes, rendering them only imperfect gene-replication vehicles for parents. From the parent's perspective, investment in any one offspring diverts energy and resources from the production of additional offspring, as well as investment in other existing or future offspring (not to mention other collateral kin). Consequently, parental provisioning mechanisms should be designed in a way that allocates resources most efficiently between reproduction and caregiving, on the one hand, and caregiving across multiple offspring on the other. Trivers made clear how these discrepant interests of infant and mother lead to a variety of predictable conflicts, including sibling rivalry (i.e., with respect to obtaining parental resources for oneself vis-à-vis siblings) and conflict over the timing of weaning (with mothers trying to wean as early as possible, and infants trying to delay weaning as long as possible).

Moreover, any given infant is a useful gene-replication vehicle (from the parent's perspective) only if it survives to reproductive age in a sufficiently healthy state to mate and reproduce. Offspring consequently vary in their *reproductive value* as a function of numerous factors that are predictive of the likelihood of this happening, including the physical condition of the infant; the mother's health, age, and resources; the availability, willingness, and ability of a father to contribute resources; the presence and ages of other offspring; and various ecological conditions that influence the costs and benefits of parental caregiving at a given point in time (Daly & Wilson, 1987; Trivers, 1974). It is therefore a highly dubious assumption that parents are (or ancestral parents were) universally motivated to provide maximal quality parental care to their offspring. Instead they display *discriminative parental solicitude* (Daly & Wilson, 1987), varying the quality of care they provide as a function of the factors noted earlier (see Belsky, 1999, and Simpson, 1999, for reviews). The extreme case is infanticide: It is not at all uncommon in the animal world for certain offspring to be killed or entirely neglected by mothers, or for mothers (as in many bird species) to turn a blind eye while older siblings or other adults do the dirty work. Even in humans infanticide is far more common than is typically acknowledged, and its practice is largely predicable from these same kinds of factors (see Daly & Wilson, 1988).

Consideration of the role of fathers introduces yet additional complications. High levels of *paternal* investment are actually extremely rare among mammals, including nonhuman primates. The reasons for this are clear from an evolutionary perspective, including (1) the problem of *paternity certainty* and the enormous inclusive-fitness costs incurred by a male who invests heavily in genetically unrelated offspring (particularly if this further precludes additional mating opportunities), and (2) the inclusive-fitness advantages for males of pursuing polygynous mating strategies when possible. In many preliterate cultures, in fact, fathers typically have very little role in the raising of children (Draper & Harpending, 1988). Other complications arise with respect to stepfathers: Being genetically unrelated to stepchildren, stepparents are far less likely to provide quality caregiving, and in fact represent the single greatest risk factor for child abuse and infanticide in the modern world (Daly & Wilson, 1998). The quality and/or quantity of caregiving received by infants from male caregivers must have been (and continues to be) even more variable than that received from mothers.

Individual Differences in Childhood Attachment

To the extent that the quality and nature of parental investment was highly variable in ancestral environments, we would expect natural selection to have designed the attachment system accordingly. This observation has led many theorists to question Bowlby's assumption that secure attachment represents the *normative* pattern, and insecure attachment a pathological or maladaptive deviation from this pattern. In Hinde's (1982) words, "We must be concerned not with normal mothers and deviant mothers but with a range of styles and a capacity to select appropriately between them. . . . *Natural selection must surely have operated to produce conditional maternal strategies, not stereotypy*" (p. 71, emphasis in original). Instead, numerous researchers have concluded, as summarized by Simpson (1999), that "each attachment pattern reflects a different ecologically contingent strategy designed to solve adaptive problems posed by different rearing environments" (p. 125). (For related arguments, see Belsky, 1999, and Lamb, Thompson, Gardner, & Charnov, 1985).

Chisolm (1996) offered the first attempt to explain the functions of each of the three primary childhood attachment patterns as evolved *facultative strategies*. Anxious/ambivalent attachment, he argued, is an adaptive response to parental *inability* to provide quality caregiving, whereas avoidant attachment is an adaptive response to parental *unwillingness* to do so. In effect, anxious attachment behavior reflects a strategy of fighting for more attention and encouraging greater parental effort, which might be just what is needed by a child of parents with deficient caregiving skills resulting from inexperience or stress. Such efforts would be lost on unwilling or uninterested parents. In this case the more adaptive strategy is to become independent as quickly as possible and minimize reliance on the attachment figure.[1]

ATTACHMENT AND REPRODUCTIVE STRATEGIES

A second new perspective brought by evolutionary thinking is the suggestion by several theorists that infant attachment styles not only reflect alternative strategies for coping with variability in parental caregiving, but in addition are related in important ways to subsequent adult *mating* and *reproductive strategies*. In the previous chapter I introduced the distinction between short-term and long-term mating strategies as facultative adaptations. Like the alternative childhood attachment patterns just discussed, both strategies are believed to be part of the human behavioral repertoire, because (in part) their relative adaptive value varies depending on a variety of ecological conditions.

Draper and Harpending (1982) were the first to argue for such a link, noting that the pair-bond status of the mother provides a potential cue to young children as to the kind of mating strategy that is normative in their environment. That is, the absence of a father is statistically predictive of whether long-term or short-term mating is the local norm. Draper and Harpending draw upon diverse lines of evidence suggesting that children raised in father-absent versus father-present homes differ, in puberty and adolescence, in ways consistent with the pursuit of short-term versus long-term reproductive strategies. For example, adolescent boys from father-absent homes tend to show, relative to father-present adolescents, more antagonistic attitudes toward femininity and toward women, exaggerated masculinity, and a "relatively exploitative attitude toward females, with sexual contact appearing important as conquest and as a means of validating masculinity" (Draper & Harpending, 1982, p. 257). Father-absent girls tend to show "precocious sexual interest, derogation of masculinity and males, and poor ability to maintain sexual and emotional adjustment with one male" (p. 258). Other studies show that girls from divorced households—that is, in which the biological father is absent—reach puberty earlier than those from intact households, and that children of divorce tend to marry earlier, have children sooner, and end their marriages more readily (Ellis & Garber, 2000; Ellis, McFadyen-Ketchum, Dodge, Pettit, & Bates, 1999; see Draper & Belsky, 1990, and Belsky, Steinberg, & Draper, 1991, for more extensive reviews).[2]

Other researchers have since buttressed the argument for linking early home environments with adult reproductive strategies based upon *life history theory* (Stearns, 1992). According to this theory, a species' behavioral repertoire across the lifespan is organized around the central question of how to allocate a finite amount of total resources across solutions to the basic adaptive problems of growth and development, mating and reproduction, and investment in offspring. In human infancy and childhood, for example, there are necessary trade-offs between the conflicting goals of growth and development, on the one hand, and survival on the other. Chisolm (1996) argues that in attachment theory terms, these trade-offs are reflected in the oscillation between using the attachment figure as a haven of safety (survival) and as a secure base for exploration (growth and development).

One way to flood future generations with genes is to reproduce "early and often." Humans and other long-lived creatures (particularly mammals), in contrast, devote much of the lifespan to growth and development, delaying reproduction to a late age and then investing heavily in offspring. In evolutionary biology language, *K-selected* organisms (such as humans) are characterized by lower fertility, delayed maturation, longer lifespan, and high levels of parental investment, whereas *r-selected* species show the reverse pattern (Pianka, 1970). Which strategy is more adaptive for a given species hinges on a variety of ecological factors, including predation rates, as in my earlier example. You can put all your eggs in one basket (almost literally) if the basket is safe, but you need lots of eggs in lots of baskets in a dangerous, unstable environment.

Although the r- versus K-selection distinction developed in relation to cross-species comparisons, variability along a similar dimension is evident *within* some species as well. This is the case particularly in reference to facultative strategies, as different alternatives may reflect different relative allocations of energy and resources across different life tasks. The distinction between long-term and short-term mating strategies, as discussed in the previous chapter, provides an important example. One way to describe the difference between these is in terms of the relative apportionment of effort and resources to mating. Differences among facultative attachment patterns can also be interpreted in this way. According to Chisolm (1996), *avoidant* attachment in childhood involves reducing investment in growth and development and shifting it toward (early) mating effort. If quality parental assistance is not forthcoming, a better life strategy is to grow up quickly and get on to the next job.

The value of life history theory is that it provides a higher-level view of organisms as organized combinations of adaptations, taking into account the relations and various trade-offs between them. Although it is easier to think about the adaptive value of particular mechanisms or systems in isolation, adaptations in fact must co-evolve in a coordinated manner over an organism's evolutionary history. A new system variation cannot evolve if it undermines the adaptive value of others, unless coordinated changes in the other system occur at the same time. Consequently, particular strategies for solving different categories of problems tend to fit together into coherent packages, or "life history strategies." In a small-prey species such as mice or shrimp, for example, it would be pointless to invest in a long period of growth and development because most individuals would become a meal before having the opportunity to reproduce; such species allocate their effort toward mating and reproduction (and lots of it).

The Belsky, Steinberg, and Draper Model

Inspired by life history theory and the work of Draper and Harpending (1982, 1988), Belsky et al. (1991) proposed a lifespan developmental model designed to tie together the evolved systems of attachment, parental caregiving, and mating. They distinguished two broad life history strategies in humans roughly parallel to the r- versus K-selection distinction noted earlier: a *quantity* strategy, which in effect amounts to "reproduce early and often," and a *quality* strategy, which involves delaying reproduction (until more experienced and more able to care for offspring), having fewer offspring, and investing heavily in those offspring (the "all your eggs in one basket" strategy). The latter links together the traditional "normative" story with respect to the three systems: high-quality parental *caregiving* (including father presence vs. father absence) leads to secure infant/childhood *attachment*, which is associated with long-term *mating* and subsequently high parental investment in one's own offspring. Conversely, experience of low quality or low quantity caregiving leads to insecure attachment, which in turn leads to short-term mating and low parental investment in one's own offspring. Life history theory provides the rationale for why the pieces fit together in this way.

Belsky et al.'s (1991) general outline of the model is reproduced in Figure 8.1. At the top, quality and quantity of parental care are influenced by a combination of ecological and personological factors. In keeping with the traditional attachment model as discussed in previous chapters, children respond to these parental caregiving patterns with conditional patterns of attachment behavior, and by developing IWMs reflecting the reliability and availability of attachment figures, the degree to which the environment is benign versus dangerous, whether people are trustworthy relationship partners or not, and so forth. There is no shortage of empirical research to support these two links in the model (see Belsky et al., 1991, for a review).

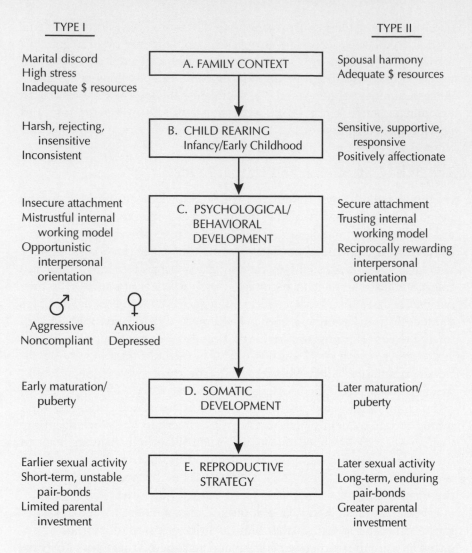

FIGURE 8.1. Developmental pathways of divergent reproductive strategies. From Belsky, Steinberg, and Draper (1991). Copyright 1991 by the Society for Research in Child Development. Reprinted by permission.

Next, in the most controversial aspect of the model, early attachment experience plays the pivotal role of triggering one or the other of these alternative developmental trajectories, tracking individuals toward one or the other of these strategies in adulthood. Proximally, early attachment patterns directly influence the rate of biological maturation or somatic development, causing children exposed to low-quality and low-quantity parenting to mature faster and reach puberty (i.e., reproductive age) earlier than others. (If this seems implausible, recall the reef-living fishes that change biological sex in response to changes in the local social ecology.) In keeping with the earlier discussion, suboptimal caregiving is likely to be a reflection of either very difficult ecological conditions that prevent parents from investing heavily, or a lack of motivation on the part of parents to do so—perhaps as a function of the parents' own (short-term) reproductive strategies. For example, poor maternal care may be a function of the mother allocating effort toward obtaining mates rather than toward parental investment, and the absence of a father suggests that paternal care is not normative in the present environment. As summarized by Belsky (1999): "By maturing earlier, individuals whose experiences had unconsciously informed them (1) that resources (including, if not especially, parental care and attention) were scarce and/or unpredictable, (2) that others could not be trusted, and (3) that relationships were not enduring would have been in a position to pursue a quantity-versus-quality reproductive strategy" (p. 149). In short, parental caregiving provides a cue as to whether the environment is one in which a quality or quantity reproductive strategy is the way to go. If the latter, the adaptive facultative response is to mature quickly, shifting one's resources away from continued growth and development and toward early mating. Although the empirical evidence for this link in the Belsky et al. model was a bit scant (though strongly suggestive) at the time of its publication, more recent longitudinal research has clearly supported the hypothesis that quality of early family relationships and father absence are predictive of differences in pubertal timing in girls (Ellis & Garber, 2000; Ellis et al., 1999).[2]

In the next phase of the model, these biological changes in maturation influence psychological and social development in a variety of ways consistent with the quantity or quality reproductive-strategy track. Considerable evidence exists linking pubertal timing to a variety of reproductively relevant behaviors, including the age at which sexual activity begins, the amount of sexual activity, quality of opposite-sex relationships and attitudes about the opposite sex, and so forth (see

Belsky et al., 1991, or Simpson, 1999, for reviews and references). In addition it is worth noting here for our purposes (although it is not central to the Belsky et al. model) that a wide range of other effects of poor-quality parenting have been observed in adolescence and early adulthood, ranging from drug and alcohol use to delinquency and criminality. Again drawing upon a broad life history perspective, it is evident that the entire constellation of effects fits together into a general "strategy" that emphasizes short-term outcomes over long-term outcomes. To the extent that poor parenting is the result of difficult environmental conditions, living in a manner that would maximize long-term outcomes is not a good bet: The odds are against living long enough to reap the rewards.

Finally, this adult reproductive-strategy orientation influences the parental style that the individual will adopt him- or herself, and thus the quality/quantity of sensitive care that he or she will be disposed to provide for offspring, beginning the cycle anew. In particular, Chisolm's (1996) later expansion of the model introduced the distinction (noted earlier) between parental willingness versus ability to invest. As Chisolm argued, reduced willingness is associated with the quantity strategy and short-term mating, and is associated with the "cold and rejecting" parenting style associated with avoidant childhood attachment—consistent with the Belsky et al. model. In turn, these differences in parenting influence one's own children's attachment patterns, consistent with the long-standing observation noted in Chapter 2 concerning the *intergenerational transmission* of attachment patterns.

Individual Differences in Adult Attachment

This developmental model of attachment and reproductive strategies provides an alternative lens through which to view some of the principal elements of traditional attachment theory and the nature of individual differences across the lifespan. At the same time, however, the perspectives are by no means mutually contradictory, and in many ways fit together rather well.

First, the reproductive-strategies model offers a new perspective on the relationship between parental *caregiving*, on the one hand, and childhood *attachment* on the other. According to the traditional view, it is mainly continuity in IWMs across the lifespan that accounts for this relationship; in the recent evolutionary view, it is because early attachment experience initiates facultative strategies that translate into, among other things, different parenting orientations in adulthood. However, these are by no means mutually inconsistent. If, as in the evolutionary account, parenting effort is part of a facultative strategy that shifts resource allocation toward mating effort and away from parenting effort, parents' "states of mind" or IWMs with respect to attachment might be expected to reflect this orientation. The reproductive-strategies approach does not discount the traditional descriptive model of how individual differences in childhood attachment and adult caregiving are interrelated; rather, it provides a deeper explanation as to why and how these systems are linked.

Second, the reproductive-strategies model offers a new perspective on the empirical relationship between childhood attachment and adult romantic attachment styles. Again, the traditional account attributes continuity of attachment across the lifespan to the continuity of IWMs of others as trustworthy and reliable (or not), and of committed interpersonal relationships as desirable and worth seeking (or undesirable and better avoided). This is entirely consistent with the Belsky et al. (1991) and Chisolm (1996) perspective, with IWMs reflecting the cognitive side of the process and/or mediating the process. And again, the reproductive-strategies model offers a distal explanation for these proximate empirical relationships, explaining why particular IWMs of parents in childhood should correspond to particular IWMs of romantic partners in adulthood.

Finally, the reproductive-strategies approach offers a new perspective on the nature of individual differences in adult romantic attachment styles. From this vantage point, such individual differences may be reflections, at least in part, of different reproductive or mating strategies. I have reviewed elsewhere a variety of research findings consistent with the notion that the secure adult attachment style(s) may largely reflect a long-term mating orientation and the avoidant style(s) a short-term mating orientation (Kirkpatrick, 1998a; see also Belsky, 1999, for a related discussion[3]). For example, recall that avoidant adults say they "do not fall in love easily," and in fact do not even believe in romantic love (Hazan & Shaver, 1987). Their mental models in general reflect a distaste for long-term committed relationships. Avoidant adults are less likely to be in a committed romantic relationship at a given point in time (Hazan & Shaver, 1987; Kirkpatrick & Hazan, 1994; Senchak & Leonard, 1992), and secure adults tend to have longer-lasting romantic relationships than other attachment groups (e.g., Kirkpatrick & Davis, 1994; Kirkpatrick & Hazan, 1994). Also consistent with a short-term mating orientation, avoidant adults report more accepting attitudes toward casual sex, having more sexual partners, and engaging in more one-night stands than the other groups (Brennan & Shaver, 1995; J. Feeney, Noller, & Patty, 1993; Hazan, Zeifman, & Middleton, 1994; Miller & Fishkin, 1997).

When viewed from Bartholomew's 2 x 2 perspective, it is the IWMs of *others*—that is, *secure* and *preoccupied* versus the two avoidant groups (*dismissing* and *fearful*)—that seem to most closely represent this dimension. The interpretation of the models-of-self dimension remains relatively unchanged from this revised perspective—though perhaps with a somewhat more specific emphasis on a specific dimension of self-esteem, namely, self-assessed *mate value*, as the crucial dimension.[4] That is, the fear of being abandoned by a mate, of not being loved by a partner, and so forth, should be related specifically the degree to which one perceives oneself as attractive to the opposite sex and one's value as a potential mate. There are good reasons to expect that our evolved psychological architecture might well contain a self-assessment mechanism specific to mate value (Kirkpatrick & Ellis, 2001).

These ideas linking individual differences in attachment with reproductive strategies have a number of interesting potential applications to the psychology of religion, which I will discuss toward the end of this chapter. Before doing so, however, it is important to consider a second recent development in attachment theory from an evolutionary perspective.

LOVE REVISITED

Although there is little doubt about the *adaptive function* of attachment in infancy and childhood, the function of the system in adulthood has been the subject of much debate. It is easy to see how the attachment system contributes to survival in infants and young children, but what are the benefits, in evolutionary currency, of attachment in adulthood? Some researchers have suggested that the nature and function of the system remains unchanged; that is, the function remains the provision of security, comfort, and protection (e.g., West & Sheldon-Keller, 1994). There is ample evidence that this remains true at least to some extent, but at the same time there are a number of evolutionary reasons that mitigate against the attachment system operating in exactly the same way in adult relationships. For example, because romantic partners are not genetic relatives, they cannot be counted upon to the same degree as mothers to behave altruistically. In addition, one's adult romantic partner, unlike one's mother, is not necessarily any more capable than oneself of providing protection and assistance with respect to adult-sized problems (see Kirkpatrick, 1998a, for additional arguments and discussion).

In contrast, Zeifman and Hazan (1997) suggest that the function of attachment in adulthood is qualitatively different from that in childhood. In adulthood, they argue, attachment is the "tie that binds" adult romantic partners together. Others have come to this same conclusion for other reasons—for example, Berman, Marcus, and Berman (1994) suggest that the function of adult attachment is "preservation of the dyadic family unit"—but Zeifman and Hazan (1997) were the first to make the argument in evolutionary terms.[5] Given the many adaptive benefits of (relatively) long-term pair-bonding and biparental investment for humans, at least under some conditions, the problem for natural selection was to "figure out" how to ensure that pair-bonds remained together sufficiently long to raise offspring at least beyond the first few dangerous years of life. Making use of the biological and psychological machinery already available in the human design, natural selection co-opted the attachment system—a suite of evolved mechanisms already well designed for the purpose of producing powerful emotional bonds, motivating commitment to a relationship, and maintaining proximity between two individuals—and reassigned the system the new function in adulthood. This process of *exaptation* (Gould, 1991), in which an adaptation for one function is later co-opted and further evolved for use in solving a different adaptive problem, is a common evolutionary process.

Love or Attachment?

Zeifman and Hazan (1997; Hazan & Zeifman, 1999) draw upon an impressive array of diverse evidence in building their case for similarities between infant–mother attachment and adult pair-bonding. For example, they note similarities between the relationship types with respect to emotional and behavioral dynamics (e.g., responses to separation; secure base and haven of safety functions), selection criteria (qualities valued in a partner), specific behaviors that tend to be restricted to only these kinds of relationships (e.g., cuddling, kissing, and other forms of intimate contact), and biological and neurochemical substrates including the roles of oxytocin, particular neurotransmitter systems, and specific brain systems. The evidence is compelling. However, I offer, as a friendly amendment, a revised conceptualization of the model that I believe resolves some troublesome problems. Specifically, it is advantageous to view the Zeifman–Hazan model as a theory of *love*, rather than of *attachment*. At the end of this chapter I show how this revised model offers a variety of interesting insights to the theory of attachment and religion.

First, it seems unlikely to me that a complex system such as the attachment system, comprising numerous mechanisms and organized around the adaptive problem of security and protection, could be co-opted for the radically different purpose of maintaining adult pair-bonds. What makes the attachment system a *system* is its organization around the solution to a particular adaptive problem, as reflected in the particular inputs that activate it, the particular behavioral and cognitive outputs it generates, and the decision rules by which it computes the latter from the former. All of this would require radical restructuring to solve the qualitatively different adaptive problem of cementing pair-bonds. For example, a system designed to provide protection and security should be activated, like the attachment system in childhood, by cues of impending danger, but a system designed to cement pair-bonds should be activated by very different kinds of threats, such as cues of infidelity. As I argued previously (Kirkpatrick, 1998), one cannot simply co-opt a radio to perform the functions of a television set: The complex interconnections among the parts are designed to receive radio waves and transduce them into sound, and cannot as a unit suddenly begin receiving television broadcasts and presenting them in a visual display.

However, to continue this metaphor, if one started with a radio and wanted to build a television, one might well utilize some of the radio's important components rather than starting from scratch. Some of the necessary parts might be the same, but some entirely new parts would need to be added, some old parts discarded, and the entire system reorganized. The emotion of love—characterized by the developmental and biological processes detailed by Zeifman and Hazan (1997)—could thus be conceptualized as one such mechanism or component. Much as certain kinds of circuits or transistors might be utilized in both radios and televisions, the love mechanism might be used by both the attachment system and the adult pair-bond system.

Second, the Zeifman–Hazan model fails to come completely to grips with the issue of variable, alternative reproductive strategies in human mating. As summarized by Buss and Greiling (1999), "A clear implication of the Zeifman-Hazan theory is that individual differences, and particularly deviations from secure attachment, represent maladaptations rather than alternative adaptive strategies" (p. 217). Although Zeifman and Hazan do explicitly acknowledge the existence and adaptive value of short-term strategies, it is not entirely clear how such strategies are to be conceptualized vis-à-vis their model other than as aberrations.

The revised version of their model I wish to offer, however, accommodates this issue more clearly and provides a theoretical link between their model of pair-bond development, on the one hand, and the reproductive-strategies literature discussed previously. If the system described by Zeifman and Hazan is viewed as a distinct love mechanism rather than the attachment system per se, individual differences in adult attachment styles and reproductive strategies can be conceptualized in terms of the *calibration* of this love mechanism. That is, one way that exposure to poor-quality caregiving might accomplish the task of "switching on" the quantity/short-term mating strategy is by calibrating the love mechanism so that it is very difficult to activate. In the adult attachment literature, such calibration may underlie the *avoidant* attachment style. In contrast, so-called *anxious* (or *preoccupied*) attachment may reflect a calibration of the love mechanism that renders it very readily activated. The kinds of findings I described previously, in the context of arguing that individual differences in adult attachment in part reflect differences in reproductive strategies, are consistent with this interpretation. For example, the observation (Hazan & Shaver, 1987) that avoidant adults do not fall in love easily (and do not even believe in the concept), but that anxious adults do, supports the love-mechanism idea quite directly.

Third, many of the resemblances between infant attachments and adult pair-bonds reviewed by Zeifman and Hazan (1997) appear to be shared by the parental *caregiving* system as well. For example, the kinds of intimate behaviors shared by adult lovers and infant–mother pairs, such as kissing, cuddling, nuzzling, and "baby talk," are also displayed by mothers (in interaction with their infants), whose behavior presumably is organized by the caregiving system rather than the attachment system. Similarly, oxytocin, which is secreted at climax in adult lovers, is secreted in both infants and mothers during nursing.

Thus, Zeifman and Hazan have identified features that are shared by adult lovers, infants, *and* mothers. If these resemblances are used to argue that adult pair-bonding involves the same system as infant attachment, however, I think this forces the conclusion that maternal caregiving involves the same system as well. However, we have already seen that caregiving is better conceptualized as a distinct behavioral system separate from attachment, and I do not think we want to argue that the attachment system has been co-opted for the adult function of maternal caregiving as well as for maintaining adult pair-bonds. Clearly there is *something* shared in all three of these contexts, but I suggest that that something is not the attachment system per se. Rather, what is shared is a *love mechanism*, a psychological–emotional–biological mechanism in its own right that is utilized for roughly the same purpose by the attachment system, the caregiving system, and the long-term mating system. The next question, then, is what this "same purpose" might be.[6]

Love as a Commitment Device

My final reason for preferring this way of thinking is that it fits nicely within a broader theory, proposed by Robert Frank (1988), of social emotions as *commitment devices*. This is a very general model that is useful for thinking about the respective roles of emotions and rationality from an evolutionary perspective. We tend to think of emotions as interfering with rational problem solving, but Frank's view suggests the opposite: In many cases, the cold and calculated solution that seems most attractive in the short run—the one that would be chosen by an entirely rational decision maker—will not be in one's best interests in the long run. For this reason, he argues, natural selection has fashioned various emotions to "commit" us to long-term strategies that are adaptive in the long run.

Suppose someone steals your $200 leather briefcase, and you know who the thief is. If you behave in an entirely rational manner you will be loath to spend hundreds or thousands of dollars, not to mention considerable time and energy, to recover it. Even if you realize that it would be in your long-term interest to prosecute (i.e., to discourage more such behavior in the future), it would be very difficult to convince yourself to do this in light of the short-term costs incurred. Now, if a would-be thief knows all this as well, then what prevents him from stealing your briefcase with impunity? Frank's (1988) answer is that if the thief steals your briefcase you likely will be become *outraged*, and as a consequence you will not hesitate to do whatever is necessary to bring him to justice. This *emotional* response provides a mechanism that effectively commits you to a course of action, namely, exacting revenge, that overwhelms the rational analyses that otherwise would lead you simply to accept the loss. If it is clear to the would-be thief that you are likely to react in this "irrational" manner, it is no longer in his or her best interest to steal the briefcase.[7]

To return to the problem of love, the commitment problem to be solved is that of determining when to end the search for the best available mate. No matter how long one searches and evaluates the mate market in choosing a partner, there is always the possibility of a more attractive alternative coming along later. What is needed is a "commitment device" that kicks in and says, "This one is it—stop looking!" Another analogy offered by Frank in this context is that of landlords and tenants, who are involved in a complex and costly search for the best available tenant and the best available apartment, respectively. At some point each must commit to a choice, or the former will continue to go on with an unrented apartment and the latter will continue to go homeless. In this case it is a lease that serves the role of a commitment device: With the potential benefits of a continued search removed (and/or costs increased), both parties are freed from the process and can get on with their lives. In the same way, a powerful emotional bond forming between two adults serves as a commitment device that frees them from the potentially interminable mate-selection process and permits them to get on with the business of childbearing and child rearing, at least for a sufficiently lengthy period to get the offspring successfully through the dangerous early years of life.

If we think of a love as a distinct evolved mechanism that operates according to Frank's commitment device model, it is easy to see how it operates in other contexts as well. A child's emotional bond to a primary caregiver "commits" him or her to that relationship, perhaps in the face of temptations to turn to other adults and away from parents when, for example, parents are punitive or temporarily uncooperative. It is generally not in a child's best interests to run away from home every time he or she gets angry. Similarly, love would play the same commitment device role in parental caregiving, which presents the commitment problem of investing in offspring despite—as any parent will tell you—many temptations to quit. A strong emotional bond to one's offspring, like a lease, functions to enforce a "decision" to maintain high levels of parental investment in spite of many competing life tasks that also seem important (see Mellen, 1981, for a related discussion). As in adult mating, differential calibration of this mechanism could help to explain variability in caregiving quality, as in the Belsky et al. (1991) model. For example, Rholes et al. (1997) found that avoidant adults (relative to secure and anxious adults) anticipated less satisfaction from caring for young children and expressed less interest in having their own. Failure of this mechanism to be activated by the usual cues could also explain cases in which mothers fail to "bond" with new infants and/or commit infanticide, as discussed earlier in this chapter.

IMPLICATIONS FOR THE THEORY OF ATTACHMENT AND RELIGION

All of this theorizing is of course speculative at this point, and it will be very difficult to design empirical studies to test the ideas directly against more traditional attachment-theoretical explanations in terms of IWMs and so forth. However, suppose for the sake of argument that these recent views are more or less correct. That is:

1. Per the "reproductive-strategies" (RS) hypothesis, the infant attachment system is connected, via evolved design, to adult reproductive strategies such that early experience with primary caregivers—including the presence or absence of a father and quality of care received—switches the developing person onto either a "quality" or "quantity" track. Those on the quality track are oriented toward long-term, committed relationships and high parental investment; those on the quantity track instead tend to seek short-term, uncommitted relationships and engage in a variety of other high-risk behaviors as part of an alternative life history strategy. Individual differences in adult attachment, as assessed by the usual measures, reflect these differences in reproductive strategy rather than (or in at least in addition to) attachment dynamics per se.

2. Per the love mechanism (LM) hypothesis, an evolved "love" mechanism is employed in the design of the attachment system in childhood, the caregiving system in parents, and the adult (long-term) pair-bonding system. According to my revised version of the Zeifman–Hazan model, individual differences in adult attachment reflect, at least in part, the calibration of this love mechanism so that it is very easily activated

(anxious) or very difficult to activate (avoidant) relative to secure individuals.

If all this is true, what are the implications for the theory of attachment and religion that I sketched in the first part of this book? Why, for example, should individual differences in long-term versus short-term mating strategies of adults be related to religious differences? And why should avoidant children be more likely to experience a sudden religious conversion later in life? In this section I suggest some (admittedly speculative) answers to these questions. Conveniently, the RS hypothesis and LM hypothesis map fairly neatly onto the general themes of *correspondence* and *compensation* as discussed previously, thus providing a clear organization for the following discussion.

Correspondence and the Reproductive-Strategies (RS) Hypothesis

In Chapter 5, we saw that mental models of religion and of romantic attachment in adulthood generally evince a pattern of correspondence: In the mainly Christian populations studied to date, avoidant adults tend to be atheists or agnostics, or to see God as distant and inaccessible; secure adults tend to have images of God as loving and feel that they have a personal relationship with God or Jesus. This was explained in terms of IWMs of attachment, particularly with respect to images of romantic partners and images of God.

The RS hypothesis provides a basis for expanding the correspondence hypothesis in several interesting directions. First, note that within Christianity, beliefs about a loving God, having a personal relationship with Jesus, and other related beliefs also tend to be correlated with a host of other religious attitudes and values which fall under the rubric "family values." In many ways the teachings of Christianity (at least most mainstream variants) read like an instruction manual for long-term reproductive strategies: to love and honor one's spouse (in some cases viewing marriage as a holy sacrament), not to lust after (much less yield to temptation with) one's neighbor's spouse, to love and care for one's children, and so forth. Being a "good Christian" in a moral sense is virtually synonymous with being a "good family man" (or woman, of course). From the perspective of the RS hypothesis, the common core shared by these diverse attitudes and values lies in the (evolved) psychology of long-term mating and parental investment. People oriented toward this general life history strategy are likely to find all of these views agreeable and attractive, whereas those oriented toward short-term mating are more likely to find them incompatible with their general worldviews.

To the extent that measured individual differences in romantic attachment styles (in part) reflect variation in reproductive strategies, we would expect to find this entire "syndrome" of family-oriented Christian views to be associated with secure rather than insecure attachment. That is, people with certain kinds of early attachment experience tend as adults both to be oriented toward "quality," long-term reproductive strategies and to agree with, and be attracted to, moral and religious belief systems supportive of such values. In this way the RS hypothesis offers a different, though related, perspective on the empirical findings reviewed previously in support of the correspondence hypothesis.

Moreover, other political and ethical values held by the so-called "Christian right" in American politics are consistent with the same interpretation. Conservative Christians tend to support women staying home to concentrate on raising children rather than going to work; strongly oppose premarital sex (and sex education courses that they fear will encourage it); and strongly oppose abortion on the grounds, in effect, that fetuses deserve parental investment. Frankly, I have long wondered why this particular constellation of beliefs "hangs together," and why opinions on these issues are so forcefully argued and held, until it occurred to me to think of it from this perspective. An interesting direction for future research would be to examine the empirical relationship between individual differences in attachment and these various kinds of sociopolitical attitudes; specifically, it would be interesting to determine whether attachment predicts variability in such attitudes above and beyond what can be predicted from orthodoxy, fundamentalism, and other traditional measures of religiosity.

A more traditional social-scientific explanation for these various links would probably assume a simple socialization model: Christians hold certain combinations of attitudes because their church (and/or their parents, etc.) teaches them. But as discussed in Chapter 5, this simple hypothesis fails to explain, at a deeper level, why exactly such socialization or cultural transmission should be effective, when it clearly is not so in many other contexts. It also fails to explain how these particular kinds of attitudes came to be packaged together in the first place. The RS hypothesis suggests that what ties all these diverse attitudes together is related to long-term reproductive strategies, and that individuals oriented toward such strategies in the domain of mating (due to early attachment experience, etc.) may find belief systems such as Christianity attractive and persuasive as a consequence.

The RS hypothesis also suggests an explanation for some other findings in the empirical research literature. For example, numerous studies have shown a positive correlation between religiousness and marital satisfaction (e.g., Hunt & King, 1978; Stanley, 1986). Although a conventional explanation for this finding focuses on the importance of shared values in reducing conflict and facilitating harmony, the RS hypothesis would explain more deeply *why* having shared values in these particular domains is so important. We know from previous research (e.g., Kirkpatrick & Davis, 1994) that romantic relationships in which one partner is "avoidant" and the other "anxious" tend not to be satisfying for either partner. One reason for this might be the conflict engendered specifically by incompatible mating and caregiving strategies, which in turn may be responsible for divergent attitudes—and thus arguments and conflict—about marriage and children. It may be that religiousness or religious compatibility has no direct effect on marital satisfaction: Instead, people who share the same long-term mating and caregiving strategies are also likely to share religious beliefs, and it is the former rather than the latter that is responsible for increased marital satisfaction.

The RS hypothesis might also help to explain a number of other known correlates of religion beyond the explicit realm of mating and child rearing. The differences between the "quality" and "quantity" strategies spill over into a variety of other domains. For example, not only does low parental sensitivity (and thus avoidant child attachment) in childhood predict earlier and more frequent sexual behavior, it is also related to a variety of behavioral problems, including aggression and disobedience (see Belsky et al., 1991, for a review). In general, the quantity strategy is a *high-risk* strategy, activated by cues in the early childhood home regarding the kind of environment generally into which one has been born. (Again, of course, children do not consciously reason this way; evolution has done the reasoning and designed systems to be calibrated in these ways.) An environment in which parental caregiving is of low quantity and quality is one calling for self-sufficiency: It's "every man for himself" (and every woman for herself). Much empirical research has shown that Christian belief is inversely correlated with many such behaviors, including drug and alcohol use and abuse (Gorsuch, 1995), delinquency (Donahue & Benson, 1995), and risk taking in general (Miller & Hoffman, 1995).

Finally, and I think of particular interest to psychologists of religion, the RS hypothesis might explain the long acknowledged and widely documented sex differences in religiousness. On virtually every kind of religion measure in virtually every (mainly Christian) population, women score higher than men on average. In the psychology of religion (as elsewhere), explanations proffered for these differences have long come in both biological and nonbiological versions (see, e.g., Batson et al., 1993, pp. 33–38, for a summary). Add the RS hypothesis to the "biological side"—but in an indirect way. As noted earlier, evolutionary theory suggests that on average, men should be more inclined toward short-term/quantity reproductive strategies given the opportunity, whereas women on average should be less so. To the extent that a comparison of religious (especially Christian) versus nonreligious persons reflects, in part, orientations toward quality versus quantity mating strategies, we would expect to find women on average to be more religious than men.

Compensation, Sudden Conversion, and the LM Hypothesis

In an earlier chapter I discussed at some length the centrality of love in Christianity, and in particular the observation by many scholars of different stripes that religious conversion is similar to falling in love. Even Ullman (1989), who started her investigation looking for a very cognitive explanation for conversion, was surprised to find that the process had little to do with cognition but a lot to do with falling in love.

The LM hypothesis makes explicit why this should be so: Religious conversion (at least in Christianity) strongly resembles the experience of falling in love because, well, it *is* falling in love. That is, the biological/psychological mechanism designed to activate love—in the service of cementing pair-bonds in committed mating relationships, for example— may be activated by a perceived relationship to God (or Jesus, etc.). "Falling in love" might not be a mere analogy for religious conversion, but a technical description of the biological and psychological processes actually involved. (Recall that this love mechanism, like the attachment system, is assumed to be distinct from sexuality.)

This perspective on religious conversion sheds additional light on several other issues surrounding sudden conversions. First, it adds another explanatory layer to the observation that adolescence and young adulthood are the most common life periods for sudden conversions. Although we noted earlier that this is typically a time of transition between attachment figures—that is, between parents and peers—it is also the time (for the same reason) that one is likely to have one's first experience of falling in love. The love mechanism is designed this way for good evolutionary reasons: The onset of sexual maturity denotes the time to begin seeking a mate. If one "falls in love" with God or Jesus, we call it religious conversion.

Second, this view of conversion as literally "falling in love" opens some new doors to the study of conversion, particularly with respect to the common distinction between gradual and sudden conversions. As reviewed earlier, Hazan and Zeifman (1999; also Zeifman & Hazan, 1997) discuss at length the process by which love bonds develop over time, both in infancy and in adulthood. In general, this is a gradual and slow process, taking a year or more in most cases as the various components of attachment are shifted, one by one, to the new attachment figure. Likewise, gradual conversions are clearly the norm with respect to religion (Hood et al., 1996). On the other hand, in both religious conversion and romantic love the process can sometimes occur swiftly and precipitously, seemingly coming out of the blue and smacking one between the eyes. The LM hypothesis suggests some interesting ways to think about how these processes might work in terms of, for example, the calibration of activation thresholds. For some people the system is activated in the way one ordinarily turns on a stereo, powering it up and then slowly increasing the volume. For others, it is more like what happens when you turn on the power and are surprised to discover that the volume knob is already set at maximum.

Third, the LM hypothesis adds an explanatory layer to the observation that sudden conversions are most likely among those with insecure attachment histories. From this perspective, *something* happens to a sizeable minority of these individuals later in life that in effect activates an otherwise dormant love mechanism. This would explain (in a slightly altered way) why the experience is so emotionally powerful: It is, in effect, tantamount to the experience of falling in love *for the first time*—an experience acknowledged by everyone as extraordinarily powerful and difficult to describe in words.

Finally, if the conversion process really does involve activation of a love mechanism, which in turn is connected to systems related to reproductive strategies, then sudden religious conversion may involve activation of the entire *suite* of mechanisms related to the "quality" reproductive strategy, including a long-term mating orientation and commitment to parental investment. Individuals whose preconversion life was characterized by the "quantity" orientation might then be expected to evince a variety of life changes related to the shift from this quantity to quality orientation. We would expect to see, for example, a renunciation of the previous high-risk lifestyle in favor of a new, conservative one—as described in the preceding section, an adoption of a "family values" orientation. Many such effects are amply documented among religious converts: Substance abusers give up their habits; criminals "go straight"; the promiscuous settle down. The Christian metaphor of being "born again" is apt: The convert in effect really does begin, in many ways, a new life, this time on the "quality" rather than "quantity" track.

Note again that a conventional "socialization" explanation for these phenomena would simply assert that the convert has adopted the teachings of the religion to which he or she has converted. It may be true that these new values are presented by a church or other external source in a convenient package, held out to the new convert as a guide for his or her new life. But the hypothesis outlined here might explain *why* the convert, by virtue of switching to a long-term reproductive strategy, finds such values intuitively appealing.

SUMMARY AND CONCLUSIONS

From the beginning of this book I have emphasized the idea that the attachment system is an adaptation—a suite of evolved psychological mechanisms constituting an important part of human nature (and indeed, many other species' natures as well). Up through Chapter 6, however, the significance of this emphasis was not necessarily apparent. Once the central tenets of the theory were established, such as the criteria for defining attachment figures, the functions of haven of safety and secure base, and the basic patterns of individual differences, evolutionary thinking did not play a crucial role in the application of the theory to religion. The same can probably be said for the majority of research conducted today in both infant–mother and adult-love contexts. Attachment researchers generally accept Bowlby's arguments with respect to the evolutionary history and adaptive function of the system, but then the evolutionary logic per se tends to be pushed into the background as a historical note rather than a direct source of theoretical guidance.

For many purposes, such as my own in Chapters 3–6, this is probably fine. However, as I have tried to demonstrate in this chapter, returning to the evolutionary roots of the theory opens up a variety of new vistas. Consideration of other midlevel evolutionary theories such as Trivers's (1972) theory of parental investment has led researchers to new ideas about the nature and origins of attachment, as well as its relationships to other systems involved in caregiving and mating. The two general directions developed in this chapter, concerning reproductive strategies and the nature of adult romantic love, led to extensions of some ideas about religion that I developed in previous chapters, such as the oft-postulated link between love and sudden religious conversion, as well as to empirically testable hypotheses about other domains of religious attitudes and values.

Chapter 4 made the point that the application of attachment theory to religion might in fact be quite limited, and I cautioned against efforts to overextend our conceptualization of the attachment system beyond its natural domain to enhance the generalizability of the theory. It might therefore seem that I have contradicted my own advice in this chapter, wherein I have suggested explanations for a variety of other religious phenomena beyond those discussed previously. Consider, however, how these new theoretical applications were achieved. The conceptualization of the attachment system per se has not really changed fundamentally in any of this discussion. Instead, what was new in this chapter was the introduction and consideration of several *other* evolved, functionally distinct psychological systems related to caregiving, mating, and love. Although these systems are related in important ways to the attachment system, both ontogenetically and phylogenetically, the discussion has expanded from attachment to other aspects of our species' evolved psychology in a manner that both acknowledges the functional distinctions between them yet also provides a framework for integrating them. In short, we have been moving away from a strictly attachment-based theory of religion toward a more general, evolutionary-psychological one. The remainder of the book will continue on this trajectory, moving further from the attachment system and introducing a variety of other functionally distinct, evolved psychological systems and mechanisms involving very different domains of behavior.

CHAPTER NINE

Religion
Adaptation or Evolutionary By-product?

It might well have occurred to you that through eight chapters of a book purported to offer an evolutionary psychology of religion, I have not said a single word about the adaptive function of religion. Nor have I offered any suggestion about the existence of any kind of religious "instinct" or religion-specific adaptation. Instead, I have focused on the attachment system, and to some extent psychological systems related to mating strategies, as adaptations presumed to have evolved as solutions to adaptive problems of survival and reproduction unrelated to (and by far predating the emergence of) religion.

In this chapter I finally make explicit the general argument that until now has been largely implicit. I argue that there indeed is no unique religious instinct (or, in contemporary terminology, no evolved psychological mechanism or system) designed specifically for the purpose of producing or guiding religious thought or behavior. I will propose instead that religious beliefs are constructed, shaped, and maintained by a host of psychological mechanisms and systems—including the attachment system—that all evolved much earlier in the (pre)history of our species for more mundane purposes, but that have been "co-opted" in more recent human history in the service of religion. Then, in the next two chapters, I will examine a variety of other psychological systems (i.e., other than the attachment system) that have evolved to enable us to successfully negotiate functionally important aspects of our physical, biological, and interpersonal worlds.

This chapter is divided into three parts. In the first, I review some of the kinds of evidence most commonly cited in support of the idea that humans do have a "religious instinct" or some kind of innate predisposition toward religion, and explain why in fact they do not constitute convincing evidence for such a claim. The second section then introduces a different set of arguments for why we should be skeptical about the religion-as-adaptation hypothesis, including a review of some of the empirical and theoretical obstacles such a hypothesis must confront. Finally, I introduce the distinction between adaptations and evolutionary *by-products*, and describe a general model of religion as the by-product of other, nonreligious adaptations.

IS THERE A UNIQUE RELIGIOUS INSTINCT?

The idea that religion is somehow "innate," "instinctive," or otherwise inherent in human nature has a very long history. Many of the standard arguments for such a position, however, cannot be taken seriously today, at least at face value. For starters, any evolutionary theory of religion (or of anything else, for that matter) dating back more than about four decades is probably wrong, or at best right for the wrong reasons. Many of the most significant advances in evolutionary biology, particularly with respect to the evolution of behavior, emerged during the 1960s and 1970s. W. D. Hamilton introduced his theory of inclusive fitness—the cornerstone of modern evolutionary biology—in 1964; Robert Trivers introduced the theory of reciprocal altruism in 1971 and the theory of parental investment in 1972. Religion theorists working prior to these important theoretical advances simply did not have the proper tools to theorize correctly about how natural selection shapes behavioral programs. This was true of Bowlby as well and, as we saw in Chapter 8, several important aspects of attachment theory have required rethinking in light of recent developments in evolutionary biology.

In this chapter I turn the spotlight of contemporary evolutionary theory on some of the older, evolutionarily inspired ideas about religion that have been proposed over the last century or so. Rather than focusing on a review of particular theories or theorists, I will organize this material by topic, discussing the general kinds of problems that undermine these older ideas when examined from the perspective of our current understanding of evolution and adaptation.

Before turning to the reasons why I think we should not assume the existence of a "religion instinct" or evolved religion-specific mechanism, let's first ask why we might find the idea of a religion instinct attractive in the first place. In this section I examine four general lines of argument that are most commonly made, none of which turns out to be convincing on closer examination.

Universality

The primary reason most people would give for seeking an evolutionary explanation for religion (or anything else) is its apparent universality across time and cultures. Donald Brown (1991) includes religion in his list of "human universals," and anthropologists (as well as psychologists, sociologists, philosophers, and others) have long observed that religion, or at least something very religionlike, can be observed in all modern cultures, and that there is evidence for religion in past cultures for tens of thousands of years in human (and perhaps even Neanderthal) history (and prehistory). Granted there are significant differences across generations and cultures, but if something recognizable as religion, at least broadly defined, appears everywhere, doesn't that suggest it is "built in"?

The first problem with this reasoning is that thorny definition problem. Specifically, if you define anything (including religion) broadly enough, you can make a case that everyone does it. (Conversely, if you define it narrowly enough, you would not find anybody who quite fits the bill.) If by "religion" you mean belief in personalized deities, religion is widespread but not universal. If you define it vaguely as "ultimate concern" then it is universal more or less by definition, because everyone has concerns and one can always be defined as ultimate among them. The hedge I slipped in about "at least broadly defined" presents real conceptual problems, not merely semantic ones. Anthropologists have gone to great lengths to distinguish religion from magic, superstition, and other related phenomena, for example. What about modern parapsychology and pseudoscience? Whether religion is universal clearly depends largely on how we define it.

A second problem concerns how we define "universal." There are considerable individual differences within most cultures with respect to religion, as particularly evidenced by modern Western societies (especially the United States) in which people may choose from a diverse menu of organized religions, not to mention individuals' personal (often private) deviations from official church doctrine or the many forms of "spirituality" many people vigorously distinguish from religion. Perhaps more to the point, two of these menu options—at least in modern times—are atheism and agnosticism. Although American psychologists of religion like to point to surveys indicating that over 90% of Americans believe in God, pray, and so forth, the numbers in many European countries are much lower. If we reduce these figures further by focusing on "true believers," setting aside the many whose religious involvement is only nominal, the numbers would drop further still. Is religion "universal" if many people are not in fact religious, but every culture includes at least some religious people? How many people per culture must be religious for that culture to count as a plus in the universality column?

A related point that is commonly overlooked is that universality varies considerably across time. It might be true that somewhere back in our species' history (or prehistory), there was a time when virtually every human was religious (by some reasonable definition of the term). Today, however, we see a great deal of variance. Perhaps some day far in the future, as Freud and many others have predicted, religion will disappear entirely from the planet. Or, suppose it were determined that all cultures, at *some* point in their (cultural) evolution, are dominated by religious beliefs, though at other points (before, or after, or both) are not. If all cultures followed a similar pattern of religious ebb and flow over time, would we say religion was "universal"? How universal religion appears, then, would depend largely on which slice of time in human history you chose to sample. Any particular slice of time you might choose, including "now," would be arbitrary.

To illustrate, consider some given topic in mathematics—something for which humans clearly do not have dedicated evolved mechanisms (though we probably do have such mechanisms for counting small numbers, distinguishing "more" from "less," and such). At some point in time not long ago, such ideas existed nowhere on earth. They now exist widely, at least within certain subpopulations of industrialized nations, and someday they might be commonplace all around the planet. Even life forms on other planets (if there are any) might share such ideas: In the science fiction novel *Contact* (Sagan, 1985) and film of the same name, a message received from an alien civilization begins with the transmission of sequences of prime numbers—the assumption being that the mathematical concept of prime numbers is universal on an intergalactic scale. But such universality surely would not establish the existence of an evolved prime-numbers mechanism in humans (or aliens).

Another, and deeper, problem with the universality issue concerns the crucial distinction between universality of *expression*—the behaviors, feelings, thoughts, and so forth of religious experience—and the universality of the psychology underlying it. As discussed in Chapter 7, there is a crucial distinction to be made between psychological mechanisms, which are thought to be universal and species-specific, and their behavioral products, which are not necessarily so. Recall that Bowlby and other attachment theorists have made the same argument concerning the distinction between the attachment system qua *system*, on the one hand, and attachment *behaviors* on the other. Examining the ethnographic record for observable signs of religion focuses on the products, not the psychological mechanisms, and the mapping is not necessarily isomorphic. Earlier I discussed the callus analogy in this context: Large individual- and cross-cultural differences are observed in the incidence of calluses, as well as their locations on bodies: People who regularly walk barefoot have calluses on the soles of their feet, and guitar players have them on their fingers. Likewise, in cultures in which everyone walks barefoot, everyone has calluses on their feet, but where everyone wears shoes few do. So, are calluses universal? No, but the underlying physiology—the callus-producing mechanism in the skin—*is* universal. A universal mechanism can give rise to highly variable observable products.

Is it possible for something to be universally observable, yet not be the product of a species-universal mechanism designed for that express purpose? Sure. Ramachandran and Blakeslee (1998) offer the example of *cooking*, and I am inclined to agree with them. Perhaps it could be argued that there is indeed some kind of "cooking mechanism," based on the potential inclusive-fitness benefits that derive from increased digestibility and decreased microbe infection, but this sounds like a stretch to me. Cooking is probably a cultural invention resulting from some early humans figuring it out, probably by accident, and then passing along the idea to others. Another example might be the game of soccer, which is virtually universal around the globe today (even in the United States, finally!). Human psychological architecture surely does not include mechanisms designed for the specific purpose of soccer playing; rather, we cobble together a diverse array of mental and physiological machinery—all of which evolved for other, nonsoccer purposes—to do the job. (Note too that this example also points up the problem of universality across time: Soccer was surely not universal 10,000 years ago, and I am willing to bet that, despite its considerable appeal, it won't be universal 10,000 years from now either.) I will return to this analogy later in this chapter.

Genetics

Some writers have suggested (e.g., Hay, 1994; Wulff, 1997) that the existence of some kind of innate predisposition toward religion is indicated by the fact that religiosity seems to be at least partly heritable (Waller, Kojetin, Bouchard, Lykken, & Tellegen, 1990). Although such data certainly do point to the fact that genetic factors are somehow involved in shaping or producing religious belief or experience, this is not at all the same thing as saying that they demonstrate the existence of a mechanism or system whose evolved function is religion.

First, there is the obvious possibility that religiousness (or some kind of predisposition toward it) is not itself heritable, but appears so only by virtue of being correlated with personality traits or other characteristics that are known to be heritable. For example, McClenon (1997) notes that religiosity is correlated with *hypnotizability*, which is known to be heritable. The apparent heritability of religiosity could be merely a statistical artifact of such effects.

Second, and more important, demonstrating that *individual differences* in something are partly explained by genetic factors is quite a different thing from demonstrating that the thing is an *adaptation*, as I discussed in Chapter 7. Individual differences frequently represent random noise, at least insofar as natural selection is concerned. Natural selection tends over time to reduce variability in traits, as less adaptive variations are weeded out and the more adaptive ones retained (Tooby & Cosmides, 1990). The genetic variation with which we are left is, from an evolutionary perspective, largely the variation that does not matter: The entire normal range (i.e., excluding mutations or developmental errors) of values for a characteristic was sufficiently adaptive in our evolutionary history to avoid having been selected out.

Consider, for example, individual differences in iris color, which are almost 100% heritable. All human eyes share the same functional design in terms of the components and their arrangement (exceptions are the result of genetic mutations, developmental errors, or disease). However, iris color does not affect vision functions, and it turns out that slightly different genetic recipes for building eyes produce, as incidental by-products, differently colored irises that are all more or less *functionally* equivalent. Natural selection has failed to weed out this variation because it is of no fitness consequence; there are no natural selection pressures favoring one color or another. If blue eyes or brown eyes conferred reproductive advantages, the less adaptive variant would have been eliminated long ago in our evolutionary past. If anything, the fact that so much heritable variation exists in eye color argues *against* the notion that, say, iris blueness or greenness is an adaptation.[1] By the same token, the heritability of religiosity does not imply that religiosity is an adaptation any more than it implies that atheism is.

Neurology

It has long been known that epileptic seizures in certain parts of the brain—specifically, a particular region of the temporal lobes—sometimes produce intense, spiritual experiences, and many people who experience them subsequently become preoccupied with religious and moral issues (Ramachandran & Blakeslee, 1998). Persinger (1987) has demonstrated a related effect experimentally in normal subjects by activating these specific brain regions using a high-tech gizmo called a transcranial magnetic stimulator. When these areas are stimulated in just the right way, people seem to experience something Godlike. Does this mean we have a "God module" built into our brains? And if so, why?

It is possible that such a mechanism exists, but this neurological evidence does not persuasively make the case. The fact that activation in a particular brain area produces a consistent set of effects does not necessarily mean that we have located a mechanism *designed for the function of producing those effects*. For one, the effects could be merely incidental by-products of the architecture of some other system designed for entirely other functions. If you tap the right spot on your knee with a hammer while sitting with one leg crossed over the other, your lower leg and foot will jerk up. It is doubtful that this effect reflects an evolved mechanism for knee jerking in response to hammers, but rather is a coincidental vulnerability resulting from the particular arrangement of tendons, ligaments, and muscles in the knee joint.

Alternatively, such effects might simply represent a kind of *malfunction* caused by any number of possible genetic, pharmaceutical, or environmental factors. Getting whacked severely on the head with the aforementioned hammer is likely to produce a cacophony of effects ranging from the experience of pain to hallucinating stars whirling around one's head, but this would not imply that our brain architecture includes an adaptation designed to produce this particular suite of effects. Temporal lobe epilepsy presumably represents a kind of brain malfunction, not an adaptation. If we do not regard temporal lobe seizures as an adaptation, why should we regard "spiritual experiences" produced by them as such?

As another example consider anxiety attacks, which phenomenologically have much in common with spiritual experiences (despite obvious differences in affective tone). Both involve "powerful feelings that seem to engulf the individual, unbidden; sensations and perceptions no longer conform to actual events; the total experience is ineffable, that is, difficult to describe in ordinary language; and there is an actual or impending dissolution of the self-as-object" (Averill, 1998, p. 117). It is doubtful that our psychological architecture contains a dedicated mechanism for producing anxiety attacks per se; it is easy to see how such experiences are terribly debilitating and almost certainly maladaptive. Instead, anxiety attacks are likely the result of hyperactivation, or activation in inappropriate circumstances (i.e., relative to the functional design of the system), of a *fear* system that ordinarily is highly adaptive. Activation of the "God module" region may well be producing something analogous to anxiety attacks—a spontaneous (or artificially instigated) misfiring of a system that works very well for other purposes in its ordinary context.

I confess that I do not know exactly what the details of such an explanation would be, but I will take a stab at outlining one possibility here in order to illustrate some general ways in which it might be done. The three most commonly identified characteristics of spiritual experiences, according to Averill (1998, p. 104), are feelings of vitality (the experience was "exhilarating," a "thrill"), connectedness ("a union with reality"), and meaningfulness ("increased wisdom," "profound understanding"). We could quibble about details, but this description overlaps markedly with the descriptions provided by Ramachandran and Blakeslee (1998) and Persinger (1987), as well as Maslow's (1963) description of "peak" experiences and Csikszentmihalyi's (1990) description of "flow" experiences. My sense is that in (usually) milder form, this phenomenological trilogy closely resembles what are commonly referred to as "A-ha!" experiences—the deeply rewarding sense of having solved a difficult problem or made a discovery that amazes you. Infants seem to have such experiences in some form when they discover their hands or that pushing a button makes the mobile over their crib rotate. Such a feedback system might well be part of the brain's evolved learning architecture. Indeed, outside of religion, one of the most common kinds of contexts known to trigger spiritual experiences is creative work (Averill, 1998). Thus religious experience could reflect a kind of hyperactivation of a system that ordinarily is not directly associated with (and not specifically designed to produce) religion per se.

Another important clue here is that the neurological activity associated with such experiences does not occur in the "higher" cognitive regions of the brain, but rather in the limbic system—the brain's *emotional* center (Ramachandran & Blakeslee, 1998). This suggests that people are having abnormal *emotional experiences*, and then imposing mystical or religious *interpretations* on them after the fact in the kind of religious-attribution process described by Proudfoot and Shaver (1975). This would explain why these experiences are "ineffable," and also why people are so willing to entertain mystical interpretations for them: Highly unusual emotional experiences cry out for highly unusual explanations. Why these interpretations take the particular form that they do remains a difficult question, but the point at the moment is simply that if something like this is what is happening, we would be loath to identify the whole lot as an adaptation shaped by natural selection to produce mystical experiences. Instead, this observation suggests that a potentially fruitful approach to the problem might be based on an understanding of the organization and (evolutionary) function of positive emotions (see Fredrickson, 1998).

In a related vein, Averill (1998) suggests that spiritual experience shares "the same genus" with other "species" of experience that include *wonder* and *aesthetics*. Another context in which spiritual experiences are commonly triggered is contemplation of music, art, and natural beauty. For my own part, I have had deeply spiritual experiences at music concerts. I am not sure that this line of thinking is very helpful from an evolutionary point of view, because to me the emotional power of aesthetics itself is a profound mystery. Why should we be so powerfully affected by beautiful things? For our immediate purposes, however, the exact explanation is not important. The point is that just because such emotional experiences can be stimulated artificially (or spontaneously in the case of temporal lobe epilepsy), we should not leap to the conclusion that the capacity for religious or spiritual experiences is built directly into our brains for the purpose (i.e., with the adaptive function) of generating such experiences.

Ethology

If the capacity for religion is somehow encoded in our genetic makeup, we might look to other species for clues to the origin and nature of religion. Sir Alister Hardy (1966) was intrigued by the ethologist Konrad Lorenz's (1952) observations about domestic dogs. Hardy quotes Lorenz at length; I have abbreviated the quote here:

> The really single-hearted devotion of a dog to its master has two quite different sources. On the one side, it is nothing else than the submissive attachment which every wild dog shows towards his pack leader, and which is transferred, without any considerable alteration in character, by the domestic dog to a human being. To this is added, in the more highly domesticated dogs, quite another form of affection. . . . The ardent affection which wild canine youngsters show for their mother, and which in these disappears completely after they have reached maturity, is preserved as a permanent mental trait of all highly domesticated dogs. What originally was love for the mother is transformed into love for a human master. (p. 173)

Hardy goes on to wonder if something similar might not happen in humans, given the well-documented degree to which human development is also highly neotenic. Confessing that this conclusion is "of course, entirely speculative," Hardy (1966) suggests that

> man, who, like the dog, has juvenile characters, e.g., this prolonged period of childhood and a strong parent–child affection, may, also like the dog, have transferred part of the submissiveness which he had shown to his tribal leader, together with his filial affection, to a new master—one of a very unusual kind. This "new master," a supposedly invisible being, is imagined by primitive man to account for the "something" real beyond the self which he felt himself to be in touch with; the something which he called by various names such as mana, wakan, or God when he was able, with coming of speech, to discuss with his fellow beings this strange feeling of the numinous. . . . Whilst it is only a suggestion of a possible origin of this important human trait, the not unsimilar devotion

in the dog shows that such a transfer is in fact biologically possible. (pp. 174–175)

Hardy notes an additional parallel as well, namely that (according to Lorenz) the attachment of domestic dogs to humans appears to occur rather suddenly at a particular stage in development—during a critical or *sensitive period* as developmental psychologists would call it—which Hardy (1966) likens to "the almost sudden 'conversion' that occurs in the religious life of many human adolescents" (p. 174).

So what do these observations mean? Does evidence of precursors or parallels of religion in other species support an argument for an evolved religion instinct or mechanism in humans? Much has been written on the value and the dangers of cross-species comparisons, and we could argue the pros and cons all day. I will not bother, however, as I doubt many readers would want to defend the position that Hardy's observations establish the existence of an innate religion mechanism in humans. Rather, observations such as these point less toward the idea of a dedicated religion mechanism or instinct, and more toward the idea I wish to develop in the remainder of this book: that religion is *not* the product of dedicated religion-producing cognitive machinery but rather can be accounted for in terms of other psychological mechanisms that were designed by natural selection to do quite different things. Hardy's speculations fit within my own framework nicely, as the evolved systems to which he points—the attachment system (though it was not labeled as such when Hardy wrote in 1966) and a system related to power and hierarchy (more about which in the next chapter)—are two among the several psychological systems or mechanisms underlying religion that I emphasize. (See Wulff, 1997, p. 146 ff., for a review of other examples in which animal behavior has been discussed vis-à-vis religion.)

PROBLEMS WITH THE RELIGION-AS-INSTINCT VIEW

In the preceding section I reviewed some of the kinds of arguments that might be made in favor of a dedicated, evolved religion mechanism or instinct, and found them wanting. In this section I discuss some additional reasons why making the case for religion (or for psychological mechanisms dedicated to it) as an adaptation is very difficult at best, and why we should be reluctant to do so.

The Problem of Identifying the Adaptive Function

The first (and perhaps biggest) problem in trying to make the case for a religion-specific psychological mechanism is that of identifying what exactly such a mechanism would *do*. What adaptive problem would a "religion mechanism" reliably solve (or, more precisely, have reliably solved for our distant ancestors)? What would be its adaptive function? The benefits of such a mechanism must translate somehow, directly or indirectly, into reproductive advantage (i.e., inclusive fitness) relative to alternative mechanisms. Making such a case well is much more difficult than it sounds, and there are a variety of pitfalls that must be avoided.

Psychological versus Reproductive Benefits

First, the adaptive function of a postulated religion mechanism cannot be confined to purely psychological benefits, such as feeling good or reducing anxiety. Natural selection is blind to such effects, and can act on them only if these effects in turn translate somehow into real reproductive advantage. Of course, ample evidence now exists that stress and other psychological factors can influence physical health: We all know that dispositionally hostile individuals are more prone to coronary heart disease, for example. However, these effects tend to operate over the long term, seldom acting early enough in life to interfere with successful mating and reproduction. Another possibility might be that stress interferes with fertility, sexual interest, or other variables that might influence reproductive success, but whether religiousness could produce sufficiently large and reliable effects to matter over evolutionary time is not at all clear.

It is worth emphasizing here the idea that natural selection is not in the business of producing happy organisms. Not only is happiness irrelevant to natural selection—unless, as noted earlier, happiness in turn translates into reproductive advantage via some additional link (e.g., Fredrickson, 1998)—but evolutionary theory rather turns our view of positive and negative affect on its head. If happiness per se were adaptive, we would all simply be happy all the time because our brains would be designed that way. Consider the fact that our taste-preference system is not designed to produce pleasurable sensations whenever we eat; it is designed to make us feel awful when we eat something toxic or spoiled and feel good when we enjoy a healthful (or at least what would have been healthful to our ancestors) feast. Positive and negative affect are not the end-states that our evolved psychology is designed to seek or avoid; they are tools used by our evolved psychology in guiding us to seek or avoid experiences which themselves have implications for reproductive success.

Group Selection versus Selfish Genes

Second, a postulated religion mechanism cannot be explained simply in terms of benefits to "the group" or "the species." As discussed previously, modern evolutionary theory acknowledges that natural selection is fundamentally about differential survival of genes, not of individuals or groups, and that simplistic group-selectionism is fundamentally flawed (Dawkins, 1976/1989; Williams, 1966). In a population of organisms designed to behave "for the good of the group," an alternative gene (allele) coding for a "cheater" strategy stands to succeed at the expense of the altruists. An individual who benefits from the generosity of others, without suffering the costs of being generous oneself, will on average be more successful; the genes coding for such a behavioral strategy will spread at the expense of the altruistic strategy.[2]

The idea that some kind of religion mechanism has evolved specifically to promote group cohesion or cooperation will therefore not hold up, unless it can be shown how such effects translate into inclusive-fitness terms. Numerous theories have emerged over the last couple of decades that combine elements of natural selection with various cultural processes in co-evolutionary and multilevel selection models in ways that support certain forms of group-level selection in more sophisticated ways (e.g., Boyd & Richerson, 1985, 1992; Sober & D. S. Wilson, 1998; E. O. Wilson, 1978, 1998), but the arguments for such models are complex and they remain controversial. If one wishes to argue for religion as a biological adaptation that evolved for the purpose of benefiting groups rather than (or at the expense of) individual self-interest, the theoretical terrain is difficult and complex.

I hasten to add, however, that this decidedly is *not* to say that religions cannot or do not have effects that benefit groups, or that people cannot construct religions (or other social institutions) with the implicit or explicit goal of promoting cooperation or group cohesion. I return to this idea in the final chapter. The point is simply that we cannot blithely assume that our evolved psychological architecture contains some kind of religion mechanism that has been naturally selected because it enhanced group cohesion, cooperation, or other group-level benefits. Any case for religion as an adaptation must be based on consideration of the inclusive-fitness benefits of the hypothesized adaptation, in terms consistent with modern evolutionary biology.

Costs versus Benefits

Third, to make the case for a religion-specific psychological mechanism, one needs to demonstrate how it reliably and predictably produces benefits that, on average, exceed(ed) potential costs. For example, McClenon (1997) proposes that humans evolved the capacity of hypnotizability to enhance suggestibility in shamanic rituals, which in turn have a variety of positive survival- and health-related effects. Similarly, in searching for an explanation for a neurophysiological "God module" in the brain, Ramachandran, Hirstein, Armel, Tecomar, and Iragui (1997) suggest that a tendency toward spiritual experiences might somehow have been useful in promoting group cohesion.

Although it is not difficult to see how such religious experiences could confer certain potential benefits, further examination reveals that it is just as easy to see their potential costs. High levels of hypnotizability might enhance the positive effects of benevolent shamanic rituals, but they would also render people susceptible to sinister forms of manipulation and deceit. To the extent that people's numinous experiences or interpretations of them vary, they are just as likely to create *conflict* within a group as harmony. As Guthrie (1993) points out, some religious beliefs are effective in reducing anxiety, fear, and stress, but they equivalently produce anxiety, fear, and stress. Heaven offers something wonderful to look forward to, but hell is terrifying; gods can be beneficent beings looking out for our interests, or they can be capricious and vicious. It will not be easy to explain how a religion mechanism could be naturally selected in a way that produced the upside without the downside.

Begging Questions

Fourth, one must avoid positing the existence of a mechanism that assumes the existence of yet some other mechanism that itself remains unexplained. We make no progress by substituting one mystery for another. In the example mentioned earlier, the hypothesis that psychological stress reliably reduces fertility or sexual interest represents another effect to be explained. Why should stress have this effect and not some other (such as the opposite) effect? This is not to say that the latter cannot also be explained, but only to highlight the fact that the job is not done. Similarly, ascribing to religion the function of satisfying our need for constructing meaning in the world, or for maintaining high self-esteem, or managing fear of death begs the question as to why humans are built to "need" these things in the first place.

There is admittedly room for reasonable debate about the specific ways in which an evolutionary perspective can usefully inform psychological theory, but it seems beyond question that such a perspective is indispensable in the context of any discussion of fundamental human needs, drives, or motivations. The field of psychology is populated with any number of grand theories purporting to identify a handful of seminal motives or needs from which all else springs, many of which appear highly dubious when scrutinized from a rigorous evolutionary perspective. For example, it is doubtful that a human self-system would be designed with the goal of maintaining high self-esteem, for the same reason our taste systems are not designed to cause everything we ingest to be experienced as delicious. Instead, self-esteem is designed as a "sociometer" (Leary, Tambor, Terdal, & Downs, 1995) for monitoring our success and failure with respect to particular adaptive problems, and then for activating differential strategies accordingly (Kirkpatrick & Ellis, 2001). It therefore seems doubtful that the maintenance of high self-esteem is some kind of fundamental human need or drive.[3]

The hypothesis that a central purpose of religion is to alleviate fear of death is worth an additional word here because it is so widespread. Pyszczynski, Greenberg, and Solomon (1999), for example, postulate that fear of death is universal as an inevitable consequence of an "instinct to survive," and that humans consequently have evolved additional adaptations—a "terror management" system—to combat its potentially incapacitating effects. Ironically, however, it is not at all clear from an evolutionary perspective that such a general "survival instinct" exists. No computer chess program contains a line anywhere that says "make good moves" or "win the game," as such commands offer no practical guidance as to what one should actually do. Instead, chess programs are designed with numerous "domain-specific" modules (i.e., program subroutines) that, when all is working properly, result in good moves and winning games. In the same way, the idea that human brains contain an evolved psychological mechanism for "surviving" is dubious; instead, our psychological architecture contains specific programs for generating adaptive behavior that, in ordinary environments, have the effect of (on average) leading to success in survival and reproduction. Again, this is not to deny that religious belief can have the effect of reducing death anxiety. The point is simply that this perspective casts doubt on the hypothesis that religion is an adaptation to solve a universal fear-of-death problem that is itself the consequence of a universal "survival instinct." (I return to this "terror management theory" later in the book and suggest an alternative view with respect to death anxiety.)

The Problem of Identifying the Design

As discussed previously, earlier conceptions of the nature of "instincts" have been replaced in recent years by more sophisticated ethological models of behavioral strategies and the design of behavioral systems. In the early 1900s, psychology saw an explosion of interest in "instinct theories" of human nature, and scholars compiled lengthy lists of purported human instincts (Bernard, 1924). Numerous theorists, such as Le Bon (1903), posited the existence of specific instincts for "religious sentiments" and the like. It did not take long for everyone to realize that for the most part these theories were entirely circular; calling something an "instinct" did not explain anything, but merely provided a label for it. Simply asserting that people have a "religion instinct" does not get us anywhere at all.

Modern ethological models provided a very different conceptualization of how "instinctive" behavior is organized, particularly with respect to motivation. Freud's model of id-based motives as a kind of boiling cauldron, in which a need or drive builds and builds under pressure until it is satisfied or leaks out sideways, is all wrong. Recall the callus example discussed earlier: The skin does not contain a mechanism hell-bent on building calluses whenever possible. You do not have to go to any great lengths to prevent them: Just avoid walking barefoot, working as a carpenter, and playing guitar. Notice, too, that if you avoid such friction, you will not eventually explode into a sea of calluses because you have been repressing the mechanism, and you do not break out in pimples or warts as a consequence of a frustrated mechanism expressing itself via an alternative outlet. Bowlby's model of the attachment system clearly exemplifies the difference; indeed, the outdated Freudian model of instinct and motivation is one of the principal errors of traditional psychoanalytic theory that Bowlby set out to correct. In the modern conceptualization, behavior is organized into systems that are activated by particular stimuli or internal states, monitored by regulatory mechanisms, and deactivated by other stimuli or internal states. Thus, a hypothesis about a religion-specific mechanism cannot merely posit a generalized "drive" or "need" for religion, but would need to explain exactly what it is the mechanism does, the conditions that activate it, the specific forms of thought, emotion, and/or behavior it produces in response to these conditions, and so forth.

The requirement that a good evolutionary theory be well specified in these ways leads immediately to a significant problem if one's goal is to explain religion in its entirety because, as we have seen, "religion" refers to such a diverse range of phenomena. It is not at all clear how a single, well-defined religion mechanism could possibly explain it all. Religion involves in varying degrees to various people in various places, beliefs in the supernatural, systems of ethics and morality, group and individual ritual, and so forth. As discussed in Chapter 1, scholars have long tried without success to find the common thread running through all religions. Particularly in light of the domain-specificity argument in its modern form, in which highly specific mechanisms are designed to solve highly specific adaptive problems, the idea that a single religion mechanism underlies all religious phenomena seems patently untenable. An evolved religion mechanism could at best explain some aspects of religion, while leaving much else unexplained. One would then have to turn to other kinds of explanations for other features of religion, leaving the job only half-done, or postulate yet additional religion mechanisms and thus complicate the problem further.

The Problem of Establishing Special Design

The central distinguishing feature of an adaptation is that it demonstrates evidence of "special design," that is, has the hallmarks of a well-engineered solution to the adaptive problem it is designed to solve. In particular, adaptations are identified by evidence of such characteristics as complexity, economy, efficiency, reliability, precision, and functionality (Pinker, 1997; Williams, 1966). A useful approach is to examine a purported adaptation from the perspective of an engineer, and ask whether the mechanism is *well* designed, in light of constraints imposed by other aspects of the organism's design. At the same time, however, it is important to keep in mind that adaptations are not necessarily designed as the *best* possible solutions we might imagine. Many adaptations are far from ideal, such as Gould's (1980) classic example of the "panda's thumb" (described later in this chapter), and often one can easily imagine how to design a better solution if one could go back to the proverbial drawing board and start over. However, natural selection can work only with the parts already available in existing organisms, and there are constraints with respect to what is and is not "evolvable." Nevertheless, evolved solutions should generally be good ones, and better than plausible alternatives.

Frankly, I find it difficult to imagine how religious belief or experience could be considered an economical, efficient solution to any particular adaptive problem. For example, consider again the hypothesis that its adaptive function is/was to make people "feel better" by, for example, providing comfort and solace in a dangerous world. As noted earlier, if "feeling better" were universally adaptive, natural selection could simply have fashioned humans to feel better all the time. We know that it has managed to fashion a much more complex set of emotions that cause us to feel better and worse at different times; it would require only a very simple change in design to turn on the feel-good button perpetually. It is much easier to turn a complex design into a simpler one than the other way around. In McClenon's (1997) version of this hypothesis, humans first evolved "suggestibility," then developed shamanic rituals that capitalize on this suggestibility, which in turn make people feel good, which again in turn produces positive physical health benefits, which (finally) in turn leads to reproductive success. This does not sound to me like an efficient, economical design for anything, particularly given that natural selection could much more easily have designed us to experience those health-promoting feelings directly without all those intervening steps. Similarly, if the adaptive function of religion were to enhance group coherence and sacrifice, wouldn't it have been much easier just to design humans to feel the same kind of emotional bond to everyone around them rather than to only, say, kin and romantic partners?

Theoretical Conservatism and the Onus of Proof

Finally, and perhaps most important, is the epistemological issue concerning what our default hypothesis should be—that is, on which side of the question the onus of proof falls. Williams (1966; see also Tooby & Cosmides, 1992, and Pinker, 1997) has argued persuasively for a theoretically conservative approach to the identification of adaptations. As noted earlier, he suggested multiple criteria that must be met to make a persuasive case that something is an adaptation. The default assumption is that it is *not*. "Adaptation" is not a term to be tossed around lightly; it should be invoked only in light of compelling evidence.

Thus, before making a facile leap to the conclusion that religion is an adaptation, we should first consider whether it can be explained satisfactorily in other ways. This is not to suggest that the existence of religion-specific adaptations has been ruled out, but only that we should begin, at least for the sake of argument, with the assumption that there are none. If observations later force us to decide otherwise, and if the strict criteria for establishing a religion-specific adaptation can eventually be met, so be it. Like reasonable doubt in the courtroom, we start with the presumption of innocence (not an adaptation), and abandon this hypothesis only in the face of conclusive evidence to the contrary. The onus of proof is on those who wish to demonstrate the existence of such a mechanism, not on those arguing against.

At any rate, my intent here is to go at the problem the other way around. That is, rather than looking at features of religion and trying to spin a "Just-So" story about how and why it evolved, my approach to the problem is to examine the evolved psychology of humans in general and then ask how it might explain features of religion. As I explain in the next section, my default assumption is that religion is not an adaptation, but rather emerges as a by-product of other psychological mechanisms that we are fairly confident *are* adaptations.

RELIGION AS AN EVOLUTIONARY BY-PRODUCT, NOT AN ADAPTATION

As explained in the previous chapter, modern evolutionary psychology hinges on the construct of *psychological mechanisms* as a crucial level of analysis. These mechanisms are the adaptations produced by natural selection, not behavior or thought patterns per se. We therefore are not looking for an evolutionary explanation of religious behavior or belief per se, but rather for the psychological mechanisms that give rise to it. One important consequence of this shift in perspective is that observed behavior need not be the product of a mechanism that was specifically designed to produce it.

Adaptations versus Evolutionary By-products

Up to this point our discussion of natural selection and evolutionary psychology has focused on *adaptations*: features or traits designed by natural selection for a particular adaptive function. More formally, Buss, Haselton, Shackleford, Bleske, and Wakefield (1998) define an adaptation as "an inherited and reliably developing characteristic that came into existence as a feature of a species through natural selection because it helped to directly or indirectly facilitate reproduction during the period of its evolution. . . . Solving an adaptive problem . . . is the function of an adaptation" (p. 535). However, it should be obvious that not every feature, trait, or behavior observed in people is the direct product of an adaptation designed for that particular purpose. Our evolved psychology does not contain mechanisms designed for computing sequences of prime numbers or playing soccer. Instead, many patterns of thought and behavior, particularly in our modern environment, are produced by mechanisms (or combinations of mechanisms) designed to do something else. Adaptations are only one product of natural selection, but there are many others.

A second product of evolution is "noise," or random effects (Buss et al., 1998). A certain amount of random genetic variability is always hanging around, as a result of genetic mutations and various arcane details of sexual recombination and meiosis. Without such variability, of course, natural selection would have nothing with which to work. Much of this variability is eliminated by natural selection over time, as a consequence of the fact that most mutations are harmful and less adaptive than the normative extant variants. (Williams, 1997, puts this ironically by noting that natural selection is largely about *preventing evolution*.) However, as discussed earlier in the context of heritability, some degree of random variability is "permitted" by natural selection to remain. For any particular parameter of a given adaptation, there exists a range of values that are all more or less equally adaptive, or at least within acceptable limits. Some people have a somewhat larger lung capacity than others, or bigger feet or smoother corneas, but within a certain range of variability the functional consequences are not sufficiently large for natural selection to favor one variant over another. At some point, however, feet that are so large as to interfere with walking would be maladaptive, and those genes have been eliminated from the pool. From the point of view of evolution, much of the genetic variability among humans is just inconsequential noise. (Of course, this does not mean that it is inconsequential from other points of view, nor that it does not potentially have large effects on the course or quality of individual lives.)

More important for our purposes is a third class of evolutionary products: *by-products* of adaptations. Gould (e.g., 1991) has discussed and labeled two particular kinds of by-products. *Spandrels* refer to features that have no adaptive value in themselves, but happen to emerge inevitably from the construction of adaptive features. One of Gould's favorite examples is the human chin, which appears as a function of the design of the lower jaw in conjunction with other facial features that do reflect adaptions (for biting and chewing, smelling, and so forth). When Candide's teacher Pangloss suggested that the bridge of the nose is exquisitely designed to hold up one's spectacles, the joke was that he was erroneously assigning an adaptive function to a spandrel. Buss, et al. (1998) offer the example of the heat generated by a light bulb, an incidental consequence of the machinery used to produce (i.e., designed for the function of producing) light.

Exaptations refer to features that evolved initially as an adaptation to perform a particular function, but later come to take on a distinctly different function (Gould, 1991). Gould's favorite example here is the "thumb" of the panda, which is a wrist bone that initially evolved as part of the wrist design but with a little additional modification has become a thumblike organ useful for stripping leaves from bamboo shoots (Gould, 1980). A "real" thumb is a complicated thing to evolve, particularly given the design of thumbless panda ancestors, so natural selection has had to make do with whatever materials it has at its disposal. An example of a hypothesized psychological exaptation is provided by Hazan and Zeifman's (1999) theory, discussed in the previous chapter, according to which an evolved attachment system later was co-opted by natural selection for the new function of cementing adult pair-bonds.

Third, there is the large class of cases in which adaptations are used in the service of other functions for which they were not designed, but also which do not necessarily have inclusive-fitness consequences (and therefore are not exaptations in Gould's sense). The term *co-opted adaptations* (Buss et al., 1998) is probably as good a label as any. Playing soccer draws upon a wide variety of evolved psychological and physical abilities and mechanisms coordinated in a particular fashion. However, soccer playing has probably never been associated with sufficiently strong adaptive benefits or costs to induce further evolution of these underlying mechanisms in a way that improves soccer playing (like the panda's thumb), nor would we want to say that natural selection is what is doing the exapting (like attachment or love mechanisms being redirected for the function of pair-bond maintenance).

I want to be careful about which term I adopt for the theory of religion I am developing here. I am reluctant to use the term "exaptation" because its intended meaning seems to be highly variable in the literature, and because Gould himself has been inconsistent in its use (Buss et al., 1998). For example, it is unclear whether the term exaptation necessarily implies the use of an evolved structure (for purpose other than its original adaptive function) in a manner that is also currently *adaptive* (other than its original "intended" function), and I do not wish to imply that religion is necessarily adaptive in a biological sense. I am also not keen on the term "spandrel" because it implies a kind of inevitability, as in the case of human chins or belly buttons, that I do not necessarily want to assume. (Whether religious belief truly is an *inevitable* consequence of human psychological architecture is a fascinating question, but one I do not wish to tackle here.) Perhaps most important, I think it will be clear throughout subsequent chapters that some aspects of religion look more spandrellike, and others look more exaptationlike. For present purposes, then, I stick with the more general term *by-product*.

The general idea that religion is not the result of any adaptations designed specifically to produce it, but rather emerges from the operation of many other psychological adaptations that were naturally selected for other purposes, has been suggested by numerous theorists. Sperber (1996, p. 75) suggests that "religious beliefs develop not because of a disposition, but because of a susceptibility" (p. 75). Read "adaptation" and "by-product" for "disposition" and "susceptibility," respectively. Evolutionary psychologists including Buss et al. (1998) and Pinker (1997) refer to religion in the context of by-products, alongside other "higher" cultural products such as art and literature. Pinker (1997) uses the term *exaptation*, but I believe his intended meaning is essentially the same as mine. Atran (2002; also Atran & Norenzayan, in press) also offers a "religion as evolutionary by-product" view that overlaps considerably with the one presented here.[4]

If religion is not in fact an adaptation, you might ask, how would an evolutionary approach be useful, or even relevant, to understanding it? Buss et al. (1998) argue that evolutionary psychology is very much relevant to understanding evolutionary by-products, though such explanations will necessarily take a form somewhat different from explanations of adaptations. Specifically, they suggest that such explanations "must involve (a) an understanding of the evolved mechanisms that make humans capable of performing the behavior, and (b) an understanding of the evolved cognitive and motivational mechanisms that led humans to exploit such capabilities" (p. 541). Although Pinker (1997) and Buss et al. (1998) refer in passing to religion as an evolutionary by-product, neither takes on the task of addressing these questions. The remainder of this book is intended to offer a general framework for doing exactly this.

Religion as an Evolutionary By-product

It is now time to recast the first half of this book in terms of the second half. The attachment theory approach to religion I sketched in the first several chapters was a religion as evolutionary by-product explanation, according to which the attachment system is one particular adaptation in humans that has been co-opted or capitalized upon by many religious belief systems. Many ideas about God activate the cognitive machinery of the attachment system, which processes the ideas in attachment terms. As a consequence, people often perceive their relationships with deities functionally in terms of attachment relationships, monitoring their sense of felt security and acting toward these deities accordingly. They use these deities as a haven of safety in times of fear and distress, and as a secure base in the absence of fear and distress. We do not have an evolved God module or psychological system whose adaptive function is to cause us to think about gods in this way. Instead, we have an evolved module or psychological system whose evolutionary function is to promote survival of helpless offspring, and which is designed to monitor parental caregiving and availability in relation to current circumstances and guide behavior accordingly. This mechanism is recruited in the context of thinking about gods and other religious figures and thus shapes religious ideas and behavior in particular ways.

In discussing evolutionary by-products, Pinker (1997) refers to music as "auditory cheesecake"—the idea being that most of us find cheesecake wonderfully delicious because it capitalizes on our evolved preferences for sweets and fats. We do not have an evolved mechanism dedicated to preparing or seeking cheesecake; instead, the invention of cheesecake capitalized on those preexisting mechanisms that evolved for noncheesecake purposes. Cheesecake is exquisitely designed (by humans, of course, not by natural selection) to maximally titillate these evolved taste-preference mechanisms. In short, I think religion is a kind of socio-emotional-cognitive cheesecake.

An Analogy: Games and Sports

Consider sports and games, which in one form or another are universal across societies and which vary in form sufficiently across societies to make a good analogy to religion. Earlier in this chapter I briefly referred to the game of soccer ("football," to most of the world) as an example of a widespread human activity that surely is not explained by the existence of any kind of evolved mechanism dedicated to soccer playing. How might an evolutionary psychologist approach the problem of explaining the psychology (and/or sociology, etc.) of soccer?

First, notice that the kinds of evidence often cited in favor of an evolved religion instinct or adaptation, as discussed in the first section of this chapter, would be readily rejected as evidence of an evolved soccer instinct or adaptation. At least among developed societies at the beginning of the 21st century, soccer is nearly universal across human cultures; we might even imagine a point in time, not far in the future, in which the game is played in every human society. It is probably the case that individual differences in soccer playing or soccer ability are partly heritable – undoubtedly as an indirect influence of individual differences in a variety of correlated (confounded) physical and psychological characteristics that are themselves heritable. Kittens playing with balls of yarn might be cited as a suggestive cross-species comparison pointing to proto-soccer mechanisms in nonhumans. Although I doubt that anyone has (or ever will) collect the data, I believe that brain-imaging techniques would show that certain parts of the brain, but not others, predictably light up when people kick soccer balls. However, none of these lines of evidence would be considered compelling in favor of the hypothesis that evolution has designed humans specifically to play soccer.

Instead, a great deal about soccer can be explained in terms of (i.e., as a by-product of) a host of mechanisms that evolved for other (i.e., nonsoccer) purposes. Playing the game draws upon a variety of perceptual (especially spatial) skills, motor skills, eye–hand (foot) coordination, and so forth. Team competition—as well as the psychology of rabid fans—has all the hallmarks of coalitional psychology, including cooperation among ingroups in opposition to outgroups. Within these groups, however, there is also competition among individuals, who strive for personal achievement as well as team achievement. The fact that (male) star players are admired by other men and seen as attractive by women implicate the activity of intrasexual competition and mating systems. The emotions associated with the thrill of victory and the agony of defeat reflect evolved systems for monitoring success and failure, such as self-esteem. I could go on, but you get the point.

There is little doubt that soccer has undergone considerable change and development—"evolution," if you will—over time. The earliest competitive games invented by humans probably differed little from real-life competitions concerning who was the most successful hunter, the best fighter, and so forth; in some sense, the earliest games probably were exactly those contests. Sometime later, contests probably became ritualized and at least partly divorced from their real-life competitive domains; one can easily imagine wrestling matches, spear-throwing competitions, or footraces emerging as contests outside the context of the real hunt. Even today, Yanomamo men of the Amazon basin compete in a ritualized contest in which they take turns whacking each other with large blunt objects until one gives in (Chagnon, 1992). In modern technological societies, sports have evolved further to take on additional social functions: Professional athletes make a living at them, for example, and the Olympic Games have taken on an important role in international affairs. Religions have no doubt evolved over time in a parallel way, beginning as relatively simple beliefs that emerged readily from preexisting cognitive, emotional, and motivational systems and subsequently have been modified, refined, and expanded into myriad forms over the centuries.

SUMMARY AND CONCLUSIONS

In this chapter I have (finally) made explicit a general perspective that had been implicit throughout the preceding chapters. Religion, I am suggesting, is not itself an adaption; humans do not possess, as part of our species-universal evolved psychological architecture, mechanisms designed by natural selection specifically for the purpose of generating religious belief or behavior as a solution to any particular adaptive problem. The attachment theory of religion outlined in the first half of the book can now be seen as simply one part of a much broader model, in which the attachment system represents just one of many domain-specific psychological mechanisms that have been co-opted in the service of religion and religious belief. When people think about God, or various other deities or supernatural figures, their thinking is in part guided and shaped by the cognitive, emotional, and behavioral machinery of the attachment system in conjunction with the details of their own individual attachment-related experience. In the next two chapters I discuss a variety of other evolved mechanisms and systems that underlie other, different aspects of people's understanding of God or gods, as well as other diverse aspects of religious belief.

Recall that the power of cheesecake is that it is well designed to titillate at least two distinct taste-preference mechanisms—specifically, preferences for both fats and sweets. The power of religion is analogous. Religious beliefs activate attachment processes but also many other psychological processes as well, and it is probably this *combination* that is responsible for its widespread success and staying power. Moreover, this diversity of psychological underpinnings enables religion itself to be shaped in different ways that are maximally well suited for appealing to different cultures or different people at different times. To abuse the analogy further, consider the fact that there are many different kinds of recipes for making cheesecake: Some varieties of cheesecake are sweeter than others, some creamier than others. One could even make low-fat cheesecake by making a few crucial substitutions. Some of these varieties are prized especially by people with a sweet tooth; the low-fat varieties are valued by people on diets. It is all cheesecake, but different components can be played up or toned down to suit the particular preferences and values of the consumer.

I think religion works in much the same way: Some religions such as Christianity—and particularly certain variants, such as evangelical and charismatic traditions—emphasize the image of deities as attachment figures; other religions emphasize other themes. Likewise, within any given religious tradition, individual-difference variability in religious beliefs and values is owed in part to the ability of people to pick and choose those aspects of the belief system that strike them as most plausible, valuable, or important in light of their own personal experience. The power of religion is attributable, at least partly, to the fact that there is "something for everybody." What evolutionary psychology brings to the table is a framework for determining what those particular somethings are and how they work.

CHAPTER TEN

Beyond Attachment

Religion and Other Evolved
Psychological Mechanisms

In the previous chapter I outlined a general framework for applying evolutionary psychology to religion, by conceptualizing religion as a by-product of numerous evolved psychological mechanisms. One of these, the attachment system, has been discussed in detail. I now turn to some of several other evolved psychological mechanisms, and suggest some examples of the ways in which the footprints of these domain-specific mechanisms are evident in some of the common forms that religion takes. Specifically, I introduce some of the other "middle-level" evolutionary theories mentioned in Chapter 7, working at a level of analysis roughly comparable to attachment theory.

One theme I emphasized in my discussion of attachment and religion was the more general issue of religion as "relationship." A great deal of religious belief and behavior involves perceived relationships with supernatural beings, as well as with religious leaders and fellow believers. Like attachment theory, all of the theories discussed in this chapter are, at core, theories of interpersonal relationships. Much of our evolved psychological architecture comprises mechanisms dedicated to tasks related to negotiating social relationships. From an evolutionary perspective, however, varieties of interpersonal relationships differ in *kind*, reflecting qualitatively distinct sets of adaptive problems. Attachment relationships are about bonds between caregivers and care recipients and characterize parent–child relationships, and psychological mechanisms underlying them evolved to maintain proximity of helpless infants to caregivers for the (ultimate) function of providing protection from predation and other environmental threats. Other kinds of relationships involve different processes, guided by other psychological mechanisms that evolved for different reasons.

POWER, STATUS, AND INTRASEXUAL COMPETITION

Status, prestige, esteem, honor, respect, and rank are accorded differentially to individuals in all known groups. People devote tremendous effort to avoiding disrepute, dishonor, shame, humiliation, disgrace, and loss of face. Empirical evidence suggests that status and dominance hierarchies form quickly. . . . If there were ever a reasonable candidate for a universal human motive, status striving would be at or near the top of the list. (Buss, 2004, pp. 344–345)

In the material replaced here by ellipses, Buss cites experimental studies showing that only minutes after groups of strangers are assembled, clear hierarchies emerge (Fisek & Ofshe, 1970) and that individuals can accurately predict their future status in the group without even having spoken to the others (Kalma, 1991).

Dominance hierarchies of one form or another are clearly evident in species from crickets and crayfish to chimpanzees (and humans). In the simplest (and perhaps most common) case, status is determined by physical size and strength. Larger and stronger individuals defeat rivals in combat, or actual fighting is avoided when the weaker sizes up the other and defaults by submitting or fleeing. In chimpanzees, size and strength are less critical in determining status than "connections": High rank is achieved by way of assembling *alliances* with other individuals who come to the dominant individual's aid when challenged (in exchange for other favors). In all of these cases, the value of status is the increased access to important resources: High-ranking individuals get the best territories, food and water, and—perhaps most important—access to preferred mates.

It is with this last point that the issue of *sex differences* emerges as an important consideration, albeit one that has hardly appeared in this book up to this point. I do not want to wander too far off into the world of sex differences, in part because this is such a controversial, emotionally charged area, and in part because sex differences are only of tangential interest in the context of this book. Nevertheless, there are places where evolutionary theory predicts such differences and empirical observation supports them, so they cannot be ignored. Sexual access to females represents an important adaptive function of dominance competition in males more than in females.[1] In many species, intrasexual competition among males takes the form of a winner-take-all contest, in which the emerging victor gains exclusive or at least preferential sexual access to reproductive females. Behind all of this is the driving force of female choice: It is the females who choose with whom to breed. It is important to note that although in many species females prefer the victors of physical contests, in many other species competition takes other forms, such as displays of qualities that advertise "good genes," including coloration and symmetry of physical features. In humans, much empirical research confirms that men are generally more strongly motivated to compete and strive for status than are women, at least in the sense of attempting to elevate themselves above others, and women all around the world value status and resource-acquisition ability in choosing mates much more strongly than do men (see Buss, 1989, 1992, for a review). There is no shortage of historical evidence to show that men tend to use high status in the service of gaining access to women, as well illustrated by kings and emperors who maintain dozens or hundreds of wives and/or concubines.[2]

Although such constructs as status, dominance, and prestige are often treated more or less as synonymous, there are good reasons to think that several functionally distinct psychological systems might need to be distinguished. Henrich and Gil-White (2001) suggest that *status* involves, at a general level, social asymmetries in power and resource-acquisition potential. In humans, however, status is attained through at least two distinct means or pathways. *Dominance*, they argue, refers to relationships in which high status is attained and enforced through the use or threat of force. In contrast, *prestige* refers to status that is freely conferred by subordinates who hope to learn and benefit from the target's recognized skills, abilities, or knowledge. Consequently, prestigious individuals are honored and revered, rather than feared, by subordinates. Behavioral differences include the observations that subordinates (sycophants) seek proximity to and eye contact with prestigious individuals, whereas subordinates maintain distance from and avoid eye contact with dominant individuals. Recent research in my own laboratory (Snyder & Kirkpatrick, 2002, 2003) has demonstrated the distinction between dominance and prestige to be crucial in the context of female mate preferences.

Supernatural Beings as Power Figures

Based on an extensive review of ancient religions, historian Walter Burkert (1996) concludes that "religion is generally accepted as a system of rank, implying dependence, subordination and submission to unseen superiors. The awareness of rank and dependence in religion is particularly clear in all the ancient religions" (p. 81). The influence of dominance/status mechanisms in God beliefs is consistent with a variety of observations about worship behavior common to many religions, including Christianity. For example, recall Hardy's (1966) suggested parallel between perceptions of gods and "canine devotion" to their masters, which (following Lorenz) he attributed partly to attachment to mothers and partly to submission to tribal leaders (or in the case of wild dogs, pack leaders). Burkert (1996) observes that behavioral expressions of veneration and submission common in religious worship, such as bending, bowing, kneeling, and touching one's head to the ground, have much in common with human surrender displays (i.e., in warfare), as well as with the submissive displays of lower-ranking individuals toward higher-ranking ones in many other primate species. Similarly, Paden (1988) suggests that massive cathedrals are designed to "declare the smallness of human stature" relative to God.

I suggested in a previous chapter that some behavioral expressions of worship might be interpreted as manifestations of the attachment system. However, the specific behaviors noted by Burkert (1996) seem clearly more consistent with submission behavior than attachment behavior. In neither chimpanzees nor humans, for example, do infants manifest the same kinds of submission displays to their parents as they do (later in life) toward dominant adults. Attachment figures are clearly perceived as more "powerful" by infants and children, but this meaning of "powerful" should not be confused with the very different sense of relative status and dominance in intrasexual competition.

Patterns of individual differences in beliefs about God, as discussed in Chapter 4, suggest that a dimension related to dominance and status is a major factor with respect to which people vary in their conceptualizations of God. Recall that factor-analytic studies widely show that after a first, attachment-related factor (God as loving, nurturing, etc.), the second major factor that typically emerges from God-image data concerns God as powerful and controlling. Benson and Spilka (1973) labeled their second (of two) factors *Controlling God*; Gorsuch (1968) named one of his factors *kingly*. In the ongoing debate concerning maternal/feminine versus paternal/masculine images of God, the latter is typically conceptualized in terms of power, strength, and dominance. Again, although some aspects of this "masculine" component might be conceptualized in attachment terms—I suggested that being strong and powerful would enhance the perceived ability of an attachment figure to provide protection and security—these beliefs about God as powerful and controlling are probably more consistent with a conceptualization of God as a "big chief" or the ultimate king. According to Burkert (1996), "Jahweh" is one of only many examples in which the word for God is essentially synonymous with "king."

Another interesting observation explained by this perspective is that in polytheistic belief systems ranging from African traditional religions to the more familiar pantheons of classical Rome and Greece, the gods invariably are perceived as displaying a status hierarchy (or multiple hierarchies) amongst themselves, with one god reigning supreme over the others (Smart, 1976). Sometimes this supreme God is perceived as so distant (metaphorically or and/or physically) from humans that they are unable to interact with him or her directly; instead, humans have direct relationships only with lower gods or with human intermediaries (Smart, 1976). Such hierarchies are typical even in belief systems characterized by more abstract (i.e., less fully anthropomorphized) "spirits" or "powers" rather than gods per se, as in the Nuer and Dinka peoples of Africa (Comstock, 1972). Such thinking seems a direct reflection of a psychological mechanism designed specifically to process information about relative dominance and status and keep track of the current hierarchy and each individual's place within it.

In the preceding discussion, prestige processes seem clearly evident in some examples and dominance processes in others. God or gods can be perceived either as prestigious figures to be honored and revered, or as dominant figures to be feared. Within Christianity, the difference is in many ways illustrated by contrasting the God of the Old Testament with that of the New Testament. An interesting direction for future research would be to devise separate measures of these dimensions in, for example, people's images of God, to determine if they display different correlates as compared to existing measures such as the Benson–Spilka *Controlling God* scale.

Human Religious Leaders as Power Figures

Apart from the gods themselves, religious institutions—like many other human cultural institutions—are at least in part social hierarchies of status, power, and dominance. The roles of shaman, priest, medicine man, and so forth in preliterate societies are important power positions that command respect and awe from other group members. Burkert (1996) refers to these perceptions of religious leaders as the "other side" of submission in religion (p. 93).

Some kind of division of labor, based at least in part on variability in specific valuable skills and abilities, is probably common to all societies. Ridley (1996) argues that specialization is by no means a modern phenomenon, suggesting that it is easily observed in contemporary hunter–gatherer peoples such as the Ache and surely was characteristic of our Stone Age ancestors as well: "One man made stone tools, another knew how to find game, a third was especially good at throwing spears, a fourth could be relied on as a strategist" (p. 49). Given the diversity and complexity of ancestral environments and social structures, it seems reasonable to assume that humans have evolved mechanisms for identifying experts in their respective domains and treating them as leaders within those domains. One such domain that represents a recognized area of expertise in most if not all societies is that of religion (and related domains such as magic).

This scenario may have special importance with respect to religion, for several reasons. First, it is much more difficult to determine objectively whether one person's expertise about, say, the desires of the gods is greater than another's. Someone's claim to be the best spear-thrower is empirically testable; someone who rarely hits the target will not be regarded as a spear-throwing expert for long. On whatever basis people decide which religious experts to trust, they subsequently treat these leaders with great deference and respect and trust their proclamations. Although such scenarios can be quite benevolent and mutually beneficial, it is easy to generate modern and historical examples of exploitation of power by people in leadership positions, ranging from the pre-Reformation Roman Catholic Church against which Luther rebelled to modern televangelist shysters.

A related reason, as suggested by several theorists, is that religious beliefs are often poorly understood by the people who subscribe to them. As will be discussed more fully in the next chapter, Sperber (1996) suggests that religious ideas are often only "half-understood," and people consequently must rely on trusted authorities to explain these beliefs to them or to tell them how to behave appropriately. In discussing the "looseness" of Fang beliefs about ghosts, Boyer (1994b) notes that "Only certain qualified speakers, such as religious specialists, make definite statements about these matters, and even they often qualify them with such comments as 'these things are obscure,' 'we are only repeating what our fathers told us,' and so on" (p. 93). Pinker (1997) summarizes the idea succinctly by noting that religion "exploits people's dependence on experts" (p. 557). As a consequence of all this, the role of religious leader, in whatever particular form it takes, is typically one imbued with high status—achieved by means of prestige rather than dominance, it might be noted—and thus one worth pursuing and achieving if possible.

It is worth noting in passing that this is one domain in which an evolutionary approach suggests hypotheses about potential sex differences in religious belief. Parental investment theory predicts that men should on average be more concerned with issues of power, status, and dominance and the negotiation of such hierarchies. This may explain why the power positions of shamans, priests, and so forth have long been held most commonly by men, as well as the fact that more recent liberalizing efforts—such as according the status of priesthood to women—often evoke strong opposition. Cox (1967) found that boys were more likely to view God as a supreme power, forceful planner, and controller, whereas girls tended to depict God more as loving, comforting, and forgiving. Similar results were reported by Nelsen, Cheek, and Au (1985) in an adult sample. Note, too, that these particular sex differences are not easily explained by a simple socialization process: Parents may buy dolls for little girls and toy trucks for little boys, and encourage them to play accordingly, but I doubt that parents (or anyone else) teach boys and girls qualitatively different lessons with respect to what God is like.

KINSHIP

The theory of *kin selection* is really an inherent component of the highest-level theory in the hierarchy, namely Hamilton's (1964) theory of inclusive fitness, but it is worth separating out here and placing it at the "middle-level" for our purposes. Once it is acknowledged that natural selection involves the relative success of genes rather than of individuals (or species), the conclusion is inescapable that behavioral strategies designed to facilitate the reproductive success of one's close kin—individuals who, by virtue of genetic relatedness through common ancestry have a greater-than-average probability of carrying the same genes as oneself—can be highly adaptive. Kin selection is one of two general evolutionary theories widely recognized to explain the evolution of *altruism*—behavior that benefits others at (usually) some cost to the self.[3] (The other theory is discussed in the next section.)

Parental investment in offspring represents a special case of kin-related altruism, one that is easily overlooked with respect to attachment. It is obvious why an attachment system is adaptive for *infants*: Seeking proximity to and protection from caregivers is clearly in the infant's survival interests. But the only reason an attachment system could evolve in the first place if it were in the interest of caregivers to provide protection and nurturance, and the existence of caregiving systems is due to the fact that parents (or, more specifically, parents' genes) have a direct (genetic) interest in the infant's fate.

Anthropologists have long appreciated the importance of kinship and recognized it as a crucial set of issues in all societies. In psychology, however, kinship represents a huge "conceptual hole" that has received surprisingly little research attention (Daly, Salmon, & Wilson, 1997). The importance of kinship psychology for understanding religion, however, is evident in a variety of ways.

Supernatural Beings and Religious Leaders as Kin

One way in which kinship psychology is manifest in religious belief is with respect to beliefs about the dead, and particularly one's ancestors. A belief in the immortality (in some form or another) of the dead occurs in all cultures (Lehmann & Myers, 1993) as does the worship (again, in some form or other) of *ancestors* (Steadman, Palmer, & Tilley, 1996). Deceased ancestors are typically seen to have rather typical kin concerns, such as "continuance of the line" and the expectation that living relatives will seek vengeance on their behalf if they had been wrongly killed (Smart, 1976). In many belief systems, ancestors are much like gods who continue to look after their living relatives. Part of our evolved psychology is the expectation that kin, more than nonkin, can be counted on for assistance and support when the chips are down. If dead ancestors continue to "live" in some way and exert influence on the world, psychological mechanisms devoted to kinship concerns may be responsible for shaping the belief that they would continue to be concerned about the welfare and continuance of their family line. I doubt that there are any societies in which the principal goals of ancestors' ghosts is to cause harm to, or impede the success of, their descendants.

The idea of God as a parent, discussed previously, is often expressed directly in kinship language, as when God is addressed or referred to as "Our Father." This is where kinship psychology—in particular, parental investment —and attachment theory converge: For God to serve effectively as an attachment figure, we must assume that God is deeply interested in us and our welfare. Kin, including (especially) parents, are the only individuals who can be counted on to provide the level of caregiving that an ideal attachment figure would provide, and thinking of a divine attachment figure in parent (kin) terms supports these beliefs. This same kind of language is similarly common with respect to religious leaders, as when priests are addressed as "Father." I suspect that this linguistic "trick" capitalizes on kinship mechanisms that, once activated, promote an enhanced level of obedience and trust that would be accorded only reluctantly to nonkin. In turn, a priest addressing a worshiper as "my son" reflects the flip side of this relationship, in a manner that may be useful in promoting an enhanced level of concern and investment in the welfare of his "children."

As we saw with respect to dominance and status hierarchies, perceptions of the relationships among multiple gods tend to reflect people's understanding of human relationships. In the classical Roman and Greek pantheons, gods beget other gods and evince complex systems of kinship. If you think about it, there is no logical or necessary reason why gods should be conceived of as parents or children of other gods. At least one god must be the first, the child of no other god. So why not simply believe that all gods have existed forever, or appeared at the same time? I suggest it is because human brains/minds are built to parse human relationships largely along kinship lines, and naturally apply these kinship schemata when trying to discern the minds and lives of the gods.

Ingroup Members as Kin

Batson (1983) observed that prosocial behavior is enhanced by the use of kinship imagery for this reason, particularly in the context of religion. Worshipers often refer to one another as "brothers and sisters," as do monks and nuns; religious ethics promote "brotherly love" (but more on this in the next section). The reason these linguistic tricks are effective is that they activate kin mechanisms and motivate mutually altruistic behavior. The same modus operandi is evident in other social groups as well, such as fraternities and sororities. Buss (2004) points out that the phrase "Brother, can you spare a dime?" similarly owes its existence to its effectiveness in activating kinlike concerns.

This hypothesis has been developed most fully and forcefully by Crippen and Machalek (1989), who describe religion generally as a "hypertrophied kin recognition process" (p. 74). In their explicitly evolutionary view, "kin recognition mechanisms are 'usurped' to form communities of fictive kin" (p. 68), which in turn encourages "individuals to subordinate their apparent self-interest to the collectively-expressed interest of sovereign agencies" (p. 70). That is, religious beliefs represent a kind of cognitive error in which psychological mechanisms that evolved for the purpose of identifying kin (and treating them preferentially) are led to misidentify unrelated ingroup members as kin, in much the same way (this is my analogy, not theirs) that our taste-preference mechanisms can be fooled into enjoying soft drinks or potato chips flavored with artificial sweeteners and fat substitutes. Although the authors may go a bit too far in identifying these processes as a complete theory of religion, it neatly explains a variety of ways in which group members might be encouraged (tricked, really) into promoting the welfare of the group despite the absence of evolved mechanisms designed for this purpose. It also may be useful in understanding the ways in which religious beliefs are tied to such constructs as nationalism and patriotism, a topic to which I return later.

The worship of ancestors may be another way of accomplishing the same trick as other "kin-talk." Identification and reverence or worship of ancestors makes salient the group's shared ancestry, with the implication that group members are all (genetic) relatives (Steadman et al., 1996). Similarly, the related phenomenon of *totemism*, in which an animal or other natural object is recognized and revered as symbolic of the clan, may function in the same way. Like ancestor worship, totemic beliefs have the effect of making salient the relatedness among group members by virtue of common descent. (Other aspects of totemism are discussed in Chapter 11.)

Wenegrat (1990) has suggested another variation on the theme, combining the idea of God as an attachment figure with that of fellow worshipers as siblings. In his view, people "believe that they are involved in a reciprocal altruistic relationship with a deity they perceive as a universal parent, who has asked them to be their brother's keeper" (p. 74). That is, another reason for behaving altruistically toward others is that your shared "parent" implores you to do so. You owe it to God, too. I am skeptical about this idea, however, because it fails to take adequately into account the problem of parent–offspring conflict (Trivers, 1974). Because parents are equally related genetically to all of their offspring, it is in the parents' interest for siblings to promote each others' welfare as much as possible. Individual offspring, however, are more closely related to themselves (obviously) than to their siblings, so their interests in the sibling's welfare are not quite as strong. As any parent of multiple children knows, it is not as easy to get kids to cooperate as it sounds. Although children's evolved psychology does motivate them to behave more altruistically toward siblings than toward nonkin, this altruism does not quite reach the level the parents would prefer.

Be that as it may, such a "hypertrophied kin-recognition process" illustrates one way in which religion could function to promote group cohesion and mutualism, as suggested by Durkheim (1912) and many others, without recourse to dubious assumptions about the evolution of characteristics on the basis of their benefits to groups. This process is probably most effective in small, tribal societies, in which the idea of shared ancestry (i.e., of a few hundred people or fewer) may be intuitively more plausible than in larger, more diverse societies. Within the latter, however, it may also be particularly effective within small subpopulations, particularly those that are ethnically homogeneous. In an observational study of immigrant Chinese churches, Palinkas (1982; cited in Pargament, 1997) found that group members always addressed each other in familial terms (i.e., as brothers and sisters). Given that small groups of immigrants undoubtedly have a particular need to "stick together," it makes sense that such churches might be especially likely to capitalize on this process.

On the other hand, there are limits to how far this "hypertrophied kin-recognition" trick can be taken. One potential consequence is the emergence of competition for loyalties between *fictive* kin, as promoted within religious groups, and *real* kin. When push comes to shove, people understand that their "brothers and sisters" in faith are not "really" kin, and this is a tough battle for the fictive side to win. Pinker (1997, p. 439) avers that all religious (and political) movements attempt to subvert loyalty to families, one well known example being Jesus's ultimatum about choosing between God and parents. Pinker also notes that laws created by the ruling class or religious institutions have often been in the service of breaking the stranglehold of evolved nepotism. For example, incest laws have been designed to prevent consolidation of power within families via marriages between cousins, not to prevent brother–sister incest (which requires no such laws, given our evolved disinclination to mate with siblings). Similar arguments have been made concerning the medieval church's rules on sex and marriage (Betzig, 1986).

RECIPROCAL ALTRUISM AND SOCIAL EXCHANGE

I noted earlier that modern evolutionary theory provides two ways in which apparently altruistic behavior can evolve, one being via kin selection. The other is explained by the theory of *reciprocal altruism* (Trivers, 1971). In short, it is adaptive to behave in a way that benefits another if, in exchange, the benefit will be returned at a comparable level: "You scratch my back and I'll scratch yours." The evolvability of such strategies has been studied extensively using mathematical simulations and game theory. In the most famous example, Axelrod (1984) conducted a tournament for computer programs designed to play an iterated (i.e., multiple-trial) version of the classic Prisoner's Dilemma. The winner that emerged out of the round-robin, head-to-head competition turns out to be the simplest and shortest of the programs submitted: *Tit-for-Tat* cooperated on the first move, then simply parroted the opponent's previous move on each subsequent trial. Despite a huge amount of research since, Tit-for-Tat—or something closely related, such as "Two-Tits-for-a-Tat"— consistently appears a winning formula (Poundstone, 1992).

Ethological research has produced many examples of similar behavior in other species. In the famous example of vampire bats, for example, successful hunters have been observed, both in natural environments and under controlled laboratory conditions, to regurgitate food to the unsuccessful back at the cave, but only to "friends" who had done so for them in the past (Wilkinson, 1984). In humans, of course, the tit-for-tat concept is very familiar: in economics, from old-fashioned bartering to modern monetary systems, and in law and politics (for better or worse) as *quid pro quo*. In humans, however, our advanced cognitive abilities allow us to use more complex bookkeeping strategies that may at times appear as if they are not governed by rules of reciprocity (Batson, 1993).

The principal threat to reciprocal altruism, from an evolutionary perspective, is the counterstrategy of *cheating*. This is what prevents pure, indiscriminate altruism from evolving in a way that would otherwise be "good for the group": An individual (and his or her genes) can be wildly successful by enjoying a free ride, taking the benefits of others' do-gooding without incurring the costs. Therefore, if mechanisms coding for reciprocal-altruism strategies are to evolve, other mechanisms devoted to the task of identifying cheaters must co-evolve along with them. An extensive empirical research program by Leda Cosmides (1989; see Cosmides & Tooby, 1992, for a review) demonstrates the existence of a mechanism activated specifically by violations of *social contracts*. In a word, people are easily able to solve a difficult symbolic logic problem when it is posed specifically in a social-contract context—specifically, "if you take the benefit, then you must meet the obligation"—but make systematic errors in logic otherwise.

In addition, human psychology includes motivational and behavioral systems for responding to and punishing such wrongdoing. The physiological and affective components of *anger* are clearly universal human responses to perceptions of having been "done wrong" in some way. What is interesting about such responses is that they often tend to far exceed the desire to restore equity. If you have ever had a radio stolen from your car or your home burglarized, you know what I mean: Receiving a new stereo or computer from the criminal in retribution is not what is on your mind. You probably are fantasizing about how you would literally kill—and perhaps torture—the person if only you could get your hands on him or her. Frank's (1988) commitment device notion, described in Chapter 8, offers an intriguing explanation. Would-be thieves cannot steal briefcases indiscriminately because they know that the victim's powerful, emotionally laden desire for vengeance will overwhelm his or her rational assessment of the situation; the victim will not hesitate to incur disproportionate costs to see the thief punished. The visible cues of rage, Frank suggests, have evolved as an honest signal of this capacity. Thus, because would-be thieves know that their victims will respond in this way rather than in a cold, calculating manner, briefcase stealing carries immense risks that deter most from trying their luck (see also Daly & Wilson, 1988, for a similar discussion).

Supernatural Beings as Social-Exchange Partners

Perhaps the most common theme in people's perceived relationships with gods, from so-called primitive religions to modern-day Christianity, is that of some form of reciprocity. Virtually everywhere, people hope to receive benefits of various sorts from the gods, in exchange for which they assume they must meet certain obligations. As summarized by Burkert (1996),

> practically everywhere it is understood that communication with the divine should be through exchange, through mutual giving, which is reflected in the circulation of gifts within the community or hierarchy of believers. One might even be tempted to say that every form of religion is, among other things, an organization to elicit gifts. (pp. 144–145)

A reciprocally altruistic relationship with God, however, poses a unique problem: What could humans possibly offer in exchange that would be of any value to God? (Talk about someone who is difficult to shop for!) People have pushed their creativity to its limits in trying to figure out what the gods want, from gifts, monuments, and sacrifices to submissive behavior to doing good deeds. Fortunately, the evolved logic of social exchange does not demand that you understand why your contribution benefits the other—only that the other treats it as a benefit. Because gifts cannot be handed to gods directly, a common alternative is either to destroy or withdraw valuable goods from human society, or to redistribute them within society (see Burkert, 1996, for numerous examples and further discussion). Even if it is not clear that the gods would somehow benefit directly from such actions, the latter are psychologically fulfilling because they provide a sense that one has demonstrated a willingness to incur significant costs in exchange for benefits received. Consequently, the objects (or animals or people) sacrificed are selected because they are valued by the people doing the sacrificing, not necessarily by God.[4]

An alternative perspective is provided by Atran (2002; Atran & Norenzayan, in press), who argues that sacrifice represents a demonstration by individuals of their willingness to incur costs on behalf of the group. Building upon Alexander's (1987) concept of *indirect reciprocity*, "the basic idea is to help those who are known to help others" (Atran, 2002, p. 119). A crucial element of religious sacrifices from this perspective is that they are both *costly* and *hard to fake*, which leads them to be interpreted as sincere social commitment. Atran emphasizes (and I agree) that the evolution of such mechanisms could be favored by natural selection due to the (reputational) benefits to the sacrificing individuals, not because of any resulting benefits to the group as a whole (i.e., "group selection"). Nevertheless, there is no reason why such behavior could not also have auxiliary effects of enhancing social cohesion and cooperation or benefiting entire groups in other ways.

Of course, the assumption is that "if we please the gods—with sacrifices, food offerings, or prayer—we expect to be rewarded with military victory, good harvests or a ticket to heaven" (Ridley, 1996, p. 131). If we fail, however, the consequences are invariably expected to be dire. Taking the benefits without meeting those obligations is, in effect, to cheat the gods, who in turn would be expected to become enraged (recall the stolen-briefcase caper) and exact some form of revenge and/or punishment (such as damning one to hell for eternity). In many cases such understood agreements take the form of a formal agreement or covenant, as in the Old Testament. Whether explicit in this way or merely understood, reciprocal exchange agreements between gods and people are evident in nearly all religions.

An overextension of social-contract thinking to the natural world—a "hypertrophied social-exchange process," if you will—may underlie the much-researched phenomenon of "belief in a just world" (Lerner, 1980). People everywhere tend to believe the world is a place where everyone gets his or her just desserts, and where the good are rewarded and the wicked are punished. This belief, whether conscious or not, is so strong that when bad things happen to good people, we tend to infer automatically that they must not be good people after all. As shown in a variety of experiments, people tend to "denigrate the victim" when something bad happens to them for no immediately obvious reason, inferring that the fate must *somehow* be deserved (see Lerner, 1980, for a review). It therefore proves easier to alter one's (probably unconscious) perceptions of the person than to "admit" (again, probably unconsciously) that the world is sometimes unjust. In Ridley's (1996) words, "We invent social exchange in even the most inappropriate situations" and "display a steadfast refusal to believe in good or bad luck" (p. 131). A related example I find fascinating is the strong sense of gratitude we tend to feel when we benefit from some unexpected, fortuitous event that we clearly have done nothing to earn. Even atheists will confess that they feel "thankful" on such occasions, despite being at a loss to say to whom.

You may or may not agree that just-world beliefs fall within the category of "religious" beliefs. As I have suggested previously, however, it is not important where people wish to draw lines between religion and non-religion; the question is which psychological mechanisms explain which phenomena. In any event, belief in a just world often does take on an explicitly religious character by any reasonable definition. For example, supernatural beings are often seen to provide the means by which a social-exchange "contract" with nature can be enforced. The reason bad things do not happen to good people is that God does not let them; God can enforce justice. As Pargament (1998) notes, God is virtually always seen by believers as just; he does not punish or wreak havoc arbitrarily, but always for good reason (whether or not we understand that reason). The Old Testament is replete with examples of God enforcing a "just world"—at least a world that is assumed to be just in God's eyes.

Sometimes, however, this system breaks down: One is forced by some (probably emotionally distressing) circumstance to confess that something bad really did happen to a good person. When it does, it creates an extremely troubling problem—one with which philosophers and theologians have struggled for centuries (see, e.g., Kushner, 1981). The beliefs that God is good and just and that God is all-powerful simply cannot be reconciled logically with the observation of injustice. As I discuss more fully in Chapter 11, this may be simply because religious beliefs are not necessarily organized logically into a coherent system. Instead, different aspects of beliefs about God are constructed and maintained by different, functionally distinct reasoning systems, with consequences that may or may not be logically consistent. Inconsistencies can be tolerated to a surprising extent, but circumstances can sometimes force the issue in a manner that creates something of a psychological crisis.

Finally, an evolutionary perspective on social exchange and cheater detection offers insights into the phenomenon of *forgiveness*, which has received increased attention of late in the psychology of religion litera-ture (e.g., McCullough, Pargament, & Thoreson, 2000). Pingleton (1989) summarizes the meaning of forgiveness concisely as "giving up the right to hurt back" (p. 27). That is, our evolved psychology leads us to expect and/or demand compensation or vengeance for a misdeed, whether the punishment comes from the victim or a third party (such as God). Once the idea is in place that God is all-knowing (thus, is aware of your misdeeds or sins) and all-powerful (thus, capable of exacting re-venge or punishing you), an inevitable result must be anxiety and fear about some impending retribution; this is a direct product of the activity of our evolved social-exchange reasoning processes.

There are only a few logically possible solutions to this problem. First, we could (theoretically) avoid ever committing any misdeeds, but of course this is impossible. The fallibility of human nature is emphasized by most religions, thus explicitly ruling out this option. A second possi-bility is to have available a way of undoing or compensating for misdeeds, and of course many religions provide implicit or explicit sets of rules for doing "good acts," penance, or somehow providing remuneration. The third possibility is simply to be forgiven: to hope that God will give up the right to punish you, as a straightforward act of unconditional grace. One or the other of these latter two options can be found in nearly any religion that includes belief in all-knowing and all-powerful god(s).

Mutual Helping and Social Support

We have already seen how kinship mechanisms can be misdirected to en-courage mutual helping and altruism within religious communities. But this is not the only aspect of our evolved psychology that can have this effect. Unrelated individuals form relationships among each other based on reciprocal altruism and other social-exchange processes as well. Pargament (1997) discusses at length the many ways in which people provide mutual social support within religious congregations and fellow-ships. Such processes are not unique to religious groups, of course: Social exchange is a common form of interpersonal relationship in a wide vari-ety of settings. Pargament notes, however, that mutual social support in the context of religious fellowships might be particularly important, be-cause they often provide continuity across longer periods of time than many other, more ephemeral institutions. People drift in and out of clubs, colleges and universities, and other social settings, whereas their association with a church or religious fellowship tend to remain more stable across time.

A distinguishing characteristic of relationships based on reciprocal altruism is that they must be, well, reciprocal; they will dissolve if perceived inequities become too great. Maton (1987) studied mutual helping in congregations and found that "unidirectional givers" often felt resentment toward those they helped, whereas "unidirectional receivers" suffered from feelings of indebtedness and inferiority. We have evolved a psychology that prevents us from giving away resources in ways that on average do not ultimately enhance inclusive fitness and that compel us to reciprocate favors (or expect some sort of negative consequences if we do not). This component of expected reciprocity—if you take the benefit you must meet the obligation—is the crucial difference between social-exchange relationships and attachments. Parents do not expect their infants to in any way reciprocate the caregiving they provide, and infants do not feel guilty about failing to do so.

Morality and Ethics

Most religious belief systems include reference to, if not emphasis on, ethical rules and norms: They are to at least some extent prescriptive programs for correct behavior. Despite considerable cross-cultural variability, certain moral precepts appear to be universal. Perhaps most evident among these are ethical mores reflecting the principles of reciprocal altruism, fair social exchange, and the detection and punishment of cheaters. Virtually all such codes, from Christianity to Confucianism, include some variation on the Golden Rule theme "Do unto others as you would have them do unto you," which is about as explicit a statement of reciprocity as one could hope to find. Treat others well, and expect to be treated well in return. (However, these rules may not be seen to apply to everyone, as discussed in the next section.) Numerous theorists have argued that morality is largely a direct outgrowth of evolved mechanisms designed to promote mutualism or reciprocal altruism (e.g., Alexander, 1987; Ridley, 1996).

Conversely, moral systems (including religious ones) typically deal with the issue of retribution or retaliation against wrongdoers. The idea of "an eye for an eye" seems to go hand-in-glove with the Golden Rule, and similarly appears a fairly direct reflection of the operation of our evolved psychology. Reciprocal altruism can evolve only if concomitant mechanisms are in place to detect cheating and motivate punishment of cheaters, as evidenced (with respect to humans) in the research by Cosmides and Tooby (1992) on mechanisms for detecting cheating on social contracts. In the Old Testament, for example, considerable space is devoted to detailed civil codes for determining the precise retribution required for specific offenses. In this way ethical systems, including religious ones, reflect our evolved patterns of reasoning about social exchange.

From another perspective, Daly and Wilson (1988) suggest that "an eye for an eye" is not so much a moral proscription for encouraging retribution, but rather an injunction against *excessive* retaliation—in other words, "*only* an eye for an eye." Left uncurbed, the powerful emotional response and desire for vengeance in response to being cheated or victimized (Frank, 1988) may well lead us to respond with a level of violence far in excess of what would rationally be considered equitable. If so, then moral injunctions against excessive vengeance may not so much result directly from our evolved psychology, but rather represent social or cultural strictures designed to combat or rein in our evolved psychology. In the absence of such external constraints, (excessive) vengeance provokes further retaliation, which can easily lead to an escalating cycle of violence that is bad for everyone around. Such ongoing exchanges typically involve families and other kin groups and take the form of blood feuds, which are an extremely common phenomenon in human societies (see Daly & Wilson, 1988, for a review). In modern societies, the task of punishing criminals is turned over to the state, which (ideally) is more capable than the parties involved of determining and carrying out an equitable form of retribution that (again, ideally) serves to inhibit further escalation—to the benefit of all parties (and particularly the innocent bystanders comprising the remainder of the group). Religions contribute further to these cultural value systems by invoking God (or other deities) as both the giver and enforcer of such laws.

COALITIONAL PSYCHOLOGY

Another central feature of our evolved psychology, one shared with many of our primate cousins, concerns coalitional psychology. The hierarchy of evolutionary theories presented earlier does not currently include a specific middle-level theory for this (i.e., one comparable to the theories of parental investment or reciprocal altruism), perhaps because the psychology of coalitions, alliances, and intergroup conflict involves elements of parental investment (i.e., with respect to competition for resources and mates), kinship (along which lines large social groups, such as tribes, are often at least partially defined), and reciprocal altruism (the foundation of alliances other than kin-based ones). Nevertheless, this domain points to a number of important issues that have not yet been addressed, but cannot be omitted from any comprehensive theory of religion.

In short, our evolved psychology appears to contain a suite of mechanisms for distinguishing the good guys from the bad guys, or the ingroup from the outgroup, and then giving preferential treatment to the good guys. In chimpanzees, shifting coalitions and alliances are a crucial factor in determining dominance hierarchies; the alpha male is not necessarily the biggest and strongest, but rather the one most successful in recruiting others to his cause and maintaining loyalty among his collaborators (which include both males and females, incidentally). When allegiances shift, so do leadership and dominance (de Waal, 1982; Diamond, 1992).

In humans, these mechanisms operate with remarkable speed and efficiency. In the classic "Robbers Cave" study, groups of boys in summer camp who were randomly divided into two groups quickly became extremely competitive with one another, to the point that the investigators eventually had to devise a way to bring them back together and prevent further escalation of conflict (Sherif, Harvey, White, Hood, & Sherif, 1961). More recently, social identity theorists have argued that group memberships, such as national and ethnic identities, are central to individuals' ("social" or "collective") self-esteem (Luhtanen & Crocker, 1992; Tajfel, 1982; Tajfel & Turner, 1986). Research using the so-called "minimal-groups" paradigm, an extension of the Robbers Cave idea used with adult participants, has repeatedly demonstrated that assigning people to groups on an entirely arbitrary basis has immediate and powerful effects in promoting differential treatment of ingroup versus outgroup members.

Coalitions and alliances are universally important to humans and chimpanzees not only with respect to within-group competition for status and dominance, but also with respect to competition and conflict between populations. In chimpanzees, groups of males regularly form raiding parties that go off in search of outnumbered groups from neighboring chimpanzee groups and attack them. Chagnon (1983, 1992) has documented the lifestyle of the Yanomamo of South America, whose neighboring villages are in a virtually constant state of warfare. Every so often, periods of peace are broken by parties from one village raiding another in retribution for a previous raid or to kidnap females. And, of course, a quick perusal of the daily newspaper quickly reveals that border skirmishes, warfare, and ethnic cleansing are as common around the world today as ever.

Ingroup Cooperation and Morality

In this chapter we have seen several ways in which religious beliefs can promote within-group cohesiveness and cooperation by capitalizing on kinship mechanisms and providing a context for mutually beneficial social-exchange and friendship relations. Coalitional psychology provides a third way: Shared religious beliefs and labels define ingroups, and fellow ingroup members receive preferential treatment vis-à-vis outgroups. Shared beliefs and interests help to cement the ties within smaller, homogeneous tribes and villages, or within subpopulations within larger, heterogeneous societies, as in the modern West. Even in larger nations, religious and nationalistic interests may converge for the majority of society members, such that the two combine into a single group identity; patriotic and religious fervor may become indistinguishable. The country of Israel provides perhaps the most salient modern example. Newspapers reported widely that in a stadium appearance by the Pope in Mexico City a few years ago, the crowd broke spontaneously into a chant of "Mexico, always faithful!" Religious self-identification can work psychologically in much the same way as national identity, in terms of association with a coalition from which people derive self-esteem and feelings of empowerment. In fact, there are many ways in which religious congregations resemble the relatively small, partly kin-based groups in which our ancestors are thought to have evolved.[5]

Any number of psychological theories propose that people have a "need to belong" and that such group inclusion represents a central source of self-esteem (e.g., Baumeister & Leary, 1995; Leary et al., 1995; Tajfel & Turner, 1986). The psychology of religion provides numerous examples of ways in which religious groups may serve this function, with religious fellowships providing a sense of community and belonging among parishioners (Pargament, 1987; Wenegrat, 1990). Research on religious cults particularly emphasizes this theme. For example, Lofland

and Stark (1965) found that religious converts were generally alienated from family, friends, and spouses, and Galanter (1989) has developed a general theory of religion focused largely on the central role of group-affiliation needs in religious groups including cults. Numerous researchers have documented the ways in which cult-recruiting practices are designed to capitalize on this psychological dynamic, for example by targeting recruitment efforts on the lonely and disaffiliated, and the use of "love bombing" and other techniques to quickly make recruits feel valued as group members. Although cults illustrate the process vividly and perhaps in an extreme form, there seems little doubt that the same coalitional-psychological processes are at work at various levels in other religious settings.

For example, proselytizing is a common activity among many religious groups, particularly in religiously heterogeneous cultures; cult recruiting is just a particularly salient example. From a strictly rational perspective, why should believers be motivated to convert others to their cause? One possibility that has been suggested concerns the need for social confirmation of one's own beliefs. Another motive, however, may be the (conscious or unconscious) desire to strengthen one's coalitions. There really is strength in numbers, and recruiting others to the cause is in the interest of the proselytizer, who benefits from the increased strength of the alliance. Winning others to one's particular point of view may be less important than winning others to one's *side*.

While I was a graduate student, a national organization called "Fundamentalists Anonymous" (FA) appeared on the scene. FA was designed as a kind of self-help group, modeled very loosely on Alcoholics Anonymous, for people who had "deconverted" from fundamentalist religions. I attended a number of the local chapter's meetings, in which 15 or 20 people showed up to exchange stories and discuss the problems they had faced in leaving their churches. What struck me most was a common complaint about harassment in various forms from members of the groups they had left behind, some so severe that they were genuinely frightened about physical danger; many had moved from their homes. As with proselytizing, this poses a question as to why continuing church members would be so concerned about someone leaving their fold; after all, there is no rational reason to believe that the loss of a member would harm them in any way.

From the perspective of coalitional psychology, this phenomenon makes sense. The only thing worse than an outgroup member is an ingroup member who defects: a traitor. Research by Rutherford, Kurzban, Tooby, and Cosmides (1997) highlights this phenomenon: Using a variation of the Prisoner's Dilemma game, Rutherford et al. showed that people were more "forgiving"—that is, less retaliatory in response to noncooperative plays by the opponent—of ingroup members than outgroup members early on in the game. However, if the opponent switched from cooperative to uncooperative behavior late in the series— in essence, defected from a previously cooperative alliance—he or she was more severely punished in retaliation than those who were uncooperative from the beginning. (See Boyd & Richerson, 1992, for a discussion of the evolution of punishment in small groups.) In the same way, FA members were viewed by the groups they left not merely as people who had adopted a new worldview, but as traitors defecting from the ingroup to the enemy beyond.

In Chapter 4, I raised the question of whether attachment theory can or should be drawn upon to explain "attachment" to religious groups. It should now be clear why I think the answer to this question is largely no. Coalitional psychology offers a set of solutions to a qualitatively different set of adaptive problems, and hence requires a qualitatively different set of evolved mechanisms. Consistent with this domain-specific view, Bruce Ellis and I have argued that humans possess distinct self-esteem "sociometers" (Leary et al., 1995) for monitoring inclusion in different kinds of interpersonal relationships (Kirkpatrick & Ellis, 2001). Functionally distinct kinds of relationships, such as infant–mother attachment, coalitions, adult pair-bond relationships, and so forth operate by different principles encoded into distinct psychological mechanisms, and the provisions offered by one differ from those afforded by another.

Outgroup Discrimination and Conflict

The darker side of coalitional psychology, of course, is that favoritism toward ingroup members necessarily entails the opposite treatment for outgroup members; they are two sides of the same coin. There can be little doubt that although religious group affiliation can have positive effects on self-esteem and intragroup cooperation, it also has a long history of fostering hatred and conflict. I will not insult the reader's intelligence by providing a lengthy list of bloody conflicts promoted and/or perpetuated by religion. In many cases, of course, religious differences are confounded with ethnic and/or nationalistic ones, resulting in multidimensional ingroup/outgroup definitions that are particularly potent.

Perhaps the oldest and most vexing question in psychology of religion is how religious traditions that preach brotherly love can simultaneously be a source of such hatred and warfare. In one sense there really is no paradox, because the prescription to "love thy neighbor" typically applies only to real neighbors—that is, other members of one's ingroup. Anthropologists and linguists have long recognized that in most languages, the self-referential proper noun used as the name of the local people is actually the word for "the people" or something quite similar; outsiders, by definition, are not even "people." Consequently, killing them does not even count as a crime.

Religious teaching "has almost always emphasized the differences between the in-group and the out-group: us versus them; Israelite and Philistine; Jew and Gentile; saved and damned; believer and heathen; Arian and Athanasian; Catholic and Orthodox; Protestant and Catholic; Hindu and Muslim; Sunni and Shia" (Ridley, 1996, p. 191). Hartung (1995) has examined in depth the ethics of the Old Testament and concluded that it clearly reflects "in-group morality." All of the rules dictating fair treatment, tolerance, and mutualism are intended, he argues, to be applied only within the local population. It is not a coincidence, Hartung points out, that major religions such as Judaism and Christianity, with their strong ingroup morality, originated historically within the context of oppressed minority groups. Genocide is seen to be sanctioned by God, and the Bible endorses the idea of women as spoils of war (Pinker, 1997, p. 511).

A closely related topic that has also been central to psychology of religion from its beginnings is the relationship between religion and prejudice or discrimination against minorities. Allport and Ross (1967) attempted to rescue religion from the charge of promoting prejudice by distinguishing an extrinsic dimension of religion correlated with prejudice from an intrinsic dimension that was not. Allport's definition and measurement of the so-called extrinsic dimension reflected, in large part, social motivations for religion, one of which (I would argue) is the degree to which one's religious beliefs reflect the operation of coalitional psychology. To the extent that one's religious beliefs are driven by perceptions of one's religious group as a coalition, those outside the fold comprise the outgroup—and thus become victims of outgroup biases.

Indeed, Allport was probably closer to the correct answer in 1954, well before he introduced the intrinsic–extrinsic distinction of which the psychology of religion has since been enamored. In *The Nature of Prejudice*, he observed, "The chief reason why religion becomes the focus of prejudice is that it usually stands for more than faith—it is the pivot of the cultural tradition of the group" (p. 446). His argument is that it is really the distinction between ingroups and outgroups along ethnic, national, or other coalitional lines that breeds prejudice and discrimination, and that religion tends to become confounded with these distinctions. Allport (1954) later concludes that

> if one looks at the matter closely, it becomes doubtful whether bigotry ever is or can be exclusively religious. Differences of creed there are; realistic conflicts can occur. But bigotry enters only when religion becomes the apologist for in-group superiority and overextends itself by disparaging out-groups for reasons that extend beyond deviation in creed. (p. 449)

This perspective also helps to explain why at least some forms of religion are related to prejudice against ethnic minorities, rather than only religious outgroups. From an evolutionary perspective, there is no reason to believe that humans would have evolved psychological mechanisms for automatically categorizing others along racial lines, because our distant ancestors would rarely if ever have encountered a person of another race; racial prejudice per se is not "in our genes." In support of this view, Kurzban, Tooby, and Cosmides (2001) demonstrated that contrary to the assumption of much social-psychological research on stereotyping and prejudice, race is *not* a basic category into which human minds categorize individuals automatically; rather, race acts as a proxy for outgroup membership in person evaluations. (In contrast, *sex* is such a basic category, consistent with an evolutionary perspective.) It is not one's skin color, for example, that activates outgroup categorization but rather the inference (which itself may be based in any number of sources) that someone of a different skin color is not part of the ingroup. Kurzban et al. showed that race-based categorization was readily superseded by other group-membership markers in experimental social cognition tasks. Such findings are consistent with applied research showing that the most effective way to reduce interracial biases is to induce people of different races to work together collaboratively in the context of a shared goal (e.g.,

Aronson, Stephan, Sikes, Blaney, & Snapp, 1978; Sherif et al., 1961), which serves to redefine the criteria for dividing ingroup from outgroup.

This approach also explains why certain measured dimensions of religiousness and related constructs correlate more strongly with prejudice than others, particularly fundamentalism (Kirkpatrick, 1993) and right-wing authoritarianism (Altemeyer & Hunsberger, 1992; see Hunsberger, 1995, for a review). Religious fundamentalism has long been conceptualized by sociologists and some psychologists with respect to its "boundary maintenance" function (e.g., Ethridge & Feagin, 1979). Fundamentalism is largely about establishing and defending a particular set of beliefs and practices that define an ingroup; those failing to accept and live by these particular standards are assigned to the outgroup. Thus, fundamentalism may largely reflect an orientation toward religion in which coalitional psychology, as opposed to other psychological processes discussed in this book, is predominant. More recently, Laythe, Finkel, and Kirkpatrick (2001; see also Laythe, Finkel, Bringle, & Kirkpatrick, 2002) have shown that when authoritarianism is statistically controlled, the predictive relationship between fundamentalism and racial prejudice not only becomes less positive, but actually reverses in direction. It appears that authoritarianism, which smacks strongly of coalitional, good guy/bad guy concerns, is the perpetrator.

Coalitional psychology may also help to explain a variety of other details about religion that may otherwise seem mysterious or merely inconsequential. For example, food taboos are common in religious (and other cultural) belief systems, but such taboos rarely can be explained in terms of practical, health-related reasons. Pinker (1997) suggests that food taboos are a culturally defined mechanism for maintaining ingroup–outgroup differentiation, noting further that foods defined as taboo in one group are frequently a staple or favorite of a neighboring group: It is difficult, he observes, to be friends with someone if you cannot share a meal with him or her.

Finally, this may be another area in which sex differences emerge as an important factor. Kurzban, Tooby, and Cosmides (1995) showed, using a variety of different methodologies, that automatic ingroup–outgroup membership categorization occurs more readily and more strongly in men than in women, and with respect to male more than to female targets. From an evolutionary perspective, warfare against neighboring tribes and the use of alliances in the service of status striving within the local group are primarily male activities. (See Tiger, 1969, for an extensive discussion of sex differences in coalitional psychology.) Attention to such potential sex differences might be warranted in future research on the empirical relationships between various forms of religion and discrimination.

Supernatural Beings as Coalition Partners

Coalitional psychology may also provide another perspective on beliefs about gods and deities. I suggested earlier that perceptions about God may in part reflect psychological mechanisms dedicated to processing information about dominance and status, that is, God as the "big chief." Inherent in this notion is the idea that God is "on our side"; he is *our* big chief. God is part of our coalition, and thus leads us into battle with our enemies. Just listen to postgame interviews with professional athletes after winning a big game: Although they usually seem to try hard to avoid claiming that God is on their team, the inference inevitably leaks out in one form or another.

One interesting consequence of this perspective is that under certain extraordinary circumstances, God can be perceived as a *traitor*. In Chapter 3 I discussed several studies reviewed by Pargament (1997) in which concentration-camp survivors and combat veterans described the experience of feeling that God had abandoned them. I interpreted these results in terms of the effects of experiencing loss of an attachment figure, but we now see a potential alternative interpretation in which God might instead have been perceived as having abandoned "our side" for the enemy.

Finally, coalitional psychology may shed some light on beliefs about Satan, the devil, or whatever more or less anthropomorphized form the forces of evil take in any given belief system. If God is the leader of our group, who is the leader of the opposition? In some cases a human leader of the opposition is easily identified and vilified, such as the tribal chief of the next village or Adolf Hitler. But the enemy is not always clearly defined, and belief in a supernatural bad-guy figure provides a convenient answer.

SUMMARY AND CONCLUSIONS

In Chapter 4 I suggested that although it is in many cases tempting to try to extend attachment theory beyond the context of perceived relationships with deities in monotheistic systems, to do so might be a mistake. Perhaps attachment theory could be stretched, squeezed, or otherwise tweaked to try to account for a variety of other religious phenomena. But if we take a step back for a larger perspective, we can see that there is no need to do so. When the attachment system is seen properly as just one among a very large collection of evolved psychological mechanisms designed to guide social relationships in a variety of ways, each of which operates according to different principles, we have a framework within which to look for alternative explanations for those aspects of religion that do not clearly seem to fall under the purview of attachment theory. Rules of reciprocal altruism are largely irrelevant within the context of attachment relationships, but social-contract thinking is clearly evident in many beliefs about gods and how these gods should be appeased. Attachment theory would be hard pressed to explain the relationship between many forms of religion and prejudice; instead, coalitional psychology appears to be implicated. Ancestor worship is a tempting topic to attack from attachment theory, but other mechanisms designed for regulating kinship relations fit more naturally. Each of these families of mechanisms can be seen to operate in different aspects of religious belief, to different degrees in different cultures and different individuals.

Each section of this chapter could easily have been a book unto itself, or at least a set of chapters analogous to Chapters 2–6. In principle, I could have begun this book with five chapters on parental investment theory, or five chapters on kin selection, and reviewed in much greater detail the many ways in which this particular suite of psychological mechanisms explains a variety of aspects of religious belief. In this case I started with attachment theory, but only because I have been working on this particular approach to the psychology of religion for almost 20 years. (I hope someone will eventually write those other books.)

I suggested in an earlier chapter that perceived relationships with God might represent a more "pure" form of attachment than adult romantic relationships, because the attachment system's role in God relationships tends not to be confounded with the sexual/mating and caregiving systems as in adult pair-bonds. It should be clear from this chapter, however, that attachment to God may not be so "pure" after all, as it is likely to be confounded by a different set of evolved systems. God may be perceived as an attachment figure, but also as a "big chief," a social-exchange partner, and a coalition partner. For any particular person, beliefs and reasoning about God are potentially influenced by all of these systems, as well (no doubt) as others not discussed here. For different people in different places, as well as for any given person at different points in time, the relative weighting of each system with respect to how one thinks about God probably varies in response to local conditions. Moreover, as I suggested in the previous chapter, the power of the God idea may lie in the fact that God can (psychologically) be any or all of these things.[6]

The focus on interpersonal relationships in these theories and their applications to religion, however, still leaves unanswered some more fundamental questions. I have tried to explain in this chapter why it is that, given that people believe in gods, these beliefs tend to take certain forms that reflect the operation of evolved cognitive machinery for thinking about attachment figures, social-exchange partners, kin, and so on. This approach begs the important question as to why people believe in gods in the first place, or in less anthropomorphized forces such as spirits or "mana." This is the topic of the next chapter.

CHAPTER ELEVEN

The Cognitive Origins of Religious Belief

In the previous chapters I discussed how a diverse collection of psychological mechanisms or systems, evolved for guiding social behavior in various ways, lies beneath religious thinking. Supernatural beings are perceived as having the characteristics of an attachment figure, and/or a powerful leader of a local coalition; ethical principles reflect the operation of evolved algorithms for monitoring social exchange; within-group cooperation is fostered by our evolved coalitional psychology, and so on. Evolutionary psychology offers a way to predict and interpret the particular contents that religious beliefs are likely to evince, shaping our perceptions and inferences about the world along the lines dictated by our evolved psychology.

However, we eventually need to confront a more basic issue, which is how such beliefs can get started in the first place. Attachment theory explains nicely why beliefs about personalized deities tend to take certain forms, for example, but cannot explain why people find the idea of God or other supernatural phenomena plausible to begin with. Moreover, as discussed in Chapter 4, a comprehensive framework for understanding religion must be capable of explaining religious belief systems not characterized by personal gods, and should be able to explain the origins and (cultural) evolution of religious beliefs over human history, beginning with historically ancient religious or protoreligious beliefs. Whether religion evolved historically from a starting point of animism (Tylor, 1873), magic (Frazer, 1890/1935), or a primitive form of monotheism (Schmidt, 1931)—the resolution of this debate need not concern us here—the earliest religious and protoreligious beliefs must have emerged more or less spontaneously from our ancestors' evolved psychology. In this chapter I review some recent evolutionary perspectives on the cognitive origins of religious beliefs that may shed light on how this might have occurred, and that provide the psychological foundation for the more specific forms of beliefs discussed in previous chapters.

EVOLVED MECHANISMS FOR THINKING ABOUT THE NATURAL WORLD

In recent years, the classical Piagetian view of the sequential development of a few, domain-general reasoning abilities has begun to give way to a view tracing the development of multiple, domain-specific perceptual and inferential modules. In particular, three major domains of concepts and concept formation have been studied extensively by developmental and cognitive psychologists, reflecting three "major domains of understanding for human beings, in that they encompass much of the reality with which all people—children and adults—interact" (Wellman & Inagaki, 1997). These are the domains of *physical objects* and their movements, *plants and animals* and their behavior, and *other people* and their mental lives. The psychological systems inferred to process information within these domains are known respectively as *naive* (or *folk* or *commonsense*) physics, biology, and psychology.

Much of this research in the fields of cognitive development and cognitive neuroscience is not organized or guided explicitly by an evolutionary perspective. Whereas cognitive and developmental researchers have identified the whats and the hows of this modularized organization of the brain/mind, evolutionary psychologists have approached the same problems by considering the *whys* in terms of adaptive function. As Cosmides and Tooby (1994) observe in reference to these cognitively oriented researchers, "It is as if they had laboriously built a road up one side of a nearly impassable mountain range into unexplored terrain, only to find themselves met at the top by a foreign road construction crew—evolutionary functionalist researchers—who had been building a road upward to the same destination from the far side of the mountains" (p. 85).

Much of the data for this modular cognitive organization comes from research with children of various ages, in which the development of specific reasoning abilities is traced. The argument for innateness with respect to such mechanisms generally is based on the observation that certain forms of concept acquisition and reasoning abilities seem to emerge very early, spontaneously, and in the absence of explicit training or experience. These are the same kinds of arguments used by Chomsky (1957) in support of his claim for the existence of an innate "language organ" (see Pinker, 1994, for a review and extension of this position). This is not to suggest that experience, learning, and teaching are irrelevant, which of course they are not, but the fact that certain kinds of experience are required for these systems to develop properly should not be construed as an argument against their "innate" nature. Although genes are widely described metaphorically as blueprints, a better analogy is that they are like *recipes*; they are not depictions of the final products of development, but rather instructions for constructing organisms through a step-by-step developmental program under expectable conditions (Dawkins, 1986). As demonstrated in classic studies by Hubel and Weisel (1965), the proper physiological development of the visual system (in kittens) is strongly contingent on growing up in a "normal" visual environment. For example, raising kittens in artificial environments containing only vertical lines severely impairs development of other parts of the visual system (Stryker & Sherk, 1975). The point is that evolved perceptual and cognitive systems, such as those discussed in this chapter, develop reliably and predictably under a wide (but not unlimited) range of normal environments—specifically, those of the environment of evolutionary adaptedness (EEA).

Humans (like all other organisms) evolved in a world in which many aspects of the natural environment were fairly stable and predictable as a function of physical and biological laws. Moreover, humans (like only some other organisms) evolved in a highly social environment in which, due to a species-universal evolved psychology, the behavior of other people was at least somewhat predictable and stable. It makes good sense then that humans have evolved a suite of psychological mechanisms that reflect recurrent and predictable properties of their physical and social worlds, as they related to adaptive problems of survival and reproduction. Although debate continues to rage (as in so many areas of psychology) about the processes by which such abilities develop and the relative roles of "nature" and "nurture," there is fairly widespread agreement that these three particular domains are distinct and basic (Pinker, 1997; Wellman & Inagaki, 1997).

Previous research on *religious* development across childhood has in general yet to catch up with these changes in the field of cognitive development. The extant research in this area has long been guided by the classic Piagetian perspective. Much research in this tradition has shown that the complexity of children's thinking about God, prayer, and other religion-related topics follows a predictably progressive trend across age (Elkind, 1971; Goldman, 1964; Harms; 1944). Of course, it could hardly be otherwise; virtually any developmental theory would predict that the development of simpler forms of reasoning should precede that of more complex forms. A domain-specific perspective on these processes, however, promises a more refined picture of why and how different aspects of religious belief may change across time. As I argue in this chapter, these evolved mechanisms provide the fundamental building blocks upon which religious thinking (as well as much nonreligious thinking) is founded.

Naive Physics and Psychological Animism

Much research now demonstrates convincingly that children are aware of a variety of basic principles of physics at a much younger age than can reasonably be attributed to direct experience and logical inference. By the age of 4–6 months, children seem to understand that objects tend to move as cohesive units along continuous trajectories; that two solid objects cannot occupy the same space (e.g., one cannot move through another); that unsupported objects fall down; that objects meeting no obstacles continue to move in the same direction; and that there is "no action at a distance" (e.g., one object cannot influence the path of another without coming into contact with it; Baillargeon, 1987; Baillargeon & Hanko-Summers, 1990; Leslie &Keeble; Spelke, 1990; see Boyer, 1994b, 2001, and Pinker, 1997, for reviews). Such abilities are typically referred to as *naive*, or *folk*, *physics*.

Of greater interest to us here, even infants appear to be able to distinguish animate from inanimate objects, presumably based on cues about motion and behavior that are inconsistent with the principles noted in the preceding paragraph (Premack, 1990). In particular, objects that display self-propulsion, or whose trajectories of motion defy expectations about inanimate objects, appear to be classified differently by infants as young as 3 months of age, leading them to have different expectations about these objects and to attempt to influence them in different ways (Bullock, 1985; Gelman, Spelke, & Meck, 1983; Richards & Siegler, 1986). The ability to distinguish living from nonliving objects in the environment is obviously a crucial and fundamental skill for negotiating and predicting the environment, and it should come as no surprise that our brains are designed to acquire this knowledge rapidly.

Naive Biology and Natural Kinds

A second body of research on cognitive development amply demonstrates that very young children understand the ontological difference between living and nonliving objects and reason in fundamentally different ways about them. For example, Keil (1986) provided information about fictitious (and thus unfamiliar) objects to kindergartners, such as that "hyraxes are sometimes sleepy" and that "throstles need to be fixed." When given the opportunity to draw inferences about other aspects of these objects, the children inferred that, for instance, a hyrax might be hungry, but denied that it could be made of metal (and vice versa for throstles). Similarly, children understood that one kind of artifact could be transformed into another by switching or adding parts, but that this was not true of living species; that is, one kind of animal cannot be turned into another simply by altering its physical appearance or behavior.

Further, young children readily understand that various "living kinds" differ among themselves in fundamental ways, and distinguish between deep and superficial differences among types. In one study, 4-year-olds were shown pictures of dolphins and of tropical fish and told how each breathes (i.e., above the surface and underwater, respectively). They were then shown pictures of sharks, which bore a much stronger visual resemblance to dolphins than to the tropical fish pictured earlier. When told that sharks are actually a type of fish, most of the children correctly inferred that they breathe underwater (Gelman & Markman, 1986). Moreover, as summarized by Boyer (1994b), "children seem to make such kind-based inductive generalizations more easily if the properties chosen are 'inherent' properties of the exemplars, such as ways of breathing and feeding . . . not weight of a given animal or the fact that it moves fast" (p. 106).

At the heart of reasoning about living kinds appears to be the implicit assumption that each species or group is characterized by a sort of Platonic ideal, a phenomenon referred to as *psychological essentialism* (Gelman, Coley, & Gottfried, 1994; Medin & Ortony, 1989). As summarized by Gelman et al. (1994), people seem to believe implicitly that

> categories are discovered rather than arbitrary or invented; they carve up nature at its joints. The underlying nature, or category *essence*, is thought to be the causal mechanism that results in those properties that we can see. For example, the essence of tigers causes them to grow as they do—to have stripes, large size, capacity to roar, and so forth. (p. 344)

One can bleach a tiger and sew on a mane, but even second graders understand it remains a tiger and does not thereby become a lion; its essential "tigerness" has not been altered (Keil, 1989). There is some kind of essence of tigerness and lionness that makes tigers and lions fundamentally different at a deep level.[1] Other evidence suggests that children believe such essences to be on the "inside" of organisms, giving rise to the observable characteristics (including developmental trajectories) of different organisms. (See Gelman et al., 1994, for a review of many lines of evidence of psychological essentialism.)

Naive Psychology and Theory of Mind

A third well-established category of innate reasoning mechanisms concerns *naive psychology* or *theories of mind* (Baron-Cohen, 1995; Carruthers & Smith; Leslie, 1994), which interpret other people's behavior in terms of beliefs, desires, and other (unobservable) mental states (i.e., *belief–desire psychology*). As summarized by Boyer (1994b), belief–desire psychology is "a set of tacit principles and expectations which govern our understanding of mental phenomena and observable behavior . . . do not constitute a full-blown psychology . . . but form the basis on which subjects construct all ordinary causal attributions" (p. 110). Of course, such theories of mind, once in place, guide our thinking about other people throughout the remainder of our lives; we are all amateur psychologists.

One crucial developmental landmark is the cognitive ability to distinguish between actual states of affairs and people's mental representations of them, which appears at about the age of 5. This landmark is characterized by the emergence of the understanding that mental representations can be either true or false—that is, the realization that beliefs can be mistaken. A raft of research has documented this developmental event using so-called false-belief tests. In the typical design, a child is shown a hidden object, the location or identity of which could clearly not be known by a certain third person; the child is then asked what or where the third person will believe the hidden object to be (e.g., Leslie & Frith, 1987). The timing of the developmental shift to correct responses on such tasks has been replicated in other cultures, such as among Pygmy children (Avis & Harris, 1991), consistent with the idea that such reasoning is based on innate mechanisms that come on-line at this age.

Interestingly, it does not take much to activate a theory of mind inappropriately in regard to mindless things. In a classic experiment, Heider and Simmel (1944), created an animated film in which dots moved around on the screen in various ways. Adults as well as children readily described what they saw in terms of beliefs and desires of dots or groups of dots—for example, that one was chasing or trying to escape from another. Guthrie (1993) reviews a variety of studies of this type as well, demonstrating the general principle that people readily interpret the behavior of nonhuman objects as if they had human feelings, emotions, and goals. If you have doubts, just think about the last time you cursed at your computer.

THE PSYCHOLOGY OF COMPLEX THINKING: HOW THE MIND WORKS

The Swiss Army-knife model of the human mind, as a collection of numerous domain-specific mechanisms each designed to solve mundane problems of survival and reproduction in ancestral environments, may seem intuitively not to square with everyday experience and observation. Humans are capable of such remarkable flexibility and creativity in their thinking and behavior that such a model seems far too simplistic as an explanation for it. Instead, it seems, we must have brain/minds that are instead built as powerful, domain-general information-processing systems, capable of learning and/or creating virtually anything. I suspect that this alternative view is particularly compelling if one's everyday experience involves being an intellectual and interacting with scientists, philosophers, and poets in art galleries and at the theater. However, the observation of flexibility and creativity in human thought is not inconsistent with that of a highly modular and ancient brain/mind. In this section I briefly describe some ways in which the former can emerge from the latter to produce, among other things, religious thought.

So how does one get creativity and flexibility out of highly domain-specific psychological mechanisms? In his extraordinary book, from which I borrowed the title of this section, Pinker (1997) provides the most comprehensive explanation to date of "how the mind works." Combining the latest work from the recent explosions of both cognitive neuroscience and evolutionary psychology, Pinker discusses many ways in which complex reasoning and behavior are created by cobbling together and exchanging information between simple mechanisms designed to solve simple problems, and/or applying mechanisms designed for reasoning about one kind of problem to a new kind of problem. Minsky's (1985) classic society-of-mind model demonstrates how highly complex tasks can be solved by large numbers of hierarchically arranged, stupid mechanisms, each slavishly and uncreatively following simple computational rules. In Pinker's version of this argument, "higher" forms of complex thinking and reasoning are constructed from innate psychological mechanisms for reasoning about the physical, biological, and psychological world—the kinds of mechanisms discussed earlier in this chapter and in the previous chapters of this book—along with processes of language understanding and acquired knowledge about the world.

Pinker identifies the principal trick of complex thinking as the use of *analogy* and *metaphor*—that is, the application of inferential modules to tasks outside the particular content domains for which they were intended. Pinker points out, for example, that metaphors of location in space and physical force pervade language. Borrowing from linguistic research by Jackendoff (e.g., 1994), he illustrates the point by observing that we use words such as "go" and "went" in a wide variety of ways other than to refer to changes in physical locations: for example, "The meeting went from 3:00 to 4:00" and "The light went from green to red." Why?

> It is not just to co-opt words but to co-opt their inferential machinery. Some deductions that apply to motion and space also apply nicely to possession, circumstances, and time. That allows the deductive machinery for space to be borrowed for reasoning about other subjects. . . . This sharing is what makes location and other concepts *good* for something,

and not just resemblances that catch our eye. (Pinker, 1997, p. 353; emphasis in original)

To Pinker, even the "highest" forms of thinking are not a profound mystery, only a set of puzzles (though not simple ones, to be sure) to be solved by a computational theory of mind and evolutionary psychology:

> Even the most recondite scientific reasoning is an assembly of down-home mental metaphors. We pry our faculties loose from the domains they were designed to work in, and use their machinery to make sense of new domains that abstractly resemble the old ones. . . . To do academic biology, we take our way of understanding artifacts and apply it to organisms. To do chemistry, we treat the essence of a natural kind as a collection of tiny, bouncy, sticky objects. To do psychology, we treat the mind as a natural kind. (p. 359)

For example, symbolic logic draws upon cheater-detection mechanisms, mathematics draws heavily on spatial reasoning skills, and so forth. And if mathematics, symbolic logic, and other "recondite scientific reasoning" can be explained in terms of the operation and interaction of evolved psychological mechanisms, then so too should religious beliefs.

The general idea that minds use analogy and metaphor to create complexity from domain-specific simplicity has appeared in many different forms. In his well-known theory of multiple intelligences, for example, Gardner (1983) suggests that although the various domains of intelligence are more or less discrete and autonomous, they interact with each other and operate smoothly as a (partially) integrated system. Other researchers, including Boden (1990), Rozin (1976), and Karmiloff-Smith (1992) have also concluded that the trick to creativity and intelligence involves applying knowledge or processes from one domain to other domains. (See Mithen, 1996, for a review.) There are some important differences among researchers with respect to their definitions of "domains," but they are all in agreement on the general principle or process.

More recently, Mithen (1996) has similarly focused on analogical reasoning as a basis for an account of how evolution might have created modern minds. His argument, in a nutshell, is that early *Homo sapiens*, as of, say, 100,000 years ago, possessed a highly modularized psychology.[2] The domains upon which he focuses conform essentially to the three categories of mechanisms discussed earlier in this chapter—naive physics, biology, and psychology (renamed as "technological," "natural history," and "social" domains, respectively)—plus language ("linguistic"). Per their evolutionary design, social mechanisms were used to think about and guide social relations, natural history ones to think about and guide behavior with respect to other living organisms, and so forth. Over the next 50,000 years or so, Mithen argues, a significant evolutionary advance occurred that gave rise to the modern mind: The barriers preventing information exchange across mechanisms broke down. As a consequence, a door was opened to an exponential increase in the ability to form new thoughts and sets of inferences that were previously impossible. Historically, this resulted in the great cultural explosion (the "Great Leap Forward"; Diamond, 1992) that archaeologists and anthropologists agree occurred approximately 30,000–60,000 years ago, characterized by a variety of new technologies and (inferred from these) behavioral patterns.

This hypothesis neatly explains not only why a species that had already existed for several hundred thousand years could suddenly evince radical technological and behavioral change, but how this could occur in the absence of a concomitant significant increase in brain size (which actually occurred much earlier, presumably for other reasons). The evolutionary change is one of organization within an existing design, rather than the simple addition of more brain. It also provides an evolutionary explanation for how human brains/minds came to exist as they are, reconciling the domain-specificity view of evolutionary psychology (for which the theoretical arguments are indeed compelling) with the observation of creativity and flexibility in modern human thinking, without appealing to a mysterious, all-purpose general-information-processor model as in the Standard Social Science Model (SSSM). (Mithen does include discussion of a "general intelligence" module, but it is in addition to the other evolved mechanisms and refers specifically to basic, widely applicable learning principles such as trial-and-error learning strategies.) In the SSSM, the all-purpose mind is a black box; those who subscribe to the notion give little thought to how it might work or what exactly might be inside. What is inside are numerous domain-specific mechanisms, each designed by natural selection to solve a particular adaptive problem, with rich interconnections among them.

Arguing mainly from archeological data, Mithen provides numerous examples of how interaction of mechanisms across the domains he discusses gives rise to the kind of technological advances associated with the cultural explosion. For example, it is during this time that we first see evidence of jewelry. Mithen's suggestion is that earlier ancestors' evolved technological abilities were focused entirely on creating tools for use as weapons in hunting; it was not until the cognitive barrier between the technological and social domains was lowered that it would occur to humans to use their tool-making skills to construct items that could be used to adorn oneself and communicate information about, for example, one's social status and identity. Similarly, Mithen suggests that social knowledge might also have been used in the service of hunting, with theory-of-mind knowledge employed to more effectively anticipate the behavior and movements of prey animals.

In summary, then, the basic idea behind both Pinker's and Mithen's theories is that natural selection designed a highly modularized brain/mind comprising domain-specific mechanisms, each adaptive for (and thus activated by) particular problem contexts: one tool for each task. More complex thinking is the product of applying a particular psychological mechanism—or, more likely, a combination of mechanisms—to perform a novel task for which it was not specifically designed. A screwdriver is designed specifically for tightening loose screws, but a little creative thought reveals that it can be used to pry apart two surfaces, dig a hole, scrape paint off a board, or, serve as a doorstop. Psychological mechanisms similarly can be drafted into service for purposes other than those for which they were primarily designed.

THE COGNITIVE BUILDING BLOCKS
OF RELIGIOUS BELIEF

The theories of Pinker (1997), Mithen (1996), and others suggest that complex reasoning involves the application of evolved psychological mechanisms beyond the stimuli for which they were "designed" by natural selection. Many aspects of religious thought are understandable from this perspective, particularly with respect to the psychological domains of naive physics, biology, and psychology. In this section I briefly review some examples of this with respect to the reasoning domains discussed earlier.

Animism

Most animate objects in ancestral environments were animals of various kinds, and most inanimate objects were not. However, situations abound in which brains misinterpret inanimate objects as animate. "All humans and many animals display animism: mechanics see tools as rebellious, runners see distant fire hydrants as dogs, horses see blowing papers as threats, and cats see fluttering leaves as prey" (Guthrie, 1993, p. 6). Chimpanzees have been observed engaging in angry threat displays in response to the onset of heavy rains, sudden strong winds, waterfalls, and rapid streams (Goodall, 1986; van Lawick-Goodall, 1971). However, they do not respond in this way to other forms of movement; for example, they do not seem to "interpret" a falling leaf or branch as if it were alive. Likewise, human gods are, to my knowledge, not typically invoked to explain why a thrown object eventually falls to the ground, or why solid objects cannot move through each other.

Animism—in the sense of belief in spirit beings—has long been regarded by anthropologists as characteristic of some of the earliest or most "primitive" forms of religious belief. Tylor (1873), for example, thought belief in spirit beings and souls resulted from early man's attempts to explain dreams and death. Guthrie (1993) reviews a variety of criticisms that have been leveled against this view, including the charge that it is too "rationalistic." That is, it views early humans as philosophers and scientists attempting to solve the mysteries of nature, when it is more likely that they were much too busy looking for food and avoiding predators.

Guthrie's (1993) own view is both simpler and more broadly sweeping: He suggests an animistic bias is essentially built into our perceptual system. When confronted with ambiguous stimuli—and most perceptual stimuli are, in fact, ambiguous—it is generally safer to assume a "higher" level of complexity than a lower one. A hiker in the woods does not have time to ponder whether the object just ahead is a bear or a boulder, or whether the object at his feet is a poisonous snake or a harmless stick. Just one instance of mistaking a bear for a boulder, or snake for a stick, however, and the hiker will be nobody's ancestor. It is a "safer bet" to assume bear or snake and be possibly be wrong, than to assume boulder or stick and be wrong. With respect to religion, then, it should come as no surprise that gods and spirits of the earliest known religions frequently are associated with environmental objects that appear to display self-propulsion or other characteristics that distinguish animate from inanimate objects, such as the sun, moon, and stars, and weather phenomena such as storms, rain, and wind. Guthrie argues that these processes are extremely common, not only in religion but in the arts, philosophy, and the sciences.

Although Guthrie never spelled out his safe bet argument explicitly in evolutionary terms, Atran (2002; Atran & Norenzayan, in press) has since done so. Atran argues that the evolved human agency-detector mechanism is designed to operate on a hair trigger, leading to frequent errors in attributing agency to inanimate objects or unseen forces influencing them. We return to this issue from an evolutionary perspective later in this chapter.

Psychological Essentialism

The natural intuitions about inherent differences among living kinds and psychological essentialism permeate a variety of common themes in religious thinking. For example, a central defining aspect of religion, in the view of at least some researchers, concerns the imbuing of "sacred" or "holy" status to objects, thoughts, or people (e.g., Greeley, 1972; Pargament, 1997). Virtually anything can be sacralized, according to Greeley and Pargament, including sports teams and national flags as well as divine beings. In any case, however, the crucial psychological factor seems to be the perception that something holy or sacred has a distinct *essence* that defines it as a different "natural kind," and that is unaffected by superficial transformations. The belief among many preliterate peoples in "a hidden or secret force which operates silently and invisibly in things and persons that are in some way especially powerful, impressive, or socially important" and that "resides in the tribal chieftain, in animals, plants, and rocks of a significant kind"—*mana*, as labeled by anthropologists (Smart, 1976, p. 29)—seems little more than a matter of making such implicit thoughts explicit.

A second example concerns the widespread phenomenon of *totemism*. Citing a variety of anthropological researchers, Hirschfield (1994) notes "the rich exploitation of analogies between the natural and social domain found throughout the world," of which "the best known example is totemism" (p. 202). In totemic systems, the "essence" of a living species is seen to be shared with one's family or tribal group, in a manner that imbues the group with some of the essential qualities of that species. Although there is ongoing debate about whether such thinking involves the transfer of natural-kinds (naive biological) reasoning to human groups, or whether distinct psychological mechanisms exist for thinking about social kinds, psychological essentialism appears to be at the core of totemic belief.

The widespread if not universal belief in life after death may also have its roots in psychological essentialism. Although the details of such beliefs vary greatly, from reincarnation to eternal heaven or hell, they always revolve around the core idea that some kind of internal essence (e.g., "soul") of a person transcends physical form and continues to exist after death. That is, physical death is seen merely as a kind of "superficial transformation" to which a living being's essence is impervious, much as painting stripes on a lion does not change it into a tiger. The general idea of a person's ghost, spirit, or essence being released from the body at death is seen in virtually all religions, from those of traditional cultures such as the Nuer (Evans-Pritchard, 1956) to Buddhism to modern Christianity. Such beliefs are not confined to churchgoers or the traditionally religious, either: Even among Americans who do *not* belong to a church, nearly 60% believe in some form of afterlife (Gallup & Castelli, 1989). Even our extinct Neanderthal cousins might have had a similar (protoreligious?) idea, as reflected in the famous burial sites in the caves of southern France (see, e.g., Mithen, 1996).

Another interesting application of such thinking concerns perceptions of religious leaders of various sorts. Boyer (1994b) argues that shamans, priests, and other human spiritual figures are typically perceived to be of a different "natural kind" than other social groups, almost as if they were a different species. Such leaders are often believed to have special, internal qualities and powers that distinguish them qualitatively from other humans. In many belief systems such leadership positions are explicitly "person-based"—that is, having such a distinct essence is an explicit qualification for the job. Interestingly, it is also common for such social roles to be passed down from father to son, under the apparent (and presumably implicit) assumption that this "special essence" is biologically heritable. Boyer argues that even in belief systems in which religious leadership roles are officially "criterion-based" rather than "person-based," and in which orthodoxy dictates explicitly that such individuals do *not* possess any special, internal attributes (but rather, simply appropriate training and accomplishments), people tend to perceive them as having special qualities, abilities, or essences, anyway—often much to the dismay of other orthodox leaders.

Anthropomorphism

Perhaps the single most important domain among these "folk theories" for understanding religious belief is *theory of mind*, and the process of psychological *anthropomorphism* by which theories of mind are (mis)applied to nonhuman objects or creatures. Once a target is identified by the mind as human-like, and theories of mind whir into action, people assign the target desires, beliefs, motivational states, and emotions, on the basis of which they draw further inferences in regard to how they themselves should behave in interaction with these beings.

Indeed, to Guthrie (1993) religion *is* anthropomorphism. Guthrie reviews at length examples of anthropomorphic thinking not only in religion, but also in the arts, philosophy, and science. The only difference between religion and these other disciplines, he argues, is mainly that religion makes humanlike beings "central." His explanation for the readiness to anthropomorphize is analogous to his explanation for animism: Given ambiguity as to whether an animate object is human or nonhuman, it is a "safer bet" to assume the higher level of complexity; it is usually better (i.e., less costly) to mistake an animal for a person than the other way around. In other words, anthropomorphism represents a kind of inevitable error resulting commonly from the design of our evolved psychology. Although he does not describe it this way, his depiction of anthropomorphism is that it represents a *spandrel* (per the discussion in Chapter 9) of our evolved psychology. (Again, see Atran, 2002, for an extensive discussion.)

Wenegrat (1990) makes a related point, at a more general level of analysis, in observing the degree to which psychological anthropomorphism is evident in religion. Human brains are largely designed not as general, all-purpose information-processing devices, but specifically are designed in large part as dedicated *social*-cognitive systems. A great deal of the brain is designed specifically for processing social information, from facial identification to complex modules for negotiating and keeping track of social-exchange relationships. Our heads contain a warehouse full of social-cognitive machinery waiting for something to do, and the engines start up at the first sign of possible applicability. "Humans, in short, are social game players, and social game players are prone to invent gods who will then be used in social games" (Wenegrat, 1990, p. 112).

The power of the human tendency to anthropomorphize is impressive. Research on the development of children's religious beliefs (e.g., Harms, 1944) has consistently shown that some of the earliest versions of God concepts held in childhood are fully anthropomorphized ones—including the stereotypical old man with a long white beard. This concrete idea of God in a literally human form is rejected by adults, at least contemporary Western Christians, as childish and contrary to orthodoxy.

Nevertheless, it proves remarkably difficult even for adults to think about God in abstract terms without falling back into anthropomorphism. As Guthrie (1993) notes, even "recent theologians and philosophers continue to struggle with anthropomorphism" (p. 182). They would like to eliminate anthropomorphism from ideas about God, but "virtually all writers, however, agree theologians can guard *only* against its grosser forms, because eliminating all forms eliminates religion" (p. 182, emphasis in original).

Evidence for the anthropomorphizing inherent in people's reasoning about God has been demonstrated in the laboratory. In a clever experiment, Barrett and Keil (1996) found evidence that anthropomorphic thinking does indeed underlie people's reasoning about God. In a narrative comprehension task, participants read stories about God acting in relation to humans—for example, responding to human prayers. Subsequent memory tests were carefully designed to assess the degree to which participants misremembered aspects of the story in an anthropomorphized way. The results demonstrated clearly that people regularly misremembered facts in the ways one would expect if they were drawing upon psychological inference mechanisms dedicated to processing information about humans and human behavior. For example, one story involved simultaneous prayers by two different people in different places: Participants frequently recalled that in the story, God finished answering one prayer in one place before responding to the other, something that was not mentioned in the story. Other examples of common errors included "God's moving, being in a particular place, requiring sensory input to gather information, performing only one task at a time, having a single focus of attention, having sensory limitations and being unable to process competing sensory stimuli distinctly" (Barrett & Keil, 1996, p. 614). The results were subsequently replicated by Barrett (1998) in India using Hindu (and some Muslim) respondents, demonstrating that the finding is not specific to Western Christian culture.

Barrett (2000) has recently expanded his research on these processes to the study of children's conceptions of God. In a typical false-belief task, 5- and 6-year-olds were (as usual) shown to understand that ordinary human beings such as their own mothers would not know the contents of a box if they could not see inside it (because it was dark, or because the box was closed). However, the same children believed that God *would* know. Similar results have been reported among Yukatek Mayan speakers in Mexico, who by age 7 appreciate that God is not fooled into false beliefs under the same conditions in which people are (Knight, Barrett, Atran, & Ucan Ek', 2001; cited in Atran, 2002). Moreover, these children appeared to understand a kind of hierarchy of theories of mind with respect to their polytheistic religion, in which other specific deities and spirits vary along the continuum between people and God in terms of their susceptibility to false beliefs.

WHY RELIGIOUS BELIEFS SUCCEED

The idea that religious beliefs represent analogical extensions of our evolved psychology seems straightforward, but raises some intruiging questions about how and why this happens. Of all the possible mechanisms that could be "misapplied" to new domains, for example, why are certain analogical forms of reasoning common and others rare? That is, why are religious beliefs in particular so successful? In this section I review two sets of insights about these issues that emerge from an evolutionary-psychological framework—one focusing on characteristics of psychological systems, the other on characteristics of religious belief—that suggest some answers to this question.

Evolved Psychological Mechanisms: Calibration and Bias

Although it may seem intuitive that natural selection would have designed psychological mechanisms to be as accurate as possible, this is not necessarily true. The important fact to keep in mind is that the criterion by which evolution determines what stays and what goes is not *accuracy*, but *adaptiveness*. As Alcock (1995) observes, rabbits are designed to make a lot of Type I errors in determining when to run for cover; it is much more costly for a rabbit to mistake a predator for a benign rustling of leaves than the other way around. Ancestral rabbits with unbiased predator-detection systems did not become rabbit ancestors. The same is no doubt true for many other psychological mechanisms of both rabbits and people. Like our cravings for fats and sweets, cognitive systems that were designed to solve ancestral problems may or may not serve us well in modern environments.

In any kind of binary choice situation there are two kinds of errors: You can choose A when B is true, or choose B when A is true. Moreover, it is generally true that adopting a decision strategy that minimizes one kind of error tends to increase the likelihood of the other. A familiar example to psychological researchers, of course, is the Type I and Type II errors of statistical hypothesis testing, in which minimizing the likelihood of the former (by, for example, using a more stringent alpha level such as .001) tends to increase the likelihood of the latter (i.e., reducing statistical power). If, with respect to an adaptive problem faced commonly by our ancestors, one kind of error was routinely more costly (in inclusive-fitness terms, over the long run) than another, natural selection is likely to have designed the corresponding mechanism with a built-in bias, in the same way that researchers use small alpha levels in statistical hypothesis testing in order to minimize Type I errors (i.e., claiming evidence for a hypothesis when the data might simply be due to chance), but at the cost of increasing Type II errors (i.e., failing to acknowledge support for a hypothesis that is in fact true).

Haselton and Buss (2000) have applied this reasoning in a series of experiments on "cross-sex mind reading," in which they showed that men are likely to overinterpret ambiguous signs of sexual interest displayed by females (i.e., more likely to make Type I errors), whereas women are likely to underinterpret signs of commitment displayed by men (i.e., more likely to make Type II errors). The evolutionary reasoning (following from parental investment theory) is that for men, a missed mating opportunity is more costly than is rejection of an overeager advance; for women, mating with a male who is unwilling to commit resources to child rearing is more costly than a missed mating opportunity. According to Haselton and Buss's (2000) *error management theory*, similar reasoning can be applied to any number of evolved inference modules, using evolutionary theory as a guide to predicting the kinds of errors toward which different systems are likely to be biased (and why). (See also Haselton, 2003; Haselton & Buss, 2003.)

Another example, from a different domain, is that of self-serving biases in attribution and self-concept processes. It is well known that most (nondepressed) people tend to give themselves more credit for positive outcomes than they normatively deserve, be more optimistic about the future than is objectively justifiable, and think more highly of themselves and their abilities than is logically possible (Gilovich, 1991; Taylor & Brown, 1988). It makes sense for evolution to have designed the self-esteem system with a positive bias, as a kind of self-deception that leads us to behave as if we were "better" than we are and thus induce others to consequently treat us accordingly (Kirkpatrick & Ellis, 2001). This bias gets deactivated, however, when repeated failure dictates that a frank re-assessment is called for, as seen in depressed people who are "sadder but wiser" (Alloy & Abramson, 1979).

Such biases are evident in many forms of everyday thinking, and some are particularly relevant with respect to religion. This idea is the basis of Guthrie's (1993) theory of religion in terms of animism and (especially) anthropomorphism, as discussed earlier. As summarized by Atran (2002), the explicit evolutionary argument is that

> natural selection designed the agency-detector system to deal rapidly and economically with stimulus situations involving people and animals as predators, protectors, and prey. This resulted in the system's being trip-wired to respond to fragmentary information under conditions of uncertainty, inciting perceptions of figures in the clouds, voices in the wind, lurking movements in the leaves, and emotions among interacting dots on a computer screen. This hair-triggering of the agency-detection mechanism readily lends itself to supernatural interpretations of uncertain or anxiety-provoking events. (p. 78)

Just as rabbits are designed to "interpret" a vast array of stimuli as potential predators, resulting in a great many (but harmless) Type I errors and few (lethal) Type II errors, human perception is designed to err on the side of animism and anthropomorphism.

Thus, religion is just one of many common forms of human reasoning that reflects adaptive biases in the calibration of evolved mechanisms. To explain why religious ideas have been so enormously successful, however, there must also be something about religion that is particularly effective in capitalizing on these biases.

Religious Beliefs: Combining the Intuitive and the Counterintuitive

Boyer (1994a, 1994b, 2001) observes that there is an important difference between religious beliefs and other kinds of beliefs that is crucial for understanding why religious ideas in particular are accepted and transmitted: Religious beliefs are different from other kinds of beliefs in that they are (or involve the) *extraordinary*, and people generally acknowledge them as such. Boyer takes issue with anthropologists who have long assumed that beliefs of a foreign culture, while appearing bizarre or strange to outsiders, "seem perfectly natural" to those within the local cultural context. In fact, he argues, the subjects of this research themselves typically recognize that beliefs about the supernatural are different from other kinds of beliefs. When the Fang people talk of invisible ghosts flying on banana peels, for example, they are fully aware that they are describing an event qualitatively different from ordinary events.

This is a crucial point because, according to Boyer, it is the (acknowledged) extraordinary aspects of religious beliefs that make them so intriguing, wondrous, exciting, and thought-provoking—and thus worthy of remembering, pondering, and repeating. In Boyer's words, "Religious claims take their attention-demanding quality, which is crucial for their acquisition and transmission, precisely from the fact that they are not entirely compatible with ordinary intuitive expectations" (p. 59). Specifically, he argues that central to a religious belief are one or more strongly *counterintuitive* ("nonschematic") aspects. These are counterintuitive specifically in the sense of violating the kinds of innate knowledge and reasoning structures described earlier in this chapter, and they are attention- and thought-provoking for this very reason. These counterintuitive aspects are what put the *super* in *supernatural*: Supernatural beings possess characteristics that violate ordinary laws of physics (e.g., are invisible, can be in more than one place at once), biology (e.g., never die or contract diseases), and/or psychology (e.g., have extraordinary mental abilities such as mind-reading).

Constrained by these culturally specific counterintuitive beliefs, people then fill in the gaps and draw further inferences based on other principles of intuitive physics, biology, and psychology. The most powerful ideas are those that achieve what Boyer refers to as a *cognitive optimum*: a combination of intuitive and counterintuitive beliefs that involves enough of the former to be plausible, but enough of the latter to be intriguing, exciting, and memorable. Boyer and others have observed that supernatural beings, for example, invariably are characterized as having just one or a few "super" characteristics, but otherwise are perceived in utterly mundane terms. In Pinker's (1997) words, all supernatural objects and individuals are common ones with "a property crossed out and new one written in" (p. 556). Although a god might be perceived as omniscient and invisible, for instance, he or she otherwise thinks and behaves just like a person—for example, displaying the full range of human emotions, having his or her own beliefs and desires, engaging in coalitional bonds and conflicts with other gods, having offspring, and so forth.

Thus, "religious concepts need little in the way of overt cultural representation or instruction to be learned and transmitted. A few fragmentary narrative descriptions or episodes suffice to mobilize an enormously rich network of implicit background beliefs" (Atran, 2002, p. 96).

One reason such admixtures of intuitive and counterintuitive beliefs are successful in being transmitted and spread throughout a culture is that they have an advantage in memorability over mundane, ordinary beliefs. Several studies demonstrate clearly that at least certain kinds of counterintuitive beliefs are indeed recalled better than intuitive ones (e.g., Barrett & Nyhof, 2001; Boyer & Ramble, 2001). More important, Norenzayan and Atran (2003) examined memorability of combinations of beliefs varying from intuitive and ordinary through various degrees of counterintuitiveness. Of the various kinds of beliefs sets examined, the one that contained mostly intuitive beliefs, combined with a few "minimally counterintuitive" beliefs, evinced the greatest memorability over time. As summarized by Atran and Norenzayan (in press), "This is the recipe for a successful transmission of cultural beliefs, and it is the cognitive template that characterizes most popular folktales and religious narratives" (p. 15).

Sperber (1996) makes much the same argument about the role of counterintuitive beliefs in the context of his general theory of cultural transmission. He notes that religious beliefs are typically "half-understood" ideas, to which we are particularly susceptible because they cannot be evaluated rationally (e.g., in terms of identifying logical inconsistencies). The role of trusted authorities then becomes crucial: We rely on supposedly knowledgeable authorities to help us sort through the half-understood combination of intuitive and counterintuitive ideas to determine what to believe and what to reject. I suspect that American children's belief in Santa Claus is psychologically quite similar: Santa is humanlike in all aspects except a few extraordinary ones, and children no doubt only "half understand" how Santa can be so humanlike and so extraordinary simultaneously. (Note, by the way, that Santa's supernatural characteristics nicely illustrate violations of naive physics [How does he get in and out of houses without chimneys?], biology [Since when can reindeer fly?], and psychology [How does he know if you've been naughty or nice?].) Despite this confusion, however, most children are willing to continue to go along with the story so long as trusted authorities (parents and, increasingly with age, older peers) sanction it—and so long as the beliefs come with other rewards (presents!) and cause no harm.

Boyer (1994b) also argues that, again contrary to anthropological orthodoxy, religious beliefs in most cultures are in fact poorly understood by most ordinary people. Western students of religion, he suggests, have a mistaken tendency toward "theologism," according to which we conceptualize religious belief systems as detailed, internally consistent theological networks from which specific beliefs are logically derived. In contrast, however, Boyer argues persuasively that most belief systems are not like this at all: People understand some parts but not others, happily ignore contradictions and logical inconsistencies, and so forth. Instead, religious belief systems are better conceptualized as loosely knit combinations of imperfectly related ideas. There typically are a handful of central assertions and episodic stories about the main characters, and then people are left to fill in the gaps, make connections, and draw inferences. When definitive statements about such matters are needed, specialists are called upon to explain them—and even the experts "often qualify [their statements] with such comments as 'these things are obscure,' 'we are only repeating what our fathers told us,' and so on" (Boyer, 1994b, p. 93).

Anthropologists have struggled mightily to make logical sense of seemingly paradoxical and illogical combinations of beliefs in traditional societies. Comstock (1972) observes that both Evans-Pritchard (1956) and Leinhardt (1961) ran into the same problem in their studies of Nuer and Dinka religion, respectively: simultaneous belief in a single God ("Spirit" or "Divinity," respectively, as translated by the researchers) as well as a variety of gods ("spirits," "divinities"), in a manner that seems at once monotheistic, polytheistic, and pantheistic. It is common to attribute such confusion on the researchers' part (the research subjects themselves seem not at all confused) to difficulties of translation and linguistics, but I suspect that Boyer is correct: People just do not fully understand these ideas.

Even within modern Christianity, which over centuries has developed into something much closer to (multiple variations of) a unified, detailed theology, the situation is not very different for either average believers or experts. Philosophers of religion and theologians, along with ordinary folk, have long wrestled with fundamental paradoxes and apparent logical inconsistencies within their belief system. The paradox of the Holy Trinity—somehow three and one simultaneously—poses virtually the same problem as the one-and-many divinities/spirits of the Dinka and Nuer. Other examples abound: How can Jesus be both divine and human? How can God be all-good and all-powerful, yet there is evil in the world? If God created the universe and everything in it, where did God come from? These are of course the oldest and most stubborn problems in the philosophy of religion, and there is no sign of a consensus about how to answer them.

BEYOND RELIGION: OTHER FORMS OF THOUGHT AND BELIEF

In the first chapter, I argued for an approach to the psychology of religion that begins with a top-down view, beginning with a metatheoretical framework containing many distinct but integrated theories and applying it to religion. One advantage of this approach over the more common bottom-up approach is that the problem of defining religion went away. If we start from the psychology side, we can apply our (meta)theory to any set of topics we wish to call "religion," perhaps using only parts of it to explain more narrowly defined topics and more of it to explain larger chunks. We can draw any arbitrary perimeter around "religion" that we wish, and apply our psychological tools to the task.

One problem in attempting to define religion is that however one chooses to do it, there are always gray areas around the edges: "Religion" shades into various other forms of thinking, belief, and experience that some definitions include and others exclude from consideration. It follows from my general argument, then, that the framework I have proposed should be applicable to these marginal cases as well. In this section I address a few such cases to illustrate how this might be done. As we move further from what is conventionally called "religion," we eventually will find ourselves on the other side of even the most liberal definition of religion, and will turn the evolutionary psychology paradigm on science itself. In the final section of the chapter, I use the science example as a hook on which to hang a more general discussion of the uniquely human phenomena of rationality and culture to demonstrate, if only in rough form, the way in which these complex issues can be integrated within an evolutionary psychology of religion and culture.

Parapsychology and Other Supernatural Beliefs

One domain of phenomena that seem clearly related to religious beliefs in some ways is that of parapsychology and other supernatural beliefs. I doubt many scholars would categorize modern belief in ghosts as "religious," but where does one draw the line between, say, the ghosts of horror movies and ancestor worship or belief in gods or spirits?[3] If shamans in nonliterate cultures are "religious figures," then what about modern clairvoyants, palm readers, or astrologers? I believe the same psychological principles are at work.

Consider, for example, claims about clairvoyance, extrasensory perception (ESP), and telepathy. First, one might note that psychological *essentialism* and beliefs about *natural kinds* (i.e., *naive biology*) are immediately evident: The person with such abilities is believed to have some kind of special powers, abilities, or essence that makes him or her importantly different from the rest of us—as with beliefs about shamans, clergy, and other religious leaders as discussed earlier in this chapter.

Second, such beliefs typically reflect *combinations* of intuitive and counterintuitive ideas as discussed by Boyer with respect to religious beliefs. The ability to "see" the future (clairvoyance), or to move objects using "psychic energy" (telekinesis) involve violations of naive (and real) laws of physics; bringing people back from the dead (e.g., seances) involves violations of naive (and real) biology; reading others' thoughts directly (ESP) involves violations of naive (and real) psychology. Apart from these nonintuitive claims, however, paranormal activities look entirely mundane: Telekineticists simply bend spoons or "push" objects an inch or two along a table; they do not transform spoons into pigeons or make space shuttles disappear. Stage magicians do these latter sorts of tricks, and this is why they are stage magicians and not religious heroes: The violations of intuitive scientific principles are so extreme as to render the trick unbelievable. It is fun to watch illusionist David Copperfield make the space shuttle seem to disappear into thin air, but everyone knows it is a trick.

Similar observations might be made about beliefs concerning extraterrestrial beings and flying saucers. Martians (or whoever) are certainly seen as a distinct *natural kind*—a different species, at least. Those alleged to visit our planet clearly possess one or another kind of special ability— for example, piloting saucers that defy laws of physics—but otherwise are remarkably like us. In fictional film depictions, for example, they invariably share our coalitional psychology, coming to Earth to defeat us in battle or colonize us; alternatively, they come to join together with us in some kind of cross-galaxy alliance, or to engage in some sort of equitable social exchange with us. They typically are assumed to have their own beliefs, desires, and motivations; to share our own emotions, feelings, and goals; and otherwise obey all of the basic principles of naive psychology. For example, they get angry when confronted, or feel homesick and phone home.

Several writers have examined beliefs in a variety of other paranormal (or at least dubious) phenomena and shown how they clearly reflect common, fundamental biases in human cognition—biases which themselves reflect the operation of evolved psychological mechanisms. Gilovich and Savitsky (1996), for example, discuss how the *representativeness heuristic*—the intuitive belief that things that are similar "go together"—underlies pseudoscientific beliefs in homeopathic medicine, astrology, and naive handwriting analysis. Penmanship characterized by large, loopy letters is assumed to reflect an emotional, extroverted personality; individuals whose astrological sign is Leo, like (the stereotype of) lions, are confident and courageous.

Beliefs about *magic*—which is usually distinguished from "religion" by scholars but which clearly has much in common with it—provides many other examples. For example, Vernon (1962) suggests that the rationales underlying homeopathic (imitative), repetitive, and contagious magic are, respectively, "that like produces like," "that events which have been observed to occur simultaneously or to follow a particular sequence will continue to follow the same pattern," and "things which have once been together must forever afterward . . . have a magical influence on one another" (pp. 65–67). Each of these seems to reflect evolved inferential rules of naive physics or biology. More specifically, the last seems to reflect the evolved psychology of *disgust*—a psychological mechanism designed to encourage avoidance of potentially disease-laden objects which do in fact conform to a "law of contagion" (Rozin, 1996). In Pinker's (1997) words, "Disgust is intuitive microbiology" (p. 383). It is also noteworthy that the goals of magic are typically entirely mundane and reflect the same evolved desires and motives as other kinds of behavior, such as acquiring resources, attracting mates, thwarting competitors, and assisting kin.

If the psychological processes underlying fascination with science fiction or stage magic are similar to those underlying religious belief, one might reasonably ask why people devoutly believe the latter to be true but not the former. Science fiction and disappearing acts ask us to do much the same thing as do religious beliefs (per Boyer), namely, accept one or two extraordinary (counterintuitive) assumptions in the context of situations and persons that are otherwise ordinary. (Have you ever noticed that centuries from now, in distant galaxies, conflicts apparently are still resolved via fistfights?). The simple answer is that science fiction is, by definition and name, *fiction*, and the word *magic* in modern culture has come to connote make-believe. That is, stage magic and science fiction are presented to us from the beginning as untrue. Nobody is claiming, or asking us to accept, that the starship *Enterprise* really exists or that Copperfield's space shuttle is really gone. Note, however, that when the rare illusionist *does* claim to actually possess extraordinary powers, as did spoon-bender Uri Geller during the 1970s, many people *do* in fact believe it (Randi, 1982).

Commonsense Knowledge and Reasoning in Everyday Life

Just as modern beliefs about a variety of paranormal phenomena shade into "religion" through a wide gray swath, these beliefs in turn shade into other, more mundane forms of everyday thought and commonsense reasoning. Alcock (1995) goes so far to claim that

> nothing is fundamentally different about what we might think of as "irrational" beliefs—they are generated in the same manner as other beliefs. We may not have an evidential basis for belief in irrational concepts, but neither do we have such a basis for most of our beliefs. For example, you probably believe that brushing your teeth is good for you, but it is unlikely that you have any evidence to back up this belief, unless you are a dentist. You have been taught this, it makes some sense, and you have never been led to question it. (p. 15)

This might be a bit of an overstatement, depending (as usual) on how you wish to define religion. From Boyer's perspective, for example, a crucial distinguishing characteristic of religion is the presence of one or more strongly counterintuitive beliefs, a feature clearly absent in the case of toothbrushing. Toothbrushing also does not hold much fascination for us either, for exactly this reason. Moreover, as Boyer (1994b) has argued cogently, people generally are aware that there is something extraordinary about their religious beliefs, which is not generally true with respect to their beliefs about dental hygiene.

Nevertheless, Alcock's point is well taken that the cognitive mechanisms underlying everyday beliefs and religious beliefs are very much the same. The general model of "how the mind works" offered by Pinker (1997) and others is generally applicable. Our psychological architecture comprises numerous, domain-specific mechanisms evolved initially to solve particular adaptive problems, but which we now are able to apply beyond their "intended" domains in acts of creative thought. Whether beliefs or inferences are categorized as "religious" or "superstitious" or "everyday reasoning" is another matter; the cognitive processes underlying them are largely the same. This is why I have suggested that the notorious problem of defining religion is a red herring when it comes to trying to explain religious belief.

Research on everyday reasoning in social psychology has long focused predominantly on the problem of identifying and explaining *errors* in human information processing and "judgments under uncertainty." We play the lottery even though we know our chances of winning are poor; we read about a particular car's wonderful repair record in *Consumer Reports* but then do not buy one because a friend had a problem with hers. The work of Tversky and Kahneman (e.g., 1974; Kahneman, Slovic, & Tversky, 1982), in which they and others have shown in many, many experiments that certain kinds of reasoning errors are common, is probably the best known of this tradition. Their general form of explanation is that we tend to process information under certain circumstances according to *heuristics*—cognitive shortcuts or rules of thumb that work correctly most of the time but can be made to fail miserably in experimental tasks. According to this research, people fail to take base rates adequately into account when solving probability problems, tend to overestimate the power of generalization from small samples, and make a variety of other well-known cognitive *faux pas*. The underlying assumption of this heuristics approach is that humans are "cognitive misers." Because information-processing resources are limited, the theory goes, people use cognitive shortcuts whenever possible, bringing to bear their more refined and powerful logical skills only when necessary.

Why this preoccupation with errors? One reason, which I suggest only half facetiously, is that they are amusing. It is fun to point to bonehead mistakes that otherwise very intelligent people make. A second, more serious reason, is that examination of errors can provide a very useful window into the cognitive processes that generate them, in much the same way that neurologists learn about the organization of the brain by studying the effects of lesions in particular locations.

However, I think there is a third and far more insidious reason for the interest in inferential errors, one that emerges from a very wrong set of assumptions about the nature of the human mind. Errors are surprising and interesting in large part because we implicitly tend to assume that the brain/mind ought to produce *right* answers. According to the Standard Social Science Model (Tooby & Cosmides, 1992), the brain/mind is seen to be a general, all-purpose problem-solving device that somehow "knows" fundamental rules of logic and is expected to use them effectively to generate normatively correct inferences. Errors in reasoning are therefore exceptions to the general rule, signs that something has unexpectedly gone awry.

An evolutionary perspective turns this set of assumptions on its head. As I have discussed previously, the brain/mind has evolved via natural selection in ways that, in ancestral environments, were *adaptive*—in the strict sense of reproductive fitness—not necessarily accurate or correct. Recall the highly adaptive yet frequently erroneous paranoia of rabbits. From this perspective, what is remarkable is not that people sometimes error on statistical or logic problems, but rather that they can do them correctly at all. We have seen several reasons why systematic errors in reasoning are expectable, such as inherent biases in cognitive systems (e.g., paranoid rabbits) and mismatches between evolved mechanisms and modern environments (e.g., attempting to solve artificial problems designed by devious experimenters in the laboratory). On the other hand, we are *able* to solve complex problems when the structure of a problem corresponds to one in our cognitive toolkit, as when logic problems conform to the logic of detecting cheating in reciprocal-altruism relationships (Cosmides & Tooby, 1992). Everyday reasoning is (perhaps) surprisingly often tolerably accurate, but errors of various sorts are also common.

Science

I have been suggesting here that the problem of defining religion is in part a slippery-slope problem: We can imagine a kind of continuum from religion "proper" to other forms of paranormal and supernatural beliefs, to superstitition and erroneous reasoning in everyday life. My argument has been that all of these ways of thinking can be understood in terms of the same evolved psychology. By the same reasoning, then, we might continue slipping down the slope and ask about forms of thought that are intended to be "unbiased" and "objective." In particular, we might ask about science itself, which is the "form of thought" I have adopted in this book.

The general evolutionary perspective I have outlined does not bode well for an enterprise such as science in which the ultimate goal is to be "correct." The brain/mind is designed to produce inferences that are (were) adaptive in the strict sense of enhancing survival and reproduction, irrespective of any norms we might impose with respect to accuracy or correctness. Sometimes, of course, these criteria converge: Being right surely is (or was, in ancestral environments), in many cases, more adaptive than being wrong. But if our explicit goal is to be right about something, we cannot take for granted that our cognitive machinery is well suited for the task.

"Being right" is the explicit goal of science: to understand how the world "really" works. But if science is just another product of our evolved psychological architecture like so many other ways of thinking, why is science any better? Is there really anything special about it? There is no shortage of critics who think not, even (maybe especially) within academia itself. It has become *de rigueur* in many intellectual circles to point out that attaining objectivity in science is a myth. "Deconstructionists" and "social contructionists" from many academic disciplines, particularly within the humanities, argue that the emperor has no clothes. Science, they say, is just another group of "texts" to be interpreted in an open-ended manner, subject to whatever one's personal biases and cultural context happen to be. Scientific theories are "just theories" ("theory" somehow becoming a pejorative term in the process), and hold no special status in competition with nonscientific perspectives (Gross & Levitt, 1994).

The principal argument usually comes down to the indisputable observation that scientists, as people, are incapable of being objective and unbiased, and consequently their perspectives are biased by their own personal motives and beliefs as well as their local cultural context. Although the problem is seldom framed in evolutionary terms, it is easy to generate examples of how many of the psychological mechanisms discussed in this book strongly influence the activity and thinking of scientists. Guthrie (1993) illustrates a variety of ways in which anthropomorphism sneaks into science and philosophy despite the best efforts to suppress it. For example, Newton had to free himself from intuitive physics that reflect the behavior of objects on a planet with atmosphere to make his momentous discoveries about how bodies might behave unencumbered by friction. If, as evolutionary psychology assumes, scientists are working with the same basic psychological architecture as everyone else, they are as vulnerable to cognitive biases and inferential errors as everyone else. Evolved psychological mechanisms are both enabling and constraining in doing science, and consequently can be the source of creative, insightful ideas—or really bad ones.

In addition to these kinds of cognitive biases, science as a profession is a context in which other motivational systems complicate matters further. For example, consider the degree to which striving for excellence and recognition in research and teaching reflect (often quite transparently) competition for status, power, and resources. The most successful receive accolades from their peers, rake in grant money, and wield power in the politics of their departments and their fields. Within any field everyone knows which journals are the most prestigious, and we endeavor to publish in these as often as we can. Professional conferences are (among other things) places to strut one's stuff. Successful academics are widely perceived as arrogant (and they really are; Feist, 1998), and often are perceived as unapproachable by those of lower status. Likewise, there can be little doubt that coalitional psychology is rampant beneath the common turf wars between academic disciplines, subdisciplines, and theoretical camps.

In short, scientists are people, and the psychology of science can therefore be understood in terms of the science of psychology (Feist & Gorman, 1998). To the extent that evolutionary psychology provides a useful metatheoretical framework for organizing research and theory in psychology, it also provides a potentially powerful perspective on the psychology of science.

SUMMARY AND CONCLUSIONS

In this chapter, along with the previous chapters, I have suggested a variety of evolved psychological mechanisms that appear to be involved in processing information and belief about gods and other religious phenomena. Mechanisms for naive physics, biology, and psychology provide a psychological basis from which supernatural beliefs—including animism and anthropomorphism—are built by analogy and metaphor. Cognitive metaphors common to religion are driven in part by adaptive biases in the calibration of psychological mechanisms, and by blending intuitive and counterintuitive ideas in proportions that render them both intriguing and mysterious, on the one hand, but not so much so to be entirely implausible. Once anthropomorphized, details of beliefs about gods' intentions and actions are molded by other mechanisms dedicated to social-cognitive inferential processes designed to negotiate dominance hierarchies, attachment, and coalitional relationships, as discussed in previous chapters. In this way evolutionary psychology provides a coherent framework for itemizing the various components of cognitive machinery that contribute to the acquisition, maintenance, and modification of religious beliefs.

These same theoretical perspectives can be applied with equal force to topics around the definitional edges of religion, such as magic, superstition, and parapsychology. In particular, these areas appear to be, at least in part, manifestations of psychological systems related to naive physics, biology, and psychology, and to follow principles laid out by Boyer with respect to the reasons many people find them salient, fascinating, and believable. Indeed, the same perspectives can also be brought to bear on other forms of thinking that clearly fall outside the scope of anyone's definition of religion. Everyday reasoning, with respect to both correct inferences and erroneous ones, can be approached in the same way. Our evolved psychology in many ways leads us intuitively to accurate inferences and conclusions, and in other ways leads to systematic errors. (Note that, again, it does not matter which of these is the case for religion or any particular religious belief as far as the theory is concerned.) The same is true of science as well.

On the other hand, science *is* different from other ways of acquiring and evaluating knowledge, for reasons that illustrate some larger themes about the nature of religious beliefs that I have been skirting for the last couple of chapters. Indeed, a comprehensive theory of religion ultimately will need to be very much more complex than what I have laid out so far, as we will see in the next chapter.

CHAPTER TWELVE

Beyond Genes
Learning, Rationality, and Culture

U p to this point, my "religion as evolutionary by-product" view has generally cast human thinking and behavior—and especially religion—as simply spilling out of our evolved psychology, like water running down a hillside. The peaks and valleys of the landscape represent, in this metaphor, our evolved psychology; religion is the water following the natural contours of the land, flowing down from the peaks and winding through the valleys (Atran, 2002). We come equipped with specialized mechanisms that guide our everyday thinking about our natural and social worlds, which when applied overly zealously produce religion and related phenomena. Belief in spirits or mana appear to be rather straightforward extensions of psychological essentialism; animism and anthropomorphism emerge easily and readily from biases inherent in our evolved systems of naive physics and biology. Some aspects of beliefs about God flow easily from the attachment system, whereas others emerge from the application of psychological systems for thinking about power and prestige, coalitional psychology, and reciprocal altruism. The "Golden Rule" seems to represent a codification of social-exchange principles already embedded deeply within our psychological architecture.

In stark contrast, however, is an alternative perspective with a long intellectual history that views religion in precisely the opposite manner: as a cultural construction that has emerged *in spite of*, and whose function is that of *opposing* or *constraining*, our evolved psychology. Freud (1927/ 1961) was probably the most (in)famous proponent of this alternative view, arguing that civilization in general, including religion in particular, was fundamentally about taming our base animal instincts. A more contemporary (and evolutionarily more sophisticated) version of the idea was espoused by Donald Campbell (1975). In Campbell's view, religious traditions reflect the experience and knowledge of many generations, accumulated via a lengthy process of trial-and-error learning, that function to keep our biology under control. Like Freud, Campbell adopts a hydraulic model, according to which our biological nature is pushing in one direction, and religion (culture) is pushing back against it from the other direction. In contrast to the metaphor of water flowing down a hillside, religion from this perspective looks more like a set of dams constructed by humans to stem the flow.

Most of what I have written in this book so far reflects the downhill metaphor, but I have mixed in a few examples more consistent with the dam metaphor without (I now confess) acknowledging having done so. In Chapter 10, for example, I introduced several examples in which religious beliefs appear well designed to "trick" people into behaving in ways contrary to the ways they would ordinarily be inclined to behave otherwise. "Kin-talk," for example, was discussed as a gambit designed to induce altruism toward people who otherwise would be treated differently. The ethical systems inherent in most organized religions, as illustrated by the Ten Commandments and proscriptions against the Seven Deadly Sins, read like lists of base desires upon which, we fear, we will all be tempted to act unless prevented from doing so. One interpretation of the common eye-for-an-eye stricture was as an effort to discourage the excessive level of retaliation that would likely occur spontaneously in response to an insult or injury, rather than to encourage revenge.

Such examples pose an obvious problem for evolutionary explanations. Adaptationist hypotheses are clearly useful for explaining adaptive behavior, more or less by definition, but explaining *maladaptive*—that is, from a strict inclusive-fitness perspective—behavior requires additional work. Critics like to point to dams as evidence against evolutionary psychology. Students and colleagues frequently ask, for example, how evolutionary psychologists could possibly explain the voluntary use of condoms or other forms of birth control, behavior that seems to fly in the face of natural selection. In the realm of religion, critics ask why, if behavior is adaptive and "in our genes," monks or nuns would ever vow to be celibate. Because religion, like most human thought and behavior, clearly includes a variety of adaptive, nonadaptive, and maladaptive (from a strict inclusive-fitness perspective) manifestations, a theory of religion (or anything else) grounded in evolutionary psychology must be capable of explaining all of these cases.

The short answer, of course, is that there is far more to explaining human thought and behavior, including religion, than evolution and genetic fitness. The causal path from genes to religion is a long and circuitous one, with many levels of analysis interposed in between. Although natural selection (and its criterion of reproductive success) is a *distal* or *ultimate* cause in the production of any behavior, many other *proximal* levels of analysis mediate the causal path from genes to behavior. Moreover, each of these levels operates according to different principles—that is, principles other than inclusive fitness—which produce behavioral choices according to criteria other than success in gene propagation.

Each of these levels of analysis could be (indeed, has been) the subject of many books in itself. Numerous theoretical models have been developed that attempt to combine and integrate the processes of biological (genetic) evolution with those of *cultural* evolution. Such models go by names such as *gene–culture co-evolution* (Lumsden & Wilson, 1981; E. O. Wilson, 1978), *multilevel selection* (Sober & D. S. Wilson, 1998), and *dual inheritance* (Boyd & Richerson, 1985). Although differing in many ways, such models are all in agreement that social learning and cultural transmission give rise to Darwinianlike processes in the selection of ideas and behaviors at the cultural level, in ways that sometimes parallel and sometimes diverge from processes of biological evolution at the level of genes. A review of these models would be far beyond the scope of this book. However, in this chapter I offer some ways in which higher levels of analysis (i.e., beyond biological evolution) can be conceptualized.

There are several reasons for including this discussion here. First, as suggested earlier, it is necessary to consider these issues in order to explain behavior, including many examples in the context of religion, that appears to be maladaptive or nonadaptive from the perspective of natural selection. Second, such a discussion expands upon the idea, first proposed in Chapter 9, that religion is an evolutionary by-product, by illustrating a variety of processes through which such by-products emerge. Third, no discussion of religion (or most other complex human phenomena) would be complete without reference to familiar psychological processes such as learning, rational thinking, and culture. A primary purpose of the chapter is to point to ways in which such processes are on the one hand independent of those of biological evolution, yet on the other hand cannot be properly understood outside the context of biological evolution.

NATURAL SELECTION, GENES, AND INCLUSIVE FITNESS

One of the most persistent criticisms of evolutionary explanations of behavior is that they are "reductionistic" in their attempts to explain all behavior in terms of inclusive fitness. To the extent that such approaches do this, the criticism is apt. Natural selection does not produce behavior; it produces physiological and psychological systems that in turn, in interaction with the environment, produce behavior. This distinction between psychological mechanisms and the behavior they produce is crucial for a proper evolutionary understanding of behavior (Cosmides & Tooby, 1987).

The criterion by which systems and mechanisms are designed by natural selection is that of inclusive fitness: The system designs that have been naturally selected are those that, by virtue of their effects on survival and reproductive success, resulted in more copies of their own genetic recipes being represented throughout the species than alternative designs. However, applying such explanations directly to a behavior or class of behaviors—religion, for example—is often inappropriate and potentially very misleading. Behavior can and often does appear maladaptive or nonadaptive from an inclusive-fitness perspective. There is nothing inconsistent about this: Nature selects and discards adaptations based on their overall average track records, not particular episodes or events.

Consider again the hypervigilant predator-detector system in rabbits. An explanation of why it is adaptive (in inclusive-fitness terms) for rabbits to be paranoid comes easily in terms of enhancing survival (and thus reproductive) prospects. Each time a rabbit successfully evades a predator in this way, it appears to be behaving adaptively. But each time it races for cover at the sound of a harmless rustling leaf it wastes valuable foraging time, consumes calories, and generally appears to be behaving in a maladaptive manner. This particular instance of behavior appears maladaptive, but such "errors" are very much a part of the adaptive design of the system—a feature rather than a bug, so to speak. It is the over-all system design that is adaptive, not any particular behavior or class of behaviors it produces.

The same argument applies with equal force to religion. Indeed, the analogy of paranoid rabbits is particularly fitting with respect to Atran and Norenzayan's (in press; also Atran, 2002) emphasis on the role of a hypervigilant "agency-detector" mechanism in the production of beliefs about gods and other supernatural forces. Along with Boyer, Atran, and others, I have argued that religious beliefs are explained in part by the overly zealous application of evolved mechanisms of folk physics, folk biology, and so forth that were "designed" to guide (adaptively) thinking about the natural world. Such systems have proved over thousands of generations to be more adaptive on average than competing designs. Sometimes these systems produce beliefs about gods or spirits. These beliefs might or might not be adaptive in a strict inclusive-fitness sense; the point is that it does not really matter for explaining them. Most of what I have said in this book fits in this category, and demonstrates what I mean in claiming that religion is an evolutionary by-product rather than an adaptation: Psychological systems related to attachment, social exchange, dominance and prestige, and so forth are all adaptations that evolved for purposes unrelated to religion, but sometimes produce religious beliefs as a kind of side effect of their overall design. Whether particular instances of these side effects appear "adaptive" or not is beside the point.

Of course, if the design of these psychological systems reliably produced highly maladaptive by-products, this would have led to the entire system being selected against, or at least being recalibrated. The level of paranoia in rabbits characterizing rabbits is the result of a long history of natural selection balancing the average costs of false alarms against the average costs of predator-detection failures. If rabbits were any more paranoid, they would be unable to stay in one place long enough to eat, mate, or do other important (adaptive) rabbit things. Likewise, had it been the case in ancestral environments that the religious (or religionlike) by-products of psychological systems were consistently maladaptive, natural selection would have recalibrated the systems to reduce such effects. For example, perhaps people would be less likely to imagine gods as attachment figures because they would generally be more reluctant to identify other humans as attachment figures.

Another way in which apparently maladaptive behavior can be reliably produced by a naturally selected system is when the environment in which it occurs differs in important, functionally relevant ways from the ancestral environments in which the systems evolved. Recall the example of our evolved taste preferences turning against us in, in the form of an obesity epidemic, in a world of fast-food restaurants. The functioning of an adaptive system, in terms of both its "intended' products and its various by-products, can differ in many ways from its ancestral form (and original design) in the context of modern environments that differ in important, functionally relevant ways from the environment of evolutionary (EEA). As discussed in Chapter 6, for example, it has been argued that the structure of modern Western societies (e.g., geographical dispersion of family members) provides less support for bereavement than would have been likely in ancient environments; as a consequence, the attachment system might be more readily activated with respect to God in times of bereavement than was once the case (cf. Caudill, 1958; Loveland, 1968). Any number of differences between modern and ancestral environments, ranging from mass media to urban crowding, might play important roles in the degree to which evolved psychological systems give rise to religious belief and behavior in modern environments. Such effects might be adaptive, maladaptive, or simply nonadaptive with respect to inclusive-fitness criteria.

Though not central to the main arguments in this book, it is important to at least note in passing one additional way in which apparently maladaptive thought or behavior can emerge from an adaptive psychological system: *malfunction*. Genetic mutations, environmental insults, and other kinds of developmental perturbations sometimes cause the operation of an otherwise well-designed system to function differently than "intended." Countless physical and psychological syndromes are due to such errors, some of which are extremely maladaptive and others inconsequential with respect to genetic success. With respect to religion, profound spiritual experiences can be triggered by bouts of temporal lobe epilepsy or schizophrenia, for example, as a result of error rather than design. It would be fruitless to attempt to explain religious beliefs emerging from schizophrenic delusions in inclusive-fitness terms.

FROM GENES TO MEMES

Although evolved psychological systems are designed strictly by the criterion of inclusive fitness or genetic success, individual behaviors produced by those systems do not necessarily—and indeed often do not—appear adaptive by this same standard. Explaining behavior for which natural selection is only an indirect cause is a rather different task than explaining the evolution of a behavior-producing adaptation. In the remainder of this chapter I outline some of the processes that occur at higher levels of analysis and operate by criteria other than inclusive fitness, and therefore lead regularly to thought and behavior—including, of course, religious thought and behavior—that appear non- or maladaptive from an inclusive-fitness perspective.

Individual Learning, Reinforcement, and the Pleasure Principle

In the simplest of worlds, evolved psychology would consist of nothing more than simple if–then rules of the form "In response to stimulus X, do Y"—where Y has proven over many generations the most adaptive available behavioral response to X. However, such decisions rules become less reliably adaptive when environments are transitory, locally variable, and complex—that is, when alternative behavioral options are differentially adaptive depending on contextual factors. Over millions of years, natural selection has hit upon a clever, alternative system design to accommodate such situations: *Learning* is a process by which behavior can be more finely tuned to local conditions to ensure adaptive responding in variable environments.

In simple terms, we experience reinforcement and punishment as cognitive–affective states such as "pleasure" and "pain," and learn to behave in ways that reliably produce the former and avoid the latter. It is important to note that natural selection does not care about the happiness—that is, the pleasure–pain balance—of individuals; it "cares" only about the relative success of genes in producing more copies of themselves. But it can achieve its inclusive-fitness goals by designing organisms who *do* care about their own pleasure and pain.

Thus, learning processes can be thought of as a level of analysis distinct from natural selection, in which people choose (whether consciously or not) beliefs and behavior based not on inclusive-fitness criteria, but rather on the criterion of their own individual pleasure–pain (or reward–punishment) experience. In the ancestral environments in which these systems were "designed," the criteria would (at least on average) have been more or less isomorphic: Learning where the best food was, for example, would be rewarded by the feel-good experiences of a tasty meal and full stomach, which in turn would contribute to inclusive fitness via enhanced survival (and hence reproductive) prospects. However, the two levels of criteria can easily become decoupled such that learned behavior appears non- or maladaptive with respect to genes.

First, learning systems make errors. A classic example of particular relevance to religion and everyday knowledge is *superstitious behavior*, by which I refer to the specific phenomenon well studied in pigeons and other laboratory animals by which individuals "learn" behaviors that happen coincidentally to get paired with reward in random reinforcement schedules (Skinner, 1948). I doubt that many people, upon learning of this phenomenon, have failed to jump immediately to thoughts of human "superstition" (in the colloquial sense of the term), astrology, and various aspects of religion. If one dances in a certain way and a thunderstorm arrives within a short time thereafter, or if one prays for an outcome that eventually occurs, a new cultural ritual or faith in God might be born. Such errors are analogous to the kinds of errors made by inferential systems discussed in the previous section, such as the false alarms frequently produced by rabbits' predator-detection systems.

Second, the adaptiveness of an evolved learning system can be compromised in novel environments that present rewards or punishments different from those in the EEA, leading us to behave in ways that feel good to us as individuals, but not necessarily in ways that benefit our genes. Amusing animal tricks performed in circus acts or by your pet dog provide a good illustration. Humans are immensely creative at figuring out ways to fool Mother Nature, and to capitalize on novel (relative to ancestral environments) opportunities to obtain pleasure and avoid pain, irrespective of genetic fitness consequences. People know that it is pleasurable to have sex with a desired partner, eat a slice of cheesecake, be admired by others, and so forth, and we learn all kinds of creative ways to achieve these states using the tools available in our local cultural setting. In the extreme, we can bypass the design of our psychological systems entirely with psychotropic drugs, obtaining the feel-good payoff without going through all the trouble to "earn" this state in the ways designed by natural selection. Religion, as Marx famously proclaimed, can function like an "opiate" as well, to the extent that religious beliefs or behaviors are psychologically rewarding in one way or another.

This line of reasoning provides a context for reconciling the many theories in the psychology of religion that focus on the ways in which religious beliefs and behaviors are rewarding or reinforcing to individuals (e.g., Galanter, 1989; Stark & Bainbridge, 1987), as well as the countless psychological theories that posit emotional or cognitive functions of religion, such as providing a sense of security, meaning, or control; ameliorating fear of death; reducing anxiety; producing peak experiences; and so forth. It is not at all inconsistent to say on the one hand that people pray, for example, because they find the experience rewarding (or pleasurable, etc.) and on the other that they do so as a consequence of an attachment system that evolved via natural selection. Most theories of religion that focus on learning, reward, or some form of emotional deprivation as the principal mechanism are deficient not because there is anything wrong with this level of analysis, but rather because such analyses are merely circular unless informed by an understanding of *why* these behaviors or beliefs are rewarding. Although learning processes in some ways represent a fundamentally distinct level of analysis from natural selection, a proper understanding of it requires that it be placed in evolutionary perspective.

Learning is not an alternative to evolved design, but rather an example of it. No species, including humans, possesses a domain-general, all-purpose learning device capable of learning all things in all contexts with equal ease. As demonstrated convincingly in many now-classic studies that contributed to the demise of radical behaviorism, animals do not learn all things equally well; moreover, these differentiated learning abilities make good evolutionary sense. For example, rats learn to associate nausea with particular foods far more quickly than other kinds of stimulus pairings (Garcia, Ervin, & Koelling, 1966)—the so-called "Garcia effect"—and people acquire fears of snakes and spiders much more readily than of fast-moving cars or live electrical outlets (Seligman & Hager, 1972). Similarly, the design of our psychological systems enable people to "learn" quickly that the rain dance was successful, that gods were looking over them when danger was narrowly avoided, or that their prayers have been answered.

Complex Reasoning and Higher-Order Cognitive Processes

The metaphors of the flowing river and the dam are reminiscent of a long-standing distinction in psychology between rational and nonrational thought, or between our "animal instincts" and "higher levels" of human nature. Freud, for example, differentiated *primary process* thinking versus *secondary process* thinking; the former reflects stuff bubbling up from the id over which we have no control, whereas the latter is composed of ego processes involving reason. More recently, numerous major papers or books have appeared in the cognitive and social-cognition literatures distinguishing, for example, *associative* versus *rule-based* systems (Sloman, 1996), *heuristic* versus *analytic* processing (Evans, 1989), *implicit cognition* versus *explicit learning* (Reber, 1993), *intuitive cognition* versus *analytic cognition* (Hammond, 1996), *automatic* versus *controlled* cognitive processes (Devine, 1989; Fiske & Neuberg, 1990), and an *experiential system* versus a *rational system* (Epstein, 1994), to name just a few (for reviews, see Evans & Over, 1996; Gigerenzer & Regier, 1996; Sloman, 1996). Although there are important differences among these various schemes, they all point to thinking and reasoning processes that are more complex, more controlled (i.e., less automatic), more effortful, less spontaneous, and more likely to be accessible to conscious awareness than the kinds of psychological systems I have discussed so far.

I have no intention of attempting to define or explain the nature of "rationality," nor to speculate on how exactly it works. Numerous theorists have speculated about the adaptive function of our advanced reasoning abilities and "consciousness." Humphrey (1976, 1984) suggests, for example, that consciousness evolved as a tool for simulating and predicting the social behavior of other people, which in a highly social species such as ourselves would confer obvious benefits in negotiating social relationships. Mithen (1996), as discussed previously, provides many examples of ways in which new connections between previously independent psychological mechanisms could be useful in solving diverse adaptive problems, as in the use of certain theory of mind mechanisms in predicting the behavior of prey animals or the use of technological skills for creating decorative jewelry. Miller (2000) argues that our high level of intelligence owes largely to the process of *sexual selection*, because its products were attractive to potential mates rather than because of any particular survival benefits per se. I will not take a position on this matter, but merely take for granted that we are capable of complex reasoning processes (of which we are sometimes consciously aware).

Rationality and consciousness are probably best understood not as distinct systems with their own unique goals or motives, but rather a set of cognitive *tools* or abilities that evolved in the service of other extant, functionally organized systems. Their emergence changed how (and how well) we accomplished the goals of negotiating social relationships, attracting mates, and so on; it did not change the goals themselves. Your evolved taste preferences might motivate you to seek out cheesecake, but your advanced reasoning systems are indispensable for locating a bakery in the phone book, driving there in your car or negotiating the city bus system, and transacting the purchase. That is, one way in which our rational/consciousness systems work is to find more effective ways to achieve goals encoded into our evolved psychology, from figuring out the best pickup line to attract a desirable mate to computing the most efficient path to the grocery store on your way home from work. In such cases, rationality is a tool that can operate as a kind of extension of natural selection in ways that promote inclusive fitness.

However, rational thinking need not be—and indeed typically is not—restricted to enhancing inclusive fitness. Contrary to common misunderstanding (and some earlier versions of sociobiology that preceded the emergence of modern evolutionary psychology), people are not designed as "fitness-maximizers" whose decision-making behavior is guided by calculations of the inclusive-fitness consequences of their behavioral options. Perhaps the strongest evidence against the "humans as fitness maximizers" hypothesis is that evolutionary biologists and geneticists, who presumably understand the concept of inclusive fitness better than anyone, do not (so far as I know) generally evince higher levels of it than the rest of us. Complex thinking is often, if not usually, guided by criteria other than inclusive fitness.

One particular way in which cognitive skills are helpful is that they enable us to calculate and anticipate the consequences of events and behaviors without actually engaging in them. In this way they function as a kind of *learning simulation*, in which we attempt to reckon reinforcements and punishments before acting rather than after. As such, it leads to potential decoupling of behavior from inclusive-fitness criteria in the same ways discussed in the previous section. When we do such computations to choose, for example, a course of action intended to achieve a particular goal, the criteria by which we do the reckoning largely concern the question of what will bring us (as individuals) pleasure and avoid pain, not what will most enhance our inclusive fitness. For the person deciding whether or not to drive to the bakery for a cheesecake, the dilemma concerns the anticipated costs and benefits (pleasure–pain) to the individual decision maker, not which course of action will better propagate copies of his or her genes.

This is why people in modern societies often make choices that clearly would be considered maladaptive from an inclusive-fitness perspective, such as using condoms or deliberately remaining childless: They typically have decided that life without children will be more pleasurable for them than life with children, perhaps because they will have more time and energy to pursue other activities they find more rewarding. Many religious behaviors that appear inconsistent with an adaptationist perspective can be explained in this way. Monks or nuns vowing to be chaste are not that different from the large number of us who actively choose to give up parenting; they have just decided to give up sex too. In less extreme ways, people following religious proscriptions frequently choose to forgo various earthly pleasures in lieu of other goals.

As with the learning processes discussed earlier, one important source of discrepancies between inclusive-fitness and feel-good criteria is differences between the EEA and modern environments. We use our rational systems to compute strategies for attaining goals that are themselves often products of learning in local environments, and which for reasons discussed previously may be disassociated—sometimes radically—from fitness consequences. Heroin addicts become remarkably resourceful in designing complex plots to obtain their next fix, with disastrous consequences. Psychological tools, like any kind of tools, are inherently neither benign nor malevolent, but can be used for either kind of purpose.

In addition, rational processing can lead to another level of decoupling of behavior from inclusive-fitness criteria. Unlike simple learning processes, complex reasoning processes permit us to go beyond the most immediate and obvious consequences of our actions and consider much longer-term plans and goals. Without a rational system you might well jump at a slice of cheesecake placed in front of you, or seek one out if you caught a whiff of one's aroma. But you would never come upon the solution of driving to the bakery to buy one or going shopping for the ingredients to make one. (And, of course, there would not be automobiles or bakeries anyway if other people had not had rational systems to enable them to construct them.) Nor would it occur to you to pass on the cheesecake in favor of a diet, in the service of such long-term goals as remaining physically attractive to potential mates or decreasing health risks. Choosing between short-term and long-term goals is a mental task with which most of us are confronted almost continually in day-to-day life. Giving up alcohol or other immediate pleasures in exchange for an expected eternity in heaven (and/or avoiding an eternity in hell) is a perfectly reasonable decision for anybody convinced of the reality of these afterlife alternatives.

It might seem that the ability to forgo short-term benefits for long-term ones would be highly adaptive in the genetic/biological sense; indeed, one might be tempted to speculate that this is precisely the function of complex reasoning systems. The cheesecake example illustrates how rejecting short-term pleasures for long-term goals can indeed be inclusive-fitness enhancing—in this case, potentially lengthening the lifespan and thus increasing opportunities for reproduction, caring for children and grandchildren, and so on. However, this is not necessarily the case, for a reason that might seem surprising. Natural selection tends to design mechanisms that produce reproductive benefits as early in the lifespan as possible, for the simple reason that we might well not survive into old age to reap any benefits of late-blooming adaptations. Postponing parenting until midlife in order to pursue status and resources in early adulthood is a fitness-enhancing strategy if all goes well, but a lot can happen (including death) before one gets around to reproducing. Indeed, many adaptations designed to maximize reproductive success early in the lifespan have deleterious long-term consequences (Williams, 1957). Ironic as it may seem, living longer is not necessarily adaptive. From natural selection's perspective, a short, reproductively successful life beats a long barren life every time.[1] We as individuals, however, tend to care deeply about living longer and often choose to take steps to increase our lifespans.

In Freud's early version of dual-processing theory, religion was regarded as mainly a product of primary process thinking. Wenegrat (1990) similarly concludes from an extensive literature review that religious thinking is largely automatic and spontaneous, and reflects a lack of higher forms of critical thinking. It should be clear from this discussion that the common misconception of religious belief as fundamentally "irrational"—presumably in contrast to science or other intellectual pursuits—is overly simplistic. Like any other form of thought, religious belief involves a combination of complex, analytic processes and deep cognitive and motivational biases. Some religious beliefs, such as the intuition that living things contain spirits or that God is a reliable attachment figure, emerge largely from non- or prerational thought. On the other hand, one would be hard pressed to find a better example of analytic reasoning than theology or the philosophy of religion, or a more extreme example of delaying gratification based on computations of long-term costs and benefits than spending one's entire life preparing for heaven. Religious beliefs, like everyday thinking and science, represent varying blends of "experiential" and "rational" processes.

Finally, rational thinking leads potentially to yet another level of disconnect between behavior and inclusive-fitness criteria: the ability to consider and evaluate potential courses of action not only with respect to one's own outcomes, but also those of *other people*. This opens the door to another set of complexities and levels of analysis to which we return later in this chapter.

Social Learning, Socialization, and Cultural Transmission

In focusing up to this point on individual learning and cognition, I have virtually ignored the fact that humans are fundamentally social creatures. The next level of complexity arises out of the fact that we learn from and communicate with one another through behavior and (especially) through language. Social learning can be a particularly effective "short-cut" because we can benefit from the learning of others; rather than reinventing the wheel, each individual can begin his or her own individual learning process with products of others' prior learning experience (Boyd & Richerson, 1985).

Social learning adds a layer of complexity to the problem of understanding religion and other psychological and cultural phenomena in several fundamental ways. First and most obviously, the pool of potential ideas and behaviors with which an individual has to work is a function of those currently held by others. This is of course one important reason why people are more likely to adopt religious beliefs with which they are surrounded: People growing up in rural Iowa only rarely become Buddhists, and virtually no one there adopts Fang beliefs about witches flying on banana peels.

The next level of complexity emerges from the fact that social learners and teachers are typically embedded in larger cultural groups containing a diversity of ideas and behavior patterns, and a diversity of potential models and teachers, from which to choose. This gives rise to a variety of cultural-transmission processes unique to this level of analysis, including various forms of *biased transmission* (Boyd & Richerson, 1985).

To some extent, preferences for particular ideas or behaviors rather than others are predictable from the lower levels of analysis discussed earlier in this chapter and in previous chapters of this book. People gravitate spontaneously toward certain variants and away from others by virtue of their current psychology, by which I mean their evolved psychological architecture combined with the products of their individual learning history. Some variants are attractive to all people by virtue of their shared evolved psychology; others are preferred by some people more than others by virtue of their idiosyncratic learning histories and reasoning. Like individual learning, social learning is not independent of evolved psychology but rather a reflection of it. As in the "Garcia effect" noted earlier, not all things are socially learned equally well. For example, monkeys quickly learn to avoid snakes after observing other monkeys displaying fear responses to them, but the same observational learning does not occur when flowers are substituted for snakes as the fear stimuli (Mineka, 1992). Boyd and Richerson (1985) refer to the success of certain behavioral variants rather than others within a culture resulting from this process as *direct bias*. As discussed in a previous section of this chapter, much of the material discussed in this book (prior to the present chapter) would fit this description. For example, the idea of a loving, personal God is attractive to people by virtue of the design of their attachment systems, as discussed in previous chapters.

Other dynamic processes at the population level, however, are unique to this level of analysis, including what Boyd and Richerson refer to as *indirect biases*. Two examples of indirect bias are particularly important for the understanding of religion. *Frequency-dependent biases* are those based on the relative frequency or distribution of variants currently extant in the population. For example, a *conformity bias* is evident when individuals choose variants by virtue of their popularity. Boyd and Richerson (1985) suggest that human evolved psychology contains epigenetic rules along the lines of "when in doubt, do what others are doing." It is easy to see how such a strategy could be, like social learning in general, an effective shortcut to learning. In most cultural settings—including, surely, those of our distant ancestors—anything that "everybody is doing" is probably a behavioral strategy with a proven track record. As noted in the previous section, people tend to adopt the religious beliefs, along with other customs, norms, and behavioral patterns, with which they are surrounded.

A second example of indirect bias in cultural transmission is that of *prestige-based bias* (Boyd & Richerson, 1985; Henrich & Gil-White, 2001). Doing what everyone else is doing is fine so long as everyone is doing the same thing, but how to choose when different people do things differently? A useful strategy in this case would be to choose as models or teachers those individuals who seem most knowledgeable or skilled with respect to the particular domain in question. People therefore benefit from clustering around prestigious individuals to acquire their knowledge and skill. The prestigious individuals, in turn, receive benefits from their clienteles in exchange for their teaching services.

It is hardly mysterious that people would be well served by seeking out experts in many domains: One clearly would benefit from learning how to make spears from the best spear-maker, to make boats from the best boat-maker, and so forth. It is perhaps less obvious, however, why people would turn to experts in the domain of religion such as shamans or priests, or why they would bestow prestige upon people by virtue of their acknowledged expertise in that domain. For starters, how would one determine what constitutes religious expertise? It is a relatively straightforward manner easy to determine whether someone is an expert boat-builder or hunter, for example, by simply observing whether his boat sinks or he regularly comes home from the hunt empty-handed. But when it comes to the nature of the gods and unobservable supernatural forces, how does one determine expertise? This is a crucial question, because to the extent that prestigious models are preferred, certain individuals wind up playing a disproportionately greater role in the cultural evolution of religious ideas; the beliefs of an entire population might be determined by a single shaman and his or her idiosyncratic view.

An interesting evolutionary perspective on this question is provided by Miller (2000). To fully appreciate his argument requires a short digression on an important evolutionary process that up until now I have largely ignored in this book. Miller suggests that the process of *sexual selection*, as sometimes distinguished from natural selection (beginning with Darwin, 1859) has long been underrated with respect to its role in fashioning the human mind (see Cronin, 1991, for a detailed discussion and history). The basic idea is that traits might be favored over the course of evolution not because they enhance survival, but simply because they are preferred by potential mates. If females of a bird species come, for whatever reason, to favor a particular pattern of plumage or color of beak, then males carrying genes for that trait will be more successful in obtaining mates and passing those genes to its offspring (which in turn are more likely to have the same features and be reproductively successful, etc.). Moreover, the process can lead to unusually rapid evolutionary change as a consequence of the fact that female preference for the trait will co-evolve with male exhibition of the trait, because females who carry genes causing them to choose such males are more likely to have male offspring displaying the same trait, and female offspring who prefer it. The result is a runaway process (Fisher, 1930) driven by a positive feedback loop.

The interesting thing about sexual selection is that it can drive the evolution of traits that are entirely arbitrary in terms of survival value, or even that actually *hinder* survival. The latter case is exemplified by the classic example of the peacock's tail. Such enormous and colorful plumage is terribly costly to produce (in terms of nutritional resources, for example), interferes with the ability to run and fly, and renders its bearer conspicuous to predators. The answer comes from Zahavi (1975; Zahavi & Zahavi, 1997). According to his *handicap principle*, elaborate ornamentation such as peacock tails have evolved via sexual selection in large part *because* of its potential survival and/or nutritional costs. A peacock displaying a large, brightly colored, and symmetric tail is in effect advertising that he is *so* (genetically) fit and healthy that he can afford to carry this ball-and-chain around with him; he has survived successfully in spite of it. Because weaker and less healthy animals simply are not capable of producing such high-quality tails, a good tail functions as an *honest signal* of genetic fitness. Markers or traits that cannot be faked—that is, that can only be produced by the most fit—are valuable diagnostic tools for mate choice. Thus, the argument goes, peahens have come to favor extravagant tails, which has led peacocks to produce ever more elaborate tails as a function of mating competition.

Many of our psychological systems and capacities have survival value and have evolved through natural selection, such as the attachment system. However, scholars have long puzzled over the reasons for the evolution of "higher" cognitive capacities in humans. What is the survival value of an aesthetic sense, for example? It seems clear that the ability to design and construct strong, sharp spears or solid, watertight bowls would have survival value to ancestral humans, but why would they come to value the ability to fashion beautiful, creatively ornamented versions of these objects? Miller's (2000) answer is that many of our cognitive abilities, such as those related to morality, language, and creativity, are the product of sexual, rather than natural, selection. In a word, he suggests that many of these "higher" abilities represent a kind of cognitive ornamentation—an intellectual peacock's tail, if you will. The human mind is designed as much as an amusement park as a survival machine.

Religion, like art and other creative endeavors, provides a forum within which people compete to demonstrate their wit and intelligence. Creative storytelling about such topics as the nature and origins of the world and the objects in it is a way of displaying, to both potential mates and intrasexual rivals, one's intellectual prowess, much as feats of strength display one's physical prowess. As a consequence, listeners may well evaluate competing stories not so much in terms of veridicality or accuracy, but rather intrigue and entertainment value. We therefore admire those who entertain and fascinate us with their creative thinking and storytelling, at least partially independent of their (unknowable) truth value, thereby providing an explanation for many forms of prestige bias as per Boyd and Richerson (1985).

This leads us back full circle to the question of what kinds of ideas people find fascinating and entertaining, while simultaneously plausible and worthy of retention and transmission, in the first place. In light of the discussion in the previous chapter, based on the work of Boyer (1994a, 2001), Atran (2002), and others, we would expect that prestigious religious leaders would be those who most masterfully weave stories combining the ideal blend of intuitive (based on evolved psychology) and counterintuitive elements, such as gods who are largely humanlike except for one or two supernatural traits or abilities. The fact that one or a few such individuals can disproportionately influence the beliefs of an entire community injects a certain level of arbitrariness into cultural evolution that render it notoriously difficult to predict: Specific beliefs about gods, for example, may differ substantially from one village to the next for no obvious (e.g., ecological) reason. On the other hand, however, our shared evolved psychology imposes predictability and consistency across belief communities at a deeper level. Specifically, the counterintuitive elements (e.g., invisible witches flying on banana peels) of religious beliefs are highly arbitrary, but the intuitive elements are highly thematic and understandable based on evolutionary psychology (Boyer, 2001).

To return now to the main point, the *population-level characteristics* of social learning represent another level at which human thought and behavior are decoupled from the inclusive-fitness criteria by which their psychology was designed. A belief or set of beliefs widely held within a group is not necessarily one that benefits individuals in an inclusive-fitness sense, nor even necessarily in terms of their personal pleasure–pain balance: Within a social group, a particular idea can become popular by virtue of the storytelling abilities of a single prestigious individual (prestige bias), and popularity of an idea can snowball into even greater popularity (conformity bias). An important consequence of this process is that behavioral variants should become relatively homogeneous within groups while potentially diverging widely across or between groups (Boyd & Richerson, 1985). In this way, belief systems can have the effect of enhancing within-group social cohesion—a principal "function" of religion according to Durkheim (1912) and many others—even though it would be misleading to say that religion evolved via natural selection with this adaptive function.

Cooperation, Competition, and Manipulation

The advantages of social learning to the learner seem straightforward enough: Believing or doing what most others believe or do is probably a safe strategy; learning from those who are best at what they do seems better still. However, the world of information exchange is not uniformly benign. Communicators and learners do not necessarily share the same goals and motives, and often they are at cross-purposes, and therein lies the potential for deception and manipulation. The downside of social learning—and the basis for another level of disconnect between natural selection's inclusive-fitness criteria and human behavior—is the danger that what one learns socially might be not in one's own interests so much as someone else's.

Irrespective of one's own beliefs, it often is to one's own advantage for *others* to hold certain beliefs. It comes as no surprise, then, that as long as there have been religious beliefs—and other kinds of beliefs for that matter—people have used them to manipulate others to their own advantage. We do not always practice what we preach, but hope instead that others will do the practicing. Loving one's neighbor as one loves oneself is very good for neighbors. Similarly, beliefs about the virtues of giving alms to the poor and reaching out to help the underprivileged are very much in the interests of the poor and underprivileged. As Badcock (1986) notes, Christianity and other altruism-fostering religions all originated among poor urban dwellers—that is, among the kinds of people who stood most to gain from promoting such beliefs. And as Pinker

(1997) notes only semifacetiously, ancestor worship looks like a good idea to people who are about to become ancestors themselves.

Perhaps the most obvious (and also most cynical) example with respect to religion concerns the use of beliefs as a tool for promoting one's own power and status, and for acquiring the benefits associated with such power. There is no shortage of examples of unscrupulous religious leaders who take full advantage of their positions to line their pockets with all sorts of personal and family benefits. Luther led a revolt against a powerful Catholic Church hierarchy riddled with corruption, and the news today regularly brings tales of televangelists spending viewers' well-intended dollars on their own lavish lifestyles. An example particularly interesting (and transparent) from an evolutionary perspective is the common practice by male cult leaders to promulgate belief systems that afford themselves exclusive sexual access to female group members. Pinker (1997) suggests that rules against incest (which often are embedded within religious ethical systems) have historically been designed by powerful leaders to prevent consolidation of wealth within extended families, and that food taboos (which typically involve favorite foods of neighboring groups) have been designed to keep insiders from fraternizing with outgroup members.

History suggests that one particularly effective way to promote one's own power is to link it to people's beliefs about God's power. As summarized by Burkert (1996),

> Submission and sovereignty inhabit the same hierarchic structure. Dependence on unseen powers mirrors the real power structure, but it is taken to be its model and to provide its legitimization. It is a two-tiered sovereignty that stabilizes itself through this structure; god is to ruler as ruler is to subjects. This lends theoretical support to the ruler, who ceases to be alone at the top of the pyramid as a target of potential aggression. (p. 95)

Indeed, some theorists have suggested that religion is primarily a tool employed by the powerful to manipulate and control the masses (e.g., Diamond, 1997; Marx, 1842/1972).

Beliefs promoted by people in power need not have detrimental consequences to others, however. As Machiavelli (in)famously explained, it is often in the interests of leaders to preside over a happy and healthy populace in order to retain their status and power and forestall revolt. In previous chapters we saw how many religious beliefs can enable high levels of co-operation and cohesion within social groups, not because our evolved psychology motivates such attitudes and behavior but rather by "tricking" our evolved psychology into producing altruism where it would otherwise not occur. For example, thinking of others as our "brothers and sisters," or emphasizing shared ancestry via totemic systems, can encourage kin-based altruism toward nonkin. Thus individuals in power may encourage or mandate such beliefs, at least in part because it is in their own interests to enhance social cohesion and within-group cooperation.

As noted earlier, cultures and societies are collections of individuals whose separate inclusive-fitness interests differ from one another's, often sharply. I am motivated to enhance my own personal welfare and that of my close kin and social-exchange partners, and you to look out for you and yours. Your personal welfare, and your kin and social-exchange partners, are not in general the same as mine (although they might overlap). To some extent, these conflicting goals can be managed in ways that complement each other, with principles of social exchange providing the basis for cultural products to provide benefits to all parties. Bakeries, for example, benefit cheesecake lovers by providing a cost-effective way of obtaining cheesecake, and benefit bakers by providing a venue for social exchange, from which they obtain resources to use subsequently in the service of their own goals and desires.

On the other hand, though, some products of culture represent solutions to group-level problems that are unique to the cultural level of analysis. Disparate goals among individuals are bound to lead to conflicts that are not readily resolved by simple social exchange, and that are bound to produce unpleasant experiences for everyone. In designing psychological mechanisms concerning interpersonal competition (for mates, resources, etc.), natural selection was utterly unconcerned about the fact that winner-take-all contests produce one happy winner and many unhappy losers. From Nature's detached perspective, the losers are just statistics; any psychological pain that might be caused is irrelevant. However, a human reasoner faced with the unpleasant prospect of being one of those losers, and able to realize that statistically, this is any particular individual's most likely fate, might well decide to steer clear of winner-take-all competition in lieu of less risky behavioral strategies more likely to produce future pleasure. Groups of individuals might then be motivated to construct cultural institutions, rules and regulations, policing agencies, and other group-level solutions to minimize the adverse psychological effects of competition.

For example, polygynous mating systems appear to emerge "naturally" given the opportunity (e.g., ability of men to horde valuable resources) and absence of cultural constraints (Daly & Wilson, 1988). Such mating systems might on first blush appear "good for" men, but in fact they are good only for a small proportion of men. Each additional wife acquired by a powerful male reduces the available mate pool for all other men, so that the vast majority of men are losers and only a few are winners. It therefore behooves this majority of men to cooperate in constructing a social system that precludes the hoarding of mates by the powerful. It has been suggested that the institution of marriage represents, in essence, agreements among men governing mating competition, thereby reducing the amount of intrasexual rivalry and conflict that would otherwise create a very unpleasant living environment for everybody (Daly & Wilson, 1988; Pinker, 1997; Wright, 1994).

Moreover, group living creates needs for, and offers potential benefits of, large-scale, cooperative ventures that benefit everyone—for example, the oft-cited example of a village wall to protect the group against invasion from outside. Our evolved psychology often renders these problems difficult. For example, the so-called "tragedy of the commons" (Hardin, 1968) refers to the unfortunate reality that when people share a common resource that benefits everyone, such as a grazing pasture for livestock, each tends to take more than their fair share, thereby depleting the resource to the point that it no longer benefits anybody (see Ridley, 1996, for a discussion). Similarly, people tend to contribute somewhat less than their fair share to cooperative ventures when they can get away with it, yet continue to take their share of the benefits provided by the common venture—the so-called *free rider problem*. Many cultural institutions and laws (including religion) are, at least in principle, about resolving these problems. Drawing upon our rational systems, we are capable of realizing that we have these conflicting interests, and that not everybody will be able to satisfy their own individual desires without interfering with others' attempts to do the same. Further calculation can then lead us to ideas such as the goal of producing the greatest good for the greatest number, or the most happiness for the most people. We can design our cultural milieu in a manner dictated not by the invisible warfare between genes, but by our own common desire to pursue happiness. Leases, taxation systems, and many other social institutions enable humans to engage in higher levels of mutually beneficial cooperation than natural selection alone could have designed us to do (by functioning essentially as *commitment devices*; Frank, 1988). All this is crucial in the present context because it introduces yet another level of analysis at which behavior can become decoupled from inclusive-fitness criteria. Behaviors and institutions can now be selected or constructed based not on individuals' genetic or personal interests, but rather the interests of the group as a whole.

The idea of *group selection* was excised almost completely from evolutionary biology in the 1960s in the face of theoretical insights by Williams (1966), Hamilton (1964), and others. It has made some inroads on a comeback in recent years, thanks especially to the work of D. S. Wilson (1975; Sober & Wilson, 1998), though as a mechanism of genetic/biological evolution it remains controversial. However, there is little debate about the potential for group-level selection to occur with respect to *cultural* products. Cultures clearly do construct institutions, laws, and other systems designed to benefit the society as a whole, even (or particularly) when the goals of society conflict with those of individuals. A world without such cultural constructions would be perfectly satisfactory as far as natural selection is concerned, but rather unpleasant for many of us as individuals. Without legal and police systems, people would take it upon themselves to avenge perceived wrongdoings, leading to escalating feuds, increased violence, and, inevitably, innocent victims. Without public support of science and other intellectual pursuits, we would be incapable of developing the countless technologies that enhance the quality of our lives today, in developed and increasingly in developing countries.

Religious systems can be seen in this context to represent cultural phenomena that have emerged, or been deliberately designed, to benefit groups in their local ecologies. Such a perspective is consistent with Durkheim's (1912) observation that religious institutions are generally characterized by *secular utility*, providing solutions to practical problems of existence and group living. D. S. Wilson (2002) analyzes several religious systems along these lines, from the water system and gods of Bali to Judaism and early Christianity, in these terms, concluding that "religions exist primarily for people to achieve together what they cannot achieve alone" (p. 159).

Memes and Viruses of the Mind

The central point of this chapter is that although our evolved psychology was designed by natural selection strictly according to inclusive-fitness criteria, the proximal processes by which these systems produce behavior involve higher levels of analysis that often involve very different criteria.

Systems that are designed to produce behavior that is good for genes give rise to learning principles that lead individuals to choose what is best for them as individuals, irrespective of their genes; our evolved capacity for social learning gives rise to manipulation by others in ways that can lead to choosing what is actually best for someone else; rational processes can be employed in the service of all of these criteria, as well as making possible the consideration of additional goals such as choosing what is "good for the group." In addition, processes occurring at the cultural level, such as prestige-based and frequency-dependent biases, can give rise to thought and behavior that are not necessarily good for anyone or anything, merely because, for example, popularity can beget popularity. Products of these various levels of analysis may be consistent with (i.e., adaptive), inconsistent with (maladaptive), or simply irrelevant (nonadaptive) to genetic success, and as such provide a variety of vehicles by which thought and behavior can become decoupled from inclusive-fitness concerns.

This way of thinking about things leads naturally to the perspective offered by the modern field of *memetics* (e.g., Blackmore, 1999). Dawkins (1976/1989) first introduced the concept of the *meme* to represent a unit of analysis in culture analogous to genes in the context in biology, such that cultural evolution could be understood in a manner parallel to genetic evolution. (Lumsden & Wilson, 1981, later offered the alternative term *culturgen* and defined it in cognitive terms as being equivalent to a node of semantic memory.) In the same way that some versions of genes (technically, alleles) are more successful than others in propagating copies of themselves in future generations, some ideas or concepts are more successful than others in propagating copies of themselves in the heads of other people.

For example, consider a catchy commercial jingle that gets stuck in your head for no obvious reason. There is nothing about the jingle that benefits your genes, or your pleasure–pain balance (indeed, it might be extremely annoying), or the group in which you live. Although we could perhaps trace the particular "catchy" quality to some aspect of our evolved psychology or experience, it may well be a totally nonfunctional one. That is, vulnerability to a particular meme may be a kind of spandrel (see Chapter 9), such that the memorability or transmittability of the meme is functionally irrelevant at all levels of analysis other than *memetic fitness* itself.

Memeticists in effect recast all of the issues discussed here into the frame of reference of the meme. Rather than starting from processes of biological and cultural evolution and asking how they produce certain memes, memeticists start with the question of why some memes have greater memetic fitness than others, and reach down through the various other levels of analysis discussed in this chapter for answers. For example, memeticists would probably agree that the idea of God as an attachment figure is successful because of the evolved nature of human psychology and the design of the attachment system; they would merely shift the focus to the meme's perspective and characterize this aspect of human psychology as providing an unwittingly hospitable habitat for certain memes.

One particularly interesting insight that emerges from this line of thinking is that certain properties of ideas themselves may contribute directly to their memetic success, quite independent of the other levels of analyses reviewed in the preceding pages. Consider the simple self-referential idea "copy me." This is essentially the instruction that a virus transmits to a host cell, leading to effective production of virus copies, (often) at the expense of the victim. Chain letters and computer viruses operate on the same principle, containing a built-in mechanism for ensuring rapid "reproduction" from victim to victim (Blackmore, 1999). No one, and no thing, benefits from such a system except the "copy me" meme itself.

Dawkins (1993) suggests that religion can be understood generally as a kind of "virus of the mind," which succeeds because religion memes are particularly good at self-replicating by jumping from mind to mind in this way. A crucial idea central to many modern belief systems is that *faith despite of lack of evidence* is both desirable and virtuous. Once this notion is accepted, it inoculates all faith-based beliefs to which it refers against rejection in the face of contrary evidence (Dawkins, 1993). The faith-without-evidence belief is not successful because it benefits any particular genes, nor any individual's pleasure–pain balance, nor the success of any group or population of individuals: The only beneficiary of this quality is the memetic success of the beliefs themselves. As such, memetic success can represent yet another level of analysis in which thought and behavior can become decoupled from inclusive-fitness concerns.

Whether memetics as a general perspective proves over the long run to have memetic fitness itself remains to be seen. The strength of this approach is its ability to recast all of the levels of analysis into a single perspective by viewing everything in terms of the differential survival and reproduction of memes. Unfortunately, as is often the case with such grand perspectives, this strength is also the greatest weakness. In collapsing many levels of analysis into one, the numerous complex and distinct processes occurring at each level and interacting between levels are glossed over. Our evolved human psychology is a given from which memetics begins; the meme's-eye view cannot help to explain the process of natural selection by which the attachment system evolved. The memetic perspective is useful for understanding why chain letters are successful, with their built-in "copy me" instructions, but cannot explain why—in stark contrast to a biological virus—some unscrupulous hacker was motivated to create the first link. Similarly, it is not mere happenstance that the catchy pop tune in your head will not go away; it was created by one or more prestige- and mate-seeking musicians with precisely that goal. The same goes for the commercial jingle produced by a cooperative coalition (company, business) in the context of its competition with other coalitions for your money. The memetic perspective may explain nicely why these phenomena are successful at surviving and reproducing, but a complete understanding of any of them would also need to include an account of how and why they came about in the first place. To answer these questions, it is necessary to abandon the meme's-eye view and analyze the problem from other biological, psychological, sociological, and anthropological perspectives, beginning with evolutionary psychology.

SCIENCE REVISITED

In the last chapter I argued that religion is by no means the only kind of thinking that falls naturally out of our evolved psychology: In addition to related forms of thinking such as superstition and other paranormal beliefs, everyday thinking and even science show the unmistakable signs of our evolved psychological architecture, which was clearly not designed to produce objectively "true," veridical ideas about the world. Like those of everyone else, scientists' minds are biased to process information in ways that were on average adaptive, but not necessarily accurate, in ancestral environments. Although most of us would like to think that we are motivated only (or at least primarily) by an idealistic search for the truth, in reality we are probably motivated (consciously or not) by the rewards of scientific success—not so much money, perhaps, but at least prestige.

So what exactly is it about science that makes it unique, and that warrants confidence in its claim to be the most effective means to determining "objective" truth? The answer is its *methodology*: the system of rules by which observations are made, evaluated, and disseminated. The rules for conducting scientific research are arranged specifically to neutralize (or at least minimize) the impact of perceptual, cognitive, emotional, and social biases that threaten to undermine the goal of finding "the truth." Observations are made, and reported in scientific publications, in ways designed to enable replication by other researchers with different goals and biases. The effects of perceptual biases are defeated through machine-based measurements, or by examining empirically the interrater reliability of multiple human observers. The use of placebo controls and double-blind procedures neutralize the effect of researchers' and participants' expectations and hopes. Paper-and-pencil questionnaires are useful in avoiding some of the pitfalls of subjective interpretation of open-ended interviews. Our tendency to overinterpret results of small or nonrepresentative samples is combated by sampling techniques and statistical analysis, and inferential statistics provide an objective way of determining whether an apparent effect can be adequately explained by dumb luck, or whether it is sufficiently strong to "reject the null hypothesis" and thus be worthy of a substantive explanation. Human cognitive and perceptual bias cannot be eliminated, but scientists can arrange their observations in such a way that these biases are prevented from systematically skewing the empirical results.

Moreover, although scientists cannot be objective as individuals, science (or a particular field or subdiscipline) as a *whole* can be much more so, at least over the long run. Science is a self-correcting system designed to defeat, at the collective level, the biases that operate at the individual level. Consider, for example, the status-competition motivation that potentially leads scientists to seek confirmation of their own theories, misconstrue or misrepresent the views of competitors, and so forth. Such personal biases are exacerbated by extreme levels of competition for scarce resources of prestige, grant dollars, and journal space. At the same time, however, the system simultaneously offers incentives to competitors. For every researcher who succeeds at selling shoddy work and inaccurate conclusions, a dozen others have an opportunity to make a career out of undermining and correcting the work. The same motivation that can lead to errors in the first place also leads to corrective action by others. To the extent that scientists' biases are different—as is true by definition with respect to individual self-interest—the system as a whole can converge on "truth" in a way that no individual could ever hope to do. Although "cheating" may be tempting for its short-term benefits, scientists have the foresight to know that it will not pay in the long run. The system is arranged in such as way that the biggest payoffs (in resources, grants, and prestige) go to those whose data and ideas will hold up to critical scrutiny over time.

Science therefore stands as an exemplar of human ingenuity in recognizing the kinds of biases, distortions, and agendas that come with our evolved psychology, and finding ways to choose to be otherwise. The various kinds of processes discussed in this chapter have provided the means by which this has been possible. In the end, science represents a cultural construction that on the one hand recognizes that veridical understanding of the empirical world can lead to enormous benefits for everyone, but that can only be accomplished by arranging circumstances carefully in ways that either prevent our unscientific evolved psychology from interfering with the process (e.g., double-blind experiments), or harness the power of this psychology to achieve other ends (e.g., rewarding scientific accomplishment with prestige).

In these ways, science is similar to many other cultural institutions and mechanisms. Our adversarial legal system is based on the assumption that the only way to arrive at the truth about a crime or other conflict is to allow each competing side to bring to the table its full complement of bias and self-interest. Democratic governments are designed in recognition of the fact that "power corrupts" and no single individual can be entrusted to act fairly on behalf of all the people of a society; such systems consist of features such as multiple government branches with numerous built-in "checks and balance," representative legislatures, and so forth, designed with the idea that what is best for the society as a whole can be produced despite everyone acting in their own self-interests. Many aspects of religion, including its various systems of morality and ethics, can be conceptualized in much the same way.

SUMMARY AND CONCLUSIONS

The path from genes to religious belief is a very long and circuitous one. The fundamental nature and content of our evolved psychological architecture, as outlined in previous chapters, plays a crucial role in providing the raw materials and basic psychological processes for producing religious belief. However, many levels of higher-order processes are layered on top of this basic evolved psychology. In this chapter I have outlined some of these, in bare-bones form, from individual and social learning through cultural evolution and memetic selection. The distribution of religious beliefs that we observe today—or would observe at any other given point in time throughout human history—ultimately is a product of this complexity.

There were several purposes to this discussion. First, a number of important issues were clarified (I hope) in regard to the nature and scope of the evolutionary-psychological perspective I have adopted throughout this book. For example, we saw how individual and social learning processes represent complex adaptations that, while introducing new levels of analysis to explanations of human behavior, are made possible by and cannot be understood independently of our evolved psychology. A variety of processes discussed illustrate how humans are not fitness maximizers, that is, they should not be expected to always behave in ways that are adaptive from a genetic perspective.

This latter issue leads back to my argument that religion is not an adaptation, but rather a by-product of evolved mechanisms designed for other purposes. I suggested in Chapter 9 that as such, religion could potentially be adaptive, maladaptive, or neutral with respect to inclusive fitness, but gave only a few illustrations to explain how this could be. The present chapter offers a way to conceptualize the by-product problem in terms of levels of analysis and the differential criteria for behavior selection beyond that of genetic fitness that drive each of these respective levels. Each such level presents the opportunity for behavior to become decoupled from the inclusive-fitness criteria by which the systems producing it were designed. It turns out to not be necessary, or even advisable, to focus on the ways in which religion might or might not promote inclusive fitness per se. In some cases religious belief systems appear to do so, as in the directive to "be fruitful and multiply" or the promotion of whatever reproductive strategy is most adaptive under local ecological conditions (Reynolds & Tanner, 1983). But in many other cases the opposite may be true, as when monks or priests vow to be chaste.

Third, this levels-of-analysis perspective provides a larger framework within which to fit the countless theories of religion extant in psychology, sociology, anthropology, and related fields, including the many that have never been conceptualized from an evolutionary perspective. As illustrated throughout the chapter, many psychological theories of religion focus on the roles of learning, socialization, or rational thought; any such theory, I maintain, can be reconceptualized within the framework outlined here. Some theories focus on the ways in which religion appears to be "instinctive" and flows naturally from our evolved nature, whereas others focus on the ways in which it appears designed to tame those instincts; both such perspectives, as well as many others in between, can be understood within this perspective. Sociological and anthropological theories focusing on issues such as cultural transmission, the value of religion in enhancing group cohesion, the ways in which religions as institutions adapt to local social and physical ecologies, and how religion has been used historically as a tool of manipulation and control all have a place in this hierarchy.

Notwithstanding the importance of emergent properties that appear anew at each higher level of analysis, an understanding of the nature, content, and processes that make up human evolved psychology is essential for a proper understanding of all these levels. Learning processes must be understood in terms of psychological mechanisms designed to learn some things readily but not others. Rationality, consciousness, and other "higher" forms of thought are enabled and constrained by our evolved psychology. Our minds are not all-purpose computing machines armed with general rules of symbolic logic; moreover, these advanced cognitive abilities are employed in the service of evolved motives and goals. Social learning represents an evolved suite of motivations and capacities that appear unique to humans, and that in turn unleash the possibilities of cultural transmission and evolution. Although unique evolutionary processes emerge at the cultural level, our evolved motives and cognitive biases are crucial to their operation, as exemplified in conformity and prestige biases.

Consider a metaphor, adapted from Atran (2002), for the scientific study of religion as analogous to the scientific study of the behavior of water in a mountain range, with natural selection representing the snowcap and the melted water representing the many forms of religious belief and behavior. A simplistic adaptationist perspective claiming that humans have "religious instincts," and that focuses on those aspects of religion that appear to emerge directly from our evolved psychology as solutions to adaptive problems, would be well suited for explaining those areas in which large volumes of water rush in a torrent down steep slopes or down sheer drops in waterfalls. But such a perspective would be hard pressed to explain why the vast majority of water flowing down the mountain slopes does not do so in waterfalls, and instead displays much more complex, circuitous paths. More important still, such a theory would be helpless to explain why large volumes of water, collecting in puddles, small ponds, and lakes, never make it to the bottom of the hill.

Now consider the many extant theories of religion that have been developed and researched with no reference to evolutionary psychology. We might imagine learning theorists or rational-choice theorists focusing on the details of the countless twists and turns followed by any stream. Researchers studying the social learning and cultural transmission of religious belief and ritual might be represented as focusing on the ways in which multiple streams sometimes merge into a single river, or at other times split among multiple forks. Theories of religion as cultural institutions—particularly those that focus on the ways that religion enhances ingroup solidarity or provides other benefits to groups—offer descriptions and explanations of the lakes and ponds dotting the landscape. Cultural evolutionists observe how all of these features change across time—rivers changing course, lakes appearing and disappearing, and so forth—in response to snowfall and temperature variation and geological activity.

In principle, at least, each of these perspectives would provide a potentially useful, and often accurate, description and (partial) explanation for the behavior of water in the mountains. Theorists working in each domain would provide a basis for understanding how particular features of the geology give rise to particular patterns of water flow (or nonflow). But imagine now that none of these theories acknowledge the role of *gravity*. Even to the extent that such gravity-blind theories might be accurate, with researchers eventually learning from their incorrect predictions and modifying their theories accordingly, they would still be deficient. As well as such a theory might explain how water flow responds to particular local variations in the landscape, none would ever be able to fully explain *why* it responds this way and not some other. It would forever remain a profound mystery as to why water generally flows downhill, rather than uphill, in the first place.

CHAPTER THIRTEEN

Toward an Evolutionary Psychology of Religion

In Chapter 1, I suggested that this book is in some sense written backwards. The first half or so was devoted specifically to attachment theory and religion—the focus of much of my own research over the last 10 years or so. I then introduced a broader evolutionary perspective within which the attachment approach fits, and suggested a variety of directions beyond attachment theory for guiding future theory and research in the psychology of religion. This sequence was appropriate for the task at hand, namely, a book primarily about attachment theory and religion but in which the final chapters were designed to sketch a rough outline for going beyond this particular theory in the scientific study of religion. Moreover, it was a natural way for me to present the material, as it follows my own path of study and thinking in roughly chronological order, beginning with my earliest ideas and empirical research on attachment and religion and concluding with my more recent thoughts about how this specific view fits within a larger evolutionary psychological framework.

Having led you down the path in this direction for these reasons, however, I now wish to retrace our steps in reverse to see what it looks like going the other way. I want to suggest now that we actually began near the *end* of a path—the application of attachment theory to the psychology of religion—and traced the path backward to its point of origin.

(This is by no means the true end of the path, however; there remains much research to be done regarding attachment and religion.) When we turn around to see whence we have come, we can now see that there are numerous paths originating from here, and we have many different directions from which to choose next. Because this clearing is where I am leaving you—namely, a general evolutionary-psychological framework for conceptualizing religion and related phenomena—I want to describe the scene as it looks from here.

In the first half of this chapter I therefore present a brief summary of my general argument from this (more or less) reverse perspective. In doing so I will review many of the major points presented throughout this book, though I hope they will look somewhat different from this direction. My goal here is not to present the same material again, but rather to illustrate a new conceptual arrangement of it. In the second half of the chapter I conclude by summarizing some of the major reasons that this evolutionary psychological approach—as now seen from the new perspective that follows—offers a promising direction for the psychology of religion.

A PRÉCIS IN (MORE OR LESS) REVERSE

I argued in Chapter 1 that the psychology of religion must begin from the *psychology of* side rather than the *of religion* side of its moniker. We need a comprehensive theoretical perspective for understanding human psychology in general, which can then be applied to specific phenomena of interest such as religion. In reverse perspective, then, the path of my argument begins with evolutionary psychology.

Evolutionary Psychology and Adaptation

The point of departure for evolutionary psychology is the realization that the brain, the primary source of all thought and behavior, is an organ designed by natural selection over eons of evolutionary time, and that this fact has numerous specific and crucial implications for understanding what it is designed to do and how it is designed to accomplish these goals. In turn, the presumption is that knowing these hows and whys is immensely useful for understanding *what* it does including, among other things, generating and embracing religious ideas (or not) and behaving in accord with them (or not). Some of the most important implications, which provide the background assumptions for evolutionary psychology, include the following.

Like other parts of the body, the brain is an *adaptation*—or, more precisely, a large collection of adaptations—that evolved to solve adaptive problems faced by our prehuman ancestors. Such problems include, at a general level, the survival problems of identifying, finding, procuring, and ingesting appropriate food and liquids; avoiding predation; shelter and/or other defense against natural elements such as climate and weather; identifying, procuring, and perhaps defending appropriate mates; managing complex social relationships of many types (e.g., coalitions, kinship relations, reciprocal-exchange relationships); and so on. In addition, the process of *sexual selection* has led to the evolution of other features that do not confer survival benefits per se, but rather the reproductive benefits associated with successful mating.

In either case, the term *adaptive* has a highly precise meaning in evolutionary theory that should not be confused with other kinds of purpose or function. Natural selection operates at the level of genes: Evolution itself refers to nothing more than changes in relative gene frequencies across time. A trait or feature is "adaptive" if it causes, either directly or indirectly, the genes containing the developmental recipe for constructing it to increase relative to alternative designs. Thus our bodies and minds are *not* designed in ways that necessarily are good "for the species," or for our social groups, or even for any of us as individuals. As mentioned in a previous chapter, a chicken is just an egg's way of making another egg.

The basic principles of natural selection have given rise to a number of general, second-tier theories that can be derived more or less directly from inclusive-fitness theory. These include, for example, theories of *kin selection*, *reciprocal altruism*, and *parental investment*. It has been suggested that Bowlby's theory of *attachment* be placed at this level of analysis. At a more specific level, many evolutionary theories have been proposed—some from the middle-level theories noted here and others independently—regarding virtually all domains of human behavior.

Like other parts of the body, the organization of the brain reflects the fact that because adaptive problems are highly *domain-specific*, specialized mechanisms and systems designed to solve particular problems are more effective than domain-general solutions. Much as the body comprises a digestive system, circulatory system, and so forth, which in turn comprise specific organs and tissues designed for highly specific roles, the brain/mind contains numerous domain-specific psychological mechanisms (and systems thereof), each organized in a manner specific to its adaptive task. These mechanisms are conceptualized as algorithms designed to respond to environmental inputs in particular ways, and as such offer a coherent interactive model of nature and nurture. In this book I focused on psychological mechanisms/systems related to understanding, predicting, and behaving in the natural world (naive physics, biology, and psychology) and the social world (attachment, kinship, coalitions, social exchange, and dominance/status).

From Genes to Behavior

Natural selection produces and designs physical and psychological systems, which in turn give rise to thought and behavior. Thus evolution by natural selection is not the direct or *proximal* cause of any behavior, but rather a *distal* or ultimate *cause*. To understand thought and behavior therefore requires consideration of a variety of complexities, including evolutionary by-products and additional, higher-level causal processes. The causal path from genes to behavior can be a long and circuitous one.

Evolutionary by-products are (for our purpose) effects of adaptations on thought and behavior other than those "intended" by natural selection. *Spandrels* are side effects of adaptations that are adaptively neutral, such as the human chin and navel, which "fall out of" the design of adaptive features of facial and reproductive-system design respectively. *Exaptations* refer to the use of adaptations that, once in place, might be used for other purposes, as the aforementioned chin might be used, with a strap, to hold a helmet in place. Explaining the existence or helmet-attaching use of chins ultimately resides in natural selection, but not because chins per se served an adaptive function—and certainly not a helmet-attaching one. Much human behavior, particular in modern environments, falls into the by-product category, complicating the link between evolution and behavior. I argue that religion is one of the things that falls into this category, emerging not because it (or any particularly aspect of it) served an adaptive purpose in ancestral environments, but rather as a spandrel and/or exaptation (or, perhaps more properly, a collection of spandrels and/or exaptations) of other, mundane adaptations. Understanding by-products of adaptations does not by any means reduce the importance of evolutionary process and function as an explanatory tool; the task merely shifts to one of identifying the adaptations that are involved and specifying the ways in which they have been co-opted for other purposes.

Second, various and multiple levels of other higher-level causal processes can mediate the link between genes and behavior. *Learning* systems are adaptations designed to tailor thought and behavior to local adaptive pressures, by setting in motion a selection system within individual brains/minds will choose behaviors leading (on average) to adaptive outcomes. *Rationality* and other higher-order cognitive processes enable us, for example, to simulate learning without actually behaving, a particularly useful tool when poor behavioral choices are potentially costly. *Social learning* permits ideas and behaviors to spread from brain/mind to brain/mind, and set in motion cultural evolution processes that can only be understood in terms of population-level properties and consideration of what ideas and behaviors are already in the environment (e.g., various forms of *biased transmission*). Finally, particular ideas can have properties that make them inherently more likely to be recalled and transmitted, adding another level of analysis related to *memetic fitness*. Each of these levels of analysis involves proximal causes of behavior that operate according to different principles, in which the unit of selection is ideas or behaviors (rather than genes), and the criteria by which they are selected involve actual or anticipated psychological benefits and costs to individuals or groups of individuals, or to the memes themselves.

As a consequence of these sets of factors, any particular behavior or category of behaviors may appear to be adaptive, nonadaptive, or maladaptive from the standpoint of "selfish genes." Unfortunately, it seems widely assumed by contemporary social scientists that these "complications" are of such magnitude as to trump any preexisting effects of evolutionary processes on human psychology, as if the effects of biological evolution disappeared when, for example, rationality and culture appeared. To the contrary, however, an understanding of our evolved psychological architecture is essential for investigating the ways in which its design enables and constrains rational thought and culture, and why the latter take the particular forms they commonly do and not others. This is not to say that culture, for example, is reducible to biology—this is a classic levels-of-analysis problem—but any theory of culture must be informed by and consistent with our understanding of psychology; in turn, a proper understanding of human psychology must be rooted in the evolutionary processes that gave rise to it. The nature and breadth of religion necessitate that the social-scientific study of it draws upon and integrates all of these levels of analysis.

Religion as an Evolutionary By-product

From an evolutionary perspective, the first crucial question about religion is whether religion—or one or more particular elements of it—represents an adaptation. Do humans possess specific psychological mechanisms designed by natural selection to produce religious thoughts and/or behavior specifically? It has frequently been suggested that religion is somehow "in our genes"—humankind as *Homo religiosus*—on the basis of observations regarding the apparent universality of religion across cultures, the heritability of religiosity, the neurological substrate of religious experience, and hints of protoreligiosity in other species. I argue that none of these provide convincing arguments, and that instead there are more (and better) reasons to doubt the existence of unique, evolved, religion-related psychological mechanisms. These include the difficulty of identifying what the adaptive function of such a mechanism might be, how such a system would be designed to achieve that function, and the failure of religion to display the kinds of features of "special design," such as efficiency, reliability, and functionality.

Instead, I suggest that religious belief and behavior is better conceptualized as the by-product(s) of numerous adaptations that evolved in early humans (or long before in other ancestral species) for other mundane purposes. For example, the attachment system evolved in humans (and many species, including other primates) for the purpose of maintaining proximity between helpless infants and their primary caregivers (usually their mothers) for protection against predators and other environmental dangers, but can be used to process information and organize beliefs and expectations in regard to noncorporeal entities such as God or gods. A variety of mechanisms, each designed originally for other specific purposes (i.e., to solve other specific adaptive problems unrelated to religion per se), give rise to and guide the development of religious thinking. Indeed, I believe that the power of religion, and the success of religious belief over the last several millennia, emerges from its ability to co-opt many different psychological adaptations—the attachment system serving as only one example—and thus function psychologically in very different ways for different people in different places at different times.

Such "co-opting" of evolved systems for new purposes is a hallmark of humanity, made possible in large part by our unique cognitive abilities and intelligence. Central to this process is the use of metaphor and analogy. Somewhere along our evolutionary path, a multitude of highly domain-specific psychological systems that were previously independent and mutually isolated began to swap information among themselves, probably facilitated by (or co-evolving with) the emergence of language. All of the examples of psychological mechanisms discussed in the book involve, in one form or another, the idea of mechanisms being activated by ideas, stimuli, or environments different from those for which they were initially designed, as in the case of an attachment system designed to promote certain behaviors and feelings in children about their caregivers being applied to a noncorporeal being such as God or gods.

The Psychological Origins of Religious Belief

In building a psychology of religion from this evolutionary by-product perspective, the first step would be to identify some of the specific evolved mechanisms postulated to underlie the most simple or "primitive" forms of religious belief. Before trying to understand such things as modern religious institutions and theology, we need a perspective on the question of how religious beliefs could get started psychologically in the first place.

Like Atran (2002), Boyer (2001), and Guthrie (1993), I begin with two much-studied cognitive systems for understanding the natural world, *naive physics* and *naive biology*, which provide the most fundamental cognitive building blocks for religious belief. As evidenced largely from research in developmental psychology, human brain/minds readily distinguish living from nonliving objects, but also are prone (for various reasons suggested by different authors) to err on the side of animism— thus attributing characteristics of living organisms to inanimate objects. One feature of naive biology that is activated as part of animism is psychological essentialism, by which we ascribe unique "essences" to different living kinds (including, perhaps, different "kinds" of people). The operation of these processes give rise to such religious concepts or thinking processes such as animism and spirits, totemism, special status of shamans and priests, belief in an afterlife, and the distinction between sacred and profane.

Finally, mechanisms for *naive psychology* and theory of mind give rise to anthropomorphism, including attributions to the beliefs and desires of supernatural beings or "nature" and particular patterns of inference about them. Thinking about gods, spirits, and other supernatural beings invariably follows a template or script for thinking about humans: They are subject to laws of biology (e.g., reproduction) and physics (e.g., gravity), but have motives, intentions, goals, emotions, and their own theories of mind. However, supernatural beings are always perceived as having one or more specific features that contradict the human script, such as being invisible or omniscient. These "counterintuitive" features, which are culturally specific, are what make the ideas intriguing and memorable. Our inferential systems for processing information about humans fills in all the rest. (See Boyer, 2001, for an extended discussion.)

The Social Psychology of the Supernatural

Once these mechanisms have provided the psychological foundation for belief in supernatural forces or beings, and naive psychology has provided the foundation for thinking about them in human terms, the door is open to a host of other psychological mechanisms designed specifically to guide reasoning and behavior about qualitatively different kinds of interpersonal relationships (i.e., categories of relationships that pose different adaptive problems). I focused mainly on these interpersonal or social-psychological aspects of religion. Perceived relationships with gods or supernatural forces, whether conceptualized literally as humanlike beings, play a central role in most religions. This fact, in turn, owes largely to the fact that human psychological architecture is designed disproportionally for processing social information: It is in many ways a collection of dedicated social-cognitive processing systems.

One such psychological system is the attachment system. In this book I devoted several chapters to introducing the general theory (Chapter 2) as developed originally by John Bowlby, focusing especially on Bowlby's conceptualization (which seems to have largely drifted into the background in many researchers' writings) of the attachment system as a suite of evolved psychological mechanisms. The attachment system has a distinct evolutionary function both distally (providing protection to helpless offspring) and proximally (by maintaining physical proximity between primary caregiver and infant); is activated by particular conditions relevant to its adaptive function (e.g., frightening environmental stimuli, illness and fatigue, separation from the primary caregiver); and gives rise to stable individual differences depending on early experience with caregivers.

The attachment system thus provides an illustrative example of evolved psychological mechanisms and how they work. It also clearly illustrates, as emphasized by Bowlby (1969) from the beginning, the degree of specialization of our evolved social-psychological architecture. Attachments are functionally distinct from other kinds of interpersonal relationships and are undergirded by a unique evolved psychological system. Other systems underlie functionally important classes of interpersonal relationships, our understanding of which is guided by middle-level theories derived from the theory of inclusive fitness. In a "backward" version of this book, there would be no reason to give primacy to the attachment system (other than the fact that it has been the subject of much of my own research over the last decade and that it is particularly useful for understanding many aspects of modern Christianity, the religion with which I and most readers of this book are probably most familiar).

However, attachment is only one of many dedicated social-psychological systems that can be recruited to process information about supernatural beliefs. In Chapter 10 I discussed the respective roles in religious thinking of *coalitional psychology*, *competition for status and mates*, *kinship*, *social exchange*, and *reciprocal altruism*. From an evolutionary perspective, the adaptive strategies required to successfully (in inclusive-fitness terms) negotiate relationships differs radically depending on the functional nature of that relationship. Biological kin are a privileged class of people in whose well-being one inherently and invariably has genetic interests; kin are treated differently than others because their reproductive success is in part one's own. Coalitional psychology dictates that under some circumstances, (genetically unrelated) coalitional partners may, like kin, receive preferential treatment relative to outsiders. In both cases cooperation strategies may trump competition strategies, though the latter differ in that the individuals occupying the roles of good-guy and bad-guy are variable across time and situations. Outside these two categories, cooperative relationships are guided by rules of social exchange or reciprocity. Beyond (and sometimes overlapping with) these relational categories, other persons are either potential mates (opposite sex) or competitors for mates and other resources (same sex).

The operation of each of these social-cognitive systems, along with the attachment system, is evident in diverse ways across religions. Gods and other supernatural beings might be treated psychologically as attachment figures, but also (or instead) as kin (e.g., ancestors or Father), coalitional partners ("God is on our side"), social-exchange partners (who offer particular provisions in exchange for proper behavior, sacrifices, etc.), or high-status "leaders" (God as "king"). Similarly, perceptions of and beliefs about human religious leaders, who may or may not be seen to possess special essences, may reflect one or more of these processes in the role of attachment figure, powerful leader, service-provider (social exchange), and so forth.

Conclusion

In the present book, I discussed at length the many ways in which various aspects of religious belief, particularly (but not exclusively) in Christianity, reflect the operation of attachment processes. Once gods (or other supernatural beings) are identified as human-like, the attachment system is one of many social-cognitive psychological systems that might be recruited to process information about them, filling in the gaps of culturally given knowledge and generating inferences, expectations, and behavioral plans for interacting with them. In addition, the theory addressed some other important aspects of Christianity involving, for example, relationships with religious leaders. In this book I devoted Chapters 3, 4, 5, 6, and 8 to attachment processes in religion. Material on other social-psychological relationships was squeezed into a single chapter (10). Given another, say, 20 years, I can imagine (someone) expanding the book into a massive volume, in which each of the psychological mechanisms (and many others) discussed only briefly here receives the same extended treatment as attachment theory. I doubt that I will ever write that book, but I hope that the field of the psychology of religion—or more accurately, the social-scientific study of religion generally—will eventually write that book collectively.

In short, many different psychological systems dedicated to processing information about particular classes of functional relationships are brought to bear on religious ideas and behaviors. Which particular systems are principally involved varies greatly from religion to religion, culture to culture, person to person, and within a person over time, depending on enduring ecological conditions and/or ephemeral individual circumstances. The power and success of "religion" historically is largely a function of this fact. It is not just about attachment relationships, or social exchange, or any other particular psychological processes: It is about all of these, to varying degrees in different situations and for different people.

Indeed, religion is undoubtedly about many other things as well. In this book I have tried to outline a very general approach, filling out one part of the picture (attachment) in some detail but providing only a rough sketch of the rest. I did this backward, taking the specific attachment path to the overlook provided by evolutionary psychology. Future researchers, I hope, will begin here and explore the many and varied paths available from this point. In the final section of this book, I explain why I think they should.

AN EVOLUTIONARY PSYCHOLOGY OF RELIGION FOR THE FUTURE

I began this book by laying out an agenda with the long-term goal of a *scientific, comprehensive, explanatory psychology of religion*. I then proposed that we have a better chance of achieving this goal more quickly and efficiently if we begin with a broad metatheoretical framework—a rough sketch of the "big picture"—to organize theory and research with this goal explicitly in mind from the start. In the 12 chapters since then, I tried to make the case that evolutionary psychology (including attachment theory in particular) offers a powerful and heuristically rich framework for fulfilling this agenda. In this final section of the book I offer some observations about what a future psychology of religion, organized by this perspective, might look like, highlighting some of the strengths of this approach vis-a-vis current and past approaches to the psychology of religion.

A Theoretically Rich "Psychology of . . . "

As I discussed in Chapter 1, "psychology of religion" means many things to many people with many different agendas. The perspective I advocate here supports one such agenda: the attempt to understand religious phenomena in terms of psychological science. Such a psychology of religion would be unambiguously *psychology* first, and "of religion" second: Religion would be examined as a topic of investigation in the same manner as any other domain of cognition, affect, or behavior. Indeed, as I tried to demonstrate in Chapter 11, the same evolutionary psychological perspective can be brought to bear, in much the same way, on other domains of thought and behavior, including science itself. Such a psychology of religion would fall squarely within the purview of the field of psychology proper.

One consequence of this approach is that research on religion would be integrated within the context of other, nonreligious variables. Examining some aspect of religion as a manifestation of a particular psychological mechanism or system would clearly necessitate inclusion of other variables related to that system in empirical studies; religion would not be studied in a vacuum. Though not based on an evolutionary perspective, Pargament's (1990, 1997) work provides a noteworthy example in which he starts with a psychological model of stress and coping processes in general, and examines the role of religion—alongside other factors—within each component of the model. In my own work, attachment to God is examined alongside childhood attachments to parents and adult romantic relationships in such a way that each aspect can be studied as it influences, and is influenced by, the others. Research organized in this way would be particularly effective in highlighting both the ways in which religion-related factors function similarly to nonreligious factors, and the ways in which religion is unique. For example, attachment to God functions psychologically in much the same way as human interpersonal relationships (e.g., provision of a secure base and haven of safety), but differs importantly from human relationships with respect to beliefs about God's unique powers and abilities (e.g., infallibility, constant availability, and provision of unconditional acceptance).

Many researchers have noted a paucity of good theory in the psychology of religion in recent decades. In addition to providing a metatheoretical framework, the evolutionary paradigm brings with it a host of more specific theories developed in other applications. In this book I have introduced the general, "middle-level" evolutionary theories of parental investment, kin selection, and reciprocal altruism, from which numerous, more specific theories such as social exchange theory have been derived. Any of these theories, as well as many others that might otherwise not come to the attention of psychologists of religion, can be brought to bear on the psychology of religion, in conjunction with whatever particular (nonreligious) topic they were initially constructed to address. A psychology of religion based on evolutionary psychology would be richly theoretical.

A Paradigmatic, Interdisciplinary Science

I suggested in Chapter 1 that in the best of all possible worlds, the psychology of religion would bring to the table a comprehensive, paradigmatic *psychology*, which could then be carried over into the domain of religion. Unfortunately, psychology has not been organized around a clearly identifiable paradigm since perhaps the heyday of behaviorism. Evolutionary psychology aspires to fill this void, by offering an all-encompassing metatheoretical framework—a "big picture"—within which more specific theories, hypotheses, and findings can be organized. My application of this perspective to religion in some ways puts the cart before the horse, as the evolutionary paradigm is currently in its infancy and by no means widely accepted in psychology generally. Nevertheless, the horse is making good progress as the approach gains popularity and increasingly demonstrates its potential to organize previous research and guide future study. A psychology of religion based on evolutionary psychology would be internally consistent, with the various pieces within it fitting together without theoretical gaps and overlaps.

Moreover, the evolutionary paradigm promises to integrate psychological perspectives not only across the field's various (and largely arbitrarily defined) subdisciplinary boundaries, but also with approaches from anthropology, sociology, political science, and other social sciences. Although each of these fields represents a level of analysis of religion different from psychology, each must be founded upon a clear understanding of human psychology. The ideal "scientific study of religion" must be truly interdisciplinary, not merely multidisciplinary, and a shared evolutionary perspective promises to provide a common conceptual framework and language to facilitate cross-disciplinary communication and collaboration. This is not to say that these other fields are reducible to psychology: The goal is not to collapse higher levels of analysis to a psychological level, any more than an evolutionary approach attempts to collapse psychology down to a biological level of analysis; instead, each level must be firmly founded on the levels below. (See E. O. Wilson, 1998, for a discussion.) Indeed, note that many of the religion researchers whose work most closely resembles the model advocated in this book—most notably Pascal Boyer—are not psychologists but anthropologists.

The desirability of both an *intra*disciplinary paradigm for psychology and an *inter*disciplinary paradigm for connecting psychology to other social sciences would be beneficial in countless ways for the study of virtually any topic in which psychologists and other social scientists are interested. Given the unusually complex, multifaceted nature of religion, however, such an integrated perspective is not only desirable but essential. We in psychology cannot be serious about studying "religion" without reference to, for example, the vast knowledge base in anthropology and other fields regarding religious beliefs in other parts of the world, including (perhaps especially) those of preindustrial societies. At the same time, anthropologists cannot hope to make sense of these remarkably diverse observations in the absence of a coherent model of human psychology. A psychology of religion based on evolutionary psychology would be a central part of a larger, paradigmatic field of the social scientific study of religion.

A Coherent Model of Universality versus Individual Differences

The history of attempts to understand religion from the perspective of psychology has long been characterized by two more or less mutually exclusive camps: theorists with big ideas and little empirical data, and quantitative researchers with lots of data and little theory. As the scientific psychology of religion has moved increasingly away from the former toward the latter, the big questions addressed by the grand (but speculative) theories seem to have been lost in the shuffle.

Perhaps the biggest question in the psychology of religion has always been "Why are people religious?" Anthropologists have long observed that something worthy of the title "religion" is evident in all cultures. It seems apparent that religion is somehow an inherent part of "human nature." The question of what exactly this means—including the grand "nature–nurture" conundrum—has shackled the field for a century. Evolutionary psychology offers the only coherent framework for conceptualizing the ancient nature-nurture debate. In a manner analogous to the way in which *both* friction against the skin (an environmental stimulus) and a specialized physiological mechanism (constructed based on genetic instructions) are required to produce calluses, all human behavior is the product of both environmental input and specialized, evolved psychological mechanisms designed to process it. Religious belief and behavior are neither "in our genes" nor merely "in the environment," but rather result from a combination of our particular psychological architecture interacting with specific environments. To understand it properly, then, it is necessary to begin with a coherent theory about the design and nature of the psychological architecture, specifically from the perspective of what it was initially "designed" to do, in response to what kinds of experience.

The evolutionary psychological perspective restores the centrality of "human nature" to the psychology of religion, from which (as in the rest of psychology) it has largely disappeared. Like the rest of psychology, the psychology of religion has been dominated by a Standard Social Science Model that strongly emphasizes the roles of general "learning" and "socialization" processes while deemphasizing the role of our biological nature. One consequence of this is that empirical research in the psychology of religion has come to focus almost exclusively on questions of individual differences. Indeed, the "measurement paradigm" in the psychology of religion could just as well be called the "individual differences paradigm." Of course, individual differences are a crucially important aspect of the problem, but they are only half the problem. This is well illustrated by attachment theory, which on the one hand describes a species-universal psychological system shared by all humans—that is, an aspect of "human nature"—and on the other provides a basis for explaining the common patterns of individual differences that emerge from the interaction of this system with variable environments and experience. Such a perspective provides a conceptual framework for empirical research integrating the effects of individual differences (e.g., in attachment styles) with effects of situational variables (e.g., stress, illness). Both perspectives therefore become useful and relevant for answering the big question: In part, (some) people are religious because their attachment systems are activated by, and process, their experience. An evolutionary psychology of religion would focus equally on universal aspects of religion as well as individual differences, based on a fundamentally interactive model in which the study of each of these aspects informs the other.

One particularly noteworthy individual-differences topic that remains poorly understood in the psychology of religion is that of sex differences. Although much data exists demonstrating that women are "more religious" than men in general, little is known about qualitative differences in the content of male and female religiosity. Moreover, these observations are based exclusively on modern Western societies such as Great Britain and the United States. An evolutionary perspective provides a strong theoretical basis for predicting and studying sex differences in religion, which would be expected to vary depending on the particular psychological domain in question. In this book I have said little about sex differences because theory and research on attachment suggests little reason to expect such differences in this area. Similarly, sex differences might not be expected in domains of religion related to social-exchange (reciprocal-altruism) thinking. On the other hand, the theory of parental investment leads to predictions, which have been borne out in research in many contexts outside of religion, about sex differences in domains such as that of striving for power and status. Moreover, evolutionary predictions tend to be particularly clear with respect to topics closely related to sexuality. From this perspective it should come as no surprise, for example, that male cult leaders commonly use their position to monopolize sexual access to female cult members, whereas we virtually never hear about female cult leaders doing so. An evolutionary psychology of religion would provide a strong foundation for conceptualizing, predicting, and studying empirically sex differences (or lack thereof) across different domains of religious belief and behavior.

Beyond Description to Function

I suggested earlier that an evolutionary approach to religion, in contrast to most extant approaches, provides the basis for asking deep questions about the nature of religion as well as integrating such questions with ones about individual differences. This is so because the evolutionary paradigm is, at its heart, a *functional* approach. An evolutionary psychologist is like a 4-year-old incessantly asking "Why?" because each successive answer begs the next question. Unlike other extant approaches to the psychology of religion, an evolutionary perspective begins with a strong theoretical basis for conceptualizing functions, rather than merely postulating them post hoc: Organisms are "designed" (or were designed in ancestral environments) arising from functional principles according to the criterion of inclusive fitness, and all theory flows from there. In evolution, form really does follow function.

This matter is particularly important with respect to questions about *motivation*. To illustrate, consider a claim by Gorsuch (1994) in his (laudable) attempt to reconceptualize the distinction between intrinsic and extrinsic religious motivation. He suggests that the former involves a behavior that is "carried out for its own sake," in that it "creates positive affect" or "feels like a moral obligation," as when singing a joyful song because of the joy directly associated with that singing. It may well be that people sing joyful songs because it feels good to do so, but this begs the question as to why singing some kinds of songs (and presumably not other kinds of songs) has this effect, or why some contemplated behaviors feel like moral obligations and others do not. If we knew which psychological systems were involved in producing these effects, we would be in a position to predict what kinds of differences between songs might be crucial, what other kinds of activities might have similar effects, and so forth. For example, reciprocal-altruism theory suggests that we feel obligated to reciprocate when we perceive someone has done something to benefit us at some expense to him- or herself.

Psychologists of religion have long been interested in questions of motivation, and have been quick to nominate candidate motivations for explaining religion: People are religious because it enhances their self-esteem, or creates meaning, or assuages their fear of death, and so forth. However, in the absence of a larger evolutionary framework, there is no basis for digging more deeply to ask why people would be so motivated. Why is "enhancing self-esteem" so important to people? Why is death so terrifying that fear of it requires assuaging? This is where the psychology of religion needs a strong psychology-in-general to draw upon: If we already had a clear explanation for the answers to these general questions about human motivation, the psychology of religion could simply start from there. But this is not currently the case. Indeed, I have argued in various places in this book that there are good reasons to question the assumptions that humans have an inherent "need for self-esteem" or an inherent fear of death, and have offered alternative perspectives based on evolutionary reasoning.

A commonly heard criticism of evolutionary psychology is that it is nothing more than a collection of post hoc speculations about origins and functions of observed features. It can be this, of course, in the same way that nonevolutionary approaches often are. (Indeed, most extant motivational perspectives on religion have a very speculative, post hoc quality about them.) However, the strength of the approach comes from applying it from the other direction. Rather than beginning with descriptive data and searching backward for an explanation, we can begin with theories about evolved design and functions and working forward to hypotheses about (religious) belief and behavior. In this book I have tried to illustrate this approach by organizing material by psychological mechanisms or systems (or theories thereof), rather than by religious phenomena. It could have been done the other way around, with separate sections or chapters devoted to, say, images of God, prayer, attributions of causality, and so forth. However, my goal was decidedly not to provide explanations for a litany of descriptive findings, but rather to illustrate how one could begin with a psychological theory and explore its potential applications to the phenomena of interest. An evolutionary psychology of religion would be functional rather than merely descriptive, and would provide a strong theoretical foundation for deriving and testing hypotheses about the multitude of motivations underlying religious belief and behavior. An evolutionary psychology of religion would begin with a strong theoretical foundation for thinking about function, and then apply this functional perspective to religious phenomena of interest.

Religious Nature Carved at Its Joints

Given the complex and multifaceted nature of religion, religion researchers—like scientists studying any other complex phenomenon—have long sought a framework for analyzing the subject into smaller components to be examined separately. In the absence of any clear theoretical structure, such divisions tend to be fairly arbitrary, based mainly on salient observable features, superficial similarities and differences, and intuitive judgments. As a consequence, the field has as many such descriptive frameworks as it has researchers. Moreover, there is no reason to believe that any such system will map neatly onto the functional psychological processes underlying the subject.

To illustrate, imagine trying to develop a classification system for categorizing the parts of an automobile. From a purely descriptive perspective, you might classify parts by their color, their size, or the kind of material from which they are constructed. Such distinctions would be based on criteria that happen to be visually salient to the untrained observer. They might be useful for certain applications (though frankly I am hard pressed to think of a clear example), but such a classification scheme would be of virtually no value if your goal was to understand how cars work, or if you were trying to fix one. Indeed, thinking about colors would only get in the way. Instead, for such purposes one needs to think in terms of systems (electrical, suspension, etc.) comprising numerous discrete components (battery, spark plugs, or fuel injectors), which are designed and organized according to specific functions. An evolutionary psychology of religion would look much more like an engineer's view of automobiles than the average consumer's.

For example, consider a topic such as "prayer" in the psychology of religion. This is a widely used descriptive category for a variety of forms of religious thought and behavior, though it is not clear what criteria differentiate this category from others. (Indeed, it is interesting to ponder the question of exactly what these similarities are among the items in this category, and the criteria by which a particular phenomenon is classified as "prayer" or not.) In many ways, identifying "prayer" as a category of religious phenomena might well be akin to identifying "black" or "oblong" as a category of auto parts. In terms of their psychological dynamics, certain forms of prayer probably have much more in common with, say, the practice of ritual sacrifices than with other kinds of prayer (i.e., owing to a shared, underlying psychological dynamic based on social-exchange or reciprocal-altruism mechanisms). Other forms might have more in common with certain kinds of beliefs about or images of God (e.g., as an attachment figure) than with other forms of prayer.

The problem in the psychology of religion is particularly evident with respect to the topic of motivation, as noted in the preceding section. Researchers commonly attribute religion to just one or a few vague, general motives or functions, such as enhancing self-esteem, maintaining interpersonal relatedness, or assuaging fear of death. From an evolutionary perspective, however, many such assumed functions are highly dubious. For example, interpersonal relationships are negotiated by many functionally distinct psychological mechanisms that map onto distinct adaptive problems: Attachment relationships, social-exchange relationships, coalitions, and intrasexual competitions are all negotiated by different psychological processes according to highly differentiated inferential rules, many of which are not mutually compatible. (For example, note that adopting a social-exchange/reciprocity stance towards your best friend or love partner would be deemed insulting, because it suggests that altruistic behavior on your part is motivated by expectation of payback rather than on love and commitment.) As I have tried to illustrate throughout this book, it is crucial to distinguish these functionally diverse kinds of relationships to understand the psychology behind them.

The still popular intrinsic–extrinsic distinction in the psychology of religion illustrates the problem in the extreme: In the traditional interpretation, intrinsic religious motivation refers to religion "for its own sake"—as if it were somehow devoid of motivation—and extrinsic motivation refers to everything else (see Kirkpatrick & Hood, 1990). The later distinction between "social" and "personal" extrinsic motives, which was based purely on statistical analysis of existing scales for measuring I (intrinsic motivation) and E (extrinsic motivation) (Kirkpatrick, 1989), is hardly better. Gorsuch's (1994) proposal of distinct "affective" and "moral value" dimensions within the intrinsic category is similarly much too vague.

The design of the human mind is a direct reflection of evolutionary (adaptive) function, with discrete (though sometimes overlapping) cognitive mechanisms and systems, each designed as solutions to (ancestral) problems of survival and reproduction. Specifically, an evolutionary perspective provides a clear theoretical basis for "carving nature at its joints" in constructing an organizational scheme for the psychology of religion (or anything else). Rather than arbitrarily dividing religion into descriptive categories such as images of God, prayer, or causal attributions, it provides a means for dividing up the terrain in functional ways that are more likely to lead to theoretical progress. An evolutionary psychology of religion would move us beyond arbitrary, intuitive classification systems toward nonarbitrary, highly differentiated functional ones.

Another, related feature of an evolutionary psychology of religion is that it would bring back into focus the *content* of religious belief. The so-called "measurement paradigm" in the psychology of religion has produced, to a large extent, a conceptualization of religious variability in terms of highly abstract dimensions, such as intrinsic–extrinsic orientation, quest orientation, fundamentalism, and spiritual development. Lost in these abstractions has been the details of what people actually *believe*. The idea of summarizing religion in terms of abstract dimensions is consistent with an assumption that human psychology can ultimately be understood in terms of a small number of highly domain-general principles. This assumption is flatly rejected in the evolutionary view, according to which our psychological architecture is highly domain-specific and content-dependent. The specific content of beliefs dictates the psychological systems likely to be activated to process them and the kinds of inferences likely to be drawn from them. An evolutionary psychology of religion would shift the focus away from abstract intellectualizations back to what religion is really *about*.

Avoiding Major Pitfalls in the Psychology of Religion

At various points in this book I have noted particular problems that have plagued the psychology of religion since its inception, and which would be circumvented by an evolutionary paradigm for the field. Because I believe that these are some of the most important reasons why the psychology of religion has made so little progress over the last few decades, I highlight them once again here at the end.

First, I suggested that much psychology of religion has fallen into a deep *definitional trap*. In the absence of a strong theoretical (and particularly functional) foundation from which to start, researchers have tended to begin with the topic and work backward toward a theory to explain it. Such an approach would seem to necessitate that one clearly define the target of explanation before proceeding any further. However, the quest for an acceptable definition of the term *religion* itself has proved utterly intractable, leaving the field stymied. As I have tried to illustrate, this problem need not arise if one begins from the perspective of theory: Armed with a host of hypotheses about the particular kinds of psychological mechanisms and systems that comprise the human mind, as well as clearly articulated theories about what these systems were "designed" to do, a researcher can begin applying these ideas to any particular topic of interest irrespective of whether it fits one or another definition of religion. Instead of going in circles trying to agree on a definition, we can get on with the work.

Second, I argued that attempts to escape this definitional trap have tended to lead researchers into another, *measurement trap*. A common solution to the complexity and diversity of religion (and hence its resistance to a simple definition) has been to dimensionalize it based on (mainly) factor-analytic work. The hope is that analysis of descriptive data on religion will produce a multidimensional framework that both defines religion empirically and provides a basis for construction of scales to measure these various aspects. Whether dimensions so constructed actually relate empirically to psychological variables of interest is another question, the answer to which is often likely to be no. A strong theoretically based orientation, however, provides a basis for constructing measures designed specifically to tap the particular aspects of religious belief or behavior relevant to the psychological domain of interest. For example, although the attachment-related aspects of Christian beliefs about God are tapped in part by the widely used Loving God scale (Benson & Spilka, 1973), they are probably measured more validly and reliably by scales tapping specific aspects of one's perceived relationship with God as derived directly from attachment theory (see Rowatt & Kirkpatrick, 2002).

Finally, the psychology of religion has been plagued from the beginning by extrascientific evaluative assumptions: the *evaluative trap*. A central question of interest to many researchers concerns whether religion (or some particular aspect of it) is "good" or "bad" for people with respect to individual psychology, group functioning, or some other criterion. Presumed answers to these questions are often built into definitions, measurement strategies, and theoretical constructs from the start. However, it seems obvious to me that the answer to this question cannot possibly be anything other than "both." Like any complex aspect of human experience, religion can have effects that we (or any particular individual) would probably deem "good" and others deemed "bad." Once the criteria for "good" and "bad" have been identified, the questions should be decided by empirical data rather than by fiat.

There is no reason to think that evolutionary researchers, as individuals, are any less biased with respect to their personal views about religion than any other group of researchers. However, an evolutionary perspective offers a few unique insights into this problem that effectively undermine any assumptions about the degree to which we should expect religion to be inherently positive or negative, helpful or hurtful, particularly with respect to modern societies. First, according to the model I presented in this book, the human mind is not "designed" for religion; religion is a by-product of numerous cognitive systems that are well designed for other purposes. Inherent in the concept of by-product is that the utility of one for any other particular purpose is unpredictable. Incandescent light bulbs, by virtue of unintended features of their design, happen to give off heat; depending on the particular application, this heat might be considered a desirable bonus (e.g., for both lighting and heating a reptile's terrarium) or a costly problem (e.g., the danger of starting a fire). The "side effects" of pharmaceutical drugs are often undesirable, though occasionally they turn out to be quite positive, as in the discovery that aspirin (traditionally taken for relieving pain) reduces the risk of heart attacks.

Second, even if it could be shown that our brains/minds *were* designed by natural selection to produce or experience religion, there is no reason to think that it would necessarily be "good" for individuals. Evolution does not design organisms to be happy or "psychologically healthy," but only to behave in ways likely to enhance their genes' success. Moreover, there is no reason to believe that a religion designed by natural selection would necessarily be good for *other* people; indeed, much of our evolved psychology is about out-competing others at their expense.

Third, even if it were true that a religious capacity evolved in ways that *were* designed to enhance the welfare (psychological or otherwise) of individuals or groups of individuals, there is no guarantee that it would work properly in modern environments. Recall the example of our evolved food preferences, which lead us to seek and consume fats and sweets—a highly adaptive trait in ancestral environments but a highly maladaptive one in modern fast-food societies. Modern environments differ in so many crucial ways from the ancestral environments in which our species originated that one can never safely assume that what was "good" for humans at one time will be good for us now.

Finally, related to the evaluative trap is the *veridicality trap*: the common but patently false assumption that if a belief can be understood scientifically, for example, in terms of psychological processes, then the beliefs are themselves false. I suggested earlier that, in general, there is no reason why any scientific approach to understanding religion need assume that the beliefs under study are either ontologically true or false. The origins (psychological or otherwise) of a belief are logically orthogonal to the veridicality of belief; to infer otherwise is to commit the *genetic fallacy*. This holds true for any scientific approach to religion, whether evolutionarily grounded or not: Researchers can study beliefs that are demonstrably true, beliefs that are clearly false, and beliefs that are not statements about the empirical world and therefore can be neither true nor false (e.g., aesthetic preferences). Depending on one's (extrascientific) personal assumptions, the psychology of religious belief can be viewed as explaining how and why some people are able to find religious truth, or how and why people come to hold false religious beliefs.

However, I believe the evolutionary psychological approach outlined here offers an additional insight that may help us avoid the veridicality trap. As I discussed in Chapter 12, an evolutionary perspective begins with the assumption that the human brain/mind was designed according to the sole criterion of inclusive fitness; it is designed to be *adaptive*. It is decidedly *not* designed to be "accurate" or "correct" as judged by logical or other empirical standards. Often this design leads to correct intuitions and inferences; being "correct" is indeed often adaptive. Recall the example of paranoid rabbits, whose predator-detection systems are inherently biased in such a way that they make enormous numbers of false-alarm errors. Once this is acknowledged, there is no a priori reason to believe that any particular kind of belief, whether religious or not, should be expected to be correct or incorrect. The mind is designed in such a way that, depending on any number of factors, it sometimes draws correct inferences and sometimes incorrect ones. An evolutionary psychology of religion would address the question of why and how people come to hold (as well as reject, communicate, etc.) particular beliefs in which we are interested, irrespective of the question of whether they are true or false.

SUMMARY AND CONCLUSIONS

It is for these reasons that I believe evolutionary psychology provides a powerful metatheoretical paradigm for organizing all social-scientific research on religion. There is, however, one hitch in the plan: The field of psychology in general has yet to adopt the evolutionary paradigm as its own. Evolutionary psychology is certainly gaining in popularity, and it seems to me inevitable that it will eventually rise to become a leading, if not the predominant, paradigm for the field. Nevertheless, it is not at all clear how long this will take.

In the meantime, psychologists of religion can either wait for "the revolution," hopping on the bandwagon when it finally comes around, or they can go ahead and start moving in that direction and beat the bandwagon to the pass. The question is not whether evolutionary psychology will prove to be an important tool for the psychology of religion, but when. I say we might as well get started.

Notes

CHAPTER 1 NOTES

1. Indeed, there was considerable concern expressed by many about the name change, for fear that the phrase "psychology of religion" implies a narrow focus on the scientific study of religious phenomena and the exclusion of other sorts of "interests in religious issues." Only by convincing detractors that the phrase "psychology of religion" was intended to be broadly defined, and not restricted to scientific, empirical research about religion, was the name-change motion eventually passed.

2. In case you cannot wait to find out, the general argument will be that natural selection has designed human cognition according to a single criterion of inclusive fitness or reproductive success, not veridicality. Brains/minds are designed to produce *adaptive* thoughts, not necessarily "correct" ones. The fact that the evolved architecture of our brains/minds systematically and predictably produces certain kinds of inferences or beliefs more readily than others is thus entirely independent of the ontological status of those inferences or beliefs.

3. Psychologists of religion have long complained that psychology textbooks give their topic short shrift (e.g., Spilka, Comp, & Goldsmith, 1981), and I suspect that this structural problem is one of the principal reasons.

4. Actually, the problem is even worse within the psychology of religion. For example, another long-standing rift that disappeared from most of the rest of research psychology—that between the psychoanalytic tradition and other psychological perspectives—continues to thrive within the psychology of religion. Although psychological science abandoned Freud long ago, psychoanalytic perspectives on religion are very much alive and well. It is very difficult for any-

thing constructive to come out of a "dialogue" across this paradigmatic boundary because scholars on each side (quite naturally) tend to translate the terms and concepts from the other into their own way of thinking, and inevitably a lot gets lost in the translation. Moreover, as noted earlier, the psychology of religion is divided deeply by the psychology-of-religion versus religious-psychology (and other such variations) issue.

5. I cannot resist offering a few specific comments on the definition problem and how it interferes with the development of good theory in psychology of religion, but I will relegate them to this footnote so as not to detract from the remainder of the text.

First, one common solution to the problem of defining religion is to choose a definition narrow enough that one's own theory can explain it. Many scholars have defined religion, for example, in terms of an existential search for meaning, or of group rituals, or of belief in anthropomorphized deities. The problem with such definitions is that they automatically exclude from consideration many aspects of "religion" as others might define it. Focusing on one aspect of religion leaves us without a theory of the rest of it.

A second and related problem is that of defining religion in terms of its presumed function. Pargament (1997) discusses some of the pros and cons of "substantive" versus "functional" definitions of religion. One of his concerns about the former is that "substantive definitions of religion take on a static character. They speak to what religion is, not how it works" (p. 26). In my view, though, this is a strong plus, not a minus. The function of religion is what our theories should be about, and smuggling the theory in through the definition itself is, well, cheating, and does not do justice to the complexity of the problem. Hypotheses about function must be derived from theory and tested empirically, not simply imposed by fiat. If religion is to be defined for the purposes of constructing a scientific theory about it, it should be defined in terms of what it *is*—then we can develop a theory about what it *does*.

In response to the question of why anthropologists argue incessantly about the definition of religion, Boyer (1994b) points to both of these problems with the following answer:

> The reason is that anthropological "definitions" in fact constitute the outcome, rather than the starting point, of particular research programs. . . . Authors who define religion as . . . [Durkheim does] . . . are describing the particular aspects of religious phenomena their frameworks address. (pp. 33–34)

6. Another characteristic of attachment theory that incidentally makes it potentially valuable for the psychology of religion specifically concerns its historical connection to psychoanalysis. The psychoanalytic tradition remains strong in the psychology of religion, and the fundamental rift between the psychoanalytic paradigm and the rest of psychology is one of the obstacles that must

be overcome in the quest for an integrated, comprehensive theory. Attachment theory provides a potential bridge between these traditions.

CHAPTER 2 NOTES

1. I cannot overemphasize the value of reading Bowlby, especially the 1969 volume, in the original for appreciating the breadth and power of the case he develops for attachment as an evolved system. I thank my friend (and graduate-student colleague at the time) Cindy Hazan for convincing me to do so many years ago. As persuasive as the theory may seem based on summaries in secondary sources, Bowlby's treatment renders it utterly compelling.

2. A fourth category (D), labeled *disorganized/disoriented* was introduced later (Main & Solomon, 1990). It represents a kind of combination of A and C patterns. Because most empirical research, as well as extensions of attachment theory to adult relationships, has focused on the three primary patterns, the D type will not be discussed further in this book.

3. It is important to note, at least in passing, that the relative contribution of maternal behavior to individual differences in infant attachment is not beyond debate. For example, Kagan (1982) argued that such variability reflects, at least in part, genetic individual differences in infant temperament. Based on a comprehensive review of the relevant literature, however, Vaughn and Bost (1999, p. 218) recently concluded unambiguously that infant temperament cannot explain individual differences in attachment patterns. On the other hand, they do not rule out the possibility of important interactions between family environment and certain dimensions of temperament in influencing later attachment classification. For example, infants who are dispositionally irritable and "difficult" are likely to tax the average parent's energy and patience, eliciting caregiving patterns that feed back to the infant insecurity and anxiety. In any event, the temperament debate is not particularly pertinent to the case I wish to make in this book concerning attachment and religion: For my purposes it is the nature and shape of individual differences in attachment that is important, not the precise source of these differences.

4. The situation is further complicated by recent research that reveals a large "transmission gap" in existing data: The parental caregiving measures do no fully, or even substantially, mediate the statistical relationship between AAI classification and infant Strange Situation classification (Pederson, Gleason, Moran, & Bento, 1998; van IJzendoorn, 1995). Although the failure of this expected mediational model probably can be attributed at least partly to problems in the measurement of parenting, it seems likely that the AAI is capturing something else that is somehow related to infant Strange Situation classification. It is not at all clear what this something might be.

5. My apologies to the original source of this wonderful analogy (which was not originally used in the context of attachment research), who deserves much credit but whom I cannot recall.

CHAPTER 3 NOTE

1. Interestingly, the other is a strategy of compulsive self-reliance, which is related to the insecure-*avoidant* pattern of adult attachment.

CHAPTER 4 NOTES

1. Many of these studies are methodologically flawed in ways that render their findings dubious anyway (Kirkpatrick, 1986). For example, in several of these studies, correlations are computed across variables or dimensions within each subject (and then averaged across subjects), in a manner that fails to take into account the fact that the variables are scored in arbitrary directions. If any such variable were measured or scored in reverse—for example, if an item measuring "strength" were reverse-scored so as to measure "weakness"—the within-subject correlations would all change.

2. Interestingly, Suomi (1999) reviews research showing that one major individual-difference variable in maternal behavior of rhesus monkeys concerns restrictiveness in permitting exploratory behavior in their offspring. Such individual differences are related to various ecological factors, such as resource availability and dependability and changes in the local social structure. Thus even in nonhumans, controlling/restricting is a measurable and important dimension of parenting, and it stands to reason that primate infants (including humans) are sensitive to perceiving these individual differences.

CHAPTER 6 NOTE

1. These data were collected in collaboration with Cindy Hazan. Other results from this study not pertaining to religion are reported in Kirkpatrick and Hazan (1994).

CHAPTER 7 NOTES

1. Much of the "biological" and "genetic" research by which many people are troubled on ethical or ideological grounds—such as research on racial differ-

ences in intelligence—comes from behavior genetics, not evolutionary psychology. I suspect that one reason (though there are others) for the tension between the fields is that evolutionary psychologists resent that the controversies over behavior genetics inappropriately get carried over to, and tarnish, the image of evolutionary psychology. In fact, if you do not like focusing on genetic differences among people, you ought to embrace evolutionary psychology, not reject it.

2. The EEA does not refer to any particular point in time or space; instead, each adaptation has its own EEA representing the ancestral conditions under which it evolved. Incidentally, it is also worth noting here for historical purposes that the term EEA was actually introduced by John Bowlby.

CHAPTER 8 NOTES

1. Although other attachment researchers have sometimes conceptualized attachment patterns as "contingent strategies," Belsky (1997) notes that these explanations have been couched in terms of immediate consequences and survival value, and not with regard to reproductive fitness.

2. Recent research suggests another interesting twist in this story: The presence versus absence of a stepfather, in addition to (if not instead of) biological father absence, seems to play a key role in pubertal timing in girls (Ellis & Garber, 2000; Ellis et al., 1999).

3. Belsky (1999) offers an interpretation of avoidant attachment in adulthood very similar to mine in terms of an orientation toward long-term mating. His highly speculative (by his own admission) account of anxious attachment in terms of a "helper-in-the-nest" reproductive strategy—in which effort is allocated toward facilitating reproductive success of close kin rather than of oneself—is in need of greater theoretical development and empirical support.

4. Although we have not discussed the potential role of self-esteem in all this, there are numerous reasons to believe from an evolutionary perspective that one (of many) function of self-esteem is to activate alternative behavioral strategies (see Kirkpatrick & Ellis, 2001, for a full discussion).

5. From an evolutionary perspective the Berman et al. (1994) argument is problematic in its reliance on group-selectionist thinking. Natural selection has no interest in preserving family units, for the benefit of families or species.

6. In a sense, what I am suggesting is a reorganization of the original Hazan and Shaver (1987; Shaver et al., 1988) model in which romantic love was conceptualized as the integration of attachment, caregiving, and mating systems. My proposed revision conceptualizes a functionally distinct love mechanism as a component of attachment (and of adult pair-bond relationships), rather than the other way around.

7. Another interesting implication of this view is that it explains why emotions such as rage are accompanied universally by observable displays such as facial expressions. Although it is generally assumed that the function of such observable signals is the communication of emotional states to others, this presents a rather thorny problem from an evolutionary perspective: It is usually easy to see why it would be beneficial to *observers* to be able to identify others' emotional states, but much more difficult to understand how or why it would be adaptive (i.e., in their inclusive-fitness interests) for the person experiencing the emotion to communicate his or her internal states.

CHAPTER 9 NOTES

1. I do not want to overstate this: There certainly are examples of heritable variability that do reflect alternative adaptations, as in biological sex and other frequency-dependent characteristics, so it is not the case that heritable *necessarily* means lack of functionality or nonadaptation. However, the point here is merely to establish that heritability does not imply that a trait *is* an adaptation.

2. Although Williams (1966) showed that selection at the intergroup level was theoretically possible, he showed that this was so only under a fairly narrow set of conditions that are quite rare in nature.

3. Kirkpatrick and Ellis (2001) further argue from an evolutionary perspective that so-called global self-esteem reflects an assortment of more domain-specific components or "sociometers" designed to monitor a variety of functionally distinct aspects of the self in relation to others. For example, they distinguish among three general classes of sociometers, designed respectively to monitor social inclusion or acceptance within social groups, relative rank or status within groups, and the strength or value of one's groups relative to other groups. Recent empirical studies by Kirkpatrick, Waugh, Valencia, and Webster (2002) demonstrate the importance of differentiating functional self-esteem components in this way for understanding the relationship between self-esteem and aggression: Different domains of self-esteem predict aggressive behavior differentially (and even in opposite directions), whereas global self-esteem is unrelated to aggression.

4. Although Atran's theory and my own have much in common, they were developed completely independently: He evidently was unaware of my work when writing his—for example, he did not cite my 1999b paper outlining the religion as by-product view—and his 2002 book did not appear until the present book was under final revision. In addition to many minor issues, the major differences between our views, as I see them, are that Atran's perspective (1) is more anthropological, focusing more than mine on explaining group-level as-

pects of religious expression such as ritual; and (2) emphasizes only some of the evolved psychological systems or mechanisms that I outline here. My view obviously differs in its emphasis on the attachment system, but also with respect to other mechanisms postulated designed to guide interpersonal relations, as I outline in Chapter 10. See Kirkpatrick (in press) for further discussion of differences between the two approaches.

CHAPTER 10 NOTES

1. Parental investment theory (Trivers, 1972) explains how a seemingly trivial biological difference between two kinds of gametes cascades into diverse and far-reaching differences in the kinds of adaptive problems associated with mating faced by males and females of sexually reproducing species. The fact that eggs are produced in relatively small numbers, and require considerable investment in nutritional resources to produce, whereas sperm are highly numerous and cheap to produce, means that eggs are a scarce resource for which members of the opposite sex must compete. These differences are greatly magnified in species in which females are biologically committed to the tasks of internal gestation, lactation, and nursing, as the minimal necessary investment of time and resources for females is far greater than the minimal necessary investment for males (i.e., an often-brief act of insemination). These differences in reproductive biology have the further implication that whereas males can sire a virtually unlimited number of offspring (thus enhancing their inclusive fitness through sheer numbers) by mating with many different females, this is not true for females.

2. Detractors frequently argue that the observed behavioral and psychological differences in humans with respect to mate preferences and intrasexual competition emerge simply as by-products of differential size: As the argument goes, it is simply because men are larger and stronger than women that they have been able to "dominate" women and create patriarchal societies, and so on. However, this argument fails because it begs the question as to why men evolved to be larger and stronger in the first place. From an evolutionary perspective, the sexual dimorphism in size could not have evolved in the absence of adaptive function; males must have evolved larger size in order to use it in some way. Hardware and software evolve together. As in so many other species, males' larger size evolved *because* size and strength correlated in ancestral environments with success in intrasexual competition and thus access to quality mates.

At the same time, note that this provides a clear example of the Stone Age minds issue discussed in Chapter 7. In modern industrial environments, competition takes many forms other than actual physical combat, and physical size and strength are probably no longer correlated with reproductive success to any appreciable degree. Nevertheless, our outdated minds still lead us to value physical stature in men; for example, male height continues to be correlated with status and power, and women continue to prefer taller to shorter men as mates (see Ellis, 1992, for a review).

3. Although "at some cost to the self" has long been viewed as a crucial part of the definition of altruism, Tooby and Cosmides (1996) have argued recently that this assumption may in fact not be necessary, and that dropping this part of the definition leads to a variety of other insights into the evolution of helpful behavior.

4. I cannot resist speculating here that the stereotypical example of sacrificing virgins makes perfect sense from this perspective, in a way that only an evolutionary psychologist could possibly imagine. From an evolutionary perspective, virgins are extremely "valuable" (to men, who historically have been the ones responsible for constructing sacrificial rituals) as mates because of the adaptive problems faced by men with respect to paternity uncertainty and sperm competition. From a (Stone Age) male perspective, one could not identify a more "valuable" kind of person to offer in sacrifice.

5. Thanks to Bruce Ellis (personal communication, September 21, 2000) for this observation.

6. By the same reasoning, it seems likely that romantic relationships as well are probably far more complex than we have acknowledged here so far. In addition to involving attachment, mating, and caregiving systems (Hazan & Shaver, 1987; Shaver et al., 1988), adult pair-bonds additionally include elements of reciprocal altruism and social exchange, coalitional psychology (e.g., our partnership against other pairs and families), and so on.

CHAPTER 11 NOTES

1. I should probably point out, as do Gelman et al. (1994), that I am in no way implying that such essences truly exist—only that people's reasoning about animals and plants suggests an implicit assumption about such essences.

2. Mithen (1996) also suggests that at a still earlier stage in evolution, our ancestors had "domain-general" minds. I think this part of his argument is wrong, but in a manner that is irrelevant to the issues at hand so I will not pursue it further.

3. Actually, belief in ghosts is very much part of "religion" in some contexts, if not in the contemporary United States or Europe. For example, Boyer (1994b, 2001) frequently uses beliefs about ghosts among the Fang people of Cameroon to illustrate his ideas about religion. Nevertheless, this only serves to further underscore my point about the difficulties of defining religion.

CHAPTER 12 NOTE

1. This observation provides the basis for an important theory of senescence, explaining why our lifespans are limited, and inevitably end (should we live that long) with our bodies and brains deteriorating more or less all at once (Williams, 1957). The gist of the theory is that many of the biological processes designed by natural selection to enhance reproductive success early in life tend to have, as by-products, deleterious effects in the long run that eventually catch up. For example, elevated levels of testosterone play many important roles with respect to men's competition for mates and resources, but over the long term lead to such correlated effects as increased risk of prostate cancer.

References

Alcock, J. E. (1995). The belief engine. *Skeptical Inquirer, 19*(3), 14–18.

Alexander, R. D. (1987). *The biology of moral systems.* Hawthorne, NY: Aldine de Gruyter.

Alloy, L. B., & Abramson, L. Y. (1979). Judgment of contingency in depressed and nondepressed students: Sadder but wiser? *Journal of Experimental Psychology, 108,* 441–485.

Allport, G. W. (1950). *The individual and his religion.* New York: Macmillan.

Allport, G. W. (1954). *The nature of prejudice.* Reading, MA: Addison-Wesley.

Allport, G. W., & Ross, J. M. (1967). Personal religious orientation and prejudice. *Journal of Personality and Social Psychology, 5,* 432–443.

Ainsworth, M. D. S. (1969). Object relations, dependency, and attachment: A theoretical review of the infant–mother relationship. *Child Development, 40,* 969–1025.

Ainsworth, M. D. S. (1982). Attachment: Retrospect and prospect. In C. M. Parkes & J. S. Hinde (Eds.), *The place of attachment in human behavior* (pp. 3–30). New York: Basic Books.

Ainsworth, M. D. S. (1985). Attachments across the life span. *Bulletin of the New York Academy of Medicine, 61,* 792–812.

Ainsworth, M. D. S., Blehar, M. C., Waters, E., & Wall, S. (1978). *Patterns of attachment: A psychological study of the Strange Situation.* Hillsdale, NJ: Erlbaum.

Altemeyer, B., & Hunsberger, B. (1992). Authoritarianism, religious fundamentalism, quest, and prejudice. *International Journal for the Psychology of Religion, 2,* 113–133.

Argyle, M., & Beit-Hallahmi, B. (1975). *The social psychology of religion.* London: Routledge & Kegan Paul.

Aronson, E., Stephan, C., Sikes, J., Blaney, N., & Snapp, M. (1978). *The jigsaw classroom.* Beverly Hills, CA: Sage.

Atran, S. (2002). *In gods we trust: The evolutionary landscape of religion.* Oxford, UK, and New York: Oxford University Press.

Atran, S., & Norenzayan, A. (in press). Religion's evolutionary landscape: Counterintuition, commitment, compassion, communion. *Behavioral and Brain Sciences.*

Averill, J. (1998). Spirituality: From the mundane to the meaningful—and back. *Journal of Theoretical and Philosophical Psychology, 18*, 101–126.

Avis, J., & Harris, P. L. (1991). Belief–desire reasoning among Baka children: Evidence for a universal conception of mind. *Child Development, 62*, 460–467.

Axelrod, R. (1984). *The evolution of cooperation*. New York: Basic Books.

Baillargeon, R. (1987). Young infants' reasoning about the physical and spatial characteristics of a hidden object. *Cognitive Development, 2*, 179–200.

Baillargeon, R., & Hanko-Summers, S. (1990). Is the object adequately supported by the bottom object?: Young infants' understanding of support relations. *Cognitive Development 5*, 29–54.

Badcock, C. R. (1986). *The problem of altruism*. Oxford, UK: Blackwell.

Baker, M., & Gorsuch, R. (1982). Trait anxiety and intrinsic–extrinsic religiousness. *Journal for the Scientific Study of Religion, 21*, 119–122.

Barker, E. (1989). *New religious movements: A practical introduction*. London: Her Majesty's Stationery Office.

Baron-Cohen, S. (1995). *Mindblindness: An essay on autism and theory of mind*. Cambridge, MA: MIT Press.

Barrett, J. L. (1998). Cognitive constraints on Hindu concepts of the divine. *Journal for the Scientific Study of Religion, 37*, 608–619.

Barrett, J. L. (2000). Exploring the natural foundations of religion. *Trends in Cognitive Science, 4*, 29–34.

Barrett, J. L., & Keil, F. (1996). Conceptualizing a non-natural entity: Anthropomorphism in God concepts. *Cognitive Psychology, 31*, 219–247.

Barrett, J. L., & Nyhof, M. (2001). Spreading nonnatural concepts. *Journal of Cognition and Culture, 1*, 69–100.

Bartholomew, K. (1990). Avoidance of intimacy: An attachment perspective. *Journal of Social and Personal Relationships, 7*, 147–178.

Bartholomew, K., & Horowitz, L. M. (1991). Attachment styles in young adults: A test of a four-category model. *Journal of Personality and Social Psychology, 61*, 226–244.

Batson, C. D. (1983). Sociobiology and the role of religion in promoting prosocial behavior: An alternative view. *Journal of Personality and Social Psychology, 45*, 1380–1385.

Batson, C. D. (1993). Communal and exchange relationships: What is the difference? *Personality and Social Psychology Bulletin, 19*, 677–683.

Batson, C. D., Schoenrade, P., & Ventis, W. L. (1993). *Religion and the individual: A social-psychological perspective*. New York: Oxford University Press.

Batson, C. D., & Ventis, W. L. (1982). *The religious experience: A social-psychological perspective*. New York: Oxford University Press.

Baumeister, R. F., & Leary, M. R. (1995). The need to belong: Desire for interpersonal attachments as a fundamental human motivation. *Psychological Bulletin, 117*, 497–529.

Bearon, L. B., & Koenig, H. G. (1990). Religious cognitions and use of prayer in health and illness. *Gerontologist, 30*, 249–253.

Becker, E. (1973). *The denial of death*. New York: Free Press.

Beit-Hallahmi, B. (1974). Psychology of religion: The rise and fall of a psychological movement. *Journal of the History of the Behavioural Sciences, 10*, 84–90.

Beit-Hallahmi, B. (1989). *Prolegomena to the psychology of religion*. Lewisburg, PA: Bucknell University Press.

Beit-Hallahmi, B. (1992). Between religious psychology and the psychology of religion. In M. Finn & J. Gartner (Eds.), *Object relations theory and religion: Clinical applications* (pp. 119–128). Westport, CT: Praeger.

Beit-Hallahmi, B., & Argyle, M. (1997). *The psychology of religious behaviour, belief and experience*. London: Routledge.

Belsky, J. (1997). Attachment, mating, and parenting: An evolutionary interpretation. *Human Nature, 8,* 361–381.

Belsky, J. (1999). Modern evolutionary theory and patterns of attachment. In J. Cassidy & P. R. Shaver (Eds.), *Handbook of attachment: Theory, research, and clinical applications* (pp. 141–161). New York: Guilford Press.

Benson, P., & Spilka, B. (1973). God image as a function of self-esteem and locus of control. *Journal for the Scientific Study of Religion, 12,* 297–310.

Benson, P. L., & Williams, D. L. (1982). *Religion on Capitol Hill: Myths and realities.* San Francisco: Harper & Row.

Berman, W. H., Marcus, L., & Berman, E. R. (1994). Attachment in marital relations. In M. B. Sperling & W. H. Berman (Eds.), *Attachment in adults: Theory, assessment, and treatment* (pp. 204–231). New York: Guilford Press.

Bernard, L. L. (1924). *Instinct.* New York: Holt.

Betzig, L. L. (1986). *Despotism and differential reproduction.* New York: Aldine.

Blackmore, S. J. (1999). *The meme machine.* Oxford, UK: Oxford University Press.

Boden, M. (1990). *The creative mind: Myths and mechanisms.* London: Wiedenfeld & Nicolson.

Bowlby, J. (1956). The growth of independence in the young child. *Royal Society of Health Journal, 76,* 587–591.

Bowlby, J. (1969). *Attachment and loss: Vol. 1. Attachment.* New York: Basic Books.

Bowlby, J. (1973). *Attachment and loss: Vol. 2. Separation.* New York: Basic Books.

Bowlby, J. (1980). *Attachment and loss: Vol. 3. Loss.* New York: Basic Books.

Boyd, R., & Richerson, P. J. (1985). *Culture and the evolutionary process.* Chicago: University of Chicago Press.

Boyd, R., & Richerson, P. J. (1992). Punishment allows the evolution of cooperation (or anything else) in sizable groups. *Ethology and Sociobiology, 13,* 171–195.

Boyer, P. (1994a). Cognitive constraints on cultural representations: Natural ontologies and religious ideas. In L. A. Hirschfeld & S. Gelman (Eds.), *Mapping the mind: Domain-specificity in culture and cognition* (pp. 391–411). New York: Cambridge University Press.

Boyer, P. (1994b). *The naturalness of religious ideas: A cognitive theory of religion.* Berkeley: University of California Press.

Boyer, P. (2001). *Religion explained: The evolutionary origins of religious thought.* New York: Basic Books.

Boyer, P., & Ramble, C. (2001). Cognitive templates for religious concepts. *Cognitive Science, 25,* 535–564.

Brennan, K. A., Clark, C. L., & Shaver, P. R. (1998). Self-report measurement of adult attachment: An integrative overview. In J. A. Simpson & W. S. Rholes (Eds.), *Attachment theory and close relationships* (pp. 46–76). New York: Guilford Press.

Brennan, K. A., & Shaver, P. R. (1995). Dimensions of adult attachment, affect regulation, and romantic relationship functioning. *Personality and Social Psychology Bulletin, 21,* 267–283.

Bretherton, I. (1985). Attachment theory: Retrospect and prospect. In I. Bretherton & E. Waters (Eds.), Growing points in attachment theory and research. *Monographs of the Society for Research in Child Development, 50*(1–2, Serial No. 209), 3–35.

Bretherton, I. (1987). New perspectives on attachment relations: Security, communication, and internal working models. In J. D. Osofsky (Ed.), *Handbook of infant development* (2nd ed., pp. 1061–1100). New York: Wiley.

Broen, W. E., Jr. (1957). A factor-analytic study of religious attitudes. *Journal of Abnormal and Social Psychology, 54*, 176–179.

Brown, D. E. (1991). *Human universals.* New York: McGraw-Hill.

Brown, S. L, Nesse, R. M., House, J. S., & Utz, R. (in press). Religion and emotional compensation: Results from a prospective study of widowhood. *Personality and Social Psychology Bulletin.*

Bruder, E. E. (1947). Some considerations of the loss of faith. *Journal of Clinical and Pastoral Work, 1*, 1–10.

Bullock, M. (1985). Animism in childhood thinking: A new look at an old question. *Developmental Psychology, 21*, 217–225.

Buri, J. R., & Mueller, R. A. (1993). Psychoanalytic theory and loving God concepts: Parent-referencing versus self-referencing. *Journal of Psychology, 127*, 17–27.

Burkert, W. (1996). *Creation of the sacred: Tracks of biology in early religions.* Cambridge, MA: Harvard University Press.

Buss, D. M. (1989). Sex differences in human mate preferences: Evolutionary hypotheses tested in 37 cultures. *Behavioral and Brain Sciences, 12*, 1–49.

Buss, D. M. (1992). Mate preference mechanisms: Consequences for partner choice and intrasexual competition. In J. H. Barkow, L. Cosmides, & J. Tooby (Eds.), *The adapted mind: Evolutionary psychology and the generation of culture* (pp. 249–288). New York: Oxford University Press.

Buss, D. M. (1995). Evolutionary psychology: A new paradigm for psychological science. *Psychological Inquiry, 6*, 1–30.

Buss, D. M. (2004). *Evolutionary psychology: The new science of the mind* (2nd ed.). Boston: Pearson.

Buss, D. M., & Greiling, H. (1999). Adaptive individual differences. *Journal of Personality, 67*, 209–243.

Buss, D. M., Haselton, M. G., Shackelford, T. K. Bleske, A. L., & Wakefield, J. C. (1998). Adaptations, exaptations, and spandrels. *American Psychologist, 53*, 533–548.

Buss, D. M., Larsen, R., Westen, D., & Semmelroth, J. (1992). Sex differences in jealousy: Evolution, physiology, and psychology. *Psychological Science, 3*, 251–255.

Buss, D. M., & Schmitt, D. P. (1993). Sexual strategies theory: An evolutionary perspective on human mating. *Psychological Review, 100*, 204–232.

Campbell, D. T. (1975). On the conflicts between biological and social evolution and between psychology and moral tradition. *American Psychologist, 30*, 1103–1126.

Campos, J. J., & Stenberg, C. (1981). Perception, appraisal, and emotional: The onset of social referencing. In M. E. Lamb & L. R. Sherrod (Eds.), *Infant social cognition: Empirical and theoretical considerations* (pp. 273-314). Hillsdale, NJ: Erlbaum.

Caplovitz, D., & Sherrow, D. (1977). *The religious drop-outs: Apostasy among college graduates.* Beverly Hills, CA: Sage.

Carpenter, E. M., & Kirkpatrick, L. A. (1996). Attachment style and presence of a romantic partner as moderators of psychophysiological responses to a stressful laboratory situation. *Personal Relationships, 3*, 351–367.

Carruthers, P., & Smith, P. K. (Eds.). (1996). *Theories of theories of mind.* Cambridge, UK: Cambridge University Press.

Caspi, A., & Bem, D. J. (1990). Personality continuity and change across the life course. In L. Pervin (Ed.), *Handbook of personality: Theory and research* (pp. 549–575). New York: Guilford Press.

Cassidy, J. (1999). The nature of the child's ties. In J. Cassidy & P. R. Shaver (Eds.), *Handbook of attachment: Theory, research, and clinical applications* (pp. 3–20). New York: Guilford Press.

Cassidy, J, & Shaver, P. R. (Eds.). (1999). *Handbook of attachment: Theory, research, and clinical applications.* New York: Guilford Press.

Caudill, W. (1958). *Effects of social and cultural systems in reactions to stress.* New York: Social Science Research Council.

Chagnon, N. A. (1983). *Yanomamo: The fierce people* (3rd ed.). New York: Holt, Reinhart, & Winston.

Chagnon, N. A. (1992). *Yanomamo: The last days of Eden.* San Diego, CA: Harcourt Brace Jovanovich.

Charnov, E. (1982). *The theory of sex allocation.* Princeton, NJ: Princeton University Press.

Chisolm, J. S. (1996). The evolutionary ecology of attachment organization. *Human Nature, 7*, 1–38.

Chomsky, N. (1957). *Syntactic structures.* The Hague: Mouton.

Clark, E. T. (1929). *The psychology of religious awakening.* New York: Macmillan.

Coe, G. A. (1916). *Psychology of religion.* Chicago: University of Chicago Press.

Collins, N. L., & Read, S. J. (1990). Adult attachment, working models, and relationship quality in dating couples. *Journal of Personality and Social Psychology, 58*, 644–663.

Collins, N. L., & Read, S. J. (1994). Cognitive representations of attachment: The structure and function of working models. In K. Bartholomew & D. Perlman (Eds.), *Advances in personal relationships: Vol. 5. Attachment processes in adulthood* (pp. 53–90). London: Kingsley.

Comstock, W. R. (1972). *The study of religion and primitive religions.* New York: Harper & Row.

Cosmides, L. (1989). The logic of social exchange: Has natural selection shaped how humans reason? Studies with the Wason selection task. *Cognition, 31*, 187–276.

Cosmides, L., & Tooby, J. (1987). From evolution to behavior: Evolutionary psychology as the missing link. In J. Dupre (Ed.), *The latest on the best: Essays on evolution and optimality* (pp. 277–306). Cambridge, MA: MIT Press.

Cosmides, L. & Tooby J. (1992). Cognitive adaptations for social exchange. In J.H. Barkow, L. Cosmides, & J. Tooby (Eds.), *The adapted mind: Evolutionary psychology and the generation of culture* (pp. 163–228). Oxford, UK: Oxford University Press.

Cosmides, L., & Tooby, J. (1994). Origins of domain specificity: The evolution of functional organization. In L. A. Hirschfeld & S. A. Gelman (Eds.), *Mapping the mind: Domain specificity in cognition and culture* (pp. 85–116). Cambridge, UK: Cambridge University Press.

Cox, E. (1967). *Sixth form religion.* London: SCM Press.

Crippen, T., & Machalek, R. (1989). The evolutionary foundations of the religious life. *International Review of Sociology*, 3, 61–84.

Crowell, J. A., Fraley, R. C., & Shaver, P. R. (1999). Measurement of individual differences in adolescent and adult attachment. In J. Cassidy & P. R. Shaver (Eds.), *Handbook of attachment: Theory, research, and clinical applications* (pp. 435–465). New York: Guilford Press.

Csikszentmihalyi, M. (1990). *Flow: The psychology of optimal experience*. New York: Harper & Row.

Curb, R., & Manahan, N. (Eds.). (1985). *Lesbian nuns: Breaking silence*. Tallahassee, FL: Naiad Press.

Cutrona, C. E., & Russell, D. (1987). The provisions of social relationships and adaptation to stress. In W. H. Jones & D. Perlman (Eds.), *Advances in personal relationships* (Vol. 1, pp. 37–67). Greenwich, CT: JAI Press.

Daly, M., Salmon, C., & Wilson, M. (1997). Kinship: The conceptual hole in psychological studies of social cognition and close relationships. In J. A. Simpson & D. T. Kenrick (Eds.), *Evolutionary social psychology* (pp. 265–296). Mahwah, NJ: Erlbaum.

Daly, M., & Wilson, M. (1987). The Darwinian psychology of discriminative parental solicitude. *Nebraska Symposium on Motivation*, 35, 91–144.

Daly, M., & Wilson, M. (1988). *Homicide*. Hawthorne, NY: Aldine de Gruyter.

Daly, M., & Wilson, M. (1998). *The truth about Cinderella: A Darwinian view of parental love*. London: Weidenfeld & Nicolson.

Daly, M., Wilson, M., & Weghorst, S. J. (1982). Male sexual jealousy. *Ethology and Sociobiology*, 3, 11–27.

Darwin, C. (1859). *On the origin of species by means of natural selection*. London: John Murray.

Dawkins, R. (1986). *The blind watchmaker*. New York: Norton.

Dawkins, R. (1989). *The selfish gene* (new ed.). New York: Oxford University Press. (Original work published 1976)

Dawkins, R. (1993). Viruses of the mind. *Free Inquiry*, 13(3), 34–41.

Deutsch, A. (1975). Observations of a sidewalk ashram. *Archives of General Psychiatry*, 32, 166–175.

Devine, P. G. (1989). Stereotypes and prejudice: Their automatic and controlled components. *Journal of Personality and Social Psychology*, 56, 518.

de Waal, F. (1982). *Chimpanzee politics: Power and sex among apes*. Baltimore: Johns Hopkins University Press.

DeWolff, M., & van IJzendoorn, M. (1997). Sensitivity and attachment: A meta-analysis on parental antecedents of infant attachment. *Child Development*, 68, 571–591.

Diamond, J. (1992). *The third chimpanzee: The evolution and future of the human animal*. New York: HarperCollins.

Diamond, J. (1997). *Guns, germs, and steel*. New York: Norton.

Dickie, J. R., Eshleman, A. K., Merasco, D. M., Shepard, A., Vander Wilt, M., & Johnson, M. (1997). Parent–child relationships and children's images of God. *Journal for the Scientific Study of Religion*, 36, 25–43

Donahue, M. J. (1995). Catholicism and religious experience. In R. W. Hood, Jr. (Ed.), *Handbook of religious experience* (pp. 30–48). Birmingham, AL: Religious Education Press.

Donahue, M. J., & Benson, P. L. (1995). Religion and the well-being of adolescents. *Journal of Social Issues*, 51, 145–160.

Draper, P., & Belsky, J. (1990). Personality development in evolutionary perspective. *Journal of Personality, 58*, 141–161.

Draper, P., & Harpending, H. (1982). Father absence and reproductive strategy: An evolutionary perspective. *Journal of Anthropological Research, 38*, 255–273.

Draper, P., & Harpending, H. (1988). A sociobiological perspective on the development of human reproductive strategies. In K. MacDonald (Ed.), *Sociobiological perspectives on human development* (pp. 340–372). New York: Springer-Verlag.

Duke, E. H. (1977). *Meaning in life and acceptance of death in terminally ill patients.* Unpublished doctoral dissertation, Northwestern University, Evanston, IL.

Durkheim, E. (1912). *The elementary forms of religious life.* New York: Free Press.

Egeland, B. & Sroufe, L. A. (1981). Attachment and early maltreatment. *Child Development, 52*, 44–52.

Elkind, D. (1971). The development of religious understanding in children and adolescents. In M. Strommen (Ed.), *Research on religious development* (pp. 655–685). New York: Hawthorn.

Ellis, B. J. (1992). The evolution of sexual attraction: Evaluative mechanisms in women. In J. H. Barkow, L. Cosmides, & J. Tooby (Eds.), *The adapted mind* (pp. 267–288). New York: Oxford University Press.

Ellis, B. J., & Garber, J. (2000). Psychosocial antecedents of variation in girls' pubertal timing: Maternal depression, stepfather presence, and marital and family stress. *Child Development, 71*, 485–501.

Ellis, B. J., McFadyen-Ketchum, S., Dodge, K. A., Pettit, G. S., & Bates, J. E. (1999). Quality of early family relationships and individual differences in the timing of pubertal maturation in girls: A longitudinal test of an evolutionary model. *Journal of Personality and Social Psychology, 77*, 387–401.

Emmons, R. A., & Paloutzian, R. F. (2003). The psychology of religion. *Annual Review of Psychology, 54*, 377–402.

Entner, P. (1977). Religious orientation and mental health. *Dissertation Abstracts International, 38*(4–B), 1949.

Epstein, S. (1994). Integration of the cognitive and the psychodynamic unconscious. *American Psychologist, 49*, 709–724.

Ethridge, F. M., & Feagin, J. R. (1979). Varieties of "fundamentalism": A conceptual and empirical analysis of two Protestant denominations. *Sociological Quarterly, 20* (Winter), 37–48.

Evans, J. St. B. T. (1989). *Bias in human reasoning: Causes and consequences.* London: Erlbaum.

Evans, J. St. B. T., & Over, D. E. (1996). *Rationality and reasoning.* Hove, UK: Psychology Press.

Evans-Pritchard, E. E. (1956). *Nuer religion.* New York: Oxford University Press.

Feeney, B. C., & Kirkpatrick, L. A. (1996). The effects of adult attachment and presence of romantic partners on physiological responses to stress. *Journal of Personality and Social Psychology, 70*, 255–270.

Feeney, J. A. (1999). Adult romantic attachment and couple relationships. In J. Cassidy & P. R. Shaver (Eds.), *Handbook of attachment: Theory, research, and clinical applications* (pp. 355–377). New York: Guilford Press.

Feeney, J. A., & Noller, P. (1996). *Adult attachment.* Thousand Oaks, CA: Sage.

Feeney, J. A., Noller, P., & Patty, J. (1993). Adolescents' interactions with the opposite sex: Influence of attachment style and gender. *Journal of Adolescence, 16*, 169–186.

Feist, G. J. (1998). A meta-analysis of the impact of personality on scientific and artistic creativity. *Personality and Social Psychological Review, 2*, 290–309.

Feist, G. J. (in press). *The origins of science: An introduction to the psychology of science.* New Haven, CT: Yale University Press.

Feist, G. J., & Gorman, M. E. (1998). Psychology of science: Review and integration of a nascent discipline. *Review of General Psychology, 2*, 3–47.

Ferm, V. (1945). *The encyclopedia of religion.* Secaucus, NJ: Poplar.

Fisek, M. H., & Ofshe, R. (1970). The process of status evolution. *Sociometry, 33,* 327–346.

Fisher, R. A. (1930). *The genetical theory of natural selection.* Oxford, UK: Clarendon.

Fiske, S. T., & Neuberg, S. L. (1990). A continuum of impression formation, from category based to individuating processes: Influences of information and motivation on attention and interpretation. In M. P. Zanna (Ed.), *Advances in experimental social psychology* (Vol. 23, pp. 1–74). San Diego, CA: Academic Press.

Flakoll, D. A. (1974, October). *Self esteem, psychological adjustment, and images of God.* Paper presented at the Meeting of the Society for the Scientific Study of Religion, Washington, DC.

Fonagy, P., Steele, H., & Steele, M. (1991). Maternal representations of attachment during pregnancy predict the organization of infant–mother attachment at one year of age. *Child Development, 62,* 891–905.

Fox, N. A., Kimmerly, N. L., & Schafer, W. D. (1991). Attachment to mother/attachment to father: A meta-analysis. *Child Development, 62,* 210–225.

Frank, R. H. (1988). *Passions within reason: The strategic role of the emotions.* New York: Norton.

Frazer, J. (1935). *The golden bough: A study in magic and religion.* New York: Macmillan. (Original work published 1890)

Fredrickson, B. L. (1998). What good are positive emotions? *Review of General Psychology, 2,* 300–319.

Freud, S. (1961). *The future of an illusion.* New York: Norton. (Original work published 1927)

Galanter, M. (1978). The "relief effect": A sociobiological model for neurotic distress and large-group therapy. *American Journal of Psychiatry, 135,* 588.

Galanter, M. (1979). The "Moonies": A psychological study of conversion and membership in a contemporary religious sect. *American Journal of Psychiatry, 136*(2), 165–170.

Galanter, M. (1980). Psychological induction into the larger group: Findings from a modern religious sect. *American Journal of Psychiatry, 137,* 1574–1579.

Galanter, M. (1989). *Cults: Faith, healing, and coercion.* New York: Oxford University Press.

Gallup, G., Jr., & Castelli, J. (1989). *The people's religion: American faith in the 90's.* New York: Macmillan.

Gallup, G., Jr., & Jones, S. (1989). *One hundred questions and answers: Religion in America.* Princeton, NJ: Princeton Religious Research Center.

Garcia, J., Ervin, F. R., & Koelling, R. A. (1966). Learning with prolonged delay of reinforcement. *Psychonomic Science, 5,* 121–122.

Gardner, H. (1983). *Frames of mind: The theory of multiple intelligences.* New York: Basic Books.

Gelman, R., Spelke, E. S., & Meck, E. (1983). What preschoolers know about animate and inanimate objects. In D. Rogers & J. A. Sloboda (Eds.), *The acquisition of symbolic skills* (pp. 297–326). New York: Plenum Press.

Gelman, S. A., Coley, J. D., & Gottfried, G. M. (1994). Essentialist beliefs in children: The acquisition of concepts and theories. In L. Hirschfeld & S. Gelman (Eds.), *Mapping the mind: Domain specificity in cognition and culture* (pp. 341–365). Cambridge, UK: Cambridge University Press.

Gelman, S. A, & Markman, E. M. (1986). Categories and induction in young children. *Cognition, 23,* 183–209.

George, C., & Solomon, J. (1999). Attachment and caregiving: The caregiving behavioral system. In J. Cassidy & P. R. Shaver (Eds.), *Handbook of attachment: Theory, research, and clinical applications* (pp. 649–670). New York: Guilford Press.

Gibbs, H. W., & Achterberg-Lawlis, J. (1978). Spiritual values and death anxiety: Implications for counseling with terminal cancer patients. *Journal of Counseling Psychology, 25,* 563–569.

Gigerenzer, G., & Regier, T. (1996). How do we tell an association from a rule? Comment on Sloman (1996). *Psychological Bulletin, 119,* 23–26.

Gillespie, V. B. (1991). *The dynamics of religious conversion.* Birmingham, AL: Religious Education Press.

Gilovich, T. (1991). *How we know what isn't so: The fallibility of human reasoning in everyday life.* New York: Free Press.

Gilovich, T ., & Savitsky, K. (1996). Like goes with like: The role of representativeness in erroneous and pseudoscientific beliefs. *Skeptical Inquirer, 20,* 34–40.

Glantz, K., & Pearce, J. (1989). *Exiles from Eden: Psychotherapy from an evolutionary perspective.* New York: Norton.

Godin, A., & Hallez, M. (1965). Parental images and divine paternity. In A. Godin (Ed.), *From religious experience to a religious attitude* (pp. 65–96). Chicago: Loyola University Press.

Goldman, R. (1964). *Religious thinking from childhood to adolescence.* New York: Seabury.

Goodall, J. (1986). *The chimpanzees of Gombe: Patterns of behavior.* Cambridge, MA: Belknap Press.

Gorsuch, R. L. (1968). The conceptualization of God as seen in adjective ratings. *Journal for the Scientific Study of Religion, 7,* 56–64.

Gorsuch, R. L. (1984). Measurement: The boon and bane of investigating religion. *American Psychologist, 39,* 228–236.

Gorsuch, R. L. (1994). Toward motivational theories of intrinsic religious commitment. *Journal for the Scientific Study of Religion, 33,* 315–325.

Gorsuch, R. L. (1995). Religious aspects of substance abuse and recovery. *Journal of Social Issues, 51*(2), 65–83.

Gould, S. J. (1980). *The panda's thumb.* New York: Norton.

Gould, S. J. (1991). Exaptation: A crucial tool for evolutionary psychology. *Journal of Social Issues, 47,* 43-65.

Graham, B. (1984). *Peace with God.* Nashville: Word Publishing.

Granqvist, P. (1998). Religiousness and perceived childhood attachment: On the question of compensation or correspondence. *Journal for the Scientific Study of Religion, 37,* 350–367.

Granqvist, P. (2002a). Attachment and religion: An integrative developmental framework. Acta Universitatis Upsaliensis. *Comprehensive Summaries of Uppsala Dissertations from the Faculty of Social Sciences, 116.*

Granqvist, P. (2002b). Attachment and religiosity in adolescence: Crosssectional and longitudinal evaluations. *Personality and Social Psychology Bulletin, 28,* 260–270.

Granqvist, P. (in press). Attachment theory and religious conversions: A review, and a resolution of the classic and contemporary paradigm chasm. *Review of Religious Research.*

Granqvist, P., & Hagekull, B. (1999). Religiousness and perceived childhood attachment: Profiling socialized correspondence and emotional compensation. *Journal for the Scientific Study of Religion, 38,* 254–273.

Granqvist, P., & Hagekull, B. (2000). Religiosity, adult attachment, and why "singles" are more religious. *International Journal for the Psychology of Religion, 10,* 110–124.

Granqvist, P., & Hagekull, B. (2001). Seeking security in the new age: On attachment and emotional compensation. *Journal for the Scientific Study of Religion, 40,* 529–547.

Granqvist, P., & Hagekull, B. (2003). Longitudinal predictions of religious change in adolescence: Contributions from the interaction of attachment and relationship status. *Journal of Social and Personal Relationships, 20,* 793–817.

Granqvist, P., & Kirkpatrick, L. A. (in press). Religious conversion and perceived childhood attachment: A meta-analysis. *International Journal for the Psychology of Religion.*

Greeley, A. (1972). *The denominational society: A sociological approach to religion in America.* Glenview, IL: Scott, Foresman.

Greeley, A. (1977). *The Mary myth: On the femininity of God.* New York: Seabury.

Greeley, A. (1981). *The religious imagination.* New York: Sadlier.

Greeley, A. (1990). *The Catholic myth: The behavior and beliefs of American Catholics.* New York: Scribner's.

Gross, M. R. (1996). Alternative reproductive strategies and tactics: Diversity within sexes. *Trends in Ecology and Evolution, 11,* 92–109.

Gross, P. R., & Levitt, N. (1994). *Higher superstition: The academic left and its quarrel with science.* Baltimore: Johns Hopkins University Press.

Guthrie, S. G. (1993). *Faces in the clouds: A new theory of religion.* New York: Oxford University Press.

Hall, G. S. (1904). *Adolescence* (Vols. 1 & 2). New York: Appleton.

Hamilton, W. D. (1964). The evolution of social behavior. *Journal of Theoretical Biology, 7,* 1–52.

Hammond, K. R. (1996). *Human judgment and social policy.* New York: Oxford University Press.

Hardin, G. (1968). The tragedy of the commons. *Science, 162,* 1243–1248.

Hardy, A. (1966). *The divine flame.* London: Collins.

Harlow, H. F. (1958). The nature of love. *American Psychologist, 13,* 673–685.

Harms, E. (1944). The development of religious experience in children. *Journal of Sociology, 50,* 112–122.

Hartung, J. (1995). Love thy neighbor: The evolution of in-group morality. *Skeptic, 3*(4), 86–99.

Haselton, M. G. (2003). The sexual overperception bias: Evidence of a systematic bias in men from a survey of naturally occurring events. *Journal of Research in Personality, 37,* 34–47.

Haselton, M. G. & Buss, D. M. (2000). Error management theory: A new perspective on biases in cross-sex mind reading. *Journal of Personality and Social Psychology, 78*, 81–91.

Haselton, M. G., & Buss, D. M. (2003). Biases in social judgment: Design flaws or design features? In J. P. Forgas, K. D. Williams, & W. H. von Hippel (Eds.), *Social judgments: Implicit and explicit processes* (pp. 23–43). New York: Cambridge University Press.

Haun, D. L. (1977). Perception of the bereaved, clergy, and funeral directors concerning bereavement. *Dissertation Abstracts International, A37*, 6791A.

Hay, D. (1994). "The biology of God": What is the current status of Hardy's hypothesis? *International Journal for the Psychology of Religion, 4*, 1–23.

Hazan, C., & Shaver, P. (1987). Romantic love conceptualized as an attachment process. *Journal of Personality and Social Psychology, 52*, 511–524.

Hazan, C., & Shaver, P. (1994). Attachment as an organizational framework for research on close relationships. *Psychological Inquiry, 5*, 1–22.

Hazan, C., & Zeifman, D. (1999). Pair bonds as attachments: Evaluating the evidence. In J. Cassidy & P. R. Shaver (Eds.), *Handbook of attachment: Theory, research, and clinical applications* (pp. 336–354). New York: Guilford Press.

Hazan, C., Zeifman, D., & Middleton, K. (1994, July). *Attachment and sexuality.* Paper presented at the 7th International Conference on Personal Relationships, Groningen, The Netherlands.

Heider, F., & Simmel, M. (1944). An experimental study of apparent behavior. *American Journal of Psychology, 57*, 243–259.

Heiler, F. (1932). *Prayer.* New York: Oxford University Press.

Heller, D. (1986). *The children's God.* Chicago: University of Chicago Press.

Henrich, J., & GilWhite, F. J. (2001). The evolution of prestige: Freely conferred deference as a mechanism for enhancing the benefits of cultural transmission. *Evolution and Human Behavior, 22*, 165–196.

Hesse, E. (1999). The Adult Attachment Interview: Historical and current perspectives. In J. Cassidy & P. R. Shaver (Eds.), *Handbook of attachment: Theory, research, and clinical applications* (pp. 395–433). New York: Guilford Press.

Hiebert, P. G. (1992). Conversion in Hinduism and Buddhism. In H. N. Malony and S. Southard (Eds.), *Handbook of religious conversion* (pp. 9–21). Birmingham, AL: Religious Education Press.

Hill, P. C., Pargament, K. I., Hood, R. W., Jr., McCullough, M. E., Swyers, J. P., Larson, D. B., & Zinnbauer, B. J. (2000). Conceptualizing religion and spirituality: Points of commonality, points of departure. *Journal for the Theory of Social Behavior, 30*, 51–77.

Hinde, R. A. (1979). *Towards understanding relationships.* London: Academic Press.

Hinde, R. A. (1982). Attachment: Some conceptual and biological issues. In C. M. Parkes & J. Stevenson-Hinde (Eds.), *The place of attachment in human behavior* (pp. 60–76). New York: Basic Books.

Hine, V. H. (1969). Pentecostal glossolalia: Toward a functional interpretation. *Journal for the Scientific Study of Religion, 8*, 211–226.

Hirschfeld, L. A. (1994). Is the acquisition of social categories based on domain-specific competence or on knowledge transfer? In L. Hirschfeld & S. Gelman (Eds.), *Mapping the mind: Domain specificity in cognition and culture* (pp. 201–233). Cambridge, UK: Cambridge University Press.

Hood, R. W., Jr. (1994). Psychology and religion. In V. S. Ramachandran (Ed.), *Encyclopaedia of human behavior* (Vol. 3, pp. 619–629). New York: Academic Press.

Hood, R. W., Jr., Spilka, B., Hunsberger, B., & Gorsuch, R. (1996). *The psychology of religion: An empirical approach* (2nd ed.). New York: Guilford Press.

Hrdy, S. B. (1999). *Mother Nature: Maternal instincts and how they shape the human species.* New York: Ballantine.

Hubel, D. H., & Wiesel, T. N. (1965). Binocular interaction in striate cortex of kittens reared with artificial squint. *Journal of Neurophysiology, 28,* 1041–1059.

Hughes, P. J. (1989). *The Australian clergy: Report from the combined churches survey for faith and mission.* Melbourne, Australia: Acorn Press.

Humphrey, N. (1976). The social function of intellect. In P. P. G. Bateson & R. A. Hinde (Eds.), *Growing points in ethology* (pp. 303–317). Cambridge, UK: Cambridge University Press.

Humphrey, N. (1984). *Consciousness regained.* Oxford, UK: Oxford University Press.

Hunsberger, B. (1995). Religion and prejudice: The role of religious fundamentalism, quest, and right-wing authoritarianism. *Journal of Social Issues, 51*(2), 113–129.

Hunt, R. A., & King, M. B. (1978). Religiosity and marriage. *Journal for the Scientific Study of Religion, 17,* 399–406.

Hyde, K. E. (1990). *Religion in childhood and adolescence: A comprehensive review of the research.* Birmingham, AL: Religious Education Press.

Jackendoff, R. (1994). *Patterns in the mind: Language and human nature.* New York: Basic Books.

James, W. (1902). *Varieties of religious experience.* New York: Longmans, Green.

Jenkins, R., & Pargament, K. I. (1988). Cognitive appraisals in cancer patients. *Social Science and Medicine, 26,* 625–633.

Johnson, P. E. (1945). *Psychology of religion.* New York: Abingdon-Cokesbury.

Johnson, P. E. (1959). Conversion. *Pastoral Psychology, 10,* 51–56.

Jolley, J. C. (1983, April). *Self-reg:arding: attitudes and conceptions of deity: A comparative study.* Paper presented at the Meeting of the Rocky Mountain Psychological Association, Snowbird, UT.

Jones, S. L. (1994). A constructive relationship for religion with the science and profession of psychology: Perhaps the boldest model yet. *American Psychologist, 49,* 184–199.

Jubis, R. (1991). *An attachment-theoretical approach to understanding children's conceptions of God.* Unpublished doctoral dissertation, University of Denver, Denver, CO.

Kagan, J. (1982). *Psychological research on the human infant: An evaluative summary.* New York: W. T. Grant Foundation.

Kagan, J. (1984). *The nature of the child.* New York: Basic Books.

Kahneman, D., Slovic, P., & Tversky, A. (Eds.). (1982). *Judgment under uncertainty: Heuristics and biases.* Cambridge, UK: Cambridge University Press.

Kahoe, R. D. (1974). Personality and achievement correlates of intrinsic and extrinsic religious orientations. *Journal of Personality and Social Psychology, 29,* 812-818.

Kahoe, R. D., & Dunn, R. F. (1975). The fear of death and religious attitudes and behavior. *Journal for the Scientific Study of Religion, 14,* 379–382.

Kalma, A. (1991). Hierarchisation and dominance assessment at first glance. *European Journal of Social Psychology, 21,* 165–181.

Karmiloff-Smith, A. (1992). *Beyond modularity: A developmental perspective on the cognitive sciences*. Cambridge, MA: MIT Press.

Kaufman, G. D. (1981). *The theological imagination: Constructing the concept of God*. Philadelphia: Westminster.

Keil, F. C. (1986). The acquisition of natural kind and artifact terms. In W. Demopoulos and A. Marras (Eds.), *Language learning and concept acquisition: Foundational issues* (pp. 133–153). Norwood, NJ: Ablex.

Keil, F. C. (1989). *Concepts, kinds, and cognitive development*. Cambridge, MA: MIT Press.

Kelley, D.M. (1972). *Why conservative churches are growing*. New York: Harper & Row.

Ketelaar, T., & Ellis, B. J. (2000). Are evolutionary explanations unfalsifiable? Evolutionary psychology and the Lakatosian philosophy of science. *Psychological Inquiry, 11*, 1–21.

Kildahl, J. P. (1972). *The psychology of speaking in tongues*. New York: Harper & Row.

Kirkpatrick, L. A. (1989). A psychometric analysis of the Allport-Ross and Feagin measures of intrinsic–extrinsic religiousness. In M. Lynn & D. Moberg (Eds.), *Research in the social scientific study of religion* (Vol. 1, pp. 1–31). Greenwich, CT: JAI Press.

Kirkpatrick, L. A. (1992). An attachment-theoretical approach to the psychology of religion. *International Journal for the Psychology of Religion, 2*(1), 3–28.

Kirkpatrick, L. A. (1993). Fundamentalism, Christian orthodoxy, and intrinsic religious orientation as predictors of discriminatory attitudes. *Journal for the Scientific Study of Religion, 32*, 256–268.

Kirkpatrick, L. A. (1996). New developments in adult attachment: A call for re-Bowlbyization [Review of *Attachment in adults: Clinical and developmental perspectives*, ed. by M. B. Sperling & W. H. Berman, and *Patterns of relating: An adult attachment perspective*, by M. L. West & A. E. Sheldon-Keller]. *Contemporary Psychology, 41*, 811–813.

Kirkpatrick, L. A. (1997). A longitudinal study of changes in religious belief and behavior as a function of individual differences in adult attachment style. *Journal for the Scientific Study of Religion, 36*, 207–217.

Kirkpatrick, L. A. (1998a). Evolution, pair-bonding, and reproductive strategies: A reconceptualization of adult attachment. In J. A. Simpson & W. S. Rholes (Eds.), *Attachment theory and close relationships* (pp. 353–393). New York: Guilford Press.

Kirkpatrick, L. A. (1998b). God as a substitute attachment figure: A longitudinal study of adult attachment style and religious change in college students. *Personality and Social Psychology Bulletin, 24*, 961–973.

Kirkpatrick, L. A. (1999a). Attachment and religious representations and behavior. In J. Cassidy & P. R. Shaver (Eds.), *Handbook of attachment: Theory, research, and clinical applications* (pp. 803–822). New York: Guilford Press.

Kirkpatrick, L. A. (1999b). Toward an evolutionary psychology of religion. *Journal of Personality, 67*, 921–952.

Kirkpatrick, L. A. (in press). The evolutionary social psychology of religious beliefs [commentary on Atran & Norenzayan]. *Behavioral and Brain Sciences*.

Kirkpatrick, L. A., & Davis, K. E. (1994). Attachment style, gender, and relationship stability: A longitudinal analysis. *Journal of Personality and Social Psychology, 66*, 502–512.

Kirkpatrick, L. A., & Ellis, B. J. (2001). An evolutionary approach to self-esteem: Multiple domains and multiple functions. In G. J. O. Fletcher & M. S. Clark (Eds.), *The*

Blackwell handbook of social psychology: Vol. 2. Interpersonal processes (pp. 411–436). Oxford, UK: Blackwell.

Kirkpatrick, L. A., & Hazan, C. (1994). Attachment styles and close relationships: A four-year prospective study. *Personal Relationships, 1*, 123–142.

Kirkpatrick, L. A., & Hood, R. W., Jr. (1990). Intrinsic–extrinsic religious orientation: The "boon" or "bane" of contemporary psychology of religion? *Journal for the Scientific Study of Religion, 29*, 442–462.

Kirkpatrick, L. A., & Shaver, P. R. (1990). Attachment theory and religion: Childhood attachments, religious beliefs, and conversion. *Journal for the Scientific Study of Religion, 29*, 315–334.

Kirkpatrick, L. A., & Shaver, P. R. (1992). An attachment-theoretical approach to romantic love and religious belief. *Personality and Social Psychology Bulletin, 18*, 266–275.

Kirkpatrick, L. A., Waugh, C. E., Valencia, A., & Webster, G. D. (2002). The functional domain-specificity of self-esteem and the differential prediction of aggression. *Journal of Personality and Social Psychology, 82*, 756–767.

Knight, N., Barrett, J., Atran, S., & Ucan Ek', E. (2001, October). *Understanding the mind of God.* Paper presented at the annual meeting of the Society for the Scientific Study of Religion, Columbus, OH.

Kobak, R. (1999). The emotional dynamics of disruptions in attachment relationships: Implications for theory, research, and clinical intervention. In J. Cassidy & P. R. Shaver (Eds.), *Handbook of attachment: Theory, research, and clinical applications* (pp. 21–43). New York: Guilford Press.

Kox, W., Meeus, W., & Hart, H. (1991). Religious conversion of adolescents: Testing the Lofland and Stark model of religious conversion. *Sociological Analysis, 52*, 227–240.

Krol, J. (1982). [Young people's image of father and its influence on their image of God.] *Roczniki Filozoficzne: Psychologia, 30*, 73–103.

Kuhn, T. (1962). *The structure of scientific revolutions.* Chicago: University of Chicago Press.

Kurzban, R., Tooby, J., & Cosmides, L. (1995, June). *Detecting coalitions: Evolutionary psychology and social categorization.* Paper presented at the Human Behavior and Evolution Society Conference, Santa Barbara, CA.

Kurzban, R., Tooby, J., & Cosmides, L. (2001). Can race be erased? Coalitional computation and social categorization. *Proceedings of the National Academy of Sciences, 98*(26) 15387–15392.

Kushner, H. S. (1981). *When bad things happen to good people.* New York: Shocken Books.

Lamb, M., Thompson, R., Gardner, W., & Charnov, E. (1985). *Infant–mother attachment: The origins and developmental significance of individual differences in Strange Situation behavior.* Hillsdale, NJ: Erlbaum.

Lamb, M. E. (1978). Qualitative aspects of mother– and father–infant attachments. *Infant Behavior and Development, 1*, 265–275.

Lambert, W. W., Triandis, L. M., & Wolf, M. (1959). Some correlates of beliefs in the malevolence and benevolence of supernatural beings: A cross-societal study. *Journal of Abnormal and Social Psychology, 58*, 162–169.

Laythe, B., Finkel, D., Bringle, R., & Kirkpatrick, L. A. (2002). Religious fundamentalism as a predictor of prejudice: A two-component model. *Journal for the Scientific Study of Religion, 41*, 623–635.

Laythe, B., Finkel, D., & Kirkpatrick, L. A. (2001). Predicting prejudice from religious fundamentalism and right-wing authoritarianism: A multiple-regression approach. *Journal for the Scientific Study of Religion, 40*, 1–10.

Leary, M. R., Tambor, E. S., Terdal, S. K., & Downs, D. L. (1995). Self-esteem as an interpersonal monitor: The sociometer hypothesis. *Journal of Personality and Social Psychology, 68*, 518–530.

Le Bon, G. (1903). *The crowd.* London: Fisher Unwin.

Lehmann, A. C., & Myers, J. E. (1993). Ghosts, souls, and ancestors: Power of the dead. In A. C. Lehmann & J. E. Myers (Eds.), *Magic, witchcraft, and religion* (pp. 283–286). Mountain View, CA: Mayfield.

Leinhardt, G. (1961). *Divinity and experience.* New York: Oxford University Press.

Lerner, M. J. (1980). *Belief in a just world.* New York: Plenum Press.

Leslie, A. (1994). ToMM, ToBy, and Agency: Core architecture and domain specificity. In L. Hirschfeld & S. Gelman (Eds.), *Mapping the mind: Domain specificity in cognition and culture* (pp. 119–148). Cambridge, UK: Cambridge University Press.

Leslie, A., & Frith, U. (1987). Meta-representation and autism: How not to lose one's marbles. *Cognition, 27*, 291–294.

Leslie, A., & Keeble, S. (1987). Do six-months-old infants perceive causality? *Cognition, 25*, 265–288.

Lindenthal, J. J., Myers, J. K., Pepper, M. P., & Stern, M. S. (1970). Mental status and religious behavior. *Journal for the Scientific Study of Religion, 9*, 266–268.

Lofland, J., & Stark, R. (1965). Becoming a world-saver: A theory of conversion to a deviant perspective. *American Sociological Review, 30*, 862–875.

Lorenz, K. E. (1935). Der Kumpan in der Umvelt des Vogels [Companionship in bird life]. *Journal of Ornithology, 83*, 137–213

Lorenz, K. E. (1952). *King Solomon's ring: New light on animal ways.* New York: Crowell.

Loveland, G. G. (1968). The effects of bereavement on certain religious attitudes. *Sociological Symposium, 1*, 17–27.

Luhtanen, R., & Crocker, J. (1992). A collective self-esteem scale: Self-evaluation of one's social identity. *Personality and Social Psychology Bulletin, 18*, 302–318.

Lumsden, C. J. & Wilson, E. O. (1981). *Genes, mind, and culture: The coevolutionary process.* Cambridge, MA: Harvard University Press.

Maccoby, E. E., & Martin, J. A. (1983). Socialization in the context of the family: Parent-child interaction. In E. M. Hetherington (Ed.), *Handbook of child psychology* (4th ed., Vol. 4, pp. 1–101). New York: Wiley.

Maccoby, E. E., & Masters, J. C. (1970). Attachment and dependency. In P. H. Mussen (Ed.), *Carmichael's manual of child psychology* (Vol. 2, 3rd ed., pp. 73–157). New York: Wiley.

Main, M., Kaplan, N., & Cassidy, J. (1985). Security in infancy, childhood, and adulthood: A move to the level of representation. In I. Bretherton & E. Waters (Eds.), Growing points of attachment theory and research. *Monographs of the Society for Research in Child Development, 50*(1–2, Serial No. 209), 66–104.

Main, M., & Solomon, J. (1990). Procedures for identifying infants as disorganized/disoriented during the Ainsworth strange situation. In M. T. Greenberg, D. Cicchetti, & E. M. Cummings (Eds.), *Attachment in the preschool years* (pp. 121–160). Chicago: University of Chicago Press.

Marx, K. (1972). Religion and authority. In F. Bender (Ed.), *Karl Marx: The essential writings*. New York: Harper. (Original work published 1842)

Maslow, A. H. (1963). Lessons from the peak experiences. *Journal of Humanistic Psychology, 68*, 111–124.

Matas, L., Arend, R. A., & Sroufe, L. A. (1978). Continuity of adaptation in the second year: The relationship between quality of attachment and later competence. *Child Development, 49*, 547–556.

Mattlin, J. A., Wethington, E., & Kessler, R. C. (1990). Situational determinants of coping and coping effectiveness. *Journal of Health and Social Behavior, 31*, 103–122.

McClain, E. W. (1978). Personality differences between intrinsically religious and nonreligious students: A factor analytic study. *Journal of Personality Assessment, 42*, 159–166.

McClenon, J. (1997). Shamanic healing, human evolution, and the origin of religion. *Journal for the Scientific Study of Religion, 36*, 345–354.

McCullough, M. E., Pargament, K. I., & Thoreson, C. E. (Eds.). (2000). *Forgiveness: Theory, research, and practice*. New York: Guilford Press.

Mealey, L. (1995). The sociobiology of sociopathy: An integrated evolutionary model. *Behavioral and Brain Sciences, 18*, 523–599.

Medin, D., & Ortony, A. (1989). Psychological essentialism. In S. Vosniadou & A. Ortony (Eds.), *Similarity and analogical reasoning* (pp. 179–195). Cambridge, UK: Cambridge University Press.

Mellen, S. L. W. (1981). *The evolution of love*. New York: Freeman.

Miller, A. S., & Hoffman, J. P. (1995). Risk and religion: An explanation of gender differences in religiosity. *Journal for the Scientific Study of Religion, 34*, 63–75.

Miller, G. F. (2000). *The mating mind: How sexual choice shaped the evolution of human nature*. New York: Doubleday.

Miller, L., & Fishkin, S. (1997). On the dynamics of human bonding and reproductive success. In J. Simpson & D. Kenrick (Eds.), *Evolutionary social psychology* (pp. 86–101). Mahwah, NJ: Erlbaum.

Mineka, S. (1992). Evolutionary memories, emotional processing, and the emotional disorders. *Psychology of Learning and Motivation, 28*, 161–206.

Minsky, M. (1985). *The society of mind*. New York: Simon & Schuster.

Mithen, S. (1996). *The prehistory of the mind: A search for the origins of art, religion, and science*. London: Thames & Hudson.

Moller, H. (1965). Affective mysticism in Western civilization. *Psychoanalytic Review, 52*, 259–274.

Myers, D. G. (1992). *The pursuit of happiness*. New York: Morrow.

Nelsen, H. M., Cheek, N. H., Jr., & Au, P. (1985). Gender differences in images of God. *Journal for the Scientific Study of Religion, 24*, 396–402.

Nelson, M. O. (1971). The concept of God and feelings toward parents. *Journal of Individual Psychology, 27*, 46–49.

Nelson, M. O., & Jones, E. M. (1957). An application of the Q-technique to the study of religious concepts. *Psychological Reports, 3*, 293–297.

Nesse, R. M., & Williams, G. C. (1994). *Why we get sick: The new science of Darwinian medicine*. New York: Times Books.

Norenzayan, A., & Atran, AS. (2003). Cognitive and emotional processes in cultural transmission of natural and nonnatural beliefs. In M. Schaller & C. Crandall (Eds.), *The psychological foundations of culture* (pp. 149–169). Mahwah, NJ: Erlbaum.

Oates, W. E. (1967). A Sociopsychological study of glossolalia. In F. Stagg, E. G. Hinson, & W. E. Oates (Eds.), *Glossolalia: Tongue speaking in biblical, historical, and psychological perspective* (pp. 76–99). New York: Abingdon.

O'Brien, M. E. (1982). Religious faith and adjustment to longterm hemodialysis. *Journal of Religion and Health, 21*, 68–80.

Paden, W. E. (1988). *Religious worlds: The comparative study of religion.* Boston: Beacon.

Palinkas, L. A. (1982). Ethnicity, identity, and mental health: The use of rhetoric in an immigrant Chinese church. *Journal of Psychoanalytic Anthropology, 5*, 235–258.

Pargament, K. I. (1990). God help me: Toward a theoretical framework of coping for the psychology of religion. *Research in the Social Scientific Study of Religion, 2*, 195–224.

Pargament, K. I. (1997). *The psychology of religion and coping: Theory, research, practice.* New York: Guilford Press.

Pargament, K. I., & Hahn, J. (1986). God and the just world: Causal and coping attributions to God in health situations. *Journal for the Scientific Study of Religion, 25*, 193–207.

Pargament, K. I., Steele, R. E., & Tyler, F. B. (1979). Religious participation, religious motivation, and individual psychosocial competence. *Journal for the Scientific Study of Religion, 18*, 412–419.

Parker, G., Tupling, H., & Brown, L. B. (1979). A parental bonding instrument. *British Journal of Medical Psychology, 52*, 1–10.

Parkes, C. M. (1972). *Bereavement: Studies of grief in adult life.* New York: International Universities Press.

Pederson, D. R., Gleason, K. E., Moran, G., & Bento, S. (1998). Maternal attachment representations, maternal sensitivity, and infant–mother attachment. *Developmental Psychology, 34*, 925–933.

Persinger, M. A. (1987). *The neuropsychological bases of God beliefs.* New York: Praeger.

Pingleton, J. P. (1989). The role and function of forgiveness in the psychotherapeutic process. *Journal of Psychology and Theology, 17*, 27–35.

Pinker, S. (1994). *The language instinct.* New York: Morrow.

Pinker, S. (1997). *How the mind works.* New York: Norton.

Plog, S. (1965). UCLA conducts research on glossolalia. *Trinity, 3*, 38–39.

Poggie, J. J., Jr., Pollnac, R., & Gersuny, C. (1976). Risk as a basis for taboos among fishermen in southern New England. *Journal for the Scientific Study of Religion, 15*, 252–267.

Pollner, M. (1989). Divine relations, social relations, and well-being. *Journal of Health and Social Behavior, 30*, 92–104.

Poloma, M. M., & Gallup, G. H., Jr. (1991). *Varieties of prayer: A survey report.* Philadelphia: Trinity Press International.

Potvin, R. H. (1977). Adolescent God images. *Review of Religious Research, 19*, 43–53.

Potvin, R. H. (1985). *Seminarians of the eighties.* Washington, DC: National Catholic Educational Association.

Potvin, R. H., & Suziedelis, A. (1969). *Seminarians of the sixties.* Washington, DC: Centre for Applied Research in the Apostolate.

Poundstone, W. (1992). *Prisoner's dilemma.* New York: Doubleday.

Pratt, J. B. (1920). *The religious consciousness.* New York: Macmillan.

Premack, D. (1990). Do infants have a theory of self-propelled objects? *Cognition, 36*, 1–16.

Proudfoot, W., & Shaver, P. (1975). Attribution theory and the psychology of religion. *Journal for the Scientific Study of Religion, 14*, 317–330.

Pyszczynski, T., Greenberg, J., & Solomon, S. (1997). Why do we need what we need? A terror management perspective on the roots of human social motivation. *Psychological Inquiry, 8,* 1–20.

Pyszczynski, T., Greenberg, J., & Solomon, S. (1999). A dual-process model of defense against conscious and unconscious death-related thoughts: An extension of terror management theory. *Psychological Review, 106,* 835–845.

Ramachandran, V. S., & Blakeslee, S. (1998). *Phantoms in the brain.* New York: William Morrow and Company.

Ramachandran, V. S., Hirstein, W. S., Armel, K. C., Tecoma, E., & Iragui, V. (1997). The neural basis of religious experience. *Society for Neuroscience Abstracts, 23*(part 2), 1316.

Randi, J. (1982). *Flim-flam! Psychics, ESP, unicorns, and other delusions.* Buffalo, NY: Prometheus.

Reber, A. S. (1993). *Implicit learning and tacit knowledge.* New York: Oxford University Press.

Reed, B. (1978). *The dynamics of religion: Process and movement in Christian churches.* London: Darton, Longman & Todd.

Reite, M., & Boccia, M. L. (1994). Physiological aspects of attachment. In M. B. Sperling & W. H. Berman (Eds.), *Attachment in adults: Clinical and developmental perspectives* (pp. 98–127). New York: Guilford Press.

Reynolds, V., & Tanner, R. E. S. (1983). *The biology of religion.* London: Longman.

Rholes, W. S., Simpson, J. A., Blakely, B., Lanigan, L., & Allen, B. (1997). Adult attachment styles, the desire to have children, and working models of parenthood. *Journal of Personality, 65,* 357–385.

Richards, D. D., & Siegler, R. S. (1986). Children's understandings of the attributes of life. *Journal of Experimental Child Psychology, 42,* 1–22

Richardson, J. T. (1973). Psychological interpretations of glossolalia: A reexamination of research. *Journal for the Scientific Study of Religion, 12,* 199–207.

Ridley, M. (1996). *The origins of virtue: Human instincts and the evolution of cooperation.* New York: Viking.

Roberts, F. J. (1965). Some psychological factors in religious conversion. *British Journal of Social and Religious Psychology, 4,* 185–187.

Rohner, R. P. (1975). *They love me, they love me not.* New Haven, CT: HRAF Press.

Roof, W. C., & Hadaway, C. K. (1979). Denominational switching in the seventies: Going beyond Stark and Glock. *Journal for the Scientific Study of Religion, 18,* 363–379.

Roof, W. C., & McKinney, W. (1987). *American mainline religion: Its changing shape and future.* New Brunswick, NJ: Rutgers University Press.

Ross, M. G. (1950). *Religious beliefs of youth.* New York: Association Press.

Rowatt, W. C., & Kirkpatrick, L. A. (2002). Dimensions of attachment to God and their relation to affect, religiosity, and personality constructs. *Journal for the Scientific Study of Religion, 41,* 637–651.

Rozin, P. (1976). The evolution of intelligence and access to the cognitive unconscious. In J. Sprague & A. N. Epstein (Eds.), *Progress in psychobiology and physiological psychology* (pp. 245–277). New York: Academic Press.

Rozin, P. (1996). Towards a psychology of food and eating: From motivation to module to model to marker, morality, meaning, and metaphor. *Current Directions in Psychological Science, 5,* 18–24.

Rutherford, M. D., Kurzban, R., Tooby, J., & Cosmides, L. (1997, June). *Cooperation and punishment in groups: Economic tradeoffs*. Paper presented at the Human Behavior and Evolution Society Conference, Tucson, AZ.

Sagan, C. (1985). *Contact*. New York: Simon & Schuster.

Scharf, B. R. (1970). *The sociological study of religion*. New York: Harper & Row.

Schmidt, W. (1931). *The origin and growth of religion: Facts and theories* (H. J. Rose, Trans.). London: Methuen.

Seligman, M., & Hager, J. (1972). *Biological boundaries of learning*. New York: Appleton-Century-Crofts.

Shaver, P. R., & Hazan, C. (1988). A biased overview of the study of love. *Journal of Social and Personal Relationships, 5*, 473–501.

Shaver, P. R., & Hazan, C. (1993). Adult romantic attachment: Theory and evidence. In D. Perlman & W. Jones (Eds.), *Advances in personal relationships* (Vol. 4, pp. 29–70). London: Kingsley.

Shaver, P. R., Hazan, C., & Bradshaw, D. (1988). Love as attachment: The integration of three behavioral systems. In R. J. Sternberg & M. Barnes (Eds.), *The anatomy of love* (pp. 68–99). New Haven, CT: Yale University Press.

Sherif, M., Harvey, O. J., White, B. J., Hood, W. E., & Sherif, C. W. (1961). *Intergroup conflict and cooperation: The Robbers Cave experiment*. Norman: University of Oklahoma Press.

Silverman, D. K. (1991). Attachment patterns and Freudian theory: An integrative proposal. *Psychoanalytic Psychology, 8*(2), 169–193.

Simmonds, R. B. (1977). Conversion or addiction: Consequences of joining a Jesus movement group. *American Behavioral Scientist, 20*, 909.

Simpson, J. A. (1999). Attachment theory in modern evolutionary perspective. In J. Cassidy & P. R. Shaver (Eds.), *Handbook of attachment: Theory, research, and clinical applications* (pp. 115–140). New York: Guilford Press.

Simpson, J. A., Rholes, W. S., & Nelligan, J. S. (1992). Support seeking and support giving within couples in an anxiety-provoking situation: The role of attachment styles. *Journal of Personality and Social Psychology, 62*, 434–446.

Skinner, B. F. (1948). "Superstition" in the pigeon. *Journal of Experimental Psychology, 38*, 168–172.

Skolnick, A. (1985). *The ties that bind: Attachment theory and the social psychology of close relationships*. Paper presented at the annual meeting of the National Conference on Family Relations, Dallas, TX.

Sloman, S. A. (1996). The empirical case for two systems of reasoning. *Psychological Review, 119*, 3–22.

Smart, N. (1976). *The religious experience of mankind* (2nd ed.). New York: Scribner's.

Snyder, J., & Kirkpatrick, L. A. (2002, June). *Opposite sex mating preferences: The roles of dominance and prestige*. Poster presented at the annual meeting of the Human Behavior and Evolution Society, New Brunswick, NJ.

Snyder, J., & Kirkpatrick, L. A. (2003, June). *The dominance dilemma: Dominance, status, and female mate preferences*. Poster presented at the annual meeting of the Human Behavior and Evolution Society, Lincoln, NE.

Sober, E., & Wilson, D. S. (1998). *Unto others: The evolution and psychology of unselfish behavior*. Cambridge, MA: Harvard University Press.

Solomon, J., & George, C. (1999). The measurement of attachment security in infancy and childhood. In J. Cassidy & P. R. Shaver (Eds.), *Handbook of attachment: Theory, research, and clinical applications* (pp. 287–316). New York: Guilford Press.

Spelke, E. S. (1990). Principles of object perception. *Cognitive Science, 14,* 29–56.

Sperber, D. (1996). *Explaining culture: A naturalistic approach.* Oxford, UK: Blackwell.

Sperling, M. B., & Berman, W. H. (Eds.). (1994). *Attachment in adults: Clinical and developmental perspectives.* New York: Guilford Press.

Spilka, B., Addison, J., & Rosensohn, M. (1975). Parents, self, and God: A test of competing individual–religion relationships. *Review of Religious Research, 16,* 154–165.

Spilka, B., Armatas, P., & Nussbaum, J. (1964). The concept of God: A factor-analytic approach. *Review of Religious Research, 6,* 28–36.

Spilka, B., Comp, G., & Goldsmith, W. M. (1981). Faith and behavior: Religion in introductory psychology texts of the 1950s and 1970s. *Teaching of Psychology, 8,* 158–160.

Sroufe, L. A. (1983). Infant–caregiver attachment and patterns of adaptation in preschool: The roots of maladaptation and competence. In M. Perlmutter (Ed.), *Minnesota Symposium in Child Psychology* (Vol. 16, pp. 41–91). Hillsdale, NJ: Erlbaum.

Sroufe, L. A., & Fleeson, J. (1986). Attachment and the construction of relationships. In W. W. Hartup & Z. Rubin (Eds.), *Relationships and development* (pp. 51–71). Hillsdale, NJ: Erlbaum.

Sroufe, L. A., & Waters, E. (1977a). Attachment as an organizational construct. *Child Development, 48,* 1184–1199.

Sroufe, L. A., & Waters, E. (1977b). Heart rate as a convergent measure in clinical and developmental research. *Merrill-Palmer Quarterly, 23*(1), 3–27.

Stanley, S. M. (1986). *Commitment and the maintenance and enhancement of relationships.* Unpublished doctoral dissertation, University of Denver.

Starbuck, E. D. (1899). *The psychology of religion.* New York: Scribner's.

Stark, R., & Bainbridge, W. S. (1987). *A theory of religion.* New York: Peter Lang.

Stark, R., & Glock, C. Y. (1968). *American piety: The nature of religious commitment.* Berkeley: University of California Press.

Steadman, L. B., Palmer, C. T., & Tilley, C. F. (1996). The universality of ancestor worship. *Ethnology, 35*(1), 63–76.

Stearns, S. (1992). *The evolution of life histories.* New York: Oxford University Press.

Stouffer, S. A., Lumsdaine, A. A., Lumsdaine, M. H., Williams, R. M., Jr., Smith, M. B., Janis, I. L., Star, S. A., & Cottrell, L. S. (1949). *The American soldier: Combat and its aftermath* (Vol. 2). Princeton, NJ: Princeton University Press.

Strahan, B. (1991). *Parenting and religiosity amongst SDA tertiary students: An attachment theory approach.* Unpublished manuscript, Avondale College, Australia.

Strickland, B. R., & Shaffer, S. (1971). I-E, I-E, and F. *Journal for the Scientific Study of Religion, 10,* 366–369.

Strickland, F. L. (1924). *Psychology of religious experience.* New York: Abingdon.

Strunk, O. (1959). Perceived relationships between parental and deity concepts. *Psychological Newsletter, 10,* 222–226.

Stryker, M. P., & Sherk, H. (1975). Modification of cortical orientation selectivity in the cat by restricted visual experience: A reexamination. *Science, 190,* 904–906.

Sulloway, F. J. (1996). *Born to rebel: Birth order, family dynamics, and creative lives.* New York: Pantheon.

Suomi, S. J. (1999). Attachment in rhesus monkeys. In J. Cassidy & P. R. Shaver (Eds.), *Handbook of attachment: Theory, research, and clinical applications* (pp. 181–197). New York: Guilford Press.

Symons, D. (1979). *The evolution of human sexuality*. New York: Oxford University Press.

Symons, D. (1992). On the use and misuse of Darwinism in the study of human behavior. In J. H. Barkow, L. Cosmides, & J. Tooby (Eds.), *The adapted mind* (pp. 137–159). New York: Oxford University Press.

Tajfel, H. (1982). Social psychology of intergroup relations. *Annual Review of Psychology, 33*, 1–39.

Tajfel, H., & Turner, J. C. (1986). The social identity theory of intergroup behavior. In S. Worchel & W. Austin (Eds.), *Psychology of intergroup relations* (2nd ed., pp. 7–24). Chicago: Nelson-Hall.

Tamayo, A., & Desjardins, L. (1976). Belief systems and conceptual images of parents and God. *Journal of Psychology, 92*, 131–140.

Tamminen, K. (1991). *Religious development in childhood and adolescence: An empirical study*. Helsinki: Suomalainen Tiedeakatemia.

Taylor, S. E., & Brown, J. D. (1988). Illusion and well-being: A social psychological perspective on mental health. *Psychological Bulletin, 103*, 193–210.

Thouless, R. H. (1923). *An introduction to the psychology of religion*. New York: Macmillan.

Tiger, L. (1969). *Men in groups*. New York: Random House.

Tooby, J., & Cosmides, L. (1990). On the universality of human nature and the uniqueness of the individual: The role of genetics and adaptation. *Journal of Personality, 58*, 17–67.

Tooby, J., & Cosmides, L. (1992). The psychological foundations of culture. In J. H. Barkow, L. Cosmides, & J. Tooby (Eds.), *The adapted mind* (pp. 19–136). New York: Oxford University Press.

Tooby, J., & Cosmides, L. (1996). Friendship and the banker's paradox: Other pathways to the evolution of adaptations for altruism. *Proceedings of the British Academy, 88*, 119–143.

Tooby, J., & Cosmides, L. (1997). *Evolutionary psychology: A primer*. Retrieved September 13, 2000, from *http://www.psych.ucsb.edu/research/cep/primer.html*.

Trivers, R. L. (1971). The evolution of reciprocal altruism. *Quarterly Review of Biology, 46*, 35–57.

Trivers, R. L. (1972). Parental investment and sexual selection. In R. B. Campbell (Ed.), *Sexual selection and the descent of man: 1871–1971* (pp. 136–179). Chicago: Aldine.

Trivers, R. L. (1974). Parent-offspring conflict. *American Zoologist, 24*, 249–264.

Tversky, A., & Kahneman, D. (1974). Judgment under uncertainty: Heuristics and biases. *Science, 185*, 1124–1131.

Tylor, E. B. (1873). *Primitive culture* (2nd ed.). London: John Murray.

Ullman, C. (1982). Change of mind, change of heart: Some cognitive and emotional antecedents of religious conversion. *Journal of Personality and Social Psychology, 42*, 183–192.

Ullman, C. (1989). *The transformed self: The psychology of religious conversion*. New York: Plenum Press.

van IJzendoorn, M. (1995). Adult attachment representations, parental responsiveness, and infant attachment: A meta-analysis of the predictive validity of the Adult Attachment Interview. *Psychological Bulletin, 117*, 387–403.

van Lawick-Goodall, J. (1971). *In the shadow of man*. London: Collins.

Vaughn, B. E., & Bost, K. K. (1999). Attachment and temperament: Redundant, independent, or interacting influences on interpersonal adaptation and personality development? In J. Cassidy & P. R. Shaver (Eds.), *Handbook of attachment: Theory, research, and clinical applications* (pp. 198–225). New York: Guilford Press.

Ventis, W. L. (1995). The relationships between religion and mental health. *Journal of Social Issues, 51*(2), 33–48.

Vergote, A., & Tamayo, A. (Eds.). (1981). *The parental figures and the representation of God*. The Hague: Mouton.

Vernon, G. M. (1962). *Sociology of religion*. New York: McGraw-Hill.

Vetter, G. B., & Green, M. (1932). Personality and group factors in the making of atheists. *Journal of Abnormal and Social Psychology, 27*, 179–194.

Vivier, L. (1960). *Glossolalia*. Unpublished doctoral dissertation, University of Witwatersrand, South Africa.

Waller, N. Kojetin, B., Bouchard, T., Jr., Lykken, D., & Tellegen, A. (1990). Genetic and environmental influences on religious interests, attitudes, and values: A study of twins reared apart and together. *Psychological Science, 1*, 138–142.

Weinfield, N. S., Sroufe, L. A., Egeland, B., & Carlson, E. A. (1999). The nature of individual differences in infant-caregiver attachment. In J. Cassiddy & P. R. Shaver (Eds.), *Handbook of attachment: Theory, research, and clinical applications* (pp. 68–88). New York: Guilford Press.

Weiss, R. S. (1973). *Loneliness: The experience of emotional and social isolation*. Cambridge, MA: MIT Press.

Weiss, R. S. (1974). The provisions of social relationships. In Z. Rubin (Ed.), *Doing unto others* (pp. 17–26). Englewood Cliffs, NJ: Prentice-Hall.

Weiss, R. S. (1982). Attachment in adult life. In C. M. Parkes & J. S. Hinde (Eds.), *The place of attachment in human behavior* (pp. 171–184). New York: Basic Books.

Weiss, R. S. (1986). Continuities and transformations in social relationships from childhood to adulthood. In W. W. Hartup & Z. Rubin (Eds.), *Relationships and development* (pp. 95–110). Hillsdale, NJ: Erlbaum.

Wellman, H. M., & Inagaki, K. (Eds.). (1997). *The emergence of core domains of thought: Children's reasoning about physical, psychological, and biological phenomena* (New Directions for Child Development, No. 75). San Francisco: Jossey-Bass.

Wenegrat, B. (1990). *The divine archetype: The sociobiology and psychology of religion*. Lexington, MA: Lexington Books.

West, M. L., & Sheldon-Keller, A. E. (1994). *Patterns of relating: An adult attachment perspective*. New York: Guilford Press.

Wilkinson, G. W. (1984). Reciprocal food sharing in vampire bats. *Nature, 308,* 181–184.

Williams, G. C. (1957). Pleiotropy, natural selection, and the evolution of senescence. *Evolution, 11*, 398–411.

Williams, G. C. (1966). *Adaptation and natural selection: A critique of some current evolutionary thought*. Princeton, NJ: Princeton University Press.

Williams, G. C. (1997). *The pony fish's glow: And other clues to plan and purpose in nature*. New York: Basic Books.

Wilson, D. S. (1975). A general theory of group selection. *Proceedings of the National Academy of Sciences, 72*, 143–146.

Wilson, D. S. (2002). *Darwin's cathedral: Evolution, religion, and the nature of society*. Chicago: University of Chicago Press.

Wilson, E. O. (1978). *On human nature*. Cambridge, MA: Harvard University Press.

Wilson, E. O. (1998). *Consilience: The unity of knowledge*. New York: Knopf.

Wood, W. W. (1965). *Culture and personality aspects of the Pentecostal Holiness religion*. The Hague: Mouton.

Woodberry, J. D. (1992). Conversion in Islam. In H. N. Malony & S. Southard (Eds.), *Handbook of religious conversion* (pp. 22–40). Birmingham, AL: Religious Education Press.

Wright, R. (1994). *The moral animal: The new science of evolutionary psychology*. New York: Pantheon.

Wright, S. A. (1987). *Leaving cults: The dynamics of defection*. Washington, DC: Society for the Scientific Study of Religion.

Wulff, D. M. (1997). *Psychology of religion: Classic and contemporary views* (2nd ed.). New York: Wiley.

Yalom, I. D. (1980). *Existential psychotherapy*. New York: Basic Books.

Young, K. (1926). The psychology of hymns. *Journal of Abnormal and Social Psychology, 20*, 391–406.

Zahavi, A. (1975). Mate selection: A selection for handicap. *Journal of Theoretical Biology, 53*, 205–214.

Zahavi, Am. & Zahavi, Av. (1997). *The handicap principle: The missing piece of Darwin's puzzle*. New York: Oxford University Press.

Zeifman, D., & Hazan, C. (1997). Attachment: The bond in pair-bonds. In J. A. Simpson & D. Kenrick (Eds.), *Evolutionary social psychology* (pp. 237–263). Mahwah, NJ: Erlbaum.

Index

f indicates figure; *n* indicates note; *t* indicates table